The Behaviour of Interest Groups in Trade and Industry
Towards Monetary Policy and Central Banks

STUDIEN ZU
INTERNATIONALEN
WIRTSCHAFTSBEZIEHUNGEN

Herausgegeben von Prof. Dr. Michael Frenkel

Band 6

PETER LANG
Frankfurt am Main · Berlin · Bern · Bruxelles · New York · Oxford · Wien

Steffen Kern

The Behaviour of Interest Groups in Trade and Industry Towards Monetary Policy and Central Banks

Theory and Evidence on Germany and the Euro Area

PETER LANG
Europäischer Verlag der Wissenschaften

Bibliographic Information published by Die Deutsche Bibliothek
Die Deutsche Bibliothek lists this publication in the Deutsche Nationalbibliografie; detailed bibliographic data is available in the internet at <http://dnb.ddb.de>.

ISSN 1618-503X
ISBN 3-631-54615-7
US-ISBN 0-8204-9814-9

www.peterlang.de

Contents

List of charts

List of tables

List of abbreviations

ACEA	European Automobile Manufacturers Association
AT	Austria
BDEx	Bundesverband des Deutschen Exporthandels e.V. (Federation of the German Export Trade)
BDI	Bundesverband der Deutschen Industrie e.V. (Federation of German Industries)
BE	Belgium
BER	Deutsche Bundesbank, Regional Office, Berlin
BGA	Bundesverband des Groß- und Außenhandels e.V. (Federation of German Wholesale and Foreign Trade)
BIS	Bank for International Settlements
BoJ	Bank of Japan
CD	Canada
CEFIC	European Chemical Industry Council
CEPR	Centre for European Policy Research
CH	Switzerland
DE	Germany
DEM	Deutsche Mark
DIHK	Deutscher Industrie- und Handelskammertag (Association of German Chambers of Industry and Commerce)
DNB	De Nederlandsche Bank
DUS	Deutsche Bundesbank, Regional Office, Düsseldorf
ECB	European Central Bank
Ecfin	European Commission, Directorate-General Economic and Financial Affairs
EMS	European Monetary System
EMU	European Monetary Union
ERM	Exchange Rate Mechanism of the EMS
ES	Spain
ESCB	European System of Central Banks
EU	European Union
EUI	European University Institute
EUR	Euro
Eurochambres	Association of European Chambers of Commerce and Industry
FI	Finland
FIEC	European Construction Industry Federation
FR	France

FRA	Deutsche Bundesbank, Regional Office, Frankfurt
FTA	The Foreign Trade Association
GDP	Gross Domestic Product
GR	Greece
HAM	Deutsche Bundesbank, Regional Office, Hamburg
HAN	Deutsche Bundesbank, Regional Office, Hanover
HDB	Hauptverband der Deutschen Bauindustrie e.V. (Main Employers' Association for the German Construction Industry)
HDE	Hauptverband des Deutschen Einzelhandels (Main Association for the German Retail Trade)
HV	Hauptverwaltung (Regional Office of the Deutsche Bundesbank after 2002 Bundesbank reform)
IE	Ireland
IMF	International Monetary Fund
IT	Italy
JP	Japan
LEI	Deutsche Bundesbank, Regional Office, Leipzig
LU	Luxembourg
LZB	Landeszentralbank (Regional Office of the Deutsche Bundesbank prior to 2002 Bundesbank reform)
MAI	Deutsche Bundesbank, Regional Office, Mainz
MUN	Deutsche Bundesbank, Regional Office, Munich
NBER	National Bureau of Economic Research
NCB	National central bank
NL	The Netherlands
OECD	Organisation for Economic Cooperation and Development
Orgalime	Liaison Group of the European Mechanical, Electrical, Electronic and Metalworking Industries
PT	Portugal
SE	Sweden
STU	Deutsche Bundesbank, Regional Office, Stuttgart
UEAPME	European Association of Craft, Small and Medium-Sized Enterprises
UK	United Kingdom
UNICE	Union of Industrial and Employers' Confederations of Europe
US	United States of America
USD	United States Dollar
VCI	Verband der Chemischen Industrie e.V. (German Association of Chemical Industries)

VDA	Verband der Automobilindustrie e.V. (German Association of the Automotive Industry)
VDMA	Verband Deutscher Maschinen- und Anlagenbau e.V. (Association of the German Engineering Industry)
WVS	Wirtschaftsvereinigung Stahl (German Steel Federation)
ZDB	Zentralverband Deutsches Baugewerbe (National Federation for the German Construction Industry)
ZDH	Zentralverband der Deutschen Handwerks (National Federation of German Skilled Crafts and Trades)
ZVEI	Zentralverband Elektrotechnik- und Elektronikindustrie e.V. (German Electrical and Electronic Manufacturers' Association)

Introduction

Topic and motivation

This study investigates the behaviour of private interest groups towards monetary policy and central banks. It explores the extent to which interest groups seek to influence monetary policy and their motivations for doing so – or for refraining from doing so. Where evidence for interest group activity with respect to monetary decisions can be found, it aims to identify the ways in which groups communicate with policy makers.

Precisely why one should be particularly concerned with interest-group behaviour towards monetary policymaking may not be evident at first sight. Monetary policy decisions are rarely spectacular for observers not involved in economic and financial affairs. Monetary policy makers generally prefer to pursue their policies in a cautious, subtle manner in small steps – incremental interest-rate changes, for example, whose immediate impact on people's lives may appear negligible. In addition, monetary policy is decided outside the familiar arena of political battle through parliamentary debate, between government and opposition or among competing political parties. Monetary decisions are taken by central banks – administrative institutions whose staff is composed of experts in their field, taking decisions directed by their concern for the general welfare of the public. Why then should interest groups be concerned with this issue?

A second look at the topic seems to confirm such objections. Among the countless works – be they academic, political or journalistic in origin – on the functioning of monetary policy and its determinants, reference to private interest groups articulating their specific views on the monetary state of the economy is rare. Even less evidence exists on attempts to mediate private sector interests systematically, let alone on any significant impact of such interests on the formulation of monetary policy.

As clear as the evidence may be, the situation is nonetheless puzzling, considering the relevance of monetary policy for the private sector. It would clearly be wrong to argue that monetary policy has an insignificant impact on the economy. Central banks control the circulation of money in their economies and thereby preside over a resource that has become a central determinant of overall economic activity. Central banks set important interest rates. Their monetary policy stance heavily influences the rate of inflation as well as exchange rates. High real interest rates can significantly increase the costs of borrowing; low real interest rates, on the other hand, reduce the returns on savings. Even low rates of inflation can lead to a substantial erosion of income and wealth over time. Exchange rate movements, be they critical or secular, change the value of an economy's wealth as well as the competitive position of its industries by international comparison.

Despite the fact that objectives, channels, and economic impact are fundamentally different, a comparison of monetary policy with fiscal policy measures can be helpful in accentuating the question: The medium-term impact on real GDP of an increase in short-term interest rates by the central bank might be expected to be at least the same in quantitative terms as that of an equivalent rise in value added tax. Yet, anecdotal evidence suggests that the responses of economic interest groups, such as industry associations, employer organisations, and trade unions, to an increase in value added tax tend to be rather pronounced, while comparable increases in interest rates are noted by and large without great comment.

Central bank policymaking continuously and significantly affects the real income and wealth of all actors in the economy, be they private individuals, companies, or public entities, savers or creditors, exporters or importers. At the same time, there are important indicators strongly suggesting that market participants are far from indifferent with respect to monetary and exchange rate developments in their day-to-day operations. Thus, substantial resources are devoted by financial institutions, and also by large individual enterprises, to analysing and forecasting monetary and exchange rate developments. In addition, a large and increasing number of enterprises insure themselves against interest and exchange rate movements by means of financial market hedging.

At the same time, monetary policy remains subject to constant debate in financial markets, but also among politicians and the public at large. Such debate, including extensive forecasting activities, bears witness to the fact that despite institutional independence and limited discretionary scope monetary policy is a subject of social choice. Thus, it is widely acknowledged that monetary policy is not a mechanistic or even deterministic process. The direction and optimal size and timing of policy measures continue to stimulate professional and academic debate alike. What is more, monetary policy measures carry re-distributive implications since different economic actors are affected in different ways. Thus, a reduction in interest rates may be welcomed by net debtors, but possibly not by creditors. Similarly, monetary policy measures affecting the exchange rate may be perceived quite differently by private interests engaged in external trade, depending for example on the currencies affected and their position as exporters or importers.

As a consequence, the public interest represents a complex and fast-changing environment for policy makers, including those concerned with monetary affairs. Without prejudice to their institutional and personal independence, obtaining and processing information on the likely effects of their policies on the private sector therefore represents a natural and inherent concern. In fact, no central bank official would claim to be operating in complete isolation. Indeed, they recognise the high degree of mutual interdependence between monetary authorities and the private sector in economic terms. Successful monetary policy crucially depends on the actions of economic actors and their reactions to the monetary stance itself. With price stability as their most important objective, central banks are in control of important economic variables and can give decisive signals and incentives to market participants. Ultimately, however, prices and wages are determined by those market participants, leaving monetary policy makers at the sidelines to some extent, observing whether their measures are bearing fruit. The potential benefits of contacts with the private sector are reflected in the institutional arrangements of a number of central banks that take recourse to advisory councils staffed with experts from the private sector. However, the role of such advisory bodies and their impact on monetary policy decisions have remained limited.

All in all, the discrepancy between the significant impact of monetary policy on the private sector and the apparently hesitant approach of interest groups in this respect is the driving force of this study. It is motivated by and will explicitly deal with the following core questions:

- Do interest groups seek to influence monetary policy decision making?
- What are the factors contributing to the decision whether to express interests with respect to monetary policy, and to what extent?
- If influence on monetary decisions is sought, how are interests articulated by the relevant groups?

Scope, limitations, and definitions

Given the multitude of political and economic, institutional and behavioural, theoretical and practical facets of interest groups' attitudes towards monetary policy, there are certain aspects that go beyond the scope and intention of this analysis and will consequently have to be left un-addressed.

Most importantly, this study will not try to measure in any systematic way the extent to which interest-group activity actually influences monetary policy decisions in practice. To be realistic, it must be recognised that the probability of finding conclusive evidence on this issue is rather low. Although extensive, academic research on the quantitative effects of influence from electoral politics, e.g. by looking at the correlation between monetary policy decisions and election dates and political constellations before ballots, has so far remained inconclusive. Against this background, evidence of a significant link between the activities of interest groups and monetary policy decisions is highly unlikely to be found. The few attempts at doing so confirm this conclusion. Qualitative techniques, such as interviewing policy makers, are not likely to yield authoritative results either, since definitive answers to this question from policy makers and stakeholders cannot be expected out of consideration for sensitive current issues and long-term credibility aspects.

Similarly, this study does not seek to give answers to an important normative question that may be raised in this context. We may wonder whether interest groups should, or should be allowed to seek to influence monetary policy decisions, in particular those by politically independent central banks. Political independence is provided for monetary authorities in order to shield them as far as possible from external influence, especially from attempts at a short-term stimulation of economic growth, which may result in inflationary tendencies. In most monetary systems, this protection refers to the influence sought by elected politicians, who are perceived as particularly sensitive to inflationary tendencies, especially prior to elections. The question naturally arises as to whether enterprises and their stakeholders also fall victim to this temptation, and the evidence presented below contains a number of interesting suggestions in this regard. However, it is realistic to assume that private interests are likely to be articulated irrespective of whether their addressees are entitled to let themselves be influenced by these interests or not. In so far, it is more relevant to ask whether interest groups seek to influence monetary policy, and how they go about articulating these interests. Whether such influence is desirable or not presupposes a detailed enquiry into the motivations behind interest-group activity in this field of policymaking, which is beyond the scope of the current study.

Finally, the analysis does not explicitly address the positioning of interest groups with respect to the overall set-up of the monetary and exchange rate system, but focuses on the operation of monetary and exchange rate policy within these systems. This limitation primarily refers to the project of establishing Economic and Monetary Union in the EU (EMU) in the 1990s, but also to the earlier discussions, e.g. on the European Monetary System (EMS) and its Exchange Rate Mechanism (ERM). Although closely related and immensely important for the policy process, these structural caesuras represent singular events. Discussions in these contexts are not therefore necessarily typical of stakeholders' views on how monetary and exchange rate policy as such should be shaped in day-to-day operation. Further, structural questions are not immediately subject to the same inherent incentive problems characterising monetary policy, most importantly that of time inconsistency. Where appropriate, recourse will be taken below to the wealth of literature available on structural issues such as the EMS and EMU and the behaviour of the various stakeholders in these contexts.

Rather, this study looks at day-to-day monetary policy as a policy issue as viewed by interest groups and investigates the determinants of interest-group behaviour against the background of the issue itself, institutional factors, and interest-group dynamics. In doing so, it is exclusively concerned with the political dimension of the activities of interest groups and their members, i.e. with the aggregation and articulation of interests. The economic interdependence of the relevant interest groups and their members with monetary authorities, i.e. the impact of monetary policy on the private sector as well as the latter's influence on the success of the operations of monetary authorities, is not an object of this study in its own right and will only be touched upon in as far as it influences and shapes political communication. In the same vein, the analysis does not seek to make an original contribution to the body of related theories used therein, e.g. those taken from public affairs management, political communication, and interest group theory. Given the purpose of investigating interest-group behaviour in the specific policy context of monetary decision making, this study focuses on applying existing, well-established suitable theoretical elements.

In this context, the term *interest group* shall refer to organised and institutionalised, privately operated bodies whose predominant task is to promote and further the common interests of their members within the political system, as formulated by Truman[1]. Interest groups pursue a great multitude of concerns[2], many of them not necessarily related to economic issues and, more specifically, monetary affairs. The focus here is on economic interest groups, i.e. those groups with the explicit mandate to represent the economic interests of their members. Groups working on non-economic concerns, i.e. so-called promotional groups[3], will not be dealt with explicitly.

More specifically, the focus of this study is narrowed down to business interests in the sectors of industry[4] and trade[5]. Given the wide variety of interests potentially

---

1 Truman (1993), pp. 39-43.

2 Following Salisbury (1975), p. 175, the term *interest* shall be used below to refer to "objects toward which attitudes are directed", where "objects" means "acts of governmental authorities". The word *influence* is defined as the effect that one person or entity's activity has on another. Most frequently, it will be used in the context of interest groups seeking influence, or synonymously "taking political action", on a policy process or political institution. It is worth noting that the definitions for *interest* and *interest group* selected here are only one option when approaching the issue. Baumgartner, Leech (1998) have documented the widespread disagreement in academic literature on the appropriate definitions (on *interest* see pp. 22-25, on *interest group* see pp. 25-30). Throughout this study, the term *interest association* will generally be used interchangeably with *interest group*, as is the practice especially among American scholars (e.g. Baumgartner, Leech (1998), pp. 25-30), notwithstanding the fact that the term *association* is also used to refer specifically to formal unions of interest groups, e.g. in the form of umbrella organisations.

3 Von Beyme (1974), pp. 27-38.

4 Commonly defined as a group of productive enterprises or organisations that produce or supply goods, services, or sources of income. In economics, industries are customarily classified as the

represented even among economic interest groups, it is necessary to limit the number and kinds of interests under scrutiny in order to obtain detailed results on the perceptions and motivations of stakeholders in the field of monetary policy. The selection made here is based on four considerations. First, the sample of interest groups should be representative of the private sector economy at large in terms of the exposure to monetary developments and the related policy decisions. As enterprises in trade and industry represent a large section of the private sector, their interest associations are an important object for analysis. In the same vein, the sample should not reflect highly specific interests. First, agriculture will not be addressed explicitly, as this sector – with a share of only 1% to 5% in most industrial economies – today represents only a very small and specific segment of the economy. More importantly, however, firms in the financial sector are not covered in this study. In addition to their own corporate refinancing and investment concerns, it is the very purpose of financial enterprises to deal with financial-market developments and the associated risks. Monetary policy can have decisive influence on market developments. In addition, central banks often fulfil functions in the area of financial and prudential supervision complementary to and separate from monetary policy related responsibilities. Supervisory activities naturally condition relations with enterprises subject to central bank oversight, i.e. banks and other financial services providers, promoting compliant behaviour vis-à-vis the supervisory authority. The possibility cannot be excluded of such behavioural patterns, resulting from the central bank's role as a financial supervisor, spilling over into the behaviour of enterprises and their interest groups vis-à-vis the central bank in respect of monetary policy, thus blurring the behaviour otherwise likely to be observed. Financial enterprises will therefore presumably have very specific preferences in this policy field, making them a very important stakeholder in the political arena, but also limiting the suitability of the sector as an object for analysis in the present context.

Second, interest groups in this analysis should be exposed to monetary or exchange rate developments in a significant way. Such exposure is likely to be highest for capital-intensive and trade-oriented sectors, again highlighting the importance of industry and trade as the most suitable objects for analysis. For this very reason, specifically service-oriented sub-sectors are not covered.

---

primary – forestry, fishing, mining, quarrying, and the extraction of minerals –, secondary – manufacturing, energy-producing, and construction industries –, and tertiary sectors – service industries not producing tangible goods. The term tertiary sector is commonly used interchangeably with the term trade.

[5] Commonly defined as the sector in the economy that, while producing no tangible goods, provides services or intangible gains or generates wealth. Economic science commonly differentiates between domestic and international trade activities.

Third, the interest groups addressed in the present context should be sufficiently resourced to actually have sufficient means for conveying their interests to policy makers, provided such interests exist and are deemed worthy of pursuit, a criterion that business associations in trade and industry again fulfil.

Finally, the interest groups analysed here were selected so as to exhibit some degree of homogeneity in purpose, exposure, and interests with a view to making the underlying motivations and activities with regard to monetary affairs directly comparable. Business associations in trade and industry were thus viewed in isolation, leaving out other economic interest groups such as employer and employee organisations, whose objectives and exposure with respect to monetary policy are likely to be quite different from those of the selected associations.

The term *monetary policy* shall refer to the entirety of measures and processes that exist in an economy with respect to the supply of money and credit, the quantity of money, the rate of interest and the exchange rate, especially actions taken by central banks – as the most important monetary policy authority – to affect monetary and other financial conditions in pursuit of certain broad economic objectives[6]. The objectives of monetary policy are generally defined by the relevant policy makers and pertain to sustainable growth of real output, high employment or price stability, or a combination of these three. In order to achieve these objectives, monetary authorities can act in a completely discretionary manner or select explicit targets, which they try to achieve by using the instruments at their disposal. Targets usually refer to either money-supply, interest-rate, inflation or exchange rate targets. Monetary instruments are applied to influence the money market and include the supply of central bank money or the imposition of interest rates on the latter.

The term *central bank* will be used, together with *monetary authority*, to refer to the state institution endowed with the authority to formulate, conduct, and implement monetary policy in a specified political and geographical territory. Central banks are usually defined in functional terms. Contemporary central banks are characterised by three functions: First, they are entrusted with the issuance of fiat money, over which they enjoy a constitutionally or legally conferred monopoly. Second, they serve as a bank-of-banks, especially as a lender of last resort to the domestic credit sector. Third, they are responsible for that part of macroeconomic policy derived from its function as the issuer of money[7]. A fourth function some central banks historically used to serve, namely that of banker to the state, has been diminishing as financing operations with the state are prohibited in an increasing number of countries.

---

6 Büschgen (1997), p. 525, Bannock, Baxter, Davis (1992), p. 290, and Lindsey, Wallich (1992), pp. 740-748.

7 Bofinger et al. (1996), pp. 223-232.

Central banks in many countries serve functions directly related to the conduct of monetary policy beyond those enumerated here. Most importantly, many monetary authorities are assigned supervisory functions in the banking and financial services sectors or are responsible for the operation of national payment systems and their infrastructure. Such functions represent activities interest groups may also seek to influence, but which by the above definition are not directly related to monetary policy. For the sake of clarity, these additional tasks do not form part of the current analysis.

As a further conceptual delineation, the analysis is concerned exclusively with central banks as autonomous institutional entities separate from government and executive agencies and endowed with a certain degree of independence, granted either constitutionally, legally, or by convention. The degree of institutional independence has been identified as a decisive determinant of central bank behaviour within their political environment. Consequently, it is safe to assume that it will also be an important explanatory variable when investigating the behaviour of interest groups towards a monetary institution.

Finally, the empirical part of this study focuses on recent perceptions and practices of interest groups in Germany and at EU level[8]. Analysis of the relations between central banks and interest groups in Europe is complicated principally by the institutional caesura of European Monetary Union (EMU) and the introduction of the single European currency in 1999. Since then, monetary decisions for the euro area have been taken by the ECB. The latter, therefore, intuitively represents the most interesting object of analysis in the present context. However, patterns of communication on the part of interest groups at national and EU level are still adjusting to the new monetary regime, so that evidence from the EU level only may not be sufficiently stable to allow for strong conclusions on the behaviour of interest groups in this policy field.

In order to obtain a firm picture, it is therefore useful to base the analysis of relations between interest groups and central banks on experience at the level of the member states and to examine the impact of EMU on these relations as a separate, subsequent event. For the present purpose, Germany and the relations between German interest groups and the Deutsche Bundesbank were selected as the focus of analysis. The latter has been regarded an important institutional predecessor of the European Central Bank, providing a wealth of experience on the interaction between policy makers and

---

8 References to the institutional framework at EU level in this study are based on the legal provisions as laid down in the Treaty of Nice. Potential changes resulting from the Treaty revision in the context of the 2004 intergovernmental conference, to be manifested in Treaty amendments or an EU Constitution, are not included, as the latter had not been finally adopted at EU level by the time this study was finalised. The draft text of the Constitution at that time, however, did not foresee any material changes to the provision relating to EMU, the ESCB, or the ECB.

the private sector over more than four decades while maintaining a focus on recent perceptions and practices.

Related literature

The behaviour of interest groups towards monetary policy and central banks has not attracted much attention in scholarly literature so far. A large and important body of literature, especially in economic science, is concerned with external influences on monetary policy from politics and politicians. On the basis of game-theory and econometric approaches the most notable and widely recognised conclusion of this strand of literature is that elected politicians have an inherent incentive to inflate the economy and that central banks enjoying a relatively high degree of independence from electoral politics in general produce lower levels of inflation. Since inflation reduces public welfare, monetary policy should *ceteris paribus* be pursued by independent central banks in order to maximise general welfare. Verifying this central postulate has been the focus of a large number of studies, comparing the degrees of central bank independence and the output of monetary decision making over time and across countries.

Even though the influence on monetary policy from within the political system will not be discussed here, the literature does provide an important background in economic, political, and legal terms in as far as central bank independence may carry implications not just for communication between central banks and politicians, but also with private sector individuals or groups, whose motivations and objectives may differ substantially from those of elected politicians.

Interest groups as sources of influence on monetary policy have attracted comparatively less attention. Two strands of analysis can be identified. First, selective comments on relations with private interests can be found in political and historical accounts of specific central banks. Most prominently, Kettl[9] gives a comprehensive picture of the political context of US Federal Reserve policymaking, in which contacts between leading central bank officials and private sector participants are recorded. Similarly, Mayer[10] in his analysis of the Fed refers to relations with the financial sector. Second, there are a limited number of quantitative economic studies touching upon central bank-interest group relations. Most importantly, Havrilesky[11] systematically investigates the influences on US monetary policy, including those from the private sector, especially the financial industry. For this he takes a

---

[9] Kettl (1986).

[10] Mayer (2001).

[11] Havrilesky (1990), (1992).

quantitative approach. Following up on Havrilesky's work, Maier[12] applies a similar approach to potential influences on the Bundesbank.

These studies have inspired the present analysis insofar as they implicitly provoke the question that, if there is relatively little evidence of private sector influence on central banks, what factors may be behind the rather hesitant approach of private interest groups in respect of monetary affairs? Notwithstanding this difference in focus, reference will be made to the results of the work where appropriate. At the same time, these studies aim to establish how much influence interest groups actually exert on monetary policy makers, measured by certain indicators of interest-group activity. Beyond their scope is the question whether, and how much, influence is actually sought by interest groups, and how interests are articulated. In other words, what remains to be analysed is the reasons for interest-group activity on monetary issues – or rather their inactivity – as well as the channels by means of which they seek to influence monetary decision making. In this sense, the present study is complementary to existing findings, adding insights on the motivations and techniques of interest-group activity to the existing evidence on the impact of their work.

In so doing, the present study draws on a number of advances in the realm of economic and interest-group research. First of all, recourse is taken to basic insights on interest-group behaviour from those strands of political science concerned with the aims and objectives of interest groups and the determinants of their activities. In particular, theories on the origins and aggregation of interests are employed. Further, conceptualisations established in the literature on public-affairs and issue management serve as a valuable component for devising a framework for analysis. Second, the analysis builds on the vast economic literature on monetary policy. Monetary policy is a specific and complex policy issue. In order to explore the incentives for interest groups to deal with it, it is useful to examine the objectives, instruments and behaviour of policy makers. Understanding the channels through which monetary policy decisions impact the private sector, and in how far different actors are affected to different degrees, can deliver important indications of the factors behind interest-group behaviour. The analysis will also be concerned with the institutional environment in which interest groups need to operate when dealing with monetary policy issues. Political, economic, legal, and historical accounts of the positions of central banks within the political systems, as well as internal structures and decision-making processes, will therefore be consulted where appropriate. Finally, in the empirical section, historical accounts of central bank policymaking in the EU are taken as a basis for relating application of the findings of the theoretical section to the practice of monetary policy in EMU.

---

12 Maier (2002).

Approach and structure

To decide whether and to what extent interest groups seek to influence monetary decision making, the following analysis addresses the perceptions of monetary policy as a policy issue by interest groups. Issue perception is increasingly recognised in political literature as the single most important determinant of group activity, suggesting that interest groups and their members make a rational choice of the issues they address, given the large number of policy issues on the overall political agendas of contemporary economies[13].

The analysis is divided into three parts. Part I outlines the analytical approach this study takes, identifying institutional, issue, and interest group-related framework conditions as the most important determinants of interest group activity on a theoretical basis. Part II provides an initial analysis of these framework conditions by reviewing the relevant legal, institutional and historical properties of the environment in which interest groups operate with respect to monetary issues in Germany and at the EU level. Part III presents an empirical analysis of the perception by interest-group and central bank representatives in Germany and at the EU level of the importance of monetary issues and the interaction between interest-group representatives and central banks.

In more detail, chapters I.1 and I.2 provide a framework for analysing interest-group perceptions of monetary policy. The analysis begins by presenting a basic model of interest groups' maximisation behaviour, depicting the decision whether, and how much, political action to take. This is followed by a theoretical enquiry into the possible determinants of the costs and benefits of influencing a policy process as well as into the resources at interest groups' disposal. These determinants are primarily derived from the theories of interest aggregation and interest-group formation and organisation as well as from public affairs and issue management. Together, the model and determinants serve as the analytical framework for breaking down the factors behind interest-group activity in the realm of monetary policy.

This framework is applied to the specific contexts in which interest group-central bank relations are set. First, monetary policy is analysed in terms of the institutional setting within which it is conducted, most importantly the purpose and mandate of central banks, their internal organisation, and potential points of access for communication with the private sector. Further criteria are their role as administrative units, their resources, and the implications of institutional independence. This is followed by consideration of the characteristics of the policy issue with special reference to the perspective of the private sector. Finally, the focus is shifted to interest groups and

---

[13] Van Schendelen (2002), p. 118.

their resources in order to examine the potential contribution they can make in the specific context. The approach adopted in these sections is an interdisciplinary one, drawing on theoretical elements from political science, notably research on governmental theory and interest-group behaviour, from economics, notably monetary and institutional economics, as well as constitutional science in the context of the legal position of central banks within the political system.

From the analysis in chapter I.1, a list of propositions on the behaviour of interest groups with respect to monetary policy is derived, tracing the difficulties in establishing communication between interest groups and monetary policy makers back to the complexity of the effects of monetary measures on private individuals and the resulting difficulties in aggregating interests effectively, the institutional strength of central banks in terms of functional independence and resources, as well as the lack of resources in terms of original and exclusive information on the part of interest groups.

Part II presents the policy contexts within which interest groups in Germany operate with regard to monetary policymaking, reviewing the basic institutional, issue, and group settings in which interest-group behaviour is formed. It also introduces the basic policy-related and institutional changes resulting from the introduction of the single European currency in 1999 and the establishment of the European Central Bank.

The analysis of the attitude and behaviour of interest groups in Germany towards monetary affairs is presented in chapter III.2, following a brief outline of the research methodology in chapter III.1. In this chapter, the data from qualitative surveys among policy makers and interest-group representatives is presented and analysed to find out whether the forces identified in the theoretical part are actually at work in practice.

Following analysis of the monetary policy context in Germany, and against the background of the fundamental changes in the overall policy context as a result of introduction of the single European currency and the shift of monetary decision-making powers to the ECB, chapter III.3 enquires into the effects of EMU on the behaviour of interest groups in Germany as well as the way in which associations at EU level cover monetary affairs.

A concluding chapter summarises the major findings, derives implications for related fields of study and suggests points of departure for further research.

Part I Analytical approach

I.1 Theoretical framework

Monetary policy is but one issue interest groups may deal with. Large sectional interest groups and top associations in particular are occupied with a multitude of issues at any given moment in time. Such issues can pertain to a broad variety of subjects, ranging from wage negotiations and government tax policies to social and environmental legislation. In addition to existing issues, groups and their members are constantly confronted with new developments in their immediate operational environment, on the political stage, and in the wider societal sphere. As a result, new strategies to defend the interests of group members have to be formulated, implemented, and evaluated. In doing so, interest groups must communicate with a wide range of contacts relevant for their operations. Directions and feedback need to be collected from group members, potential allies sought for the groups' political activities and the relevant institutions in the political system and their representatives identified and contacted.

With the complexity of their operations in the background, investigating whether and to what extent interest groups are concerned with a fundamental issue like monetary policy implies asking at least equally fundamental questions about the behaviour of interest groups in general. Namely, what are the factors driving selection of the policy issues to be addressed; and what are the determinants of the selection process itself as well as of the effort interest groups have to make to succeed?

After presenting some basic assumptions on the decision making behaviour of interest groups, the determinants of interest-group behaviour thus established will be reviewed as a policy issue in the light of the specificities of monetary policy, with the aim of identifying factors encouraging or discouraging systematic activities on the part of interest groups in this field of policymaking. Further, the properties of central banks as the primary addressees of such activities will be analysed, as well as the resources interest groups have at their disposal in dealing with them. The chapter will conclude with formulation of the central propositions on the perception of monetary affairs as a policy issue resulting from the theoretical analysis.

I.1.1 Basic assumptions

The question as to how interest groups handle monetary affairs, and why they deal with the issue the way they do, essentially means enquiring into the behaviour of interest groups in a specific field of policymaking. This enquiry is composed of two elements. First, some fundamental assumptions will be made about the behaviour of interest groups in general terms. More specifically, it is necessary for the present analysis to identify how interest groups decide in principle whether to take political action on a given policy issue, and to what extent they pursue that issue. To that end, this section first presents some fundamental principles of interest-group decision making in this regard, which serve as the basic micro-behavioural assumptions on which the following analysis of interest-group activities in the field of monetary affairs rests. As argued below, we examine how interest groups arrive at the decision whether to act on a specific issue or not with reference to a basic analysis of the benefits and costs expected to accrue from political activity on that issue. Consequently, a second question to be answered is what the basic determinants of the expected costs and benefits of interest-group activity are. These determinants will form the second focus of this section.

The stylised facts outlined in the introductory chapter suggest that despite the potentially large impact of monetary decisions, interest groups have comparatively little regard for this field of policymaking. If this observation is correct, then the question arises as to why this is so. In other words, we must ask when interest groups actually become active on a given policy issue, and what factors contribute to this decision. A first step towards answering these questions is to look into the fundamental rationale of interest-group decision making in general.

This basic rationale has been formulated by Bartlett[14], employing a model in the tradition of public-choice theory[15], which is concerned with the formalisation of decision-making processes in the context of public-private interaction at large. Focusing on the economic self-interest of private sector agents, this literature has added a number of powerful models of the interaction of private interest groups and political decision making in democratic societies. Its analytical strength rests on the

---

14 Bartlett (1973), pp. 143-149. Bartlett was the first to address the question of how much political action should be taken in rigorous economic terms. His objective was to specify the alternative forms of political action and how and why they are chosen by decision makers seeking political influence. He did so by presenting a model with discrete functions for influence and costs, maximising the "profit or the net increase in [the producer's] real income from political activity". The model was developed further by Märtz (1990), pp. 75-79. Märtz presents this model "on the determination of the group-efficient level of production of political influence" in an explicit rent-seeking context. It serves as a basis for analysing the dynamics of the rent-seeking process in a competitive environment where the number of groups competing for political influence is larger than one. Compared to Bartlett (1973), the innovation lies in the incorporation of a production function of political influence, which in earlier treatments was taken as exogenous.

15 For comprehensive overviews of the public choice approach see Mueller (1979) and (1997). Overviews of the literature focusing on rent-seeking can be found in Tollison (1982), Rowley, Tollison, Tullock (1988), and Märtz (1990).

concept of methodological individualism[16] according to which individual behaviour of rational actors is the basis of economic and political decision-making.[17]

Assuming rational, utility-maximising behaviour on the part of decision makers[18], the model starts out from the observation that the decision to take political action rests on the same economic principles as any investment decision. Individual actors or interest groups weigh the expected benefits against the costs of seeking political influence and decide to what extent a deployment of resources for the purpose of exerting or intensifying political influence can be expected to generate marginal benefits. For the sake of simplicity, the model abstracts from differential preference within interest groups and assumes a uniform utility function in order to make it applicable to both individual and composite actors.

The decision process is based on three functional relationships. First, gross income from political influence (I) – including all material and immaterial benefits from political activity – depends on the amount of political pressure (p) – including all forms and qualities of influence on a decision at political level – that is exerted[19]. It is

---

16 Märtz (1990), pp. 6-7. For treatment of the concept of individualism in social choice see Buchanan, Tullock (1999), pp. 11-15 and pp. 31-39.

17 A systematic overview of the possible ways of modelling interest-group behaviour is presented by Potters (1992), pp. 7-24. He distinguishes between models with an influence function, models with a vote function and campaign contributions, and models with a composite utility function. The model chosen here belongs to the first category. Compared to the other types of models, influence-function-based models treat interest groups as independent and competitive players in the market for economic rents. They yield clear comparative static insights regarding the amount of pressure produced by interest groups. For the purposes of this paper such models are consequently better suited to illustrate the group-specific decision-making processes.

18 This assumption is warranted on two grounds. First, the objects of the present study are private households and firms, and the interest groups they are represented by, whose operational behaviour – in a market setting – is determined by rational profit maximisation. The central question in the present context is what the determinants are of the decision by these individuals to launch political activities with respect to monetary policy, aimed at maintaining or improving their economic position or welfare. It is useful to answer this question on the same basic premises as those on which the analysis of the underlying economic activities is customarily based. Second, there is no ex ante reason to believe that households and firms, or their interest representatives, behave irrationally or systematically differently from the way they act in their underlying operations. Irrational behaviour, i.e. behaviour which is not based on the intellectual faculty by which conclusions are drawn from premises, may be observed in practice but is unlikely to be of significant magnitude. Where such behaviour enters the analysis, explicit reference will be made.

19 The rationale behind the influence function can be spelt out more explicitly. Political decisions are relevant for an interest group because they may affect its own welfare or that of its members. Assuming that an interest group likely to be affected by a certain policy measure decides to remain passive and not to support or oppose the measure, the costs or benefits to the group resulting from that measure are given exogenously and will alter the group's welfare as an externality. Thus, the size of the expected impact of a policy measure, and therefore also the expected size of the benefits from political action, influences the intensity with which such benefits are sought (Mitchell, Munger (1991), p. 525).

reasonable to assume diminishing returns to scale, i.e. that the marginal increase in income from political influence will diminish with each extra unit of pressure.

– *Income function*

  $I = I(p)$, subject to $dI/dp > 0$ and $d^2I/dp^2 < 0$

Further, the amount of pressure depends on the resources (R) – including all forms of material or immaterial means mobilised by the group – that are deployed by an interest group to influence the policy-making process. The production function is also subject to declining marginal returns.

– *Production function*

  $p = p(R)$, subject to $dp/dR > 0$ and $d^2p/dR^2 < 0$

The resources deployed to influence the policy-making process also determine the costs of the political activities (C), which are assumed to increase with the resources deployed.

– *Cost function*

  $C = C(R)$, subject to $dC/dR > 0$ and $d^2C/dR^2 > 0$

The rational individual maximises the gains (G) from influencing the policy-making process:

– *Maximisation of gains*

  $\text{Max}\ [G = I[p(R)] - C(R)]$, subject to $dG/dR = dI/dP \cdot dp/dR - dC/dR = 0$

In other words, the resources spent on influencing the policy process are optimally employed when the marginal returns of political influence are equal to the marginal costs. The basic insight of this simple model is therefore that, assuming a rational, utility-maximising approach by the individual, political action with respect to a certain policy issue will only be taken if the expected income from such action exceeds expected costs. Both expected income and expected costs depend on the resources the individual has at his disposal, or is willing to devote to such activity, and on the rate at

---

The expected net impact of the policy measure on the group's income, M^e, is part of the group's cost-benefit analysis of whether to take political action on the policy measure. If the group decides to support or oppose the measure, this is likely to change the overall impact of M^e on the group's income function. The net effect of M^e therefore depends on the exogenously given potential impact of the policy measure and the degree of pressure the group is able to exert in the course of the policy process. Without changing the overall dynamics of the model, the group's influence function can therefore be interpreted in the following way:

Influence function: $I = i\ (p^e, M^e)$

Policy impact function: $M^e = m\ (p^e)$, subject to $dM^e/dp^e > 0$ and $d^2M^e/d(p^e)^2 < 0$

which deploying these resources can be transformed by the interest group into a marginal increase in income, i.e. on productivity.[20]

Given the basic insight that the decision whether to take political action on a certain policy issue is determined by the assessment of expected costs and benefits of such action, the question arising next pertains to the determinants of these expected costs and benefits. Costs and benefits can take a number of forms, making categorisation useful in the current context. The range of factors determining private sector influence on political issues is very broad, owing to the complexity of modern societal systems based on democracy and free markets. One categorisation of determinants of political activity by interest groups has been suggested by Mucciaroni[21] who differentiates between the institutional, issue, and group contexts within which private political activity evolves, drawing on the three most influential theoretical traditions in the literature on the subject, namely institutionalism, issue analysis, and stakeholder

---

[20] This framework can be extended to include uncertainty about future developments and competition among interest groups. First, monetary policy has a strong forward-looking slant. As a result, expectations on the part of policy makers and economic individuals about future economic and monetary developments, and therefore also about each other's behaviour, play a vital role in the policy-making process, as will be discussed in more detail below. Expectations and uncertainty about the course of major decision variables also influence the conception and pursuit of political action. Investment decisions in general, and those concerning investment in political influence in particular, are constrained by uncertainties with respect to the future development of the variables influencing the decision. The outcome of a policy process is difficult to account for. The policy decision itself is likely to be the outcome of a complex bargaining process. There may be a multitude of forces driving the decision, and of interests competing for influence. Consequently, it is sensible to assume that the future returns of influencing a given policy process as well as the associated costs cannot be quantified precisely before entering the political arena. It is useful for the current purpose to note that the independent and dependent variables used in the model are to be seen as expected variables. As a consequence, the shape and position of the functions, and therefore also the results the model yields with respect to the optimal amount of political influence, can be expected to change over time. In a dynamic setting, the resulting uncertainty over the potential costs and benefits and the overall pay-off of political action can be expected to increase the overall costs of political action. The general results of the model, however, remain the same in principle.

Second, interest groups rarely work in isolation, but usually compete with other interests for political influence. Competition is likely to alter the expected income of each individual group seeking political influence. *Ceteris paribus*, income falls as a result of intensified competition, and *vice versa*. In a dynamic setting, higher competition can also be expected to influence the costs of political action owing to the fact that, over time, achieving a given amount of political influence will become more expensive at the margins. As a result, the income and cost functions of the model cannot be taken as constant, but shift in amplitude and slope with the intensity of competition. Again, in principle the results of the present model remain valid after allowing for competition (see e.g. see Buholzer (1998), pp. 116-117, and Potters (1992), p. 9). A comprehensive overview over the effects of competition among interest groups is given by Daumann (1999), pp. 168-178. See also Buholzer (1998), pp. 113-117 and Märtz (1990), pp. 89-138. Formal treatments of competition among interest groups, such as Becker (1983) and Becker (1985) have focused on political influence for economic rents in return for votes and material resources needed in election campaigns. Potters (1992), pp. 7-24. See also Mitchell, Munger (1991) pp. 531-536.

[21] Mucciaroni (1995), pp. 8-25 and pp. 166-180.

analysis[22]. To start with, political action is by definition targeted at persons or institutions endowed with political decision-making power. Successful investment in political influence depends heavily on how far this institutional environment promotes the mediation of private interests vis-à-vis policy makers and offers easy accessibility to the latter. Second, the policy issue under consideration greatly influences the expected profitability of seeking political action. It defines the impact of a policy measure, be it in a negative or a positive direction, on the individual or the group and thereby also influences the expected benefits and costs of influencing political decisions. Finally, costs and benefits also depend on the way in which interests in a specific issue can be aggregated and organised. The ability to do so has been found to vary dramatically between countries, sectors and policy issues, suggesting that the interest-group context requires explicit treatment.

I.1.2 Institutional context

As to the institutional context, the behaviour and the accessibility of political decision makers represents an important determinant of interest groups' ability to influence political decision making. If interest groups want to change the monetary policy stance, they need to influence the behaviour of the policy makers to whom the relevant decisions are delegated. Influencing policy makers necessitates expenditure on material and human resources by interest groups. These up-front expenses will, however, yield returns if, and only if, policy makers are accessible, i.e. if channels exist through which they can be approached, and if they are receptive to external information or pressure, e.g. from interest groups[23].

The interaction between interest groups and political institutions has a long tradition in scientific research on interest group behaviour, both in theoretical and empirical terms. A great part of the literature, including this analysis, is concerned with the role groups play in the policy process[24] and suggests that their relations with political institutions

---

[22] For a concise summary of the issue and stakeholder analysis strands in the academic literature see e.g. Schendelen (2002), pp. 132-135.

[23] On the importance of accessibility of policy makers to interest groups see Ainsworth (2002), pp. 131-132 and pp. 216-217. On access as an interest-group objective see Truman (1993), pp. 264-265.

[24] Truman, who formulates the overarching question as being "[...] engaged in an effort to develop a conception of the political process [...] that will account adequately for the role of groups, particularly interest groups [...]", summarises the connection between groups and politics by stating that "[g]roups are a part of [...] politics [...] and they have always constituted an aspect of politics. In addition, they are so intimately related to the daily functioning of those constitutionalized groups – legislature, chief executives, administrative agencies, and even courts – that make up the institution of government that the latter cannot adequately be described if these relationships are not recognized as the weft of the fabric", (Truman (1993), pp. 46-47). For an overview of the research in this field see Baumgartner, Leech (1998), especially pp. 100-146.

can be very close, if not symbiotic[25]. At the same time, there is broad agreement among the authors that not only do interest groups shape the political process, but also that politics and political institutions shape the activities of interest groups[26].

In selecting the appropriate way of influencing a policy process, it is necessary for interest groups to identify the locus of decision-making power and to assess the decision maker's accessibility. As to the locus of decision making, interest groups have an inherent incentive to target the institution or institutions within the political system endowed with the power to take the relevant political decisions[27]. If decision-making powers are shared among more than one institution, it may be conducive to address political activities to all the institutions involved[28]. The more instances that are involved in formulating policy, the more access points the group has, but also the more resources it may feel obliged to invest in order to exhaust all possibilities of mediating its views. Similarly, if, for whatever reasons, the chances of influencing the policy process via a certain relevant institution are low, then an interest group might choose to work through different, more accessible bodies. Either way, the importance of an institution has to be assessed on the basis of its effective role in the policy process, which may differ from its constitutionally, legally or statutorily assigned mandate because of the political practicalities involved[29].

---

25 Thus, an important strand of literature argues that interest groups and political institutions can form so-called policy sub-systems on the basis of quasi-symbiotic relationships based on the mutual benefits of frequent and intensive interaction. Rather than exerting pressure as an external force, such interest groups attempt to insulate the policy sub-system so as to hinder interference from other groups. The less rigid concept of policy networks treats the relations between groups and policy makers as open and concludes that the structures of interaction are dynamic to such an extent that the dividing line between the policy network and its political environment remains rather unclear. This view has been advocated most notably by Heclo (1978). Both paradigms stand in contrast to the often adversarial nature of interest group-government relations (Wilson (1990), p. 27).

26 E.g. Baumgartner, Leech (1998), pp. 137-140, and Daumann (1999), pp. 99-117, Mucciaroni (1995), pp. 8-9, 167.

27 Von Beyme (1974), p. 87.

28 This becomes most visible in the context of the stages of the legislative process which may originate from different political institutions. These include the pre-legislative stages of proposing and drafting a piece of legislation. Depending on the constitutional provisions, legislation may for example be proposed by the government, parliament or via plebiscites. Drafting legislation may involve government and other executive officials, but also parliamentarians. During the legislative stage, addressees of private concerns will primarily be parliamentarians, but they can also include extra-parliamentary party officials, for instance. Once passed, the implementation of a piece of legislation may be influenced at the administrative level. *Ultima ratio* legislation and its implementation can be influenced at the judicial level by means of judicial review. Accordingly, the complexity of the policy-making process in most political systems requires interest groups to direct their political activities at more than one addressee. Von Beyme (1974), p. 90.

29 Mucciaroni (1995), pp. 18-23.

From the perspective of the group's maximisation problem, it does make a difference which and how many institutions need to be addressed in order to realise its interests. Both on theoretical and empirical grounds, interest groups are likely to approach different political institutions in different ways[30]. The most important analytical divide runs between the institutions that make up the political system. Comparable as the criteria may be in many respects[31], institutional accessibility differs considerably across the different types of political institutions. Thus, the accessibility of members of the legislature differs significantly from that of the executive, the bureaucracy, and the judiciary[32]. Accordingly, the costs and benefits of interest-group action are likely to differ with the type and number of institutions addressed by a group.

For this reason, it is useful to narrow down the focus to the type of institution that is likely to be most influential in a specific policy area. In the case of monetary policy, decision-making power rests to a large extent with independent bureaucracies[33]. Given that the most important central banks enjoy a great degree of political autonomy within their respective political systems, their institutional status is of particular relevance in the current context. In general, bureaucracies have become increasingly important as addressees for political pressure groups in modern welfare states[34]. Their growing importance as targets of interest-group activity has been associated with the transformation of their role in the policy process, moving from a range of activities centred around the application and implementation of rules laid down by the legislature to ever greater discretion in making rules by themselves, either on the basis of acts of framework legislation with broad scope for interpretation in implementation or by means of explicit delegation of specified acts of regulation and rule making[35].

---

30 Daumann (1999), pp. 103-130, Mény (1993), pp. 147-149.

31 Truman (1993), p. 437. He emphasises that the characteristics of different political institutions in terms of their openness to external forces are not so much similar as interdependent, since organisational structure and points of control across political institutions reflect and reinforce each other.

32 Most importantly Truman (1993), pp. 321-498.

33 Throughout the analysis, the terms *public administration*, *agency* and *bureaucracy* will, for the sake of simplicity, be used interchangeably and refer to structures of government whose primary function is to apply general rules and convert them into specific decisions for individual cases (Peters (1995), p. 2). It is recognised that, at a higher level of analytical differentiation, certain semantic and content-related differences between these terms do exist (Peters (1995), pp. 2-3). A definition of the term bureaucracy on the basis of welfare-economical principles can be found in Niskanen (1994), p. 15. Niskanen also presents a comparison of various types of definitions (pp. 21-23).

34 Von Beyme (1973), p. 116.

35 Von Beyme (1973), p. 116. The dividing line between framework legislation and delegation of specified policy areas to be administered by bureaucracies often remains unclear. In practice, legislative delegation generally involves the establishment of agencies separate from the governmental bureaucracy in the narrow sense. Central banks as well as regulatory and supervisory agencies are the most important examples.

The emergence of independent central banks is among the most important instances of this process. The greater the policy-making discretion of a bureaucracy, the more important it is likely to become as a point of access for private interests. Effective political independence – defined as an authority's freedom to pursue its objectives without being subject to formal or informal political instructions from other entities within the political system[36] – clearly amplifies a central bank's powers in fulfilling its mandate.

The accessibility of such an administrative institution from an interest group's perspective is determined first by its internal structure and processes. More precisely, exerting influence on policy decisions presupposes an understanding of the decision makers inside the institution, their position within it and how their views are aggregated in the course of the decision-making process[37].

Access for private interest groups to decision-making processes within administrations can be of a formal or informal nature. Formal avenues are granted by many institutions in the form of advisory or consultative committees or expert hearings[38]. At an informal level, interest groups can seek to influence policy makers by means of personal contacts with decision makers or through the dissemination of information in line with their objectives[39]. In both cases, formal and informal access, policy makers' willingness to consult with private interests is motivated by the potential benefits this can confer in terms of better information on the object of policymaking and political

---

[36] As initially defined by Grilli et al (1991) and presented by Bofinger et al. (1996), p. 184. Alternative definitions of central banks' political independence have been presented in literature. For a critical discussion see Bofinger et al. (1996), pp. 183-185.

[37] A detailed account of the relevance of institutional and procedural structures can be found in Truman (1993), pp. 328-332.

[38] Truman (1993), p. 457, differentiates between advisory committees and administration by groups in formal interaction with external bodies. With the former, decision makers acknowledge the importance of consulting the individuals and groups in society likely to be affected by a policy measure. Advisory committees or other consultative bodies are a formal device inasmuch as they are established by law or by executive action. The same applies to the process of administration by groups, which in principle represents an extension of the process of delegation by means of which government agencies are endowed with political discretion. Within well-defined limits, interest groups are granted self-governance under the rules laid down by law or executive acts. Further, Truman cites "administrative propaganda" as a third formal means of interaction with external bodies, referring to publicity activities by the administration aimed at associating certain external interests with it in order to secure its operations, especially in cases where the "adjustment", i.e. the support, of the interests involved was not obtained at the legislative stage. For a detailed analysis of formal participation through committees, councils and hearings see von Beyme (1974), pp. 170-192.

[39] Daumann (1999), pp. 158-160. Alternative methods of mediating interests are discussed by von Beyme (1974), pp. 160-169.

support[40]. As to the former, the existence of an information asymmetry between policy makers on the one hand and the private sector on the other hand is widely recognised. For one thing, the private sector may possess important information about the nature of the problem and the implications of a legal or administrative act that may not otherwise be available to policy makers[41]. Further, the success of such acts may depend on the private sector's action and reaction to the act itself. The greater the amount of information on the prospective response by private decision makers, the better picture decision makers will have of the viability and effectiveness of their measures[42].

Closely related to this latter point is the benefit from communication with the private sector in terms of political support. Handling a controversial policy measure, politicians and administrators can underpin their own position vis-à-vis the public as well as other public decision makers involved by drawing on the support of private interests. In doing so, they can enhance the publicly perceived legitimacy of their measure and create political momentum for pushing the measure ahead in the legislative or administrative process[43]. For both motives, information and political support, private interest groups are likely to find easier access to the relevant policy maker the less the latter possesses his own expertise[44] on a given policy issue or the more he has to rely on external political or public support on a controversial policy measure[45].

Finally, in addition to aspects related to the role and the needs of a public institution itself, accessibility is frequently associated with behavioural patterns of individuals serving the administration. Some public servants may be more open to external influence than others, depending on their own views as to the role they play within the

---

[40] Thus, Peters (1995), p. 181, notes that "[...] [pressure groups and bureaucrats] need each other to be successful. Administrators need the political support and influence of pressure groups in their external relationships with other political institutions, and they also need information supplied by pressure groups for making and defending policies. Likewise, the pressure groups need access to the political process and influence over decisions that are taken. This mutual need, given the fragmentation of decision making in modern governments, is the basic dynamic explaining the frequent cooperation between public bureaucracies and pressure groups."

[41] Truman (1993), p. 333, sees policy makers "[...] in continuous need of current information because [they are] at the mercy of changes as they occur. [...] The penalty for numerous or conspicuous decisions made in ignorance or in neglect of relevant available knowledge is disturbance in the politician's established relationships."

[42] Truman (1993), pp. 334-335, makes a distinction between technical knowledge, which private interests can provide on the content of a policy issue, and political knowledge, i.e. the information of private sector interests on the strength of competing claims and the consequences of alternative decisions on a policy issue.

[43] Truman (1993), pp. 333-334.

[44] Peters (1995), pp. 225-226.

[45] Peters (1995), pp. 226-227.

executive in general and their administrative unit in particular. Also, such behavioural patterns are likely to influence public officials' preferences for the means by which they choose to communicate with the public, most importantly whether formal and institutionalised or informal and personal sources of information are used. Insofar as public servants possess room for manoeuvre in proposing policy measures to political decision makers and in implementing policies, they enjoy political influence. How administrators use this influence depends on what they deem to be consistent with good government and proper administration. As a consequence, the political culture of public administrations and their members, their ethos and identification with their unit[46] is likely to have an impact on their attitude towards private interest groups and the extent to which private interest groups can address them[47].

I.1.3 Issue context

As to the issue context, the nature of a policy issue[48] plays a decisive role when it comes to assessing the prospective success of influencing policy decisions. The case for a systematic analysis of policy issues is made most explicitly by Mucciaroni, who states that

> "[v]ariations in policies [...] over time and across policy areas are not random outcomes. Rather, they reflect a predictable logic that emerges from analysis of two broad categories, or contexts, of policymaking: the kinds of issues that become salient in the political arena and how those issues are defined, and the capacities, incentives, and behaviour of key institutional actors in government."[49]

---

[46] Von Beyme (1974), p. 119.

[47] On identification and loyalty of administrative officials with their institutions, see von Beyme (1974), pp. 118-120, Peters (1995), pp. 45-134, Truman (1993), pp. 446-457.

[48] A *policy issue* has been defined as a concern, problem, or debate that centres on political or social cleavages and has a public character. Issues on which, as a rule, different parties take conflicting positions addressed to a counterpart perceived as responsible are in principle of a controversial nature. Issues are usually characterised, first, by the fact that they always relate to one or a group of events. Second, developments related to such events, including media coverage and interpretation, become part of the issue itself, so that the issue is a conceptually broader term than, for example, the term event. Third, an issue relates not only to one single individual, but is associated with at least an entire sub-system of society. See Liebl (1996), p. 8. Baumgartner, Leech (1998), p. 38, use the term issue as synonymous with the term *policy conflict*.

[49] Mucciaroni (1995), pp. 8-9. Looking exclusively at producer groups in the US, Mucciaroni takes a largely qualitative approach to examining the policy issues of tax expenditures, anti-competitive regulation, trade protection, and agricultural subsidies. He concludes that "[...] both issues and institutions are crucial in their own right, and any analysis that omits either one is likely to be inadequate." (Mucciaroni (1995), p. 167).

Nevertheless, contributions to the traditional literature on interest groups have dealt with the topic mainly implicitly[50]. Most importantly, the significance of political issues has entered scholarly debate via the classification of interest groups. The most common typologies are based on interest content[51] and therefore relate directly to the issues a group is concerned with, an insight that holds true irrespective of whether further categorisation is pursued along socio-economic, sectoral or policy domain lines[52]. Similarly, the relevance of policy issues is also documented by the literature on the origin of interest groups where common interest, and therefore the joint work on specified policy issues, are the basic motivation behind collective action within an interest group[53]. The systematic analysis of policy issues, in turn, has largely been dominated by the literature on public affairs and issue management. The focus of these writings lies on the implications of inter-temporal issue development for the formation of interest group strategies[54], most importantly dissecting the life cycle of an issue and the implications of the discrete phases of issue evolution for the behaviour of the stakeholders involved[55].

The analysis of monetary policy as a policy issue is a useful step on the way to a comprehensive picture of the incentives for private interests to influence monetary policy decisions. Theory and evidence point to an important relationship between the nature and characteristics of a policy issue on the one hand and the inclination of interest groups to include the issue on their political agenda on the other[56]. According to these findings, the decision whether to take up a certain policy issue is significantly influenced by a number of criteria, which can be split up into factors pertaining to the

---

50 Richardson, Jordan (1979), p. 77, argue that questions relating to the emergence of issues have been relatively ignored.

51 Salisbury (1975), p. 182.

52 For a list of typologies see von Beyme (1974), pp. 27-32. Also Truman (1993), pp. 63-65, Salisbury (1975), pp. 182-189, and Bamgartner, Leech (1998) pp. 25-36.

53 E.g. Truman (1993), p. 33: "[...] "[I]nterest group" refers to any group that, on the basis of one or more shared attitudes, makes certain claims upon other groups in the society [...].", or Olson (1965), p. 5: "One purpose that is nonetheless characteristic of most organizations, and surely of particularly all organizations with an important economic aspect, is the furtherance of the interests of their members."

54 For comprehensive introductions see e.g. Liebl (1996), Wheelen, Hunger (1998), Köppl (2000) and Mack (1997). Schendelen (2002), pp. 132-135, provides an evolutionary account of the contribution of issue analysis and issue management to the theory of interest-group behaviour, presenting the insights of this strand of literature as an important predecessor to the approach of arena analysis.

55 Schendelen (2002), p. 133.

56 Most importantly, Mucciaroni (1995). For a summary of theoretical arguments see pp. 166-170 in particular.

properties of an issue, subsumed under the heading of issue salience, and to the political environment under the heading of issue sponsorship[57].

With respect to issue salience, the impact of the issue on the individual has been identified as the most important determinant. This strongly supports the results yielded in the theoretical discussion above. Second, urgency and immediacy have a significant positive impact on the standing of an issue on the political agenda. At the same time, a high level of complexity[58] can discourage individuals and groups from dealing with an issue, since this may reduce the ability to mediate associated interests[59]. The salience and urgency of policy issues in particular are subject to variation over time. Thus, issues exhibit life cycles, which have been found to be of major importance for their management by the players involved. Their genesis commences when singular, superficially unrelated events are publicly placed in a common context by an interested party. With growing support from other sympathisers, the initial effect of publicity is amplified. Assuming sufficient public pressure, the addressee feels compelled to deal with the issue. Once this peak is reached, public interest is set to diminish until the issue has disappeared from the public agenda. The decisive aspect of the life cycle from an interest group perspective is that groups' room for manoeuvre and, consequently, their political influence depends on the public's perception of the issue and the timing of political action[60].

The category of issue sponsorship refers to the competitive environment in which interest groups seek to promote a specific issue and mediate their particular interests. For each given issue, there is likely to be more than one interest group claiming the interests of its members, competing with each other for maximum impact on the outcome of the political decision-making process. Next to other groups, an interest group is likely to find itself competing with vested interests articulated, for example, by policy makers themselves, political institutions, administrations, or voters and the

---

[57] Liebl (1996), pp. 91-92.

[58] By analogy, general and abstract formulation of a policy issue has been found to support it in the agenda-building process (Liebl (1996), p. 92).

[59] Liebl (1996), p. 91.

[60] Liebl (1996), pp. 8-9. Analysis of policy issues in the light of their life cycles can involve substantial challenges, as Baumgartner and Leech argue (1998), p. 38. Thus, "[...] there is no clear way to determine when an issue or a policy conflict has begun or ended. Three fundamental research problems flow from this simple fact. First, there can be no universe of issues from which to sample. Second, there is no single definition of an issue when issues are easily aggregated into large and interrelated groups or broken down into minute clauses, as constantly occurs in the policy process. Third, issues rise and fall on the political agenda over time, being transformed and redefined in the process. There are no apparent solutions to the difficulties created by the fluid nature of issues in the political process."

public at large[61]. Whether and to what extent an interest group is able to operate successfully in this competitive environment depends on its involvement with the issue as well as its political clout and resources[62], as will be discussed in further detail below. The same, in turn, holds true for the other interested parties with which it competes for influence. The higher the resistance of other interested individuals, groups or entities to a specific interest is, and the greater their political weight, the smaller the expected benefits of promoting it and *mutatis mutandis* the greater the cost will be[63].

Competition does not, however, start at the point when an issue is already discussed by policy makers or the public. In fact, interest groups already compete with each other to put an issue onto the policy agenda. Assuming that policy makers' capacity to deal with policy issues is limited, an interest group needs to bring the relevant issue to their attention or into the public domain before it can actually promote a specific interest. Consequently, there is negative correlation between the number and diversity of issues already on the individual and public political agendas and the chances for a new issue to arise[64].

Diagnosis of the issue context along these lines enters the income as well as the expense side of a group's or individual's cost-benefit analysis. The higher the expected positive or negative impact of an issue, the greater the expected benefit is likely to be from taking political action, be it in order to promote or discourage a certain policy measure, and *vice versa*. Other factors such as urgency, complexity or promoter influence will enter the analysis via their indirect impacts on benefits and costs. For example, instant action on an urgent issue will produce a higher income than delayed action. The higher the level of complexity of an issue, the more costly it will be to convince potential allies and the policy makers targeted of the benefits of joining forces or taking the desired political decision. A powerful existing political influence can reduce a group's marginal costs of pursuing one more incremental issue.

I.1.4 Interest-group context

Next to the nature of the policy issue and the policy maker's institutional and behavioural characteristics, the ability to influence political decisions depends on the interest-group context in which private interests are embedded[65]. According to the

---

[61] For detailed descriptions of the competitive environment of interest groups see Liebl (1996), pp. 125-127, Köppl (2000), pp. 37-42, and Wheelen, Hunger (1998), pp. 9-11.

[62] Liebl (1996), p. 92.

[63] Richardson, Jordan (1979), p. 79, Daumann (1999), p. 177. Daumann also provides an overview of the existing models of interest-group behaviour under competition (pp. 158-174).

[64] Liebl (1996), p. 91.

[65] Von Beyme (1974), pp. 49-52.

basic behavioural assumptions made above, income from and costs of political influence are both a function of the resources an interest group is able and willing to devote to such activities. As a partial-analysis model, it treats resources as given exogenously, and identifies the maximum net benefit from influencing a specific policy process. Following the preceding analysis of the determinants of the maximisation process, i.e. of the costs and benefits expected to play a role in a group's decision to influence a policy process, the question arises as to which resources interest groups have at their disposal in pursuit of their activities.

In the context of interest groups exerting influence on decisions in public policymaking, the various types of resources potentially available[66] have been subsumed under four headings, categorised according to their functional use[67]: financing potential, information potential, collective action in the political arena, collective action in the market arena.

First, organised interest groups' financing potential originates from membership fees, donations and other fund-raising activities[68]. In as far as revenues exceed the operational costs of running the interest group, group representatives can draw on these funds to finance their activities at the political level, i.e. to advertise a group's interests among policy makers, other influential persons and entities or the public at large[69].

Second, interest groups possess extensive information about their members, which in the sphere of economic interest groups generally encompasses information on the conditions relevant for their economic activities, the extent, relevance and importance of their operations, and their economic and strategic behaviour. As a result, interest groups generally enjoy detailed knowledge of their members' needs and objectives and their potential response to changes in their operational environment, enabling them to assess and judge public policy measures on these grounds[70]. The supply of information interest groups command in principle matches the information needs of political decision makers already observed above[71]. The degree to which interest groups are

---

66 For an overview see Daumann (1999), pp. 118-119.

67 Daumann (1999), pp. 120-124.

68 Daumann (1999), p. 121. Other fund-raising activities include entrepreneurial activities and asset management (von Beyme (1974), pp. 58-59).

69 Von Beyme (1974), p. 58.

70 Daumann (1999), pp. 121-122.

71 Interest groups have an incentive to pass on information to policy makers on a selective basis in order to make the messages contained in and associated with the information compatible with their own policy objectives. This selective approach also includes decisions to withhold information. Daumann (1999), p. 160.

able to use their information edge in exchange for political influence depends *ceteris paribus* on the quantitative and qualitative size of the informational asymmetry[72].

In contrast to finance and information, which can be regarded as direct elements in interest group action given that interest group representatives themselves have immediate access to these resources, collective action[73] is a resource which an interest group can dispose of only in an indirect manner. Collective action emanates from the members of a group, and therefore requires prior information, consultation, and organisation among group representatives and members[74]. It can be exerted in a political as well as a market setting. Collective action in the political sphere aims at influencing policy makers by exerting pressure on their position within the political context. Most prominently, elected politicians can be targeted by group representatives recommending a certain voting behaviour to their members. In this case, interest groups can be interpreted as organised, well-defined pools of voters[75]. Since the current analysis of monetary policymaking will be primarily concerned with politically independent administrators and less with elected politicians, collective action in this sense is likely to play a minor role.

Collective action in a market context refers to common patterns in the behaviour of interest group members in the markets on which they operate, including product, financial, and factor markets[76]. The effects of behavioural patterns in this sense can influence policy makers to the extent that the latter are either reminded of the economic potential behind a certain group or that the impact of a given policy measure on the economy is brought to their attention in an *ex ante* or *ex post* manner. Actions such as lay-offs in response to cuts in industrial subsidies or tax evasion following an increase in levies usually serve both purposes, demonstrating market power and

---

[72] Daumann (1999), pp. 159-161. Daumann also analyses the means by which the groups' information lead can be exploited. Apart from the instrumental role information plays for groups in the pursuit of their interests, the provision of valuable information services is frequently quoted as furthering, if not indeed constituting, the welfare-enhancing character of interest group activities. According to this view, potential distortions of the market and continued exploitation of consumers and taxpayers due to interest group activity are compensated or even outweighed by the net welfare gain from providing efficiency-enhancing information that would not otherwise have been available to policy makers. In this interpretation, the formation of interest organisations is merely the most efficient means of ensuring that all interests in an issue are voiced. See also Mitchell, Munger (1991), p. 528.

[73] The term collective action in this context refers to collective activities among interest group members beyond group membership itself. Its use here, as introduced by Daumann, (1999), pp. 121-124, therefore differs from the traditional application of the term, namely in the context of interest group formation, as initially stipulated by Olson (1965).

[74] Daumann (1999), p. 123.

[75] Further means of political collective action include strikes, demonstrations, and illegal activities (Daumann (1999), p. 123).

[76] Daumann (1999), pp. 123-124, Mény (1993), p. 129.

existing or potential policy impacts. Insofar as individual market behaviour in anticipation of or response to a policy measure follows directly from the pursuit of a private actor's inherent objectives, e.g. profit-maximising behaviour in the case of business firms, the desired results in terms of influencing political decision makers can be achieved without prior activities in the form of planning and co-ordination by an interest group. Thus, tax evasion generally occurs as a result of individual optimisation behaviour, requiring no separate incentives from interest groups for collective action, and can be interpreted by policy makers as a signal with respect to the effectiveness of taxation.

Financial means, informational lead and collective political and market action represent the sources and means of interest groups' influence on political decision makers. Interest groups, however, differ considerably in the extent to which they command these means, giving rise to differences in the amount of influence they are able and likely to exert[77]. Consequently, it is useful for the current analysis briefly to recapture the resource elements behind the means of influence categorised above.

Following von Beyme[78], there are five factors determining the degree to which interest groups can utilise the above means of influence: ideology, organisation, the quality of group leadership, representativeness, and sources of finance.

Ideology is used as a broad concept, referring to the objectives, values and self-image an interest group cultivates[79]. It derives its importance from, and aims at integrating, group members whose interests cannot be taken as entirely identical, and at promoting a group's cause with the public by underlining the importance of the group's specific interest for other groups and public welfare in general. Ideology will be relevant for the current analysis primarily in as far as interest group values may contain specific reference to the desired conduct of monetary policy in general, or to the code of conduct with respect to contacts with policy makers.

The relevance of interest groups' internal organisation for their ability to influence political processes is not uncontroversial. On the one hand, von Beyme rejects the idea of a causal relation between a group's internal organisation and its ability to assert itself at the political level, pointing to the theoretically substantiated importance of various other factors and the weak empirical evidence for such a relation[80]. Others, however, have argued that the group's effectiveness in activating indirect sources of influence in particular – i.e. pressure on politics and markets by means of collective

77 Mitchell, Munger (1991), p. 525.

78 Von Beyme (1974), p. 39.

79 Von Beyme (1974), pp. 39-40.

80 Von Beyme (1974), pp. 50-52.

action – depends on a number of organisational factors, first of all the group's ability to provide incentives to join in the common cause[81]. The more efficiently such incentives are provided, the easier it will be to motivate group members for activities beyond group membership itself, and the more likely the chances to correct subjective perspectives, i.e. to emphasise the importance of individual contributions to certain activities and prevent free-riding behaviour[82].

At the centre of Daumann's argument lies the observation that a fundamental problem usually associated with the formation of interest groups, namely that of individual free-riding, may in principle continue to prevail as a structural factor inside existing interest groups beyond the formative stage. Free-riding was identified as a structural impediment to group formation by Olson[83]. His argument can be summarised as follows:

> "[I]nsofar as an interest group is organised in order to bring influence to bear on government [...] or in any other way to make claims upon other groups, no rational self-interested person will join unless he must or unless he is persuaded to join for some other reason. The reason is simple. If influence is achieved and the group secures its claims against others, the individual who shares the interest involved will benefit fully without joining. In rational-choice theory and analysis this is the free-rider problem. [...] Therefore interest groups will not be successfully formed unless one of three conditions obtains. One is philanthropy, [...]. A second is compulsion, [...]. The third and most common is the use of selective benefits, those benefits offered only to members of the organisation and not available to others who may share the group attitudes but do not formally belong."[84]

Olson's logic plays an important part in the analysis of interest-group activity on monetary policy in two respects. First, the theory suggests that interest groups in the sense of formal interest groups will be formed only if one of the above criteria is fulfilled so that, in general, there will be an initial threshold that individuals need to overcome before they succeed in forming a formal interest group. With respect to

---

[81] Daumann (1999), p. 124. Baumgartner, Leech (1998), p. 163, refer to a number of studies supporting the argument that group resources and organisational structure are important influences on political strategies and the choice of tactic. Nevertheless, they conclude that the similarities among groups are more striking than the differences and that most data sets do not allow for quantitative testing.

[82] Daumann (1999), p. 124.

[83] Olson's argument applies only to political action for rents with a public-good character (Mitchell, Munger (1991), p. 515), i.e. goods for which the economic criteria of non-rivalry, non-excludability and non-rejectability in consumption apply (Ng (1992), pp. 187-189). Applicability in the current context is given since, as argued below, monetary policy and its policy outcomes can also be subsumed in the category of public goods.

[84] As quoted in Salisbury (1975), p. 192.

monetary policy, the question arises whether interest groups have managed to form whose only or primary concern is the pursuit of their interests with respect to monetary policy. Such interest groups would fall under the category of cause or promotional groups[85] organised to express a particular policy objective. Theoretically, one could think of groups exclusively promoting an anti-inflationary policy, low interest rates, or an exchange rate policy or regime conducive to the interests of the group members. Since these objectives exhibit a strong public-good character, incentives to form such groups are, in line with Olson's postulates, likely to come up against strong counter-incentives motivated by free-riding. Consequently, the establishment of promotional groups with a focus on monetary policy would require marked compensatory conditions in the form of idealism, compulsion, or selective benefits[86].

More relevant in practice, and indeed the focus of this analysis, is the case where individuals do not decide to form interest groups exclusively for the purpose of promoting their views on monetary policy, but where existing interest groups are employed to articulate such interests, be they general or specific in nature. The analytical focus in this case rests on groups based on socio-economic factors[87] usually concerned with a large and varied issue portfolio. Using such sectional groups, e.g. business and labour organisations, as a vehicle for mediating specific interests carries a number of advantages. First and most importantly, it enables individuals largely to evade the problems associated with the formation of a group solely designed for the pursuit of interest representation on monetary policy. Second, individuals can benefit from the infrastructure of the existing group, including its organisational facilities, contacts, reputation, and expertise and can thereby avoid incurring additional costs. Closely related to that, sectional groups usually comprise a large number of members, so that pooled resources and the combined economic and political weight of such a group can be expected to outweigh the overall potential of a newly formed promotional group.

These advantages notwithstanding, channelling a specific interest through large sectional groups may be accompanied by problems of its own. Once an interest group

---

[85] For different categorisations see Salisbury (1975), p. 182.

[86] There is evidence that the viability of selective benefits is limited. First, non-material benefits, such as appeals to solidarity or idealism, are restricted in their effectiveness if the actors are motivated primarily by material interests (Moe (1981), p. 536). Second, the higher the number of members of a group and the lower the frequency of group interaction, the more important material benefits become for initiating and constituting collective action (Olson (1965), p. 59). Third, the costs of enjoying the selective material benefits from membership in a formal interest group need to be lower than the costs of obtaining the same benefits by other means, e.g. on the open market. Consequently, the higher the competition on goods and factor markets, the lower the effectiveness of selective material benefits (Daumann (1999), p. 49).

[87] Salisbury (1975), p. 182.

is established, the process of selecting issues, and of aggregating and organising interests becomes a problem internal to the group. As a result, free-riding problems may prevail to some extent within an interest group. Second, the larger the sectional group, the more likely its members are to exhibit heterogeneous preferences with respect to specific policy issues. Where this is the case, aggregating interests becomes increasingly difficult the higher the degree of heterogeneity of preferences is[88].

Against the background of these intra-group problems, the influence of individual group members on the outcome of the group-internal process of interest aggregation depends on their market power and their organisational power[89]. Market power refers to the size and possible alternative use of a member's resources and depends on the significance of internal and external barriers to group exit. The higher a member's input into the group and the easier it is for him to leave the group and devote his resource profitably to other activities, the stronger his market power inside the group will be, and *vice versa*. Organisational power, in turn, refers to the constitution of the group and the extent to which individual members can influence a group's activities through its internal decision making structures[90]. All else being equal, individual members will find it more difficult to influence group strategy and get their objectives onto the agenda of the group as a whole, the weaker their market and organisational influence is within the group.

Closely related to the potential heterogeneity of interests within a group is the third element of resources, namely group leadership. The quality of group leadership has been found to correlate positively with interest groups' success in influencing policy makers[91]. Group leaders find themselves at a critical position between securing and promoting the internal cohesion of their group, devising appropriate strategies for group activity in order to satisfy members' expectations, and communicating in an effective way with policy makers[92]. The more capable group leaders and group

---

[88] Truman (1993), pp. 63-65, p. 167. Enumerating the sources of conflicts within interest groups, Truman considers the problem of overlapping group membership the most important (pp. 167-168). According to this view, being a member of or identifying with more than one interest group may create conflicting allegiances, thereby weakening the outright support given to each single interest group and hence the internal cohesion of that group (pp. 157-159). As the analysis below will be concerned with interest groups for which either overlapping membership cannot be expected or whose interests can largely be regarded as consistent so that such membership structures are unlikely to lead to the conflicts described by Truman, problems deriving from overlapping membership will not be dealt with in detail below.

[89] For a detailed description of the terminology see Daumann (1999), pp. 57-58.

[90] Daumann (1999), pp. 57-58.

[91] Von Beyme (1974), p. 59.

[92] Truman (1993), pp. 188-193, von Beyme (1974), pp. 59-61. Daumann (1999), pp. 78-98 gives a detailed analysis of group representatives' discretionary room for manoeuvre within the constraints

representatives are of fulfilling these tasks, the more effective a group will be in ensuring that its members' interests are represented adequately. However, relations between group members on the one hand and leaders and representatives on the other are inherently characterised by a principal-agent problem, as a consequence of which the preferences of the latter may differ from those of the former[93]. Thus, the benefits of institutionalised interest representation inevitably entail adding a further, albeit less severe, potential source of incoherence.

Adding up the problems related to interest groups' internal coherence owing to heterogeneous group member preferences and the differing objectives of their representatives, it would appear that interest groups' ability to operate as single unitary actors is limited. Against this background, the assumption of unity implicit in most models of interest-group behaviour, including the one employed above, is very stylised. However, this does not necessarily impair their validity in principle. In the present context, for example, differences in member preferences are a central part of the analysis and will therefore be adequately accounted for. In contrast, problems related to the principal-agent relationship between members and representatives will not be covered explicitly. This is warranted for two reasons. First, it is legitimate to assume that the effects of this phenomenon are limited, since in the long run the ability of group representatives to pursue their own objectives depends by and large on their ability to perform in accordance with the interests and preferences of the group members[94]. Second, it is a potential problem of general significance and not specific to

---

of the objectives of the group at large and its members. For techniques of group leadership see Truman (1993), pp. 193-210.

93 Contrary to the frequent assumption that the objectives of a group are exclusively a function of the preferences of its members, group representatives do not necessarily throw up a precise mirror image of aggregate interests. This follows directly from their position as agents of the group members who collectively fulfil the role of a principal delegating the tasks of interest representation to the executives of the group. Neutral representation of member interests by the agents can only be achieved if their interests on a specific issue are identical and the agents do not have agendas of their own (Daumann (1999), pp. 56-59). Since neither of these two conditions can safely be assumed (Daumann (1999), p. 56), the delegation of competencies by group members to group representatives follows the logic of a principal-agent relationship in which, given the difficulties in devising interest-compatible incentive mechanisms, the political pressure exerted by the agents is not necessarily entirely compatible with the aggregate interests of the principal. Possible short-term objectives of group leaders and representatives include preserving and enhancing their position and material benefits and increasing the institutional size of the group as well as its membership and financial resources (Daumann (1999), pp. 78-81).

94 It follows directly from the difficulties related to collective action that individual group members whose demands on group membership are not sufficiently catered for have a strong incentive to take corrective action, either by means of working towards a change in group regime or by exiting the group altogether. Both options would be opposed to the interests of group representatives. Failing to perform in accordance with the objectives of the principal would consequently be self-defeating for the agents (Dunleavy (1991), pp. 16-19, Daumann (1999), pp. 83-84).

the current topic. To keep the analysis focused, issues pertaining to group leadership will therefore be taken as exogenous unless stated otherwise.

The degree of representativeness is the fourth element determining the ability of interest groups to exert their means of influence as identified by von Beyme. Representativeness is defined, first, by the absolute number of members of a group and, second, by the degree of organisation as measured by the number of group members relative to the size of the quasi-group, i.e. the overall number of individuals sharing the interests of the group, including both *de facto* and potential group members. The higher the number of group members and the higher the degree of organisation, the more successful a group is likely to be in bringing its full political potential to bear in the policy-making process. This holds true for both the direct and indirect elements of group activity. [95] An interest group's ability to attract members and attain a high degree of organisation again ultimately depends on the homogeneity of interests within the domain of potential members[96] and the group's ability to overcome free-riding incentives by efficiently providing selective benefits from membership.

Fifth, potential group influence is determined by an interest group's financial resources. As already argued, aggregating interests and forming an interest group can incur substantial costs. The same holds true for an interest group's everyday operations. Exerting influence involves functional processes similar to those in other services sectors, such as planning, organisation, structuring, communication, co-ordination, resource planning, implementation, and budgeting[97]. Carrying out these functional tasks requires expenditure on mobile and immobile factors as well as personnel. The wider the financial room for manoeuvre is for an interest group, *ceteris paribus* the easier it will find the performance of its operational tasks. The size of the financial margin depends on the number of members, their ability and willingness to contribute to the group by means of membership fees or allowances, and the group's ability to employ financial resources efficiently[98].

I.1.5 Interim conclusions

Overall, the preceding analysis of the determinants of interest-group activity shows that, given reasonable behavioural assumptions, interest groups take decisions as to whether to address a certain policy issue, and how much activity to unfold, by assessing the institutional, issue and group contexts within which activity on a certain

---

[95] Daumann (1999), p. 124.

[96] Von Beyme (1974), p. 57, Daumann (1999), p. 124.

[97] Köppl (2000), p. 33.

[98] Von Beyme (1974), pp. 58-59.

issue will be placed. Either formally or informally, interest groups and their members have to weigh the expected benefits against the expected costs of such activity on the basis of this assessment. Consequently, interaction of the determinants summarised in table 1 below represents the basis for any interest-group activity.

Thus, communication between interest groups and policy makers requires the simultaneous existence of an economic rationale for seeking to influence a policy process, institutional access points for communication and the availability of resources on the part of the group. As the determinants of this decision-making process differ over time and from issue to issue, the extent of interest-group activity on a given policy issue becomes a matter of individual issue analysis, taking into consideration a large number of potential factors contributing to the overall analysis of expected costs and benefits of political action.

Determinants of interest-group activity – summary table

Table 1

Institutional context	**Institutional mandate** – Number of institutions involved in political decision making – Kind of institution involved in decision making – Institutional discretion in decision making **Institutional accessibility** – Complexity of decision-making process – Legal restrictions on external influence – Accessibility through formal channels – Accessibility through informal channels – Dependence on external information – Dependence on political support **Behavioural patterns** – Openness to external influence
Issue context	**Issue salience** – Impact – Complexity – Urgency **Issue sponsorship** – Issue attachment – Group resources – Competitive environment – Number of issues on the political agenda – Diversity of issues on the political agenda
Group context	**Resources** – Financing potential – Information potential – Political resources

I.2 Monetary policy context in theory

Given the importance of the institutional, issue, and group environments for an interest group's decision whether and how to take political action on a policy issue, the question arises as to how far monetary policy differs from other policy fields in these respects – and to what extent certain specificities may condition policy responses by the interest groups under scrutiny here.

This chapter approaches these questions from a theoretical angle, investigating the underlying rationale and functioning of monetary policy and the implications for the policy contexts in which interest groups operate. The aim of this review is, first, to present an initial theoretical overview of the fundamental issue properties of monetary policy. Second, given the broad range of items relevant to the calculation of potential costs and benefits of political action on monetary policy, many of which may not be specific to political action on monetary policy, it is useful to highlight those factors which are likely to be particularly relevant in this field of policymaking.

As to the first aim, the following section outlines the basic logic of monetary policy, identifying institutional and issue characteristics specific to this area of policymaking. Subsequently, these properties will be discussed in the light of the broad determinants of interest-group decision making with respect to the institutional, issue, and group contexts. Finally, a set of propositions on the specific conditions in which interest groups take their decisions on political action with respect to monetary affairs is deduced and then investigated in the empirical part of this study.

I.2.1 Economic relevance and sources of public controversy

Monetary policy encompasses all measures and processes that exist in an economy with respect to the supply of money and credit, the quantity of money, the rate of interest and the exchange rate[99]. As a result, it is a policy field in which contemporary states exert enormous influence on the economic performance and welfare of the private sector. This influence rests on two factors. First, it is determined by the economic importance of the resource which monetary policy commands, namely money. Second, it depends on the system by means of which the circulation of money is controlled.

Concerning the first factor, the importance of monetary policy for the private sector derives from the fundamental role money plays in modern economies characterised by a high degree of division of labour. By combining the properties[100] of being a

---

[99] Büschgen (1997), p. 525, Bannock, Baxter, Davis (1992), p. 290, and Lindsey, Wallich (1992), pp. 740-748.

[100] According to John Hicks, "Money is what money does. Money is defined by its functions." (John Hicks as quoted in Bofinger et al. (1996), p. 460). Accordingly, economic theory generally defines

generally accepted medium of exchange or means of payment[101], a store of value[102], and a unit of account[103], money has become an indispensable precondition for the development of complex market economies[104], in the absence of which the costs of gathering information about the relative prices of goods, assets and services would curtail, if not completely eliminate, the benefits of exchanging goods, services, capital, and labour. Market-based economic activity therefore *de facto*[105] largely depends on the existence of an asset that properly fulfils these functions.

The establishment, operation, and maintenance of money and the monetary system in contemporary economies are tasks assumed by the state[106]. So-called fiat money regimes[107] are based on the legal monopoly of state-appointed monetary institutions to

---

money in functional terms. Assets are money if, and only if, they fulfil the monetary functions of serving as a medium of exchange or means of payment, as a store of value, and as a unit of account (Jarchow (1990), pp. 15-18, Issing (1993a), pp. 1-2, Goodhart (1989), pp. 24-50). Alternative theories of the existence of money are based on an historical approach, arguing that the use of money emanates from convention based on an implicit or explicit social contract (Issing (1993a), p. 1, White (1999), pp. 1-14). An historical account of the importance of money and its functions with specific reference to the development in Western Europe can be found in Kindleberger (1993), pp. 19-36.

[101] For the current purpose of illustrating the importance of money and monetary policy for the private sector it is legitimate to use the terms "medium of exchange" and "means of payment" interchangeably. Strictly speaking, however, the concept of "medium of exchange" is a broader than that of "means of payment", since only the latter allows the final settlement of transactions (Goodhart (1989), pp. 26-27, Issing (1993a), p. 1). For a detailed account of the importance and implications of this function, see Bofinger et al. (1996), pp. 460-462.

[102] For a detailed account of the importance and implications of the store-of-value function, see Bofinger et al. (1996), pp. 462-463.

[103] For a detailed account of the importance and implications of the unit-of-account function, see Bofinger et al. (1996), pp. 463-464.

[104] Issing (1993a), pp. 1-2.

[105] This qualification applies since money may not play a role at all under certain hypothetical conditions. It has been argued, e.g. by Goodhart and Meltzer, that in a world of certainty, perfect foresight, absence of transaction costs, and an infinite time horizon all exchange activity can theoretically be maintained without an asset fulfilling the three central functions of money. In such a world, all relative prices are known by everyone from the very beginning so that present and future markets are clear and the whole time path of the economy is determined from the very outset. With all economic activity falling into the initial period, there is no need for a medium of exchange, means of payment, unit of account or store of value (Goodhart (1989), pp. 25-29).

[106] The historical transition to state-controlled public monetary institutions, which in most countries was undertaken between the late eighteenth and the early twentieth centuries, followed quite different paths across the industrialised countries. The most important cross-country comparison in academic literature is an early contribution by Vera C. Smith, published in 1935 (Smith (1990)). A thorough discussion of the micro-foundations of public monetary authorities can be found in Goodhart (1988).

[107] Fiat money regimes fundamentally differ from commodity-based regimes inasmuch as they allow discretionary adjustment of the money stock to overall economic conditions, irrespective of the natural scarcity of a commodity (see Issing (1993a), pp. 5-6). In contrast to commodity-money regimes, in which the amount of money is ultimately determined by nature and, even in the long run, is largely exogenous and beyond the scope of human intervention, monetary policy in fiat-

issue money and to control the quantity of money in circulation, i.e. to conduct monetary policy[108]. Unlike commodity-money regimes, such as e.g. the gold standard until the early twentieth century, in which gold or other specie serves as money whose supply is ultimately determined by their natural availability[109], fiat money regimes define as money paper notes and metal coin with very little inherent value. Redemption at par is guaranteed by the monetary authority and backed by reserves in commodities or securities, which often constitute only a small fraction of the nominal value of currency in circulation[110]. In as far as the existence of an asset serving as money can be seen as a vital precondition for the development of complex market economies, providing money and securing its proper functioning represents an eminently important economic activity. Since this economic activity is assumed by institutions of, or authorised by, the state and does not emanate from within the private sector, monetary policy is the object of economic interaction and the related communication between the responsible state authorities and the private sector.

Changing the amount of money in circulation affects a number of economic variables, either directly or indirectly. The overall relationship between the supply of money and economic activity is commonly illustrated by means of the quantity equation of money as rooted in classical economic theory[111], according to which real income and the price level on the one hand and the supply of money and the velocity of circulation of money on the other are directly linked[112]. Precisely how these variables are related to one another remains controversial, on both theoretical and empirical grounds[113].

---

monetary regimes can set the amount of money in circulation exogenously and freely, subject only to the objectives it is required to fulfil.

108 For a discussion of the importance of the state in assigning and legitimising currencies see Goodhart (1989), pp. 34-38; also Issing (1993a), pp. 5-6.

109 For a detailed account of the properties of commodity-money regimes see White (1999), pp. 9-11 and pp. 26-52.

110 Issing (1993a), pp. 5-6, White (1999), pp. 18-25.

111 Irving Fisher's quantity theory of money rests on the accounting identity between the product of money supply (M) and its velocity of circulation (V_T) on the one hand and the product of the price level (P) and the volume of transactions (T) on the other ($M \cdot V_T \equiv P \cdot T$). Overviews of the theory and its main critics can be found in Bofinger et al. (1996), pp. 473-491, Issing (1993a), pp. 132-147, Jarchow (1990), pp. 192-208.

112 For an adaptation of Fisher's equation to real income see Bofinger et al. (1996), pp. 473-474.

113 The various theoretical interpretations of the causal links between money, income and inflation have been categorised into three strands of literature, the classical quantity theory (for an outline see e.g. Issing (1993a), p. 135), the Keynesian tradition (for an outline see e.g. Issing (1993a), pp. 135-136, Levačić, Rebmann (1991), p. 52), and the neo-classical, neo-quantity or monetarist theory (as e.g. outlined in Issing (1993a), p. 138).

Consequently, the quantity equation by itself does not allow for judgements about the line of causation between the variables involved[114].

The controversy over the relation between monetary and real variables is the result of fundamental disagreement over the behavioural properties of basic economic variables such as the demand for money, as well as the nature of markets, namely whether and to what extent market clearing can be assumed[115]. Despite this controversy there is widespread agreement[116] that monetary policy does in practice affect both the price level and real economic activity, leaving open questions concerning the speed with which monetary impulses are translated into changes in both variables as well as their interdependence[117].

The connection between output and changes in the price level results from the interplay between demand and supply in goods, labour and capital markets in an economy. As described above, altering the availability of money implies a change in the relative prices and in the demand and supply of alternative financial assets, and, *ceteris paribus*, of goods and labour[118]. If monetary policy is inadequate to influence

---

114 Issing (1993a), p. 135.

115 For a comparative account of the controversies between Keynesian and neo-classical economic theory see Levačić, Rebmann (1991). A comprehensive up-date on the evolution of Keynesian interpretations of the viability of monetary policy is presented by Clarida, Gali, Gertler (1999).

116 This view is shared by most writers in the classical tradition, who would agree that the strict Walrasian assumptions of instantaneous market clearing underlying the classical model do not correspond entirely to the comparatively slow market adjustments observed in practice.

117 An instantaneous adjustment of the price level to changes in monetary variables, as suggested by the orthodox interpretation of the classical approach, has been dismissed as applying only under highly stylised conditions (Bofinger et al. (1996), p. 552).

118 Burda, Wyplosz (1993), pp. 236-255. One of the central relationships in this context has been depicted by the Phillips curve, which indirectly suggests a systematic relationship between price developments and income, by depicting a trade-off between inflation and unemployment. Originally based on empirical evidence in the UK between 1861 and 1957 (for historical accounts of the relationship between inflation and unemployment, see e.g. Dawson (1992); evidence on the relationship in Germany is provided by Smith (1994), pp. 254-311, and Weimer (1998), pp. 282-316, pp. 381-385, pp. 463-468.), the Phillips curve showed a relatively robust negative correlation between inflation and unemployment. This led many economists to believe that policy makers could choose between the two and reduce unemployment by, for example, relaxing the monetary stance, increasing output and lowering unemployment at the cost of a somewhat higher price level (Burda, Wyplosz (1993), pp. 236-242). Contemporary interpretations of the Phillips curve are more differentiated and take into account the dynamic adjustment of prices and wages occurring in practice. Dawson (1992), pp. 163-175, pp. 188-194, summarises the controversies over interpretation and application of the Phillips curve in contemporary scholarly writing. Accordingly, a direct trade-off between inflation and unemployment is believed to exist only for each given level of core inflation, i.e. the rate of expected inflation as assumed in the course of the price and wage negotiation process, considering both backward- and forward-looking elements. The long-term result of this process is that actual inflation reaches a higher level, while real income and unemployment remain unchanged (Burda, Wyplosz (1993), p. 249). For policy makers this implies that stimulating the real economy by means of monetary policy measures can only have short-term effects, which in the long run will lead back to the initial level of output and employment, while

real economic output in the long run, then the question arises as to how great its short-term potential to stimulate real output is, and how long such a stimulus can be expected to prevail until price and wage adjustments bring the economy back to its initial path. Given that an inherent tendency exists in competitive markets to pass on monetary stimuli through higher prices, over time it can be concluded that the more efficient markets are in translating changes in relative prices and the demand or supply of goods, capital or labour into changes in their respective prices, the faster the adjustment of overall prices, and the less pronounced the effects on output are likely to be.

- One category of factors inhibiting such quick adjustment is temporary price rigidities in goods, capital and especially labour markets. In practice, prices and wages cannot adjust instantaneously and continuously to changes in market conditions[119] due to price fixing on a trans-temporal basis[120], i.e. due to contractual arrangements that do not allow for inter-temporal price adjustment[121].
- Second, the size and duration of real economic adjustment to monetary policy changes crucially depend on expectations within the private sector regarding the future development in major economic variables, most notably inflation. In order to achieve optimal decisions, individual actors therefore have to anticipate future developments as accurately as possible, giving expectations a pivotal role in assessment of the viability of monetary policy measures[122].

---

actual inflation is elevated to a higher level. Since core inflation rises as well, future attempts at exploiting the short-term trade-off between inflation and unemployment will take place in an altogether less favourable, because more inflation-prone, environment (Burda, Wyplosz (1993), pp. 250-253).

119 In classical and neo-classical thinking transaction costs associated with price and wage rigidities are assumed not to exist, leading to the conclusion of instantaneous and continuous market clearing (Bofinger et al. (1996), p. 566).

120 Bofinger et al. (1996), p. 566.

121 Most importantly, wages are frequently fixed at a nominal level over time horizons of half a year or more. Second, producers of goods and services frequently do not adjust the prices of their products continually to changes in demand or supply, even without a contractual basis. Finally, rent and leasing contracts provide for prices fixed over long periods, often without the possibility of interim price adjustments.

Despite the costs of price rigidities from the angle of monetary policy efficiency, fixed contractual arrangements can be justified on economic grounds inasmuch as they help to minimise the transaction costs associated with changing price arrangements. Thus, fixing wage contracts on a trans-temporal basis serves to reduce negotiation costs and facilitate accounting and planning for firms. Staggered price setting by producers can reduce the costs associated with changing pricing in lists and catalogues, i.e. so-called menu costs, and helps bypass the uncertainty originating from difficulties in separating transitory from permanent shifts in demand (Bofinger et al. (1996), p. 567).

122 Issing (1993a), p. 227. Economic theory distinguishes between three forms of expectations formation – extrapolative, adaptive, and rational. The more accurately expectations are capable of

Summing up the preceding theoretical insights in the light of the relations between the private sector and monetary policy makers yields four important insights.

- First, monetary policy measures influence private-sector decision making in a wide range of ways as they change the terms of use of money and its near substitutes, i.e. the very basis of contemporary complex market economies, as well as *ultima ratio* those of all other assets that are held by private and public entities at any given point in time.
- Second, changes in private saving, investment, consumption, and production behaviour in response to monetary policy measures aggregate up to variations in economic output, making the potential force of monetary policy directly visible to the private sector. However, the real effect of monetary policy is likely to be of a temporary nature only, as changes in aggregate supply and demand in the economy will eventually feed through to alterations in the price level.
- Third, due to its impact on economic development, monetary policy is a matter of social choice. Monetary policy makers can and have to make decisions on how intensively and over what time horizon they will seek to influence the development of major economic variables, including the welfare and redistributive effects these can have. Depending on how much monetary policy decisions diverge from what is deemed necessary by the private sector, monetary policy therefore has the potential to become a highly political issue.
- Finally, monetary policy makers and private-sector individuals are highly interdependent in their decision making. Not only do monetary policy actions influence private-sector behaviour; in turn, effectiveness in achieving monetary policy objectives depends on the decisions taken in the private sector, namely on price and wage setting, the speed with which this is achieved and the swiftness with which policy signals are properly translated into private-sector decision makers' expectations.

This gives rise to the question what the objectives of monetary policy are, because the private sector will seek to bring influence to bear on a policy process only if the objectives, and the actions derived from such objectives, differ from the private

---

capturing future developments, the less pronounced the impact of monetary policy measures on real output are likely to be, since the private sector will anticipate that the effects of such policy measures will ultimately lead to changes in the price level only, leaving real economic activity untouched in the long run. In practice, this implies that the more and better information private-sector participants gather on monetary policy, and the better they are able to transpose information into expectations, the less effective monetary policy measures become in real terms. Ironically, there is indeed empirical evidence that private individuals systematically underestimate the real effects of monetary policy, implying that the formation of expectations in reality may not entirely correspond to the rational-expectations paradigm (Ball, Croushore (1995).

sector's own preferences. As discussed above, the importance of monetary policy for the private sector essentially derives from the central role money plays in contemporary economies as a means of payment, store of value, and unit of account. It is the guarantee of proper fulfilment of these functions that monetary policy makers have in mind when declaring price stability the sole or primary objective of their actions[123]. Price stability means that the prices of the different goods and services produced and consumed in an economy remain constant on average. Whenever the overall price level rises, the purchasing power of money, i.e. the goods and services a given unit of money buys, declines[124]. The process of an increase in the price level over time, measured by means of an index of the prices observed in the economy[125], is referred to as inflation[126]. The more inflationary tendencies erode the purchasing power of a currency, the less efficiently it is able to fulfil its functions[127].

Pursuing a policy of price stability has been justified on the grounds that the welfare costs associated with the loss of functional viability of money are greater than the expected benefits of inflationary tendencies. Most importantly for the present analysis, by and large the costs of inflation have to be borne by the private sector, while the benefits accrue directly to the state, leading to a disproportionately high burden from inflation for the private sector. These costs are the consequence of a combination of sub-optimal holdings of real balances, menu costs, and taxation-related effects or of a lack of price and wage adjustment as well as increased uncertainty, depending on whether private individuals anticipate a rise in inflation or not[128].

Even in the stylised case of correctly anticipated inflation, i.e. when all economic actors are able to predict exactly the rate of inflation for a given period at any moment in time, inflation will cause welfare losses to the economy.

---

[123] Bofinger et al. (1996), p. 77.

[124] Bofinger et al. (1996), p. 12.

[125] For a detailed analysis of the various methods of measuring the overall price level as well as the quantitative and qualitative problems associated with measurement see Bofinger et al. (1996), pp. 12-15.

[126] The opposite process, falling prices over time, is referred to as deflation (Bofinger et al. (1996), p. 12).

[127] Deflation, in contrast, leads to an increase in the purchasing power of money which, at first sight, may seem beneficial to money holders. However, by distorting the relative prices of goods, services and assets it eventually proves as damaging to economic welfare as inflation. Owing to the fact that it has been of little empirical relevance – the performance of the Japanese economy since the early 1990s has arguably been one major exception – in the post-war era, academic and public interest in deflation and the costs and benefits associated with it has been rather low (Issing (1993a), p. 185, Bofinger et al. (1996), p. 141).

[128] Issing (1993a), p. 235. Comprehensive overviews of the costs and benefits of price stability can be found in Issing (1993a), pp. 203-235 or Bofinger et al. (1996), pp. 22-96. A detailed econometric account of the welfare aspects can be found in Fischer (1981).

- First, inflation will cause the opportunity costs of holding money, as a non-interest bearing asset, to rise vis-à-vis other, interest bearing assets, leading to a reduction in real balance holdings in the private sector[129].
- Second, anticipated inflation generates menu costs, i.e. all the costs resulting from the continuous adjustment of nominally fixed prices and wages in order to avoid real effects from inflation[130].
- Third, the negative effects of inflation are frequently amplified via the tax system. Progressive tax rates, and maximum and allowances thresholds are usually fixed in nominal terms, so that delayed adjustment to the development in the price level generally leads to an increase in the average tax burden as tax payers grow into higher tax brackets in response to higher wage settlements[131].

---

[129] Bofinger et al. (1996), pp. 77-80. The welfare costs of inflation are part of the welfare costs of sub-optimal real balance holdings, which *ceteris paribus* requires consumers to spend more time on making the same real transactions with lower money balances. As a consequence, consumers will attempt to shorten the length of time between earning and spending their income, either by investing more time in spending their income, or by investing unused money in alternative assets, or by reducing their inventories. In times of high inflation, this can lead to a substitution of money as a means of payment, either by means of natural barter or by means of currency substitution, i.e. the use of non-domestic currency (Bofinger et al. (1996), pp. 81-82).

As the purchasing power of money declines, the consumer surplus from holding money, i.e. the difference between the marginal utility a consumer derives from holding each incremental unit of money and the costs of doing so, falls. The associated net welfare loss for society inevitably comes at the expense of private consumers, while the producers of money may even be in a position to raise their producer surplus in the event that their additional revenues from higher nominal interest rates exceed the losses from lower real money demand (Bofinger et al. (1996), p. 80). This evaluation of the welfare costs of inflation rests on the partial analysis model of the demand for real balances and assumes, besides correct anticipation of inflation, that inflation has no impact on output and that at least one alternative form of taxation exists which does not by itself cause negative welfare effects, e.g. a lump-sum tax. Otherwise, the welfare losses from inflation may be countered by lower opportunity costs from refraining from employing other, potentially more distortionary forms of taxation.

[130] Menu costs even arise in the stylised case of a perfectly anticipating and fully indexed economy, because nominal prices and wages need to be adjusted as long as money is being used for payment purposes (Bofinger et al. (1996), p. 87). Assuming that the adjustment of price lists or re-negotiation of wages incurs fixed costs, private individuals generally have an incentive to reduce the frequency of adjustment. In the presence of inflation, it pays off to adjust prices and wages more frequently, leading to an overall positive correlation between menu costs and inflation (Bofinger et al. (1996), p. 88).

[131] Detailed accounts of the process of "cold progression" can be found in Bofinger et al. (1996), p. 88, and Issing (1993a), pp. 234-235. Even if tax rates are adjusted appropriately, the time lags between assessment periods, tax payment, and tax repayment may lead to inflation-induced distortions. In addition, interest and dividend income taxation generally applies to capital income, irrespective of that fraction which merely compensates for the rate of inflation. Further, rules on the treatment of asset depreciation in corporate accounting regulations frequently do not allow for appropriate measurement of the decline in value of corporate assets as a result of inflation, leading to an overstatement of profits and a higher tax burden. As a result of these effects, inflation has an additional negative impact on the private sector via distortions in accounting, saving, investment,

The costs of inflation enumerated so far materialise even if changes in the price level are anticipated correctly by the private sector. Further costs arise after relaxing this stylised assumption and allowing for incorrect inflationary expectations in current and future pricing decisions and wage negotiations.

- Incorrect anticipation of inflation implies that nominal prices and wages, but also market interest rates or pensions, are bound to adjust insufficiently to the monetary environment, triggering distortions in the respective markets[132].
- The private sector also has to contend with the redistributive effects of unanticipated inflation on incomes and wealth.
- Unanticipated inflation heightens uncertainty among economic decision makers. Investment[133], savings, and spending[134] decisions by firms and consumers are made at higher risk, leading to a higher probability of misallocation of resources in the event that inflationary expectations are proven wrong *ex post*, or to higher costs of insuring against the risk of unexpected economic developments.
- Higher resource and transaction costs arise if prices and wages are adjusted more frequently in order to avoid real economic distortions.
- Private sector participants will find it difficult under non-predictable inflation to assess whether changes in prices are to be understood as changes in relative prices or in the overall price level, eroding the viability of the monetary system[135].

Given the negative effects of inflation, price stability is an important objective of monetary policy. Failing to adopt price stability as the sole or primary objective could only be explained if inflation also had positive effects, which could compensate for its disadvantages. Positive effects are felt by the issuer of money, i.e. the state. The potential producer surplus results from the revenues from issuing money, namely

---

and refinancing decisions of corporations (Bofinger et al. (1996), pp. 88-90, also Issing (1993a), pp. 234-235).

132 The effects of a distortion in relative prices become most visible in the context of corporate financial decisions, where changes in the value of investment projects, capital-budgeting decisions and the costs of funds can be thrown into substantial disarray, as documented *in extenso* by Agmon, Horesh (1988).

133 The description of the impacts of inflation on the private sector significantly abstracts from the complexity of the effects, especially with respect to firms. In particular, inflation has significant implications for the matching of corporate sources and uses of funds. In the case of stochastic shocks to the overall price level, managers need to set up financial planning with specific regard to inflationary effects in order to avoid continual revisions in the firm's financial policies or real investment plans. More precisely, the firm's debt ratio is the key determinant of its vulnerability to inflationary tendencies. An overview of these issues can be found in Lewellen, Kracaw (1987).

134 Holtham, Kato (1986) give a comprehensive overview of the interaction between inflation and consumption and present rich empirical date on wealth effects in the OECD.

135 Issing (1993a), p. 221.

"seigniorage"[136], and the erosion of the real value of nominal assets, namely the inflation tax[137]. Both effects represent a transfer of purchasing power from the private sector to the state, while the costs of generating these forms of revenue have to be borne by society as a whole[138].

Whether and to what extent this form of taxation is beneficial from the perspective of the aggregate welfare of society depends on the availability and efficiency of alternative forms of taxation. If government activity could be financed by means of non-distortionary taxes, i.e. lump-sum taxation only, then inflation-induced revenue would be a strictly inferior solution. Since state activity is in practice very difficult to finance by means of lump-sum taxation only[139], the marginal costs of employing inflation and alternative means of taxation have to be compared[140]. However, the comparatively well developed tax systems of contemporary economies are characterised by relatively low marginal costs of taxation. As a consequence, government finance by inflationary policies, especially the substantial risks of losing control over accelerating inflation, has been rejected in most industrialised economies over the past decades[141].

---

[136] Seigniorage is defined as the revenues from issuing money. On the one hand, seigniorage can be generated when the state borrows money from the central bank as the issuer of money either directly, by drawing a cheque on the central bank, or indirectly, by selling debt securities to the central bank, thereby creating additional base money. On the other hand, seigniorage is created in the course of money issuance within the banking system as a result of which the central bank disposes of interest-bearing assets. The revenues from holding and investing these assets can be transferred to the state, representing an additional source of government revenue. For detailed accounts on the theoretical foundations and empirical significance of seigniorage see Görgens, Ruckriegel, Seitz (2001), pp. 298-308, Bofinger et al. (1996), pp. 47-76, or Burda, Wyplosz (1993), pp. 200-201.

[137] Inflation is one form of taxation as it implies a transfer of purchasing power from money holders to the state. In effect, by issuing money the state secures goods and services from money holders. Inflation reduces the real value of money balances and thus the purchasing power of money. As the state's two most important liabilities, the monetary base and the public debt, are fixed in nominal terms, it benefits from the erosion of the value of real balances (Levačić, Rebmann (1991), pp. 396-397, Burda, Wyplosz (1993), pp. 200-201, Bofinger et al. (1996), pp. 58-60).

[138] Levačić, Rebmann (1991), p. 397. The revenue from seigniorage and the inflation tax cannot be raised at will by increasing the supply of money and the rate of inflation, i.e. the tax rate, since this by definition lowers the amount of real balances in the private sector, i.e. the tax base, so that beyond a certain rate of growth in the supply of money the state's net revenue from inflation declines. The maximum amount of revenue is a Cournot equilibrium on a Laffer curve whose shape essentially depends on the characteristics of money demand (Bofinger et al. (1996), pp. 61-76).

[139] Lump-sum taxation is generally considered to be of limited applicability due to the fact that it represents a relatively higher burden to lower wealth and income brackets than to more affluent households.

[140] Bofinger et al. (1996), pp. 71-74.

[141] Barro (1972), p. 978, concludes that "[...] Because inflation leads to higher transaction costs [...] there is a net social cost attached to inflationary finance. The [Barro's] model implies that marginal collection costs of inflationary finance exceed 50 percent for all positive rates of inflation – hence,

What follows is that owing to the multitude and weight of the undesirable effects of inflation, maintenance of price stability has become the preferred – albeit not always primary – objective of monetary policy in both theory and practice[142].

However, it does not necessarily follow from the general consensus on the benefits of price stability as the objective of monetary policy that all individuals in society agree with how monetary policy is conducted at every point in time. Diverging views on the appropriateness of the monetary stance may emerge from three sources:

– Price stability is a broad concept, leaving wide room for interpretation as to how it can be defined in practice. There is no generally accepted definition of price stability. Absolute price stability, i.e. a constant price level or zero inflation, as the strictest interpretation of the concept, has been rejected on practical grounds. Measuring price developments is accompanied by a number of technical difficulties, as a result of which inflation figures are statistically overstated[143]. Consequently, adhering to a zero-inflation target could lead to deflationary tendencies. In contrast, relative price stability permits slightly positive growth rates in the price level up to the extent that inflation is not incorporated into the private sector's relevant decisions[144]. In practice, this interpretation has been adopted throughout the industrialised world[145].

---

alternative means of raising revenue should be socially preferable [...]". Also Bofinger et al. (1996), p. 76.

[142] The major alternative monetary objective is the stabilisation of nominal income around its potential growth path. Purely income-oriented monetary policy would attempt to restore the equilibrium level of income or economic growth at the expense of a jump in the price level, running the risk of accelerating core and actual inflation. Purely price-stability-oriented monetary policy would aim at bringing the price level back to its equilibrium position by means of monetary contraction, depressing economic activity even further. Nominal-income targeting, in contrast, represents an interim solution in as far as it shares the burden of the initial shock between the two objectives of price and income stabilisation by allowing the rate of inflation to rise by precisely the amount by which income falls in response to the intermediate monetary stance. However, income-oriented monetary policies are accompanied by enormous difficulties in predicting, measuring, and targeting national income movements as well as the still largely unpredictable interaction between monetary policy measures and national income due to the complex channels of policy transmission and variable time lags. More fundamentally, income-orientation requires policy makers to tolerate rates of inflation that in certain circumstances will be above those tolerated under a price-stability objective. For extensive discussions see Burda, Wyplosz (1993), pp. 115-136, Bofinger et al. (1996), pp. 100-105.

[143] The statistical distortions have been calculated at 0.2% to 2% (Bofinger et al. (1996), p. 19, also Görgens et al. (2001), pp. 148-149).

[144] Görgens et al. (2001), p. 149.

[145] In most industrialised countries inflation rates of between 2% and 3% would be tolerated (Bofinger et al. (1996), p. 21).

- The objective of price stability is difficult to translate into precise policy rules[146], i.e. precise quantitative inflation, price-level, or exchange rate targets. Policy rules are defined as pre-determined commitments for monetary policy makers[147], codified at a constitutional, legal or statutory level. The aim of such rules is to give monetary policy makers stricter guidelines on how to pursue their policies on a day-to-day basis. Given that monetary policy objectives are generally formulated in rather general terms, rules are also used to narrow down the scope of policy-making discretion within the limits of the policy objectives. Rules refer to and define monetary policy targets, trying to overcome the problems associated with operationalising the broad policy objectives, i.e. first, the fact that monetary policy can only provide stimuli to the behaviour of private- sector actors rather than having an immediate impact on goods and factor markets; second, that the variables monetary policy objectives refer to are determined by a wide range of factors, of which monetary policy is but one; and finally, that as a result there is no clearly defined link between policy objectives and the instruments available to monetary policy makers[148]. How wide that room for manoeuvre for monetary authorities is, depends primarily on the margins for objectives and targets which policy makers define as the guidelines for day-to-day policymaking.
- The time horizons of monetary policy makers and individuals in the private sector may differ, to the extent that private individuals may be ready to make sacrifices with respect to price stability and favour short-term improvements in income instead. Given the potentially damaging impact of myopic and discretionary

---

[146] The term "policy rule" as used here refers directly to the concept of rules familiar from the "rules v. discretion" debate in monetary theory. For a detailed exposition see Bofinger et al. (1996), pp. 119-178.

[147] Pre-determined commitments can be decreed exogenously by the constitutional institutions establishing the monetary authority, representing the strictest application of the idea of rule-based monetary policy systems, as it must be adhered to and cannot be altered by the monetary authority itself. Alternatively, and in the absence of an exogenously set rule, the monetary authority can make an autonomous commitment to a policy objective or target.

[148] In order to fulfil their purpose, monetary policy targets need to satisfy four conditions. First, the targets need to lie within the sphere of influence of monetary policy, i.e. they must allow for a high degree of autonomous decision-making power on the part of the monetary authority. Second, the link between the target and monetary impulses must be such that the effectiveness of monetary policy measures in terms of their direction and intensity is observable earlier and more correctly than it is between the relevant policy objective and monetary impulses. Third, the target variable has to respond swiftly to monetary policy measures in order to enable timely evaluation and, if necessary, correction of the monetary stance. Finally, the target variable needs to allow for precise measurement of the degree of target fulfilment (Büschgen (1997), pp. 526-527). A detailed account of the various forms of monetary policy targets can be found in Bofinger et al. (1996). For money-supply targeting see pp. 248-300; for exchange rate targeting see pp. 300-326; for interest-rate targeting see pp. 327-349; for nominal-income targeting see pp. 349-365. The more recent strategy of direct inflation targeting is discussed on pp. 365-380.

behaviour on monetary decisions[149], monetary authorities are equipped with long-term, stability-oriented objectives and independence from day-to-day electoral politics on a statutory basis. Individuals in the private sector are free from such statutory constraints and may favour short-term gains over long-term objectives.

As a result, monetary policy is a matter of social choice – and therefore inviting to interest groups. Price stability has been identified as the most important objective of monetary policy. Its pursuit helps minimise the social costs of inflation and stabilise the economic environment in which the private sector operates. Accordingly, and viewed from a long-term perspective, price stability has frequently been characterised as a vital precondition rather than a contradiction to alternative social objectives such as income, growth, and employment. In the short run, however, these latter objectives may influence the preferences of policy makers in the wider sense as well as private sector individuals, making controversies over the pursuit of appropriate monetary policies likely.

Besides its purpose and objectives, a third source of importance and potential public controversy over monetary policy lies in the way it is transmitted into the economy and its economic impact on individuals and groups in the private sector. The transmission process of monetary impulses has remained inscrutable in many respects and is characterised by a high degree of complexity, which may affect the way monetary policy is perceived by interest groups.

---

[149] The fundamental insight in the literature on time inconsistency has been that even under rational expectations and a social welfare function that policy makers and private individuals have in common, the former will choose a combination of inflation and unemployment inferior to the result that could be achieved if monetary policy were obliged to stick to a zero-inflation rule. According to the model developed by Kydland and Prescott, in which policy makers optimise monetary policy by means of a social welfare function incorporating inflation and unemployment and a constraint given by an expectations-augmented Phillips curve, policy makers will depart from the optimal equilibrium of zero inflation and unemployment at its natural rate because they can achieve a higher level of social welfare by inflating the economy slightly and thereby reducing unemployment such that the marginal costs and benefits of doing so are just identical. Once this policy decision is taken, it turns out that the resulting rate of inflation is inconsistent with the private sector's initial expectations. Given rational expectations, the private sector will adjust their expectations, causing the feasible trade-off between inflation and unemployment to deteriorate. This adjustment of expectations brings the economy to a state where inflation is even higher than caused by the policy decision itself and where unemployment is in fact above (under the specific constraints applied by Goodhart (1989), pp. 363-366) the initial social optimum. As a result, the time-consistent equilibrium is strictly inferior in terms of achieving the objectives of society, i.e. low inflation and low unemployment as defined in the social welfare function, to the policy solution under a price stability-oriented monetary policy rule (Kydland and Prescott (1977), p. 480). For a complete account see Kydland and Prescott (1977), pp. 477-481. For the possibility of a "consistent" equilibrium see Goodhart (1989), pp. 363-366. The results of the model also hold true if alternative forms of taxation are explicitly excluded from the model (Calvo (1978), pp. 1411-1428).

When a central bank takes monetary decisions it assumes that by influencing certain monetary variables it will ultimately steer real variables, such as consumption, investment, employment, production and price developments, in accordance with its objectives and targets[150]. Transmission is best used to describe the impact of monetary impulses on certain real or nominal economic variables[151], and can be broken down into two stages[152].

- At the first stage, monetary impulses from changes in the policy interest rate or in base money lead to changes in financial market conditions, as reflected in market interest rates, asset prices, the exchange rate and general liquidity and credit conditions in the economy[153].
- At the second stage, the changes in financial market conditions lead to changes in nominal spending on goods and services by households and firms[154].

These two stages can be observed across a range of channels through which monetary impulses are transmitted. Starting from the initial monetary impulse, the literature differentiates between four broad channels of transmission: the effects of monetary measures on interest rates, the credit channel, balance sheets, and the exchange rate channel[155].

---

[150] Görgens et al. (2001), p. 233.

[151] Effects in the opposite direction have been referred to as monetary policy feedback (Görgens et al. (2001), p. 233).

[152] See e.g. ECB (2000) and Bank of England (2000). Berk suggests differentiation in three stages: First, the influence of changes in the instrument variables on the cost of finance, second, the influence of changes in the cost of finance on expenditure decisions of private-sector agents, i.e. on non-financial activity, and, third, the pass-through of changes in non-financial activity to output and inflation (Berk (1997), p. 8). This sequence differs from the one employed here in two respects. First, it takes a more restrictive approach to the first stage, focusing on financing conditions, while the present approach includes variables not strictly related to financing conditions, such as exchange rates. Second, it treats the transition from effects on non-financial activity to changes in output and inflation as separate steps, while the present analysis brackets these effects into one stage. These two aspects, while reflecting different forms of illustrating the process, do not result in different conclusions in the following analysis.

[153] European Central Bank (2004), p. 45, Berk (1997), p. 8, Görgens et al. (2001), p. 235.

[154] European Central Bank (2004), p. 45. Also Bank of England (2000), pp. 6-8.

[155] Excellent overviews of the transmission mechanism are Berk (1997) and de Bondt (1998). The present discussion largely follows the categorisation applied by Görgens et al. (2001), pp. 237-261. Similar discussion can be found in European Central Bank (2000a) and Bank of England (2000). Transmission via expectations is frequently treated as a separated channel of transmission, as argued below. Further, reference is made to a so-called cost channel of transmission, pertaining to the short-term effects of a monetary impulse on the ability of firms and households to meet their financial obligations with respect to the factors employed in production processes against the background of changes in their liquidity position. However, this approach has not been regarded as significant either in theoretical or empirical terns. For a discussion, see Barth et al. (2000).

- First, monetary policy operations influence economic activity through the interest-rate channel. The initial monetary impulse[156] is set by the monetary authority's use of its instruments[157]. By using their short-term instruments, monetary authorities can determine the terms on which financial institutions[158] can refinance their activities if they are unwilling or unable to satisfy their liquidity requirements in the inter-bank money market[159]. By setting reference interest rates, monetary authorities influence inter-bank lending conditions rather closely, and thereby the overall refinancing conditions of the credit sector[160]. The impulse feeds through to non-banks, since the banks will meet changes in their refinancing conditions by adjusting their interest rates on deposits and lending vis-à-vis their non-bank clients. Subsequently, there is pressure on the prices of capital-market instruments such as securities – government and corporate bonds – as well as shares to adjust to the developments in the money market[161]. From the perspective of the private

---

156 The initial impulse is sent out to the market for central bank money, i.e. the money market in the strict sense. Participants in this market are the monetary authority, commercial banks, and in exceptional cases selected large enterprises. For a detailed account of the alternative ways of steering the money market see Goodhart (1995), pp. 263-302, and Bofinger et al. (1996), pp. 386-417. For details on the strategic implications of operating on the market see Görgens et al. (2001), pp. 216-231. For details on rate setting by the Bank of England, see Bank of England (2000), p. 5.

157 Monetary authorities operate in the financial markets by means of open-market operations, standing facilities and minimum reserve requirements. An overview of these instruments can be found in Görgens et al. (2001), pp. 175-202, Bofinger et al. (1996), pp. 393-412, and Issing (1993b), pp. 63-142. By requiring banks to hold a certain fraction of their liabilities as minimum reserves in the form of deposits, monetary authorities can artificially stimulate the demand for central bank money and stabilise money-market interest rates (Görgens et al. (2001), pp. 175-176, Bofinger et al. (1996), pp. 412-417). Beyond these traditional instruments, communication with financial markets by means of moral suasion (Issing (1993b), pp. 127-130) and influencing international capital flows (Issing (1993b), pp. 131-140) have been identified as possible instruments of monetary policy.

158 Not all banks are necessarily directly involved in the operations of central banks. The liquidity in the inter-bank money market suffices smaller credit institutions in particular. Thus, end-2000 there were 7,500 credit institutions subject to the ECB's minimum reserve requirements, of which only 3,600 used the deposit facility and 3,000 the marginal lending facility. Only 2,500 financial institutions were involved in the ECB's main refinancing operations, while a mere 200 were eligible to participate in its fine-tuning operations (Görgens et al. (2001), p. 175).

159 The impact of monetary policy measures on the participants in the inter-bank money market is not homogenous. Following a monetary contraction, the banking system as a whole attracts additional funds from foreign banks. Whereas small savings banks and co-operative banks do not seem to access the inter-bank market themselves directly, they do so indirectly through the head institutions of their sectors. The inter-bank flows within these two sectors allow small banks to access funds that might help them keep their loan portfolios relatively unaffected by monetary policy measures (Ehrmann et al. (2001a) and (2001b)).

160 Bank of England (2000), p. 4.

161 The size and speed of this adjustment process throughout the financial market crucially depend on the degree to which investors and lenders regard the various financial instruments as substitutable (Görgens et al. (2001), p. 241). The determinants of the substitutability of assets are discussed by Goodhart (1989), pp. 238-241. On the implications of asset substitutability for the transmission

sector, the changes in market interest rates described have an important impact on the cost of finance, the return and allocation of investments, and income and wealth[162]. In addition, monetary policy has potential indirect effects in the form of substitution[163] and income and wealth effects[164].

– Second, monetary impulses are transmitted via the supply of credit on the part of commercial banks[165]. In contrast to the mere pass-through of money-market interest rate changes to firms and households by banks, the bank-lending and balance-sheet channels of monetary transmission refer to credit-market imperfection as a result of informational asymmetries[166] which might give rise to an amplification of the interest-rate effect and even credit rationing[167].

---

process see Meltzer (1999), pp. 3-5. Comprehensive accounts of the interaction of short- and long-term interest rates can be found in Bofinger et al. (1996), pp. 562-565, and Görgens et al. (2001), pp. 237-244. For a summary see Bank of England (2000), p. 4. A theoretical discussion of the interaction of monetary policy measures and the term structure of interest rates is offered by Goodhart (1989), pp. 238-262.

162 The immediate impact of monetary impulses on equities is discussed in Mishkin (1996), pp. 6-8. Bank of England (2000), p. 4. Mishkin (1996), p. 8 and Favero et al. (1999a) and (1999b), pp. 9-11, emphasise the importance of effects on other, non-financial assets in addition to those on equities. The cost-of-capital effect arises because a change in central bank interest rates ultimately affects the conditions at which lending from banks as well as directly from the capital market is available to firms and private individuals (see also Görgens et al. (2001), p. 244).

163 Substitution effects can be observed because of portfolio adjustments in response to monetary policy measures (Görgens et al. (2001), p. 247).

164 Income and wealth effects arise due to the redistribution of cash-flow following changes in monetary policy. Changes in the interest-rate structure alter creditors' present and future interest income and debtors' interest expenses (Görgens et al. (2001), pp. 248-249).

165 Enquiries into the specific role of banks in the transmission mechanism have been conducted in response to the observation that the traditional neo-classical and Keynesian interpretations lack explanatory power with regard to empirically observed movements in investment and output. The interest elasticity of investment in particular was found to be too low to explain the high volatility in investment in capital goods by firms (Küppers (2000), pp. 76-82). For a detailed critique of the interest-rate channel as the sole explanatory variable in monetary transmission see Hubbard (1994), pp. 2-6. Also Bernanke et al. (1995) pp. 1-4. However, Bernanke et al. (1995) note that it may not be warranted to regard the credit channel as a distinct, free-standing alternative to the traditional monetary transmission mechanism, but rather as a set of factors that amplify and propagate conventional interest-rate effects, reducing the credit channel to an enhancement mechanism, not an independent or parallel channel (see pp. 2-3).

166 The traditional analysis of the transmission mechanism largely rests on the assumption of perfect and complete markets. According to this view, banks pass on changes in their refinancing conditions passively to their clients. The credit channel explicitly rejects this view and takes into account informational asymmetries as the source of market imperfections, giving banks an explicit and active role in the determination of lending rates. A detailed analysis of informational asymmetries and their implications for the behaviour of financial intermediaries in general and banks in particular in the banking sector can be found in Küppers (2000), pp. 13-69.

167 According to Bernanke et al. (1995), p. 22, the empirical significance of the credit channel, and that of the bank-lending channel in particular, has declined over time owing to financial innovation and

– The balance-sheet channel relates to the effects of monetary policy on the balance sheet and cash flow of firms and households[168]. If monetary policy becomes more restrictive, the subsequent hike in interest rates and decline in financial asset prices leads to an increase in interest payments on the part of lenders as well as to higher financing requirements in response to the diminishing cash flow. In the case of extreme monetary policy tightening accompanied by a fall in the overall price level, the debt burden of lenders might even rise while the value of real assets would decline. Faced with a deterioration in the financial condition[169], banks have an incentive to compensate the associated risks by adding a risk premium to the interest rate such firms are charged, or by refusing to hand out credit altogether. Failure to gain access to alternative forms of external finance will aggravate the problem for firms and households. As in the case of the bank-lending channel[170],

---

the subsequent increase in the substitutability of bank credit. For a historical analysis of the size of the credit channel see Miron et al. (1993).

168 For a detailed description of the channel see Bernanke et al. (1995), pp. 11-18. Mishkin (1996) formally differentiates between the channels working through firms and those working through individual households, putting different emphasis on expenditure on capital goods and investment on the one hand and housing and consumer durables on the other (see pp. 14-16).

169 The net worth of a debtor plays a central role in the balance-sheet channel as it determines the amount and value of collateral the debtor can offer the bank. In the case of a decline in the value of collateral following the logic of the balance-sheet channel, moral hazard on the part of the debtor and adverse selection on the part of the creditor can induce the latter to ration the supply of credit (e.g. Hubbard (1994), pp. 6-9, and Küppers (2000), pp. 89-90).

170 In the US numerous studies find that small and young enterprises are significantly and comparatively strongly affected by credit rationing in response to monetary tightening. Kashyap et al. (1997) offer an extensive overview. Most importantly, Kashyap et al. (1997) and Kashyap et al. (2000) present extensive evidence in support of the bank-lending channel and the hypothesis that the channel is the more forceful the less liquid bank balance sheets are. See also Ramey (1993). These findings are supported by the fact that the statistical basis for analysis of monetary transmission via the banking system is very strong, benefiting from the detailed reporting requirements on firms and banks in the United States, which yield a rich source of official data. In addition, research into the credit channel has a strong tradition among American economists (Küppers (2000), pp. 120-124 and pp. 203-206). For contrasting results see Romer et al. (1990).

Research into the credit channel in European economies has yielded less unambiguous results, with significant variations across countries. Favero at al. (1999a) do not find evidence of a significant response by bank loans to monetary tightening in either France, Germany, Italy or Spain, where bank balance sheets were investigated. Rather than rationing credit, small banks are found to use excess liquidity to maintain existing levels of lending, while larger banks use the strength of their balance sheets to insulate loans from monetary policy fluctuations. In recent studies, the Bundesbank (2001) and Chatelain (2001) also conclude that the relevance of the credit channel is as yet unclear. Ehrmann (2000), in contrast, finds supporting evidence for the hypothesis that small firms, for which information costs can be expected to be higher and access to alternative forms of finance is more difficult, are significantly and disproportionately affected by the balance-sheet and bank-lending channels. Large firms are found to suffer more from exchange rate effects. Ehrmann et al. (2001b) find that monetary policy alters the supply of bank loans, but unlike the US, the size of banks does not generally explain their lending reactions. Küppers (2000) differentiates along the various categories of banks – savings, co-operative and large private credit institutions – and finds that only the latter adjust their credit portfolios significantly, but emphasises that this credit rationing as a result of this mechanism is likely to hit small enterprises and private households in particular[171].

- Third, monetary impulses reach the private sector via exchange rate effects. Monetary policy measures influence exchange rates by altering domestic returns on assets and therefore the incentive for foreign investors to channel funds into or away from the domestic economy[172].

At the end of the transmission process stands a change in present or future income or wealth for private-sector individuals, independent of the channel through which the monetary impulses take effect. These changes are likely to alter investment and consumption behaviour by firms and households, leading to changes in aggregate

---

does not necessarily contradict the central hypothesis of the bank-lending channel. Small banks with very close relations to their clients are simply better positioned in inter-bank competition and enjoy better access to information about their clients. Kashyap et al. (1997) reach similar conclusions, referring to the lower liquidity of small credit institutions. Following detailed study of the correlation of monetary policy changes and private consumption, de Bondt (1999) concludes that there is a significant accelerator effect via the banking system in Germany, Italy and the Netherlands, while in France, the UK, and Belgium no significant acceleration could be found. For the euro area as a whole, Peersman et al. (2002) conclude that neither the interest-rate channel nor a broadly construed financial channel emerges as clearly and exclusively dominant.

A recent study into the balance-sheet channel in Germany suggests this to be a significant, albeit secondary, path of monetary transmission (Kalckreuth (2001)).

For theoretical arguments supporting the credit-channel hypothesis see Mishkin (1996), pp. 19-20.

171 Görgens et al. (2001), pp. 257-258.

172 The cross-border capital flows associated with such investments influence the development of exchange rates, which, in turn, influences the price of exports from and imports to the domestic economy, the domestic price level, and the domestic private sector's income and wealth. More specifically, *ceteris paribus* an appreciation of the exchange rate associated with a hike in central bank interest rates reduces the international competitiveness of domestic goods and services. Simultaneously, imports become cheaper for domestic residents, stimulating demand for goods and services produced abroad. Both effects help reduce inflationary pressures but lead to a reduction in aggregate demand and production at home, hurting domestic producers. Private-sector income and wealth will be affected by exchange rate movements insofar as private firms and households receive income or hold assets denominated in foreign currencies. Recipients of foreign-denominated income will lose purchasing power because of rising exchange rates. Domestic investors holding assets denominated in foreign currency are confronted with a reduction in the value of such assets. In contrast, lenders holding debt denominated in foreign currency see their debt burden reduced by an exchange rate appreciation and benefit from a lower debt servicing burden. A rise in central bank interest rates leads *ceteris paribus* to higher capital-market interest rates and lower prices for securities and stocks, making investments in domestic assets more attractive for foreign investors. With investment capital flowing into the domestic market, demand for the domestic currency increases, causing exchange rate appreciation. As a disclaimer, it should be noted that this chain of causation does not necessarily hold true in all circumstances. Thus, should the initial interest-rate hike be met by market participants with expectations of a substantial weakening in domestic growth prospects, the subsequent capital flows may in fact go in the opposite direction, causing a drop in the exchange rate (Görgens et al. (2001), p. 252). For a detailed account of the mechanics of the exchange rate channel see Görgens et al. (2001), pp. 252-253, Bank of England (2000), pp. 4-5, Favero et al. (1999b), pp. 9-11, and European Central Bank (2000a), pp. 54-56.

demand and from there to changes in production, prices, wages and the general price level, as discussed in the context of the rationale of monetary policy[173]. Second-round effects can be expected to arise from the direct effects of monetary policy on financing and investment decisions and aggregate demand and production, touching even on those firms or individuals that might not have been significantly affected by the initial monetary measure. Thus, a company initially unaffected might face monetary repercussions only after aggregate demand in general, and demand for its specific products in particular, falls. Ultimately, the households and companies most directly affected by changes in monetary policy may not necessarily be those most seriously affected by their repercussions[174].

As a result, private-sector firms and households are affected by monetary policy measures in rather complex and in many respects diffuse ways, as illustrated in chart 1. Exactly how great the impact is, largely depends on where they stand along the general divides between lenders and borrowers and importers and exporters, but also on the instruments with which they are indebted or the assets in which their savings are invested, as well as the currencies in which their liabilities or assets are denominated. Even if an individual's position along these broad cleavages can be determined, the precise impact is difficult to assess due to uncertainties about the exact and constantly changing mechanics involved, the complex interdependence of economic variables, the time lags at play and the uncertainties associated with expectations formation[175].

---

[173] European Central Bank (2001a), p. 44, and Bank of England (2000), pp. 8-9.

[174] Bank of England (2000), pp. 8-9.

[175] In addition to the uncertainties arising from the complexity of the transmission process inasmuch as it has been explored so far, further uncertainties as to the way monetary policy affects the real sector result from a still imperfect understanding of the precise working of transmission (e.g. European Central Bank (2001a), pp. 44-45). First, important economic developments influencing the progress of central banks' objective and target variables lie outside their influence such that the line of causation between certain developments in the objective and target variables and monetary policy actions remains blurred. In addition, conceptualisation of the transmission mechanism is still incomplete. Even though the broad channels through which monetary impulses reach the real economy have been captured, operationalisation of these theoretical insights is complicated by the increasing multitude and variety of financial market instruments that investors and borrowers on financial markets and the real economy use as substitutes or complements to the instruments the monetary authority can influence most immediately. At the same time, the channels already identified are in many respects interdependent, an aspect that in various instances has not yet entered the realm of theoretical analysis. Further, modelling the precise functioning of the transmission of monetary impulses is hampered by the difficulties in incorporating market participants' expectations. In practice, expectations are frequently treated as a fourth, separate channel of monetary transmission, underlining their importance (see e.g. Bank of England (2000), p. 4, Görgens et al. (2001), pp. 262-266, Bofinger et al. (1996), pp. 565-578). As a result of incomplete knowledge of the components and reach of the transmission process it is also impossible to judge with complete certainty which economic developments in the aftermath of a policy change can legitimately be traced back to it. By analogy, it is also impossible to predict with certainty what effects a policy measure is likely to have at which time in the future, leading to

Monetary transmission process – simplified illustration

Chart 1

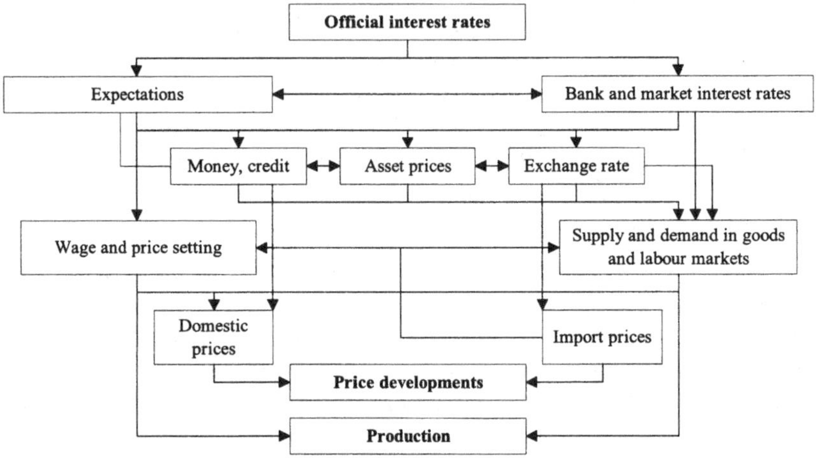

Sources: ECB (2004), p. 45, Görgens et al. (2001), p. 236

I.2.2 Institutional context: objectives and tasks of central banks

Within a given monetary area, the central bank is the key institution for monetary affairs. Even though the legal mandates underlying their establishment and operations

substantial uncertainties about the time lags involved in the transmission process. For theoretical arguments see Bank of England (2000), p. 9. Empirical evidence on the time lag of monetary policy impulses is presented by the Bank for International Settlements (1995), and Kieler et al. (1998). For a differentiated picture of the time lags in different economic variables following monetary tightening see Bernanke et al. (1995), p. 9. For a comprehensive cross-country comparison of time lags in the EU see Mojon et al. (2001). Finally, the practical relevance of the various transmission channels and their empirical weight is still disputed. While the interest rate channel is historically established in academic literature and empirically well documented, the importance of the more recently conceptualised credit channel has not yet been proved unambiguously. (For an excellent review of the literature on the empirical significance of the various channels of monetary policy transmission see de Bondt (1998), pp. 13-22. Also Angeloni et al. (2002), Favero et al. (1999b), pp. 13-18, Clements et al. (2001), and Kieler et al. (1998), pp. 4-12. Recent analyses show a solid interest-rate channel for Germany (e.g. von Kalckreuth (2001), Chatelain et al. (2001)), and other EU member states (Mojon (2000b). For aggregate euro area results see Peersman (2001). On the interdependence of the interest-rate channel and the structure of the financial system, see in particular the detailed analysis by Cecchetti (1999). In cross-country analyses in Europe, this impact has been found to be positive (Britton et al. (1997), De Nederlandsche Bank (2000) and Mojon (2000a). For a contrasting view see Mishkin (1996), pp. 18-20. On the impact of asymmetries in the structure of output, see Clausen (2001). Sgherri (2000) presents an empirical evaluation of the transmission mechanism in the UK.) Similarly, the practical relevance of the exchange rate channel for the impact of monetary policy actions on the private sector has remained unclear (for a survey of empirical evidence see Smets et al (1999)).

are individually designed and can differ substantially, the role of central banks is similar across different monetary areas in one essential respect: Charged with operation and maintenance of the monetary system, they decide on how to pursue the objectives they are assigned in their mandate, which of the instruments at their disposal they use to that end, and the use to which they put them. The effect resulting from institutional separation of the conduct of monetary policy from other policy areas is reinforced by the institutional autonomy, or independence, that the central banks considered in the present context enjoy. Owing to the incentive problems identified in the above discussion on the objectives of monetary policy, elected politicians have come to be regarded as inadequate to the consistent pursuit of a monetary policy guaranteeing price stability. In order to avoid policy decisions aimed at the short-term stimulation of economic activity along electoral cycles, monetary policy is not only separated from policy processes involving elected parliamentarians and government officials; beyond this, contemporary central bank designs seek to establish extensive independence from all external political pressures for central banks and the policy makers in them.

Central bank independence as defined above[176] is generally manifested in five provisions.

- Most importantly, central bank laws provide for institutional independence. Accordingly, central banks are established as separate legal entities, which, in contrast to other agencies or bureaux, are not subordinated to the executive branch in any legal or political sense, including the explicit prohibition of orders from any political body or person to that institution.
- Second, the independence of central bank executive personnel is generally sought by devising a pluralistic selection process, long terms of office, and restrictive impeachment procedures.
- Third, central banks are granted functional autonomy, making them the sole bearer of responsibility over monetary policy.
- Fourth, they are given instrumental independence, leaving them the choice of how to pursue their objectives within the possible confines established by law.
- Finally, central banks can be made financially independent so as to avoid material dependence on external sources.

The extent to which central banks are endowed with these various forms of independence differs in practice. Despite their national differences, however, the central banks in most industrial countries are characterised by a unique position within

---

[176] See p. 37.

their respective constitutional and political systems, laying one of the most important instruments of economic policymaking in the hands of institutions which are beyond the direct control – and in important respects even the indirect control – of the sovereign authority or its democratically elected representatives.

For all the wide-ranging discretion and autonomy they enjoy in pursuing their policies, there is still some interdependence between central banks and other constitutional organs and political institutions. The direct interdependence emanates from the fact that the central bank's very existence and the key rule governing its operations are given by the state's constitutional or legislative power. As a result, the legal basis of a central bank can in principle be amended or abandoned at any time if the law-issuing entity finds that the monetary authority no longer fulfils the tasks it is allotted. Such changes can in principle be aimed at the status of the institution in general, but also at specific aspects of its operations, its organisation or at the individual position of key policy makers, depending on the provisions of the central bank law, as discussed in more detail below. In principle, attempts from the political level aimed at a potential amendment to or abolition of the central bank law, or announcements to that effect, may ultimately influence the decisions of policy makers in that institution.

How credible and important this mechanism is in practice crucially depends on two broad considerations. First, it depends on how easy or difficult it is in practice to amend the existing central bank law. If the law enjoys legal status and can be changed by a parliamentary majority, the hurdle is much lower than if it is constitutional in nature, requiring an amendment of the constitutional basis of the polity. It follows that the higher the status of the central bank's legal basis in a polity's legal order, the more difficult it will be *ceteris paribus* to achieve a legal amendment, and the less likely it becomes for a corresponding threat to actually exert pressure on monetary policy makers. Second, amending a central bank's legal basis for the purpose of influencing monetary policy decisions is likely to impair or even destroy the credibility of the existing institutional set-up as well as that of any future arrangement, giving rise to the concern that such amendments may be repeated by the legislature any time it deems expedient with market participants.

Alternatively, the central bank's legal basis is subject to constitutional review on the part of the judiciary. The central bank law and individual provisions thereof can, on the initiative of eligible plaintiffs such as the main constitutional organs and possibly also any natural or legal public or private person, be investigated by high courts, e.g. the constitutional court and possibly also supreme administrative courts, as to their constitutionality. In a similar vein, but subject to the specific constitutional and legal provisions, it is also conceivable for a central bank to be sued for breach of its obligations under the constitution or the central bank law, e.g. in the event a plaintiff holds that the bank has failed to meet its legally defined monetary policy objectives. As with the case of legislative amendment governing the operations of the central bank, so judicial review represents an *ultima ratio* instrument for ensuring that the institution and its operations are consistent with socially desired priorities as manifested in the constitution. Rather than being a viable means for influencing monetary decision making on a regular basis, judicial review would be expected to be an option for recourse on the central bank only in exceptional circumstances.

Along with the integrity of their mandates, central banks also interact with surrounding political institutions in limited areas of their operational business. Most importantly, most central banks do not have an exclusive mandate with respect to exchange rate policies. In most cases, selection of the exchange rate system with respect to foreign currencies and the conduct of policies related to these systems are outside the scope of a central bank's mandate, being the prerogative of the legislative or executive branches of the state. In this case, central banks have to operate within the confines imposed by the exchange rate regime and participate in related decisions only on a consultative or coordinating basis.

Second, central banks are frequently held accountable to the legislature in order to secure an *ex post* review of monetary decisions with the aim of partially compensating for the lack of *ex ante* control over central bank activities. Even though regular hearings of central bank officials or written reports to parliament serve as a source of information for non-central bank policy makers and force central bank officials publicly to defend their policies on an *ex post* basis, the recommendations or conclusions of such sessions are generally non-binding and do not commit central bankers to any response in terms of future policies.

Similarly, regular or sporadic participation in committees, co-ordinating bodies and other political forums within the polity in which central bank officials meet other policy makers have no legally binding impact on the former and are generally designed to serve informational purposes.

As a result, interest groups effectively deal with a largely self-sufficient system, dominated by the central bank as the sole and independent institution in monetary affairs, as illustrated graphically in chart 2. Under normal conditions, i.e. unless exceptional economic and political crises are taken into consideration, neither the legislature nor the executive nor the judiciary have legally manifested means at their disposal to instruct, sanction or otherwise influence the central bank in its monetary policy decisions. Instruments such as legal amendment or judicial review are, essentially, of a last-resort nature and have, in practice and with respect to the banks' capacity as the monetary authority, not been invoked in recent history. The role of coordinating and consultative committees is highly limited due to the weight of the postulate of central bank independence, which keeps them at considerable distance from the decision-making process inside the central bank. The position of central banks may therefore alleviate the work of interest groups in as far as it provides clear policy responsibilities. Central bank independence, however, also has negative implications when it comes to the accessibility of the institution.

Institutional framework of monetary policy

Chart 2

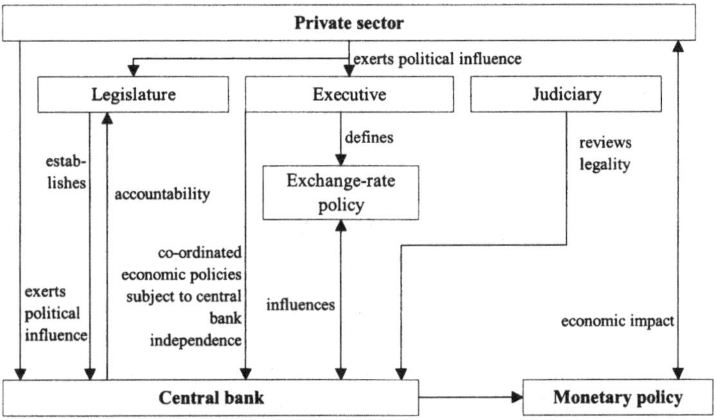

Within this institutional framework, the scope central banks enjoy in pursuing their objectives is staked out by their institutional mandate, as defined in the underlying legal basis of the bank. In general, this mandate provides that central banks have a monopoly position with respect to the operation and maintenance of the monetary system and, consequently, over the conduct of monetary policy and, in this regard, do not share responsibility with other bodies. To the extent that they do not share this responsibility with other bodies and do not need to co-ordinate their policy measures with third parties, central banks enjoy considerable freedom of action. This freedom may be limited in two respects:

– Central banks may be subject to mandatory restrictions concerning exchange rate policies, as policies related to exchange rate systems vis-à-vis foreign currencies frequently fall outside the legally drawn sphere of central bank competence[177].

[177] System-related and operational policy decisions usually have to be coordinated with the monetary authority, but final decisions rest with parliament or government. In as far as they limit the options of monetary policy, exchange rate systems can significantly curtail the framework of action for central banks. Types of systems range from freely floating rates through managed floating systems, target zones, fixed exchange rate regimes with target corridors and target rates, to completely fixed exchange rates, currency boards and ultimately replacement of the domestic currency with a

- Central banks' freedom of action is limited by the definitions of objectives and targets legislators can impose. With respect to policy objectives, the legal set-up can range from the overall absence of an identifiable objective to a detailed description of what direction central bank operations should take[178].

The decision-making processes governing monetary policy can, compared with primary and secondary legislative processes, generally be characterised as simple. Once the authority over monetary policy has been delegated to a central bank, decisions concerning operation of the monetary system in general and monetary policy in particular within that institution are taken at one level by the top decision-making body of the central bank, i.e. its council or board. The rules governing the voting behaviour on monetary policy decisions within the central bank council are generally determined internally and mostly require a broad consensus among its members. Composition of the council is determined by the central bank's legal basis and,

---

foreign denomination. The more closely the domestic currency is tied to a foreign currency, the more limited is the scope for domestic monetary policy, as the latter has to maintain the exchange rate within the agreed range or even at the agreed level, ranging from no systematic restrictions under floating exchange rates via decreasing scope for action under managed exchange rates to the complete loss of monetary policy options under fixed exchange rates and the outright surrender of an autonomous domestic monetary policy, mostly including abolition of the domestic central bank, under currency boards and currency substitution.

Depending on the exchange rate regime decided at the political level, monetary policy makers' discretion can be highly limited as a result, irrespective of the degree of independence of the central bank. This crucially implies that the focus of interest-group activity on monetary policy may have to concentrate increasingly on the political institutions in charge of choosing a country's exchange rate regime rather than on the central bank, the tighter the exchange rate system is. In the present context, especially in the subsequent empirical analysis, limitations on the discretion of monetary policy as a result of exchange rate commitments do not, however, play a central role, given that the Deutsche Mark had – save for the rules within the EMS – been floating freely since 1973, as has the euro since its inception in 1999.

[178] In practice, most contemporary central banks are equipped with a general qualitative objective pertaining e.g. to price stability, growth, employment, exchange rate stability or support for the general economic objectives of the state. Which and to what extent any of these objectives is defined or given priority can already curtail the operations of a central bank in a general way, as discussed in detail above. Thus, monetary authorities obliged to pursue the objective of price stability are bound to steer a tight monetary course and may establish clear targets e.g. for inflation, money supply growth or interest rates to that end. If growth or employment, for instance, are defined as secondary objectives, the central bank might exhaust its potential room for manoeuvre within the limits of the primary objective of price stability to support these secondary objectives, provided the monetary conditions permit. The scope for interpretation and discretionary monetary policy on the part of the central bank may widen considerably, the less clearly the monetary objective is defined, or the more open it is for alternative ends such as the wider economic conditions. How narrowly monetary objectives have to be interpreted by the central bank, however, depends on its own standing within the political system, i.e. first of all on its status as an independent institution, as well as on the types and combinations of objectives given by the legislator and the spirit in which they are defined in each individual case.

together with its organisational structure, may entail quasi-federal elements, with representatives of lower-level, mostly regional, central banks.

The second specific characteristic of the decision process in monetary policy lies in its periodicity. Unlike most other issues and policy processes, monetary policy is governed by a periodic, quasi-continuous policy- and decision-making process. Central bank councils convene regularly, mostly at weekly or bi-weekly intervals, and can if necessary gather to take decisions at any time outside the regular meetings. As a result, monetary decisions rarely lead to critical changes in the policy variables; most of the time they follow a steady path, characterised by small, incremental policy measures whose overall impact over time strongly depends on their aggregate size.

Third, monetary policy makers can exhibit a strong degree of personal independence. Monetary decisions are generally taken by the central bank's top-level policy makers, who are selected by the national government or parliament or, in the case of federal-style systems, by sub-national, state-level governments or parliaments. The selection process consequently represents one of the few occasions on which elected politicians can take influence by choosing a candidate who promises subsequently to support monetary decisions within the central bank's council that may be conducive to the objectives of the political sponsors. This is one indicator of the general outlook a future policy maker has on the policy issue. In the case of central banks, policy makers are frequently assessed by market participants in terms of their potential allegiance to orthodox, tight, stability-oriented monetary policy preferences or to a liberal, growth-oriented approach. Alternatively, central bankers may have political allegiances, which may constitute an incentive to favour monetary policy measures intended to support or run counter to the economic policies of a given government, thus influencing the chances for the latter's re-election. Further, policy makers may have professional allegiances with respect to employers or sectors in which they held positions prior to joining the central bank. Finally, local allegiances may induce central bankers in federal-type systems to support monetary policies conducive to the economic performance of a certain region within the monetary area the central bank governs. Such personal allegiances may, in turn, influence the individual accessibility of central bank policy makers, i.e. their propensity to allow or forbid certain interest group representatives to present their concerns. As investigated in different contexts, for example the selection of supreme court judges, this logic does not necessarily apply to all policy makers selected and not at all times following their selection. It is generally hoped to minimise individual susceptibility to past and present external stimuli by, first, granting monetary policy makers long terms of office; second, by limiting the possibilities of impeachment by elected politicians; and third, by limiting the option of re-appointment. These instruments can significantly diminish individual policy makers' accessibility.

Finally, central banks can enjoy a high degree of material independence. In making their decisions, central bank policy makers can take recourse to substantial resources in the form of the expertise and information generated within their institutions. In contrast to other fields of policymaking, monetary policy is a rather technical process in which econometric modelling and large-scale statistical calculations form the foundations of eventual monetary decisions. Detailed aggregate statistical data on the national accounts and detailed figures on the savings, investment, consumption and trade behaviour of economic agents serve as the basis for assessing optimal monetary policy measures as well as for forecasting future responses by the economy to these measures. Collecting and processing these data requires substantial resources in terms of capital and human expertise.

Financial resources of central banks: seigniorage and central bank expenses

Table 2

Country	Seigniorage in % of GDP, 1994	Central bank operating expenses in % of GDP, 1994
BE	0.44	0.17
CD	0.31	0.03
CH	0.45	0.05
DE	0.52	0.07
FR	0.28	0.13
IT	0.65	0.06
JP	0.42	0.06
NL	0.46	0.06
SE	0.48	0.04
UK	0.28	0.03
US	0.43	0.03

Source: Bank for International Settlements (1996)

One indicator for central banks' strong material endowment can be obtained from comparing their revenues from monetary operations with their operating expenses. While the capital resources of central banks are usually held by the state, most central banks have the right to retain all or a large part of the revenue from money issuance, i.e. seigniorage, as well as the income from re-investing their assets, most importantly central bank reserves, on the international capital markets as well as from other ancillary operations. The net gains from these operations have historically been substantial, as indicated by table 2, which compares the seigniorage across industrial countries with central bank operating expenses. The financial resources originating from these operations allow central banks to purchase the technical equipment and the personnel needed to collect and process the statistical information required to prepare monetary policy decisions.

Besides sufficient financial resources, central banks can also draw on statistical sources from the legal reporting requirements imposed on the private sector. To obtain the data needed, central banks are generally granted the right to draw on data from legally imposed reporting requirements. Where such data are not collected, they can ask the legislator to impose new requirements if deemed necessary. In addition, they can take recourse to data collected by third parties, most importantly national statistical offices.

Overall, this general review of the institutional framework conditions in which monetary decisions are taken suggests that monetary policy represents a comparatively secluded and self-sufficient policy process. Once issued with a mandate and the relevant resources needed to fulfil their legally defined objectives, central banks possess substantial scope for action and the means to take policy decisions largely independently of external political pressure or input in the form of expertise and information.

For the analysis of interest-group behaviour towards central banks, this suggests that the accessibility of central banks and their policy makers may be particularly limited from the point of view of interest groups:

- Central banks' political independence, as common practice in many legal systems including those of the EU member states, enables and obliges them to take monetary decisions in a highly autonomous manner – irrespective of political or other partial interests in society. Central banks have been committed to exclusive pursuit of the objectives established in their mandates, and only with respect to the economic area within their remit as a whole. In addition, monetary policy makers are not subject to electoral cycles, owing to the appointment and employment arrangements generally provided for central bank staff. This puts them in a position to take decisions, including unpopular and controversial policy measures, without being immediately concerned with the potential effects on support from other policy makers, political parties, interest groups or the wider public. In as far as this political independence narrows monetary decision makers' responsiveness to the views articulated by interest groups, it represents an obstacle for private interests seeking to mediate their concerns to central banks.
- Monetary authorities are unlikely to depend directly on political support from external sources. In contrast to decisions taken, say, in a parliamentary context, where political backing from policy makers, interest groups or the wider public can be of essential value in generating political majorities for a certain decision, monetary policy makers do not, as a rule, depend on such political support in their operations. *Ultima ratio* instruments for challenging central bank decisions, such as judicial review or the amendment of a bank's legal basis, can only be applied in

a credible manner in highly exceptional circumstances. Consequently, external political pressure is difficult to apply to monetary policy makers under normal conditions.

- Demand by central banks for information and expertise from external sources may be low compared to that observed in other fields of policymaking. Given their command of substantial financial, legal and human resources, central banks are regarded as highly specialised bureaucracies with a high level of expertise in their policy area. Their dependence on information, e.g. concerning economic developments or the potential impact of specific policy measures on certain sectors or the economy as a whole, can therefore be hypothesised to be extraordinarily low. In as far as used by interest groups as an instrument for mediating their interests to policy makers, the provision of sector or group-specific information and policy positions may therefore not be an effective instrument in the area of monetary policymaking.
- The institutional framework conditions are also likely to reflect on the behaviour of policy makers towards interest groups and their representatives. Considering the strong political, material, expertise-related and human resources, monetary policy makers may not only be largely independent of input from external sources; theoretically, this eminent position may also induce them to reject far-reaching contacts with external sources in their day-to-day work. As a result, monetary policy makers may not only be independent from the views of private-sector interest groups on monetary affairs, but may actually not be interested in these views.

All told, central banks and their policy makers are likely to be perceived as relatively inaccessible by interest groups and their representatives, rendering the mediation of interests difficult. This may, in their view, diminish the potential benefits from formulating and articulating policy positions vis-à-vis policy makers. Whether and to what extent the propositions identified here are observed in practice is examined in part III below.

I.2.3 Issue context: monetary and exchange rate policy

In addition to these potential institutional obstacles, the issue context of monetary policy also contains a number of elements impacting negatively on the pursuit of political action in this policy area. Potential obstacles to interest-group activity can be identified both with respect to issue salience and issue sponsorship.

Most importantly, monetary policy is likely to be a policy issue with a low degree of urgency and issue involvement as perceived by individual enterprises or their business associations. Given the theoretical insights and empirical evidence economic science has produced on the benefits of pursuing price stability as the primary objective of monetary policy, economic actors may, in practice, find themselves in strong agreement with the overall purpose of monetary policy as defined by law, as well as the policy decisions taken by central banks in pursuit of their objectives in general. Assuming that the central banks under consideration in this study do in fact pursue their policies in line with the primary objective of maintaining stable prices, the question needs to be settled empirically as to how far private-sector enterprises and their interest representatives take a long-term view on monetary issues and favour a stable monetary environment, or whether they deem discretionary policies in pursuit of short-term objectives other than price stability, such as the stimulation of growth by means of loosening monetary conditions, as acceptable or indeed desirable. Conversely, it may be asked whether interest groups reminded central banks of their obligation to maintain price stability in cases where the latter were perceived as failing to do so, or whether they sanctioned or even supported a relaxation of monetary conditions. Given the proposition that enterprises and their interest representatives generally support the overall objectives of central banks and the policy decisions derived therefrom, a second question to be answered empirically is whether instances arise in which interest groups disagree with the course of monetary policy.

Second, monetary policy may not be perceived as having a substantial economic impact on enterprises. On the one hand, monetary policy can have considerable effects on aggregate economic development. This observation is substantiated in a number of economic studies. Thus, in a summary of the state of knowledge by the Bank for International Settlements, Smets[179] reported the impact of a one per cent increase in central bank interest rates over a two-year period as producing a decline in real GDP of up to 2.09% in the case of the US, 1.23% in Japan, 0.37% in Germany, 0.36% in France, and 0.18% in the Netherlands within the five years following the initial policy measure, as depicted in chart 3. In the case of Germany, these figures compare with an estimated reaction in real GDP of a mere –0.3% in the first year, +0.1% in the second and 0.0% in the third year following a one per cent rise in value added tax[180], suggesting that in both absolute and comparative terms the immediate impact of monetary policy measures is likely to bear significantly on the economic performance of the private sector. Of particular relevance for enterprises in trade and industry is that the contraction in GDP in response to interest rate hikes results, among other factors, from a substantial decline in private investment and exports, as shown in charts 4 and 5. At the same time, the one percentage point rise in central bank interest rates simulated in Smet's study also reduces the overall price level, as illustrated in chart 6.

---

[179] Smets (1995).

[180] For a detailed analysis see Rheinisch-Westfälisches Institut für Wirtschaftsforschung Essen (1997).

Impact of monetary policy measures on real economic activity and inflation

Chart 3

– Simulated impact of a one-percentage point increase in short-term interest rates in 1994 and 1995 on real GDP in %

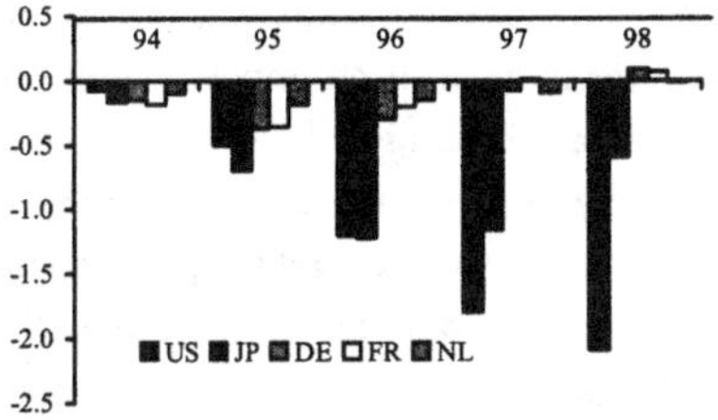

Data source: Smets (1995), p. 248

Chart 4

– Simulated impact of a one-percentage point increase in short-term interest rates in 1994 and 1995 on private non-residential investment in %

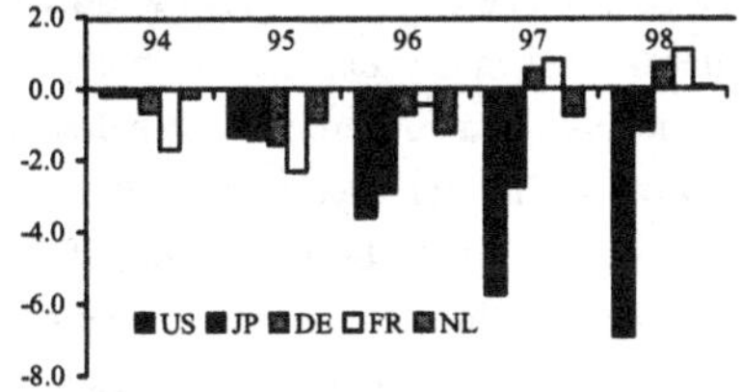

Data source: Smets (1995), p. 248

Chart 5

– Simulated impact of a one-percentage point increase in short-term interest rates in 1994 and 1995 on exports in %

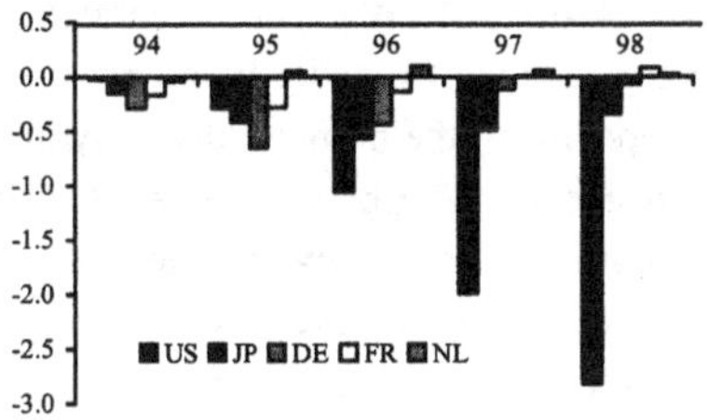

Data source: Smets (1995), p. 248

Chart 6

– Simulated impact of a one-percentage point increase in short-term interest rates in 1994 and 1995 on consumer prices in %

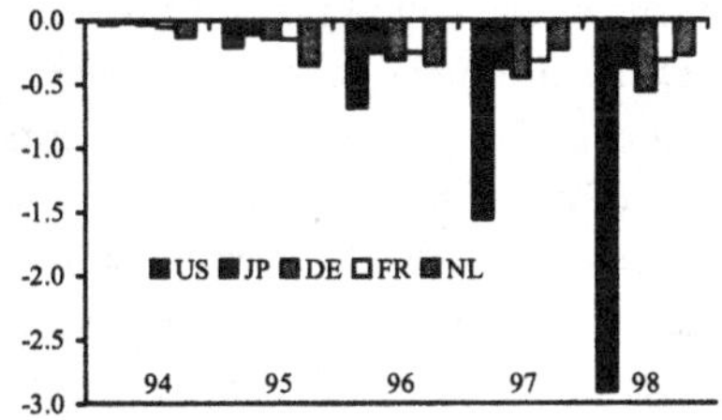

Data source: Smets (1995), p. 248

On the other hand, there is a number of factors which may diminish the perception of this impact as viewed from individual enterprises, thus weakening in practice the sense of urgency of monetary developments on the part of private sector stakeholders. Most importantly, monetary policy is transmitted to the economy in a rather diffuse and indirect manner, as discussed above. Furthermore, these changes are likely to be difficult to discern from other factors, such as, most importantly, changes in overall market conditions. In addition, the time lags encountered in the transmission of monetary impulses complicate identification of monetary policy as the source of changes in the business environment for enterprises. As a consequence, the effects of monetary policy may, in practice, be very difficult to identify and quantify, and may thus not be perceived by enterprises to have a significant effect on their operations.

Against this background, individual companies and the representatives of their interests may find it difficult to form strong preferences with regard to the day-to-day conduct of monetary policy. In this respect, the general diffusion of the economic effects of monetary conditions on individual enterprises is reinforced by the differential exposure to these effects. Thus, a company can assume debtor and creditor positions at the same time, or be exposed to both exports and imports, so that economic effects may, in practice, cancel each other out to a greater or lesser extent. In addition, even within individual firms contradicting conclusions can be drawn from the impact of monetary impulses via the different channels of transmission, e.g. in the case of enterprises heavily exposed to both external finance as well as imports, with the former implying a preference for a low and the latter for a high level of domestic interest rates. The heterogeneity of interests potentially resulting from such differential exposures is likely to be continued, if not amplified, when aggregating preferences across firms within an interest association. At interest-group level, therefore, the heterogeneity of exposures and interests may lead to substantial difficulties in interest aggregation and the formulation of a strong common policy position on monetary issues. Given the potential diversity of interests, a policy position at the lowest common denominator or even a median position may still be weak compared to other, less ambiguous policy issues.

Even after a joint policy position has been reached, it may still not be strong enough to compete against other policy issues on the political agenda of broadly based business associations. The fate of single issues critically depends on the number, diversity and strength of other issues on the political agenda in general. The higher the number of issues actively debated by decision makers and the more diverse they are, the easier it is generally regarded to place further issues on the agenda. If, however, existing issues dominate the agenda such that they largely absorb the resources and attention of the decision makers involved, placing a new issue and promoting it will be more rather than less difficult. In the present context, the competitive situation on the political agenda may also be significant, but in less straightforward ways than in the case of conventional policy issues, owing to the multitude of institutions and policy makers influencing the policy process.

One specific and important instance of the general interdependence of monetary policy with other issues is the relationship between differing views on monetary policy on the one hand and the call for central bank independence on the other. As discussed in more detail below, the independence of central banks and the policy makers in them has become regarded as an important prop for stability-oriented monetary policy, enabling central bankers to take policy decisions largely in isolation from elected politicians, who, being dependent on popular votes, are deemed susceptible to inflationary policies. Criticism by elected politicians or interest groups of the policy decisions by an independent central bank can be interpreted as an attempt at violating the independence of such an institution: Were interested parties not hoping to be able to influence the conduct of monetary policy, it would *ceteris paribus* be irrational for them to comment on it in the first place.

Consequently, if criticism or the expression of interests with regard to monetary policy decisions are met by counter-criticism that this violates the independent status of the central bank[181], that may discourage attempts at placing monetary policy-related interests onto the political agenda in the first place, since few people would in fact want to call into question or even challenge the benefits of an independent central bank[182]. Inasmuch as the conduct of monetary policy and the independence of central banks and their policy makers can be treated as two separate policy issues[183], this logic may imply the existence of a systematic bias against bringing the former onto the political agenda – especially not into the arena of public debate – in order to prevent the latter from entering the political agenda, too.

I.2.4 Interest-group context: interest heterogeneity and resource constraints

The analysis of the issue and institutional contexts suggests that interest-group action on monetary policy is likely to be difficult to organise and represent vis-à-vis the target institution, i.e. the central bank. With the potential costs of political action reaching comparably high levels by implication, the necessity for interest groups to mobilise substantial resources for their work on monetary policy is likely to be strong if effective representation of group interests is indeed intended. As the focus of this study lies with major interest associations from trade and industry, a sample that, in principle, secures significant material resources to address general economic policy issues, it is therefore being assumed that the groups examined below command sufficient resources to pursue their members' interests with respect to monetary policy, and to compete effectively with other interest groups.

However, given the specific institutional and issue properties of monetary policy, two group-related aspects become particularly relevant in the present context, influencing

---

181 The mere threat of invoking that criticism may in fact suffice to discourage interested parties from commenting negatively on monetary policy.

182 In principle, the question is whether external criticism, interests or suggestions on the conduct of monetary policy imply calling into question the independence of monetary policy makers. One argument is that the mere expression of criticism may exert pressure on the decision makers, and if the principle of central bank independence were to be taken seriously then such pressure should not be applied in the first place. On the other hand, it may be argued that total independence is unfeasible both theoretically and in practice and that the degree of independence that *de facto* exists is not necessarily damaged by a call for a change in policy. Only if the latter were linked with a credible direct or indirect threat of curtailing the independence of the institution and its policy makers, and if policy makers were to submit to such a threat, would independence be violated. A final answer to this question, though, still needs to be found.

183 The conduct of monetary policy and the independence of central banks have to be treated as one and the same issue if one assumes that the content of policymaking and the institutional structures by means of which and within which they are decided upon are inseparable concepts and require inseparable processes.

interest groups' information potential. First, as the empirical analysis below is concerned with large industry associations, the information basis is likely to be broad, representing a large number of market participants, which may give the information aggregated at the group level specific weight.

Second, the ability of interest groups to supply information can be of particular importance in the context of monetary policies with respect to the pivotal role of expectations of households, firms and the central bank concerning each others' actions in the context of price and wage formation, asset allocation and other indicators of economic behaviour. Theoretically, interest groups can be regarded as mediators of their members' expectations, increasing market transparency, reducing the impediments to market efficiency originating from asymmetric and incomplete information and promoting the effectiveness of monetary policy.

However, two potential obstacles hampering the provision of such information can be identified on the supply side. First, as a consequence of the size of major business associations, preferences within each group may turn out to be heterogeneous, along the lines of the above arguments on the complexity of the policy issue. Owing to the differential exposure to monetary measures, interest-group members may have diverging views on the preferred policy measures, complicating the collection, aggregation and analysis of information at the group level. In view of these countervailing forces – representativeness versus heterogeneity – it can be hypothesised that the formulation of a coherent common position on monetary policy measures at the interest-group level may not be possible at all times.

Further, expectations with respect to prices and wages as well as the development of monetary and financial variables may be regarded by individual firms as confidential information if considered part of corporate strategy. Especially for firms in the financial services industry, but also for industrial companies with substantial financial market exposure, sharing information with potential competitors within one and the same interest group may be perceived as disclosing vital internal information, creating an open flank in their competitive position in the market. In that case, firms may be reluctant to pass such information on to the group level, hampering the establishment of a common position on the relevant policy issues.

Next to these supply-side related arguments, the impediments to the viability of information as an instrument for expressing interest-group preferences on the demand side have already been pointed out in the institutional context above. Accordingly, central banks may be far less dependent on the provision of information by interest groups or other external sources than other policy makers. Even market expectations, which may not be directly captured by such historical accounts, can be quantified by central banks without taking recourse to the inside information of interest groups or individual households or firms. Owing to the growth of forward financial instruments and markets, data concerning the expectations of the major financial-market participants on the future development of decisive variables such as inflation, interest rates, exchange rates and growth can be extracted from market prices on spot and futures exchanges.

Not only do central banks possess substantial information in their field of policymaking, they may also have only limited demand for the kind of original information interest groups are able to contribute. Given their strong focus on pursuing the general good rather than particular interests, central banks may not be at all inclined to use industry-specific or otherwise selective information for forming their policies. In addition, should monetary policy makers use selective – in the sense of not nationally aggregated – information, they are likely to take recourse to their own ample supplies of differentiated data, rather than consulting the private sector.

As a result, the material and political resources at interest groups' disposal in the area of trade and industry may not be sufficient to bring effective influence to bear on monetary policy makers. As great as these resources are in general terms, their utility is limited in the specific context of monetary affairs by the fact that the sector or group-specific information, by itself, is of secondary importance for the analysis of monetary conditions and the formulation of monetary policy by the authorities.

I.2.5 Interim conclusions and summary propositions for empirical analysis

Recalling the puzzle motivating this study, namely the stylised fact that political activity by interest groups in trade and industry with respect to the policy field of monetary affairs was low despite the potentially substantial impact of monetary decisions on the economy, the preceding theoretical considerations have produced a number of important potential explanatory variables.

In order to explain the puzzle, a micro-behavioural approach has been suggested with the aim of investigating the basic incentives for individuals and interest groups in the private sector to take political action on monetary questions or to abstain from doing so. The decision whether to take political action or not has been presented as a cost-benefit analysis, weighing the expected benefits of identifying, aggregating and mediating individual and group interests against the potential costs. The determinants of costs and benefits have been analysed with respect to the issue, institutional and group contexts in which they originate.

The major findings with respect to monetary policy as a policy issue can be summarised in the form of the following core propositions, which are used in part III as the central criteria along which the activities of interest groups are analysed, both with respect to monetary policy in isolation as well as compared to other policy issues.

General context	
Proposition 1	In general, interests with respect to monetary or exchange rate policy are not communicated very intensively to the relevant decision makers.
Proposition 2	In general, communication of interests with respect to monetary or exchange rate policy is significantly lower than in other policy fields.
Proposition 3	Mediating interests with respect to monetary or exchange rate policy does not yield sufficient benefits relative to the associated costs.

Institutional context	
Proposition 4	Central banks are perceived as inaccessible to interests from the private sector, compared to other political bodies.
Proposition 5	Political independence is an obstacle for private interests in mediating their interests to the central bank.
Proposition 6	Given their institutional, material, and expertise-based resources, central banks are not dependent on external political support in order to fulfil their tasks in the field of monetary or exchange rate policy.
Proposition 7	Given their focus on aggregated economic indicators and their access to the relevant statistical resources, central banks are not dependent on external information with respect to monetary or exchange rate conditions and developments in order to fulfil their tasks in the field of monetary or exchange rate policy.
Proposition 8	Given the independence of central banks in terms of political, material, and expertise-related resources as well as their focus on aggregated economic indicators, central bank policy makers are not interested in the views of private-sector interest groups on monetary or exchange rate policy.

Issue context	
Proposition 9	Individual firms or interest associations agree with the objectives and the overall conduct of monetary or exchange rate policy.
Proposition 10	Interest groups rarely disagree with the monetary or exchange rate policy decisions of the central bank.
Proposition 11	Monetary or exchange rate policy is not perceived to have a significant effect on individual firms or interest associations.
Proposition 12	The magnitude of the impact of monetary or exchange rate policy on individual firms or interest associations is difficult to determine.
Proposition 13	Owing to the comparatively low and varied impact of monetary or exchange rate policy on individual enterprises, interest associations find it difficult to form strong preferences with respect to the day-to-day conduct of monetary or exchange rate policy.
Proposition 14	Given the low perceived impact of monetary or exchange rate developments and the importance of other policy fields, monetary or exchange rate policy is not perceived by interest groups as a priority issue on the economic policy agenda.

Group context	
Proposition 15	Heterogeneity of interests related to monetary or exchange rate affairs within existing interest groups weakens the formation of strong policy positions in the business sector.
Proposition 16	Interest associations and their members do not possess means of exerting economic or political pressure on the central bank.
Proposition 17	Individual firms or interest associations do not possess relevant information exclusively available to them alone, which they can contribute to the discourse with the central bank.

Part II Policy contexts in practice

II.1 Monetary policymaking in Germany

The following sections investigate the setting within which interest formation and communication occur with respect to monetary policy in Germany. The analysis commences with the institutional context, an exposition of the constitutional and institutional properties of the Deutsche Bundesbank arguing that the Bundesbank, as an independent monetary authority, provides limited access to interest representation. It subsequently turns to the issue context and reviews the major relevant monetary developments in the past decades, suggesting that monetary policy in Germany has, in general, been characterised by stability and continuity such that the risks and costs to trade and industry have, on average and in comparison to other cost factors, been rather small. The third section provides an overview of the existing interest-group infrastructure in Germany and the financial, informational and collective-action-related resources it musters, showing that with respect to information and collective action industry and trade associations do indeed have very limited resources at their disposal to use in the context of political action vis-à-vis the central bank.

II.1.1 Institutional context: the Deutsche Bundesbank

As discussed in the previous chapter, theory suggests that the institutions interest groups seek to approach and the institutional environment in which groups operate can affect the costs and benefits associated with lobbying activities. In this section, the institutional context in which monetary decisions are taken in Germany is analysed with respect to its potential implications for interest-group activities.

The present study was conducted and concluded during a period of profound change in the institutional setting of European and German monetary policy. With entry into EMU in 1999, authority over monetary policy in the relevant member states of the EU – including Germany – was transferred to the ECB. The influence of the Bundesbank on the course of monetary policy affecting Germany was thus substantially narrowed. Membership of EMU also gave rise to considerable pressure to reorganise and streamline the operations and institutional structures of the monetary authorities in the relevant EU member states, including those of the Deutsche Bundesbank. As a consequence, the Bundesbank underwent significant reform in 2002.

The breaks in the decision-making and operational structures of the Bundesbank resulting from these events can also be expected to change the shape of communication by the private sector. To analyse this, both present and past structures must therefore be taken into consideration. The present study focuses on the communication practices as they have been established within the structures given over the past decades. In institutional terms, this implies that the situation prior to entering EMU is the most relevant and important and is to the fore. Assuming that communication practices may take some time to adjust to the new institutional framework and a new equilibrium may not yet have been reached since the EMU-related amendments, such institutional developments will be analysed primarily with the aim of formulating expectations as to the potential future evolution of communication practices.

After a brief overview of the history of the institutional set-up governing monetary policy in Germany, the structures and processes will be investigated on the basis of the categories identified in the theoretical considerations, starting with a review of Deutsche Bundesbank's mandate, followed by an analysis of its accessibility from the perspective of interest groups and concluding with an examination of the behavioural aspects involved.

II.1.1.1 Historical background

The history of the monetary system of the Federal Republic of Germany can be divided into three phases. In the first phase, monetary policy lay in the hands of the Bank deutscher Länder, which operated from 1948 to 1957. The second phase commenced with creation of the Deutsche Bundesbank in 1957 and ended with Germany's entry into EMU in 1999. Membership of EMU also marked the beginning of the third phase, in which monetary decision-making was delegated in 1999 from the monetary authorities in the relevant member states to the ECB.

Germany's monetary system as it existed until entry into EMU had its origins in the far-reaching reforms of the country's political and economic structures after the end of World War II, which were initiated and implemented by the British, French and US Allied governments[184]. Regional central banks, so-called Landeszentralbanken, were established in the course of 1946 and 1947. Owned by the individual states[185] in

---

[184] The starting point for reform of the monetary system was the decision by the United States to give Germany a largely decentralised governance structure. As a result, the Deutsche Reichsbank, the central bank from 1876 to 1945, was dismantled and replaced by regional central banks in the western parts of the country. These regional central banks were referred to as Landeszentralbanken, operating under the auspices of the respective Allied governments. In the American and French zones, the Landeszentralbanken were established by Länder acts upon order by the respective Allied command and in the British zone directly by Allied decree. Regulation of the Landeszentralbanken was unified across the three zones by the Allied command as of April 15, 1949. Between 1945 and 1948, various forms of monetary governance were discussed by the Allies. In the end, a decentralised approach was adopted with legally independent regional central banks as the operating units and the Bank deutscher Länder as the bank of the Landeszentralbanken. An overview of the early history of Germany's post-war monetary system can be found in Buchheim (1998). A legal analysis is provided by Uhlenbruck (1968), pp. 14-17.

[185] The term state refers to the Länder as the basic governance units existing in Germany at that time.

Germany, their task was to oversee the circulation of money and the payment systems and to serve as a state bank in each respective state (Land). However, regional central banks did not have the right to issue money, so that they were not central banks in the strict sense. This gap[186] was closed by the establishment of the Bank deutscher Länder on March 1, 1948, which, in principle, was charged with issuing money, overseeing the circulation of money and serving as the bank of the Landeszentralbanken[187]. The act governing the Bank deutscher Länder provided for its independence from instructions by political entities other than the Allied Bank Commission[188]. This institutional, two-tier infrastructure with the Bank deutscher Länder and the Landeszentralbanken as separate entities with individual legal personalities was maintained until the establishment of the Deutsche Bundesbank almost ten years later[189].

Creation of the institutional framework was followed by the second important element of the recent monetary regime in Germany, introduction of the Deutsche Mark as the country's currency. This was achieved upon entry into force of the Issuance and Currency[190] and the Changeover[191] Acts on June 20 and June 27, 1948 respectively, which regulated the issuance as well as the distribution and exchange modalities of the new currency[192].

This first phase ended in 1957 when, after eight years of negotiations, the act establishing the Deutsche Bundesbank entered into force. According to the 1949

---

[186] In the interim period between the establishment of the Landeszentralbanken and the Bank deutscher Länder, issues pertaining to the issuance of money and coordination of the work of the Landeszentralbanken were treated separately in the Allied zones. In the American zone a Bank Council was instituted, in the French zone a Coordination Council was established, while in the British zone the Reichsbankstelle was retained and charged with the relevant tasks. For details see Buchheim (1998), pp. 103-111.

[187] The Bank deutscher Länder and its monetary policy were controlled by the Allied Bank Commission until 1951, when monetary sovereignty was transferred to the Federal Republic of Germany founded in 1949 (Buchheim (1998), p. 112. For details on the transition of monetary sovereignty from the Allied Bank Commission to the Federal Republic of Germany in 1951 see Uhlenbruck (1968), pp. 16-17). The capital of the Bank deutscher Länder was held by the Landeszentralbanken.

[188] An attempt by the first German government at making the Bank deutscher Länder subject to governmental oversight in 1951 was successfully countered by the Allied Bank Commission and the Bank deutscher Länder (Buchheim (1998), p. 114). For details on the legal aspects of the independence of the Landeszentralbanken see Uhlenbruck (1968), pp. 15-17.

[189] Despite the highly decentralised, two-tier structure the system was, in practice, operated like a unitary system in order to enable the conduct of a single monetary policy in a single economic area (Buchheim (1998), p. 117).

[190] Emissions- und Währungsgesetz.

[191] Umstellungsgesetz.

[192] For details on the 1948 currency reform see Bickerich (1998), pp. 108-133, and Weimer (1998), pp. 31-48.

German Basic Law, the Federal Republic would establish a federal bank which was to succeed the arrangements made in the immediate post-war period[193]. In this federal bank, the Deutsche Bundesbank, a number of key features of the monetary constitution in the first phase were kept and further developed. Thus, a federal, decentralised institutional and decision-making structure was retained, albeit less pronounced than that of the Bank deutscher Länder and the Landeszentralbanken prior to 1957. Further, institutional independence from politics was maintained and strengthened. Finally, the monetary authority's objective of ensuring stable prices was reinforced. Following German reunification in 1990, the Bundesbank was reformed in 1992 to the extent that the new federal states were included in the bank's existing institutional structure and a number of old and new Landeszentralbanken were merged in order to maintain a manageable number of constituent regional central banks, while leaving the overall operational structure unchanged[194].

As with the first phase, the operations of the Deutsche Bundesbank until abolition of the Bretton Woods exchange rate arrangements were shaped by the need to maintain a fixed exchange rate target vis-à-vis the US dollar[195]. The resulting constraints on monetary policymaking only disappeared with the advent of freely floating exchange rates to the US dollar on March 19, 1973[196]. At the same time, forms of exchange rate management were introduced at the European level, first in the form of the snake-in-

---

[193] German Basic Law, Article 88.

[194] Streit (1998) offers a concise account of the political debate on the post-unification reform of the Bundesbank as well as the resulting changes to the bank's structure.

[195] Issing (1993b), pp. 257-260. From the perspective of analysing interest-group behaviour, the period of completely fixed exchange rates is of lesser interest, as political controversies concentrated either on how to meet the exchange rate target, which in most cases remained a technical rather than a political controversy, or on whether the respective exchange rate target was deemed appropriate, in which case the final addressee was the Federal Government as the relevant decision maker. In the latter case, the Bundesbank may have served as an important and influential intermediary target for interest groups trying to influence federal exchange rate policies. Ultimately, however, the central bank has no decision-making authority in exchange rate related questions.

[196] Tensions within the Bretton Woods system had occurred early on, leading to the dollar crisis of 1971, when a number of countries, including Germany, suspended their fixed exchange rate to the US dollar and let their currencies float freely. These countries temporarily returned to exchange rate fixing after agreement on widening the corridor between the US dollar and the participating currencies from +/- 1% to +/- 2.25% was reached at Washington in December 1971. This was known as the Smithsonian Agreement. Following further subsequent tensions, resulting mainly from the rise in oil prices, European countries eventually ceased defending their currencies against the US dollar in March 1973. An historical overview of this decisive phase in European monetary integration can be found in Deutsche Bundesbank (1997), pp. 96-100. Walsh (2000), pp. 25-45, carefully documents the negotiations and negotiating positions of the countries involved during that period. Szász (1999), pp. 30-50, provides an inside view of the negotiations.

the-tunnel arrangement of 1972[197] and later by means of the Exchange Rate Mechanism of the European Monetary System in 1979[198]. In contrast to the Bretton Woods arrangements, however, autonomy of monetary decisions was largely maintained under the ERM, as the Deutsche Mark served as the anchor currency in this system[199].

The third phase in the history of monetary systems in Germany was ushered in by the plan to establish an economic and monetary union in the Maastricht Treaty of 1992. The final stage of that plan was reached in 1999, when the ECB took over monetary decision-making from the participating national central banks, which became integral parts of the Eurosystem and the ESCB and their decision-making structures[200]. Since the start of this third phase the Deutsche Bundesbank has no longer pursued its own autonomous monetary policy; instead, it participates in the ECB's policymaking as one of initially eleven and now twelve national central banks. Besides its participation in the ESCB and the Eurosystem, the Bundesbank plays a particular role in the EMU monetary setting insofar as a number of important Bundesbank characteristics have influenced the design of the EMU infrastructure. Thus, the high degree of independence from politics, the decentralised structure and the formulation of monetary objectives and tasks of the ESCB bear close resemblance to the Bundesbank equivalents. In response to the new monetary framework at EU level, the Bundesbank itself was subjected to an extensive institutional overhaul. As a result, the Bundesbank Act was amended in May 2002, providing for a streamlined decision-making body and distinct centralisation of its organisation.

Historical development reveals, on the one hand, that the monetary system in Germany has experienced considerable systemic breaks over time, which included substantial changes to both the institutional setting and monetary policy targets. On the other hand, institutional change has been achieved with a high degree of continuity in the most important characteristics of the monetary system, notably with respect to independence from politics as well as to the authority's policy objectives. The purpose

---

[197] In principle, the system provided for flexible exchange rates, in which autonomous control of the national supply of money by the Bundesbank was possible. For details see Baltensperger (1998), p. 475, Bofinger et al. (1996), pp. 602-605, and Szász (1999), pp. 30-50.

[198] For an overview, see Deutsche Bundesbank (1997), pp. 96-100. An economic analysis is provided by Bofinger et al. (1996), pp. 602-605, and Issing (1993b), pp. 257-260.

[199] Bofinger et al. (1996), p. 607.

[200] The historical run-up to EMU has been documented in a number of important publications. The major historical accounts include Szász (1999), Waigel (1997), and Marshall (1999). The discussions in the early nineties are covered by Nölling (1993). Specific national perspectives on European monetary integration are analysed by Walsh (2000) for Great Britain, France, and Italy. The German view has been presented by Stark (1997). Institutional aspects of the history of EMU are covered by Görgens et al. (2001), Simmert et al. (1999) and Junius et al. (2002).

of the following sections is to identify and assess the institutional properties of the Bundesbank of relevance to interest-group activity.

II.1.1.2 Institutional mandate: The Deutsche Bundesbank

One of the most important questions an interest group has to answer when shaping a strategy with respect to a certain policy issue is who takes the relevant decisions on that policy issue. The institution in charge is likely to be the primary focus of interest-group activity. Clearly, the question of responsibility is an important one and may not always be easy to answer. For one thing, responsibilities within a state may not be defined in an unambiguous manner, making it more difficult to focus interest-group work. Second, decision-making authority may be divided among more than one entity, the most important example being legislation in bicameral parliamentary systems. As discussed above in theoretical terms, dealing with one clearly identified decision-making entity is, in principle, easier for an interest group than dealing with a greater number of decision makers, especially if their responsibilities are difficult to distinguish.

In the case of monetary policy, the allocation of responsibilities has been unambiguous and ample, as the definition of the bank's objectives, powers, the scope of its business and the endowment of instruments demonstrates. Between 1957 and 1999, the Deutsche Bundesbank was the central monetary decision-making organ of the Federal Republic[201]. The Bundesbank's authority rested on the constitutional provisions of Article 88 of Germany's Basic Law, which provides for the establishment of a federal bank that should function as a note-issuing and currency bank[202]. Further provisions governing the Bundesbank are laid down in the Bundesbank Act[203].

The Bundesbank Act defines the duties of the bank as follows:

---

[201] Samm (1967), pp. 54-62. Currency, money, and coinage are exclusive legislative powers of the Federation according to Article 73 No. 4, Basic Law. Legislation relating to banking is subject to concurrent legislative powers of the Federation and the Länder, pursuant to Article 74 No. 11 of the Basic Law. Legal experts have pointed out that Articles 88, 73 No. 4, and 74 No. 11 of the Basic Law, separately or jointly, do not explicitly provide for a monopoly position on the part of the Bundesbank with respect to monetary affairs. In addition, Article 109 Paragraph 2 of the Basic Law obliges the Federation and the Länder to take due account in their budgetary planning of the requirements of overall economic equilibrium, the latter of which may include monetary questions. However, a substantial shift of the relevant activities to institutions or bodies other than the Bundesbank is generally deemed unconstitutional (Stern (1998), p. 142).

[202] "The Federation shall establish a note-issuing and currency bank as the Federal Bank.", German Basic Law, Article 88.

[203] Deutsche Bundesbank (1998a), pp. 8-55, provides the original version of the Bundesbank Act as effective until December 31, 1998 and a juxtaposition with the Act as effective from January 1, 1999, including the adjustments necessary for entering EMU.

> "The Deutsche Bundesbank shall regulate the amount of money in circulation and of credit supplied to the economy, using the monetary powers conferred on it by this Act, with the aim of safeguarding the currency, and shall arrange for the execution of domestic and international payments."[204]

Interpreting the scope of the Bundesbank's authority, however, was not left to this general definition of the bank's objectives. The Act, as effective until end-1998, also identified in detail the monetary powers of the bank, which consisted of the following elements:[205]

- Note issue: The Bundesbank had the sole right to issue banknotes, which alone were legal tender.
- Discount, lending and open market policies: In order to influence the amount of money in circulation and the amount of credit granted, the Bundesbank set the interest and discount rates to be used in its transactions and defined the principles governing its lending and open market operations.
- Minimum reserve policy: In order to influence the amount of money in circulation and the amount of credit granted, the Bundesbank had the power to require credit institutions to hold certain percentages of defined categories of their liabilities in the form of balances on giro accounts with it, i.e. as minimum reserves.
- Collection of statistics: The Bundesbank was entitled to order and collect statistics in the fields of banking and the monetary system from all credit institutions.[206]

In addition, the Act, as effective until end-1998, made detailed provisions defining and limiting the scope of the business of the Bundesbank in the following areas:[207]

- Transactions with credit institutions
- Transactions with public authorities[208]
- Open market operations
- Transactions with the general public

---

[204] Deutsche Bundesbank (1998a). Quotation refers to the act as effective until December 31, 1998.

[205] Part IV, Bundesbank Act. Summary refers to the act as effective until December 31, 1998.

[206] A concise description and early appreciation of the objectives, tasks, functions and instruments of the Bundesbank can be found in Bank for International Settlements (1963), pp. 54-96. The Bank for International Settlements also provides a direct comparison with statutory arrangements and monetary practices of the Banque Nationale de Belgique, the Bank of England, the Banque de France, the Banca d'Italia, De Nederlandsche Bank, the Schweizerische Nationalbank and the Sveriges Riksbank, based on data and evidence up to the early 1960s.

[207] Part V, Bundesbank Act. Summary refers to the act as effective until December 31, 1998.

- Certification of cheques
- Lending against and purchase of equalisation claims
- Other transactions were allowed only for the purpose of carrying out and completing authorised transactions, or for its own operations, or for its staff.[209]

The definition of the Bundesbank's mandate shows that the bank's responsibilities[210] were far-reaching and institutionally focused with respect to the essential elements of monetary policy in a strict as well as a broad definition of that issue. In the realm of monetary affairs the Bundesbank was endowed with supreme responsibilities and was therefore, in principle, the natural and sole interlocutor for interest groups on the relevant matters. The Basic Law and Bundesbank Act together placed the whole of the monetary area within the realm of central bank policy and thereby in the hands of the Bundesbank. Its activity was not limited to putting into circulation the notes required as legal tender for payment transactions, on the basis of its note-issuing privilege. Its task was the far wider one of regulating the entire supply of money to the economy, including credit institutions' deposit liabilities, and of influencing the bank's credit granting in line with the requirements of monetary and fiscal policy[211].

In addition, the Bundesbank's mandate to safeguard the currency encompassed both the internal and external aspects of stability[212]. Administering Germany's foreign exchange reserves, the Bundesbank had to deal with the closely interdependent domestic money markets and the foreign exchange markets, as any change in the amount of the country's foreign exchange reserves automatically alters supply of the domestic currency[213]. As a result, the Bundesbank also enjoyed the power to intervene in money and foreign exchange markets with the aim of stabilising the external value of the Deutsche Mark.

---

[208] After the repeal of Paragraph 20 Indent 20 No.1 and Paragraph 17, the Bundesbank's functions as the bank of the Federation have been substantially curtailed (Stern (1998), p. 164).

[209] The Basic Law does not prohibit the adoption of acts that confer additional tasks on the Bundesbank related to its role as a central bank. This has been observed in practice in a number of instances, such as banking supervision and management of the balance of payments and capital controls. In accordance with Article 88 Basic Law, however, such tasks must not impair the Bundesbank in the fulfilment of its assignment as the central bank (Stern (1998), p. 146).

[210] A detailed description of the Bundesbank's responsibilities, tasks and functions as well as a legal evaluation is provided by Stern (1998), pp. 162-178.

[211] Bank for International Settlements (1963), p. 60.

[212] Stern (1998), p. 170, Bank for International Settlements (1963), p. 60. Smits (1997) points out that the question whether the objective of safeguarding the currency also encompassed the external stability of the Deutsche Mark was subject to controversy, observing that, in practice, the term was mainly understood to refer to the internal stability of the currency only (Smits (1997), p. 184).

[213] Bank for International Settlements (1963), p. 82.

Beyond the tasks identified by the Bundesbank Act, the bank was also charged with additional responsibilities not immediately related to monetary policy. Most importantly, this included the bank's participation in supervision of the banking sector[214].

Finally, the Bundesbank was given a broad range of instruments enabling it to pursue its policy objectives. These instruments comprised the entire array of tools theoretically and practically necessary to steer monetary policy.

A second aspect of the institutional mandate of relevance to interest-group activities, besides its breadth and institutional focus, is the discretion an institution enjoys in discharging the tasks conferred upon it. As observed above, discretion in fulfilling a task is a vital factor making a decision-making body worthwhile targeting from the perspective of interest politics. A body whose room for manoeuvre is tightly limited by law, such that it is not in a position to take certain actions even if it were willing to do so, may not be a useful addressee for interest groups.

The breadth of the Bundesbank mandate as well as the broad range of instruments at its disposal are two elements indicating that the Bundesbank had wide room for manoeuvre in pursuit of its objectives. More importantly, however, extensive discretion derived from the broad definition of the bank's policy objectives. In stating that the bank should

- pursue the aim of safeguarding the currency,
- regulate the amount of money in circulation and the amount of credit supplied to the economy, and
- arrange for the execution of domestic and international payments

the legislator, at the same time, refrained from defining exactly

- how the currency should be safeguarded, which criteria and measures should be applied to the currency's stability, and which – qualitative or quantitative – goal or stabilisation standard was to be targeted by the Bundesbank, either for the internal or external value one of the currency,
- what the appropriate amount of money and credit was deemed to be, other than that it had to be in accordance with the overarching objective of safeguarding the currency, and

[214] For a detailed description of the Bundesbank's role in banking supervision see Stern (1998), pp. 172-174. As noted earlier, banking supervision and other accidental tasks of the Bundesbank fall outside the scope of the present analysis.

- how payments were expected to be executed other than that execution had to be in accordance with the overarching objective of safeguarding the currency.[215]

As a result, the Deutsche Bundesbank was endowed by the legislator with the freedom to define by itself how to safeguard the currency, when stability of the currency – internally as well as externally – was achieved and when it deviated from the self-defined benchmark of stability.

Despite the breadth of the Bundesbank's mandate and the wide scope of discretion in its policymaking, the bank also faced statutory limits which constrained its business in two respects. First, the Basic Law and the Bundesbank Act define the scope of the bank's mandate in both positive and negative terms. The pursuit of activities not explicitly mentioned in the bank's legal basis or conferred upon the institution by federal law lies outside the scope of its mandate and is, consequently, prohibited. Most importantly, this includes policies with respect to exchange rate arrangements. While the bank was put in charge of the external stability of the currency as well as of administering the country's foreign currency reserves, its activities in this respect were subordinated to bilateral or multilateral agreements by the Federation on exchange rates and their management[216]. As a result, monetary policy had to accommodate and support the exchange rate arrangements of the Bretton Woods system, the snake-in-the-tunnel and the ERM of the European Monetary System[217].

Second, the bank's legal framework suggests that the central bank does not and should not operate in isolation and that the conduct of monetary policy should not be detached from general economic policy. Accordingly, Paragraph 12 of the Bundesbank Act states that

---

[215] Bank for International Settlements (1963), p. 60.

[216] Exchange rate policy was an area of concurring powers between the Federal Government and the Bundesbank. The conclusion of international agreements in the area of exchange rate policy was reserved for the Federal Government as a rule. The rights and obligations resulting from these agreements, however, were transferred from the government to the Bundesbank by way of internal administrative acts. In the case of the agreements related to Bretton Woods and the ERM, the amendment of parities was also subject to governmental decision-making, while the Bundesbank was responsible for implementing these decisions. For details on the allocation of tasks as well as on the implications of concurring powers in cases of conflicts of objectives and interests see Stern (1998), pp. 185-189. Also Issing (1993b), pp. 257-260.

[217] Especially with respect to the snake-in-the-tunnel and the ERM, the role of the Deutsche Mark as the anchor currency and the implications of this role for the Bundesbank's policymaking were controversial. With the Deutsche Mark as the de facto anchor currency of these systems, the Bundesbank was in a position to determine its monetary policy autonomously, while the participating countries had to maintain their exchange rate obligations within the exchange rate system. The question, in theory as well as in practice, arose as to what extent the Bundesbank was obliged to support the overall system and the participating currencies. The critical role of the Bundesbank within the ERM has been documented by Szász (1999), pp. 46-85 and pp. 98-108.

> "[w]ithout prejudice to the performance of its duties, the Deutsche Bundesbank is required to support the general economic policy of the Federal Cabinet."[218]

The requirement to support the general economic policy of the Federation carries a number of important connotations. First, it implies that the Bundesbank keep itself informed about the economic policies of the government. Second, it suggests that, in doing so, the Bundesbank should not limit itself to information on economic policies of immediate relevance for its own activities, but rather that it should be aware of the government's overall economic policy stance. At the same time, the reference to general economic policy also implies that the Bundesbank is absolved from supporting specific government measures. Finally and most importantly, the provision grants clear precedence to pursuit of the Bundesbank's institutional duties, namely first and foremost safeguarding the currency.[219]

In addition to the Bundesbank Act, the Federal Act to Promote Economic Stability and Growth of 1967 defined the components of a general economic equilibrium for the Federation as comprising price stability, a high level of employment, a sound balance of payments and a stable and appropriate rate of growth[220]. The Bundesbank understood this act to confirm that its own primary objective was to secure price stability. Yet it cannot ignore general economic equilibrium because of these provisions. However, and in line with the priorities of the equivalent passage in the Bundesbank Act, the remaining objectives of federal economic policy may only play a role in the Bundesbank's policy decisions in as far as they relate to and are in accordance with the bank's primary objective. To this latter objective, general economic considerations are secondary. The relevant provisions in the 1967 Stability Act were therefore interpreted as being in the nature of a recommendation outweighed by the specific assignment of tasks in the Bundesbank Act. In summary, therefore, the Bundesbank's obligation to support general economic policies of the Federation, as manifested in the Bundesbank Act and the Stability Act, remained ambiguous insofar as no clear criteria were provided for the co-ordination of monetary and general economic policies. The weight the Bundesbank attached to the latter ultimately had to be defined in everyday practice. The latter suggests that the Bundesbank consistently

---

[218] Paragraph 12 Sentence 1, Bundesbank Act. Quotation refers to the act as effective until December 31, 1998. The latest version of the Act reads: "As far as is possible without prejudice to its tasks as part of the European System of Central Banks, it shall support the general economic policy of the Federal Government." Paragraph 12 Sentence 2, Bundesbank Act, as effective from March 28, 2002.

[219] A detailed discussion of the legal implications of Paragraph 12 Sentence 1, Bundesbank Act, can be found in Uhlenbruck (1986), pp. 53-63.

[220] Stern (1998), pp. 163-164.

gave priority to its specific monetary duties[221] and thereby largely exhausted the scope of discretion granted by law.

The third factor alongside the institutional mandate and discretion in policymaking is the kind of institution with which interest groups are dealing. As discussed in the theoretical context, the openness of an institution to external interests is related to the kind of institution it is and its position within the political arena. Parliaments, governments, courts and bureaucracies naturally differ in the extent and way in which they depend on their environment and how they communicate with it.

In this context, the Deutsche Bundesbank can best be characterised as a special part of the executive branch of the German Federation, entrusted with the responsibility for monetary and credit policy as its own particular function[222]. Starting from this general characterisation it can be concluded that, for the purposes of interest politics, the Bundesbank very much resembles the properties of a bureaucracy under the executive branch. Such a bureaucracy plays an essential part in planning and drafting policy measures and, once they have been signed off at the political level, in their implementation. From the point of view of interest politics, such bodies are vital as points of contact when bringing influence to bear on a policy measure at the conceptual stage and on the strategy applied to its practical implementation. The policy measure itself is adopted at the political level so that, in order to secure the desired outcome, interest groups may also be active – if not, indeed, particularly active – during political negotiations on the policy measure.

This characterisation, however, would not be appropriate for an analysis of the Bundesbank. Rather, the Bundesbank enjoys a particular status, which is derived from two major institutional elements. This particular status shapes the bank's openness and accessibility. First, the Bundesbank has a particular legal status, which clearly detaches it from the executive branch and its conventional bureaucracy. The bank is a separate legal entity under public law[223]. It does not come under government supervision[224], and its management bodies are on par with the highest federal authorities and are not

---

[221] Stern (1998), p. 164.

[222] Bank for International Settlements (1963), pp. 56-57. The description refers to the bank's status as effective until December 31, 1998. For details on the legal status of the Bundesbank see Eun (1994), pp. 57-201, Stern (1998), pp. 179-183.

[223] Bank for International Settlements (1963), p. 56. The Federation has therefore afforded the Bundesbank an exclusive form of legal personality previously unknown in the German legal system. Due to its uniqueness, the legal nature of the Bundesbank has been open to wide interpretation. Detailed discussions of the problem are provided by Stern (1998), pp. 151-152, Eun (1994), pp. 162-168 and pp. 177-200, and Uhlenbruck (1968), pp. 40-42.

[224] This includes the fact that the Bundesbank is not subject to full supervision by the Federal Court of Auditors. The Court of Auditors reviews the Bundesbank's annual report but has not been given the means of sanctioning in cases of objection (Bank for International Settlements (1963), pp. 41-42).

subject to instructions from the Federal Government or from any other authority[225]. Governed by public law, the Bundesbank carries sovereign responsibilities without formal transfer[226]. Its capital is owned by the Federal Republic[227]. Giving the Bundesbank an independent legal personality without direct control by the government was deemed appropriate for the kind of duties the central bank was to carry out – policy formulation in, and administration of, a narrow, clearly defined policy area – and considered superior to integration of the institution into the governmental structure as a dependent organisational complex[228]. The specific status of the Bundesbank was accentuated by the fact that, unlike the federal ministries and like other high-profile federal bodies, the Bundesbank was not headquartered at the seat of the Federal Government. Instead, it has its registered office in Frankfurt, the country's financial centre[229].

Second and closely related to its particular legal status, the Bundesbank enjoys an extraordinary degree of political independence[230]. This is rooted in the Basic Law as well as in the Bundesbank Act. The constitutional character of the Bundesbank's autonomy was subject to debate for some time. In the original wording of Article 88 of the Basic Law, independence was not explicitly mentioned as a property of the central bank's blueprint[231]. Some commentators deduced from this that the Bundesbank's independence had no constitutional basis but was established only by the Bundesbank

---

[225] Bank for International Settlements (1963), p. 56. Given this special status, the Bundesbank does not form a fourth power in addition to the executive, legislative and judiciary powers within the meaning of the public-law theory of the separation of powers. As pointed out above, its position can best be described as forming a special part of the executive branch.

[226] A formal transfer would have been necessary had the Bundesbank been established under private law (Stern (1998), p. 151).

[227] Bank for International Settlements (1963), p. 55.

[228] Stern (1998), p. 152.

[229] In principle, the Bundesbank Act provided that Frankfurt/Main was to be a temporary solution while the country was divided during the Cold War. Once unification was achieved, the Bundesbank was to be relocated to Berlin. When unification did eventually come about, this original plan was not pursued and the bank's seat in Frankfurt/Main was legally confirmed (Bank for International Settlements (1993), p. 56 and Stern (1998), p. 154). For a detailed analysis of the monetary transformation process in the wake of German unification see Streit (1998).

[230] Political independence primarily refers to the bank's functional independence with regard to the duties conferred upon it by the Basic Law and the Bundesbank Act. It does not extend to other tasks delegated to the bank by law. Also, independence primarily refers to the bank's relations to the Federal Government and subordinate authorities. In contrast, the Bundesbank is subject to federal legislation in as far as this does not affect its constitutional status, as discussed below. Also, the bank is subject to judicial review (Stern (1998), p. 185).

[231] "The Federation shall establish a note-issuing and currency bank as the Federal Bank.", German Basic Law, Article 88.

Act[232]. Others interpreted the wording of Article 88, its intention as well as the historical background of the Basic Law[233], as implying that independence was a necessary precondition for the bank to fulfil its duties and that the bank's autonomy therefore had constitutional status[234]. The answer to this question could have had far-reaching implications for the Bundesbank, not merely of a legal theoretical, but also of a practical nature. In the event of an insurmountable difference with the government or other constitutional organs, policy makers could have decided to amend the Bundesbank's legal basis, or abolish or replace the bank altogether. Had the bank's autonomy been rooted in the constitution, such a decision would have required a constitutional majority in both chambers of the German parliament. Otherwise, a simple act by the lower chamber would have sufficed[235]. In practice, a confrontation with the Bundesbank necessitating a final resolution of this question[236] never occurred[237]. Instead, the ambiguity itself has been eliminated in the meantime. In a 1992 amendment of the Basic Law, a provision was been inserted into Article 88 reading

> "[w]ithin the framework of the European Union, [the Bundesbank's] responsibilities and powers may be transferred to the European Central

---

[232] "In exercising the powers conferred on it by this Act, the Bank is independent of instructions from the Federal Cabinet.", Paragraph 12, Sentence 2, Bundesbank Act. The quotation refers to the act as effective until December 31, 1998. This position was most prominently taken by the Federal Administrative Court, which considered that political autonomy was consistent with, but not necessarily guaranteed by, the wording of Article 88, Basic Law (Stern (1998), p. 180). For a review of the coverage of central bank independence in German case law see Eun (1994), pp. 166-167.

[233] In this context, it was argued that in the pre-constitutional context – referring to the history of central banking in Germany in the form of the Reichsbank, with the exception of the Nazi era – a heritage of central bank independence had been established that the Basic Law was intended to continue (Uhlenbruck (1968), pp. 28-29, Stern (1998), pp. 180-181). A systematic review of the potential constitutional sources of the Bundesbank's independence is provided by Eun (1994), pp. 57-176, and by Samm (1967), pp. 148-191.

[234] For a presentation of the arguments in favour of and against such an interpretation see Uhlenbruck (1968), pp. 17-18 and pp. 24-32, Samm (1967), pp. 17-27 and Eun (1994), pp. 57-167. This line of interpretation was also adopted by the Federal Constitutional Court, which identified a "constitutionally independent status" in a 1989 decision (Stern (1998), p. 181).

[235] Uhlenbruck (1968), pp. 27-28.

[236] Other than the question as to how a dispute between the central bank and other state organs could ultimately be resolved, the status and degree of independence gives rise to a number of further vital questions. Most importantly, it can be asked how such an independent institution can be rationalised in social systems governed by democratic structures and processes. This question has been discussed in depth by Samm (1967), pp. 76-121.

[237] The sources, substance, and legal implications of a confrontation between the Bundesbank and other state organs are discussed by Uhlenbruck (1968), pp. 67-72 and Samm (1967), pp. 208-216.

> Bank that is independent and committed to the overriding goal of assuring price stability."[238]

The reference to the ECB, its independence and goals, has generally been interpreted as reflecting directly on the Bundesbank. Accordingly, Article 88 is today interpreted as guaranteeing autonomy for the Bundesbank at a constitutional level[239].

From the perspective of interest-group activity, it is noteworthy that – before and after entry into EMU – the bank's political independence was narrowly defined, prohibiting the bank from taking instructions from government. This implies that

- while giving or taking instructions is prohibited, it is legitimate – at least from a legal angle – for third parties to present views and express opinions on Bundesbank policies, and
- the primary addressees of this provision are the Federal Government and subordinate public authorities[240]. Political activities in the private sector are not subject to this rule.

From a legal perspective the political independence of the Bundesbank thus has no immediate effect on enterprises and interest groups in the private sector. Political and moral consistency may, nevertheless, work as incentives on the private sector not to address the Bundesbank explicitly.

The primacy of the Bundesbank's general political independence has been underscored in the Bundesbank Act by emphasising the bank's institutional and personal independence. In institutional terms, the bank has been granted a special status in the constitutional order, as already observed. The Act has refrained from giving the Bundesbank one of the conventional legal forms[241] and applies an auxiliary method by giving it a legal personality of its own. In doing so, the Act places the bank on an equal footing with government, which the latter cannot outvote[242]. The bank was deliberately created as an *institutum sui generis* in the German legal order in order to avoid any form of institutional influence on it, as would necessarily have been the case if conventional legal forms had been applied[243].

---

[238] Article 88, Sentence 2, Basic Law.

[239] Stern (1998), p. 181.

[240] Independence refers primarily to the bank's relations with the Federal Government and subordinate authorities. In contrast, the Bundesbank is subject to federal legislation in as far as this does not affect its constitutional status (Stern (1998), p. 185).

[241] Usually, organisations under public law take the form of either institutions ("Anstalt"), corporations ("Körperschaft") or foundations ("Stiftung") (Uhlenbruck (1963), p. 40).

[242] Uhlenbruck (1963), p. 40.

[243] Uhlenbruck (1963), pp. 40-41.

Second, general political independence is supported by a number of elements which can promote the personal independence of decision-making Bundesbank personnel. From 1957 to 1998, the Bundesbank's supreme decision-making body was the Central Bank Council, which determined the bank's monetary policy. It was composed of the Bundesbank Directorate, including the president and the vice president of the Bundesbank, as well as the presidents of the Landeszentralbanken. The internal structure and decision-making processes will be scrutinised in more detail at a later stage. What is important at this stage is that all members of the bank's governing bodies were political nominees:

- The members of the Directorate, including the president and the vice president of the bank, were nominated by the Federal Cabinet and appointed by the president of the Federal Republic[244].
- The presidents of the Landeszentralbanken were nominated by the Bundesrat[245] and appointed by the president of the Federal Republic[246].

In essence, therefore, the process of nomination and appointment entailed the danger of politicising the members of the bank's governing bodies. In principle, the process permitted the cabinet and Bundesrat to nominate candidates affiliated with certain political parties and espousing certain economic or monetary schools of thought or general personal attachments. With respect to potential reappointment, political appointees may have had incentives to remain beholden to the body that had initially nominated them[247]. Such political dependencies could influence decision making during the tenure of office at the central bank. From the perspective of interest groups seeking to promote a certain political party, certain economic or monetary schools of

---

[244] "The president, vice-president and other members of the Directorate are nominated by the Federal Cabinet and appointed by the President of the Federal Republic. Before making such nominations, the Federal Cabinet shall consult the Central Bank Council. Members of the Directorate are appointed for eight years, or in exceptional cases for a shorter term of office, but not for less than five years. Appointments and retirements shall be published in the Federal Gazette (Bundesanzeiger).", Paragraph 6 (3), Bundesbank Act, as effective until December 31, 1998.

[245] The Bundesrat is the chamber of Parliament representing the federal states. In practice, the nominations come from the government of the state or states in which the respective Landeszentalbank is located and are subsequently passed on to the federal president by the Bundesrat.

[246] "Presidents of Landeszentralbanken are nominated by the Bundesrat and appointed by the president of the Federal Republic. The Bundesrat submits its nomination based on a proposal by the authority appropriate under the laws of the Land or Länder concerned, and after having consulted the Central Bank Council. Vice-presidents and other members of Executive Boards are nominated by the Central Bank Council and appointed by the president of the Deutsche Bundesbank. Members of Executive Boards are appointed for eight years, or in exceptional cases for a shorter term of office, but not for less than five years. Appointments and retirements shall be published in the Federal Gazette.", Paragraph 8 (4), Bundesbank Act, as effective until December 31, 1998.

[247] Uhlenbruck (1968), p. 44.

thought or certain persons, the political nomination process could, in turn, theoretically serve as an avenue for applying political pressure.

However, there are features of the nomination and appointment process that in principle serve to discourage political dependencies. For one thing, it has been argued that political appointments were discouraged by the fact that both the cabinet and the Bundesrat were obliged by law to consult the Central Bank Council before submitting their nominations[248]. Assuming that the Central Bank Council itself behaves in a non-partisan manner, this would promote the selection of competent nominees. This logic would apply in particular if we consider that the members of the Council were required by the Bundesbank Act to command special professional qualifications[249]. Given these qualifications, Council members should be in a privileged position to make suitable suggestions to fill forthcoming vacancies on the Council. Nominating or appointing a person against opposition from the Council was deemed difficult for the cabinet or the Bundesrat to communicate to the public. As a result, the obligation to consult the Council before new nominations has been seen as limiting the scope for political appointments[250].

Further, the final appointment rests with the president of the Federal Republic. For this, the president is not bound by the nomination presented by the cabinet or the Bundesrat. He has the right and the duty to review the nominations in the context of the relevant legal requirements – most importantly, the position of the Central Bank Council and the professional suitability of the nominee – and to take care that the constitution and law are duly observed. If the latter is not the case, he has the right and duty to reject a nomination. The president's role has therefore been regarded as an important safeguard against any potential erosion of the Bundesbank's political independence[251].

An additional element working against the politicisation of high-ranking Bundesbank officials has been identified in the condition established in the Bundesbank Act that Directorate members and Landeszentralbank presidents had to command special professional qualifications[252], as already indicated above. But whether this provision has, in practice, promoted non-political appointments must be called into question on

---

[248] Paragraph 8 (4), Bundesbank Act, as effective until December 31, 1998.

[249] See Paragraph 7 (2) and Paragraph 8 (3), Bundesbank Act, as effective until December 31, 1998. Whether the assumption of non-partisan preferences of the Council in the nomination process is justified has remained open to empirical testing.

[250] For details on the role of the Central Bank Council in the nomination and appointment process, see Uhlenbruck (1968), pp. 45-46.

[251] Uhlenbruck (1968), pp. 46-47.

[252] See Paragraph 7 (2) and Paragraph 8 (3), Bundesbank Act, as effective until December 31, 1998.

purely theoretical grounds. The term 'special professional qualifications' is rather broad and, as such, does not prohibit political nominations[253].

Also, it has been argued that the plurality of the nominating, advisory and appointing bodies involved in staffing the Central Bank Council served to reduce the risk of the Council's being systematically politicised, or at least of its overall composition being politically lopsided. Given the number of bodies involved in making appointments to the Council and the fact that some of those bodies were themselves likely to be characterised by a certain degree of internal heterogeneity in terms of their political alignments – as in the case of the Bundesrat and the Central Bank Council –, the probability of a sequence of one-sided personnel decisions was judged to be limited, especially over time[254].

Finally, an important element in reducing the risk of politicisation of Central Bank Council appointments was the type and duration of employment contracts with the members of the Central Bank Council, granting Bundesbank decision makers a considerable degree of contractual independence. Thus, the members of the Directorate and the presidents of the Landeszentralbanken were appointed for a period of eight years[255], i.e. over two legislative periods in the lower chamber of parliament. The length of the term of office for Central Bank Council members is generally interpreted as giving them the opportunity to become detached from potential political ties[256]. In addition, personal independence was strengthened by allowing the Bundesbank to conclude employment contracts with the members of the decision-making organs which are not bound by general public-sector wage agreements. As a result, comparatively generous remuneration can be arranged for members of the decision-making bodies[257]. Finally, the contracts concluded with the members of the Central Bank Council cannot be terminated on political grounds. A dismissal of Central Bank Council members is, in general, possible only in cases of grave

---

[253] Uhlenbruck (1968), p. 47.

[254] Uhlenbruck (1968), pp. 47-48.

[255] In exceptional cases, a term of office of less than eight years, but no less than five years, was allowed by the Bundesbank Act (Uhlenbruck (1968), pp. 48-49, see also Paragraph 7 (3) and Paragraph 8 (4), Bundesbank Act, as effective until December 31, 1998.).

[256] Most Council members have served their full eight-year term. Unless a political decision to the contrary was taken by the relevant nominating bodies, the terms of office were generally renewed. Members of the Directorate in most cases stayed on until their retirement (Marsh (1992), pp. 90-95, also Uhlenbruck (1968), pp. 48-49).

[257] This at least applies to the members of the Central Bank Council. Ordinary Bundesbank employees are said to earn salaries comparable to those of other public servants, but significantly lower than those awarded in the neighbouring private banking sector. The most detailed insight into Bundesbank salary structures and employment conditions has been provided by Marsh (1992), pp. 116-120, who reports that – at the time – Central Bank Council members earned well above the level observed for equivalent federal civil servants. See also Uhlenbruck (1968), p. 49.

misconduct or inability to hold office[258]. By way of illustration, the appointment procedure as valid between 1957 and 2002 is depicted in chart 7.

Overview Bundesbank appointment procedures between 1957 and 2002

Chart 7

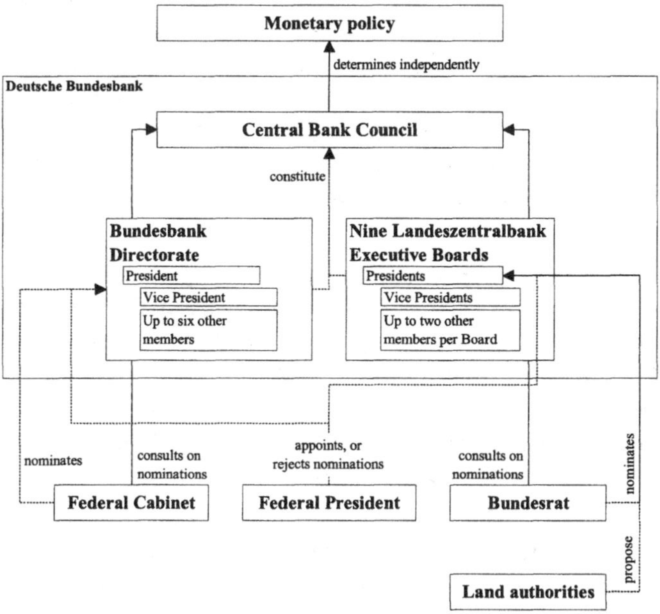

A comprehensive view of the appointment processes and employment conditions of the relevant decision makers at the Bundesbank therefore suggests that Central Bank Council members enjoy a considerable degree of personal independence, giving them the freedom fully to devote their attention to the tasks and objectives associated with their office[259] without fearing intervention from the political sphere. At the same time, it has to be noted that in practice nominations have been far from un-political. Thus, Landeszentralbank presidents were often members of the party in government in the respective state which nominated them. Many of them continued to maintain close ties with the political establishment even after assuming office at the Bundesbank[260]. To what extent the nomination process has created political dependencies or promoted

[258] For details see Uhlenbruck (1968), p. 49.

[259] Marsh (1992), p. 95.

[260] Marsh (1992), pp. 90-91. Marsh also provides an overview of the political affiliations of the relevant decision makers at the time.

certain behavioural patterns with respect to monetary policy has remained controversial and will be analysed in greater detail in the context of the behavioural patterns of policy makers below.

In contrast to institutional and personal independence, it must be said that the legislator refrained from granting the Bundesbank any form of financial independence. The Bundesbank's initial capital is held by the Federation[261]. The bank's net profits are transferred to the Federal Government after allowing for reserves and provisions as specified in the Bundesbank Act[262]. However, the Federation's capital ownership has not been regarded as an obstacle to the political autonomy of the bank. On the contrary, specific safeguards in this respect were not regarded as necessary, because influence on the bank emanating from capital ownership as such was deemed highly unlikely, if not ruled out entirely[263].

The basic properties of the institutional set-up under which monetary policy is conducted in Germany have been retained since the adoption of the Bundesbank Act in 1957. As already indicated, however, legal and institutional adjustments have recently been made in response to the establishment of monetary union at EU level. Substantial in parts, these adjustments are likely to affect the relations between monetary policy makers and interest groups. These changes extend to the mandate of the Bundesbank as well as other to institutional provisions.

Most importantly, with effect from January 1, 1999 the Deutsche Bundesbank lost its mandate as the body within the German political structure responsible for the conduct of monetary policy. As the ESCB took charge of the single monetary policy in the participating member states, i.e. in the euro area, the Bundesbank, although retaining its position as the central bank of Germany, lost its foremost assignment and, instead, became part of the ESCB. Consequently, the bank now participates in performance of the ESCB's tasks[264]. As a result, the Bundesbank is no longer in charge of safeguarding

---

[261] See Paragraph 2, Bundesbank Act, as effective until December 31, 1998.

[262] "The net profit shall be distributed in the following order: 1. twenty per cent of the profit or twenty million Deutsche Mark, whichever is the higher, shall be transferred to the legal reserves until they reach five per cent of the total amount of banknotes in circulation; the legal reserves may be used only to offset falls in value and to cover other losses; the fact that other reserves are available for this purpose does not preclude their use; 2. up to ten per cent of the remaining net profit may be used to form other reserves; the total amount of such reserves may not exceed the Bank's capital; 3. forty million Deutsche Mark, and from the financial year 1980 onwards thirty million Deutsche Mark, shall be transferred to the Fund for the Purchase of Equalisation Claims set up under the Act on the Redemption of Equalisation Claims until that Fund's dissolution; 4. the balance shall be paid over to the Federal Government." Paragraph 27, Bundesbank Act, as effective until December 31, 1998.

[263] See Stern (1998), p. 184 and Uhlenbruck (1968), p. 53.

[264] "The Deutsche Bundesbank, being the central bank of the Federal Republic of Germany, is an integral part of the European System of Central Banks (ESCB). It shall participate in the

the German currency, but is one of currently twelve central banks in the participating EU member states which together with the ECB form the Eurosystem, with the ECB carrying out the tasks of the ESCB within the euro area[265]. The ESCB and, by implication, the Eurosystem are governed by the decision-making bodies of the ECB, most importantly the Governing Board of the ECB, which is responsible for defining the Eurosystem's monetary policy and which comprises the members of the ECB's Executive Board and the presidents of the Eurosystem's national central banks[266].

For interest-group politics, this institutional change carries two major implications. First, the addressee of interest-group activities in the field of monetary affairs has changed – the ECB, an entirely new institution founded in 1998 – so that the Bundesbank is no longer the only interlocutor for the communication of private-sector interests. Second, from the perspective of interest groups in the member states, political influence on monetary decisions has diffused. The Bundesbank – still in existence and an integral part of the ESCB and the Eurosystem – is now only one of twelve national central banks participating, on equal terms, in the formulation of monetary policy for the entire euro area together with the ECB's Executive Board. The first implication suggests that interest groups will be faced with additional costs associated with the adjustment of their activities to the new institutional structures. The second implication is that, given the existence of particular interests with respect to monetary policy, mediating these interests is *ceteris paribus* likely to become more difficult as the number of potential addressees has increased. Moreover, the number of potentially competing interests may also have increased, as it is no longer merely German interest groups looking at monetary policy in Germany; instead, the entirety of interest groups in the twelve member states participating in the Eurosystem determine the relevant political arena in respect of the ECB's monetary policy. In addition, not only may the arena of competing interests grow larger, but also the breadth of interests and their intensity may increase as a result of the wider policy arena ensuing from EMU. This will be discussed in greater detail below.

---

performance of the ESCB's tasks with the primary objective of maintaining price stability, shall hold and manage the foreign reserves of the Federal Republic of Germany, shall arrange for the execution of domestic and cross-border payments and shall contribute to the stability of payment and clearing systems. In addition, it shall fulfil the tasks assigned to it under this Act or other legislation.", Paragraph 3, Bundesbank Act, as effective from January 1, 1999.

[265] Objectives and tasks related to the conduct of monetary policy in the euro area are formulated with respect to the ESCB rather than to the Eurosystem, since they were drawn up on the premise that eventually all EU member states would adopt the euro. The term euro area refers to the area comprising those EU member states which have adopted the euro. See European Central Bank (2001a), p. 9.

[266] European Central Bank (2001a), pp. 9-11. See also Articles 8, 9, 10, 11, 12, Protocol (No 3) on the Statute of the European System of Central Banks and of the European Central Bank.

Second, the aims and objectives of monetary policy have, from a German viewpoint, largely remained the same. Like the rules that governed the activities of the Bundesbank before 1999, the ESCB's objective is to maintain price stability and – without prejudice to this primary objective – to support the general economic policies in the European Community, with a view to contributing to the achievement of Community objectives[267]. As a result, there is substantial continuity in definition of the mandate that the Bundesbank, as part of the ESCB, discharges under the new regime. This objective has been re-confirmed in the latest version of the Bundesbank Act[268]. Similarly, the tasks and functions of the ESCB are, in essence, congruent with those that the Bundesbank previously exercised. This also applies to responsibilities in the context of management of foreign-exchange reserves and exchange rates. Decisions on foreign-exchange policy are a shared responsibility of the Council of Economics and Finance Ministers and the ECB. The implementation of exchange rate policies and the conduct of exchange rate management are prerogatives of the ECB[269].

Third, the primacy of political independence has been maintained and strengthened in the course of transition to EMU. Instead of referring to independence from government, as in the case of the original Bundesbank Act, the legal framework of the ESCB, which is also binding upon the member states and their central banks, provides that

---

[267] See Article 105 EC Treaty: "1. The primary objective of the ESCB shall be to maintain price stability. Without prejudice to the objective of price stability, the ESCB shall support the general economic policies in the Community with a view to contributing to the achievement of the objectives of the Community as laid down in Article 2. The ESCB shall act in accordance with the principle of an open market economy with free competition, favouring an efficient allocation of resources, and in compliance with the principles set out in Article 4. 2. The basic tasks to be carried out through the ESCB shall be: to define and implement the monetary policy of the Community, to conduct foreign-exchange operations consistent with the provisions of Article 111, to hold and manage the official foreign reserves of the Member States, to promote the smooth operation of payment systems.", and Article 2, Protocol (No 3) on the Statute of the European System of Central Banks and of the European Central Bank.: "In accordance with Article 105(1) of this Treaty, the primary objective of the ESCB shall be to maintain price stability. Without prejudice to the objective of price stability, it shall support the general economic policies in the Community with a view to contributing to the achievement of the objectives of the Community as laid down in Article 2 of this Treaty. The ESCB shall act in accordance with the principle of an open market economy with free competition, favouring an efficient allocation of resources, and in compliance with the principles set out in Article 3a of this Treaty." See also European Central Bank (2001a), pp. 9-10.

[268] "The Deutsche Bundesbank, being the central bank of the Federal Republic of Germany, is an integral part of the European System of Central Banks (ESCB). It shall participate in the performance of the ESCB's tasks with the primary objective of maintaining price stability, shall hold and manage the foreign reserves of the Federal Republic of Germany, shall arrange for the execution of domestic and cross-border payments and shall contribute to the stability of payment and clearing systems. In addition, it shall fulfil the tasks assigned to it under this Act or other legislation." Paragraph 3, Bundesbank Act, as effective from April 30, 2002.

[269] The Treaty also emphasises that exchange rate policy must be fully consistent with the primary objective of the single monetary policy. European Central Bank (2001a), p. 12.

> "[w]hen exercising the powers and carrying out the tasks and duties conferred upon them by this Treaty and the Statute of the ESCB, neither the ECB, nor a national central bank, nor any member of their decision-making bodies shall seek or take instructions from Community institutions or bodies, from any government of a Member State or from any other body. The Community institutions and bodies and the governments of the Member States undertake to respect this principle and not to seek to influence the members of the decision-making bodies of the ECB or of the national central banks in the performance of their tasks."[270]

Independence therefore now extends to any political organ, irrespective of whether it is part of the constitutional order of the EU or of one of the member states. In addition, political independence has been anchored at constitutional level in the EC Treaty, reflecting on the Bundesbank's own legal status in Germany's constitutional order, as already pointed out.

Fourth, in the wake of monetary union the Bundesbank Act was amended with the aim of adjusting the central bank to its new function within the ESCB. In particular, the latest reform[271], which entered into force on April 30, 2002, aimed at reducing the number of decision-making organs inside the Bundesbank, which was no longer deemed appropriate given that the Bundesbank no longer possesses its own monetary decision-making responsibilities[272]. As a result, the Bundesbank is now governed by one single body, the Governing Board, which is composed of eight members[273]. Following the argument that a pluralism of nominating institutions can promote institutional and personal independence, the sharing of nominating powers has been retained. Thus, the president of the Bundesbank, the vice president and two further members of the board are now nominated by the federal cabinet, while the remaining four members of the board are put forward by the Bundesrat[274]. The new appointment procedure is depicted in chart 8 below. Otherwise, the appointment process has remained unchanged, maintaining the elements contributing to the personal independence of the members of the bank's decision-making body, such as obligatory consultation of the board, appointment by the federal president, the length of office, the applicability of public law and the need to have relevant professional qualification

---

[270] Article 108 EC Treaty.

[271] For a complete review of the changes made to the Bundesbank Act in the course of the Seventh Act amending the Bundesbank Act, which became effective from April 30, 2002, see Deutsche Bundesbank (2002a), pp. 5-18.

[272] Deutsche Bundesbank (2002a), p. 6.

[273] Deutsche Bundesbank (2002a), p. 9. See also Paragraph 7, Bundesbank Act as effective from April 30, 2002.

[274] Deutsche Bundesbank (2002a), p. 9. Paragraph 7, Bundesbank Act as effective from April 30, 2002.

and experience[275]. In the same vein, federal elements in the decision-making process have been abolished. The Landeszentralbanken have been removed and replaced by regional offices headed by a president appointed by, and directly responsible to, the Governing Board[276]. With this structural alteration the legislator intended to streamline the Bundesbank's organisational procedures and make them more efficient[277].

Overview Bundesbank appointment procedures from 2002

Chart 8

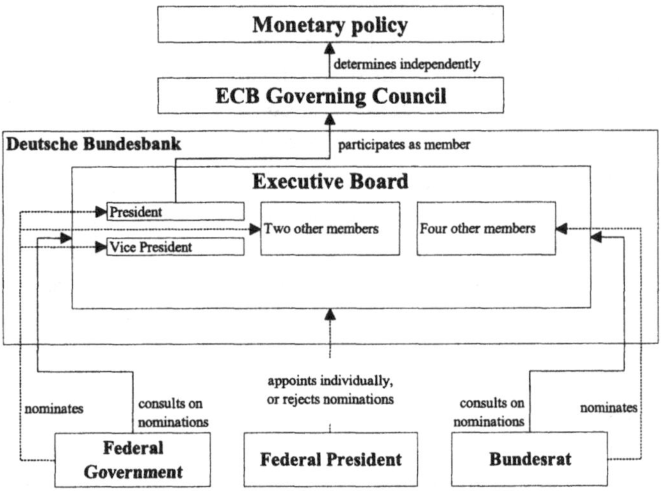

In conclusion, the institutional framework of monetary policy in Germany can, for the present purpose, be summarised as characterised by

- clear assignment of the tasks related to the conduct of monetary policy to one single institution, the Deutsche Bundesbank until 1998, and the ECB as from 1999,
- clear assignment of the conclusion of international agreements pertaining to the management of exchange rates to the Federal Government, and since 1999 to the European Council and the ECB,
- clear assignment of the tasks related to management of the exchange rate and foreign-exchange reserves to the Bundesbank, and to the ECB since 1999, and

[275] Deutsche Bundesbank (2002a), p. 10. See also Paragraph 7, Bundesbank Act as effective from April 30, 2002.

[276] Deutsche Bundesbank (2002a), pp. 11-12. See also Paragraph 8, Bundesbank Act as effective from April 30, 2002.

[277] Deutsche Bundesbank (2002a), p. 12.

thereby to highly specialised bureaucracies institutionally detached from government and other political bodies,

- a broadly defined single objective formulated in qualitative terms, namely safeguarding internal and external price stability,
- far-reaching discretion on the part of the Bundesbank, and the ECB since 1999, with regard to interpretation of the objective of safeguarding internal and external price stability as well as to the strategy, tactics and instruments applied in pursuing that objective,
- a high degree of independence from outside political influence, especially with regard to the Federal Government, designed to allow the Bundesbank and its decision makers to fulfil their tasks without politically motivated interference running counter to the bank's objectives, and which is underscored in institutional and personal respects. The regime of political independence has been reinforced in the context of EMU and implementation of the institutional provisions on the ESCB.

As suggested by theory, these institutional properties will influence the costs and benefits associated with mediating interests on monetary policy. In principle, the institutional setting in which monetary policy is determined and conducted contains a number of elements potentially affecting the activities of interest groups.

- With monetary policy tasks clearly defined and assigned to one, autonomous decision-making body, interest groups can focus their activities on this one body and do not need to target a number of concurrently responsible or otherwise involved institutions. At the same time, mediating interests can be impeded if the single responsible institution shuts itself off from external influence.
- The latter scenario is accentuated by the fact that the Bundesbank is an institution enjoying a great deal of political independence. This independent status pertains primarily vis-à-vis the government, but also versus other political entities. Exerting influence on the conduct of monetary policy via the government or other institutions and bodies in Germany's political system is therefore blocked to a great extent.
- The primacy of political independence of the Bundesbank does not, however, prevent private-sector interest groups from expressing their preferences. In principle, groups can communicate their interests, but the question is to what

extent the Bundesbank takes such interests into consideration. In any case, there is practically no way of applying political pressure on the Bundesbank[278].

- Given the definition of the Bundesbank's objectives, partial and particular interests in the economy with regard to monetary policy are of little relevance to the Bundesbank, if not indeed completely irrelevant. The bank is obliged to safeguard price stability for the monetary area as a whole. Regional, sectoral or otherwise motivated partial interests play no role in the definition of its tasks and are not relevant unless their fulfilment contributes to achievement of the bank's primary objective. This considerably limits the prospects of success for political action by interest groups and hence the potential benefits of such action.
- Since the launch of EMU, the political arena for private interests has changed enormously. In mediating their interests, interest groups have to deal with a newly established institution and compete with a greater number and broader range of interests. This complicates interest-group policymaking.

Nevertheless, the Bundesbank enjoys a considerable margin of discretion in interpreting and pursuing its objective. In as far as this discretion implies room for manoeuvre in the bank's policy decisions, interest groups can attempt to influence the bank's monetary stance as they deem appropriate.

II.1.1.3 Institutional accessibility: structures and policy processes

The preceding analysis of the Bundesbank's mandate and institutional properties shows that, on the whole, accessibility of the monetary decision-making process in general and of the Bundesbank in particular is highly limited. However, the analysis also shows that these institutional restrictions do not, in principle, prevent interest groups from mediating their interests in this policy field. This section therefore examines the second set of factors in the institutional context, namely those pertaining to the accessibility of the decision-making process. After a brief outline of the policy process, this section investigates the major restrictions on external influence, the formal and informal access points within the monetary decision process, and the dependencies policy makers face in the process.

The process of monetary decision making comprises two distinct stages: definition of the monetary decision-making framework and monetary policy decision making as

---

[278] Theoretically, political pressure can be applied in two ways: first, by threatening to change the Bundesbank Act and, second, by threatening to take the Bundesbank to court on the grounds of failure to comply with its constitutional and legal obligations. The first option is highly unrealistic since the Bundesbank's position in the political system as well as its tasks and functions are essentially defined by the EU and EC Treaties. Any amendment of the Bundesbank Act in key parts would therefore necessitate amendment of the Treaties as well as the Basic Law. The second option has not been invoked so far.

such[279]. The preceding section suggests that the monetary decision-making framework chosen in Germany, and subsequently at the EU level, anticipates two major rules on the conduct of monetary policymaking, namely that the primary policy objective is to safeguard internal and external price stability and that monetary policy decisions may be subject to commitments established as a result of exchange rate arrangements concluded at the political level. Other than that, the Bundesbank, and now the ESCB, have enjoyed a considerable degree of discretion. Most importantly, this involves

- the discretion to interpret price stability and to establish qualitative and quantitative targets for fulfilling the primary objective,
- the discretion to choose the strategy, tactics and instruments by means of which the primary objective is fulfilled.

The decision-making processes by means of which this room for manoeuvre has been exercised have changed over time, again owing to the systemic break necessitated by the realisation of monetary union. From its establishment until 1998, the Bundesbank's monetary policy was determined by the Central Bank Council. Composed of the up to eight members of the bank's Directorate and the presidents of the nine[280] Landeszentralbanken, the Central Bank Council

- determined the monetary policy of the bank,
- drew up general guidelines governing the conduct of business and administration, and

[279] This duality coincides with the economic analysis of policy rules in contrast to discretion, as presented in the theoretical section. Establishing a policy rule may encompass the assignment of tasks to a body, the definition of goals, and the modalities of operation and can theoretically go as far as defining policy targets in a qualitative or even a quantitative manner. The latter can theoretically include percentage growth targets or corridors for monetary variables such as inflation, the money supply or exchange rates, laid down by law. The more narrowly policy targets are defined at the rule – or decision-making framework – level, the less discretion the body tasked with monetary policymaking has. Taken to the extreme – e.g. by implementing a monetary rule as proposed by Milton Friedman according to which nominal central bank interest rates are fixed at zero – this task can be reduced to purely technical implementation.

[280] As from October 22, 1992, there have been nine Landeszentralbanken, located in the following areas: the Land Baden-Württemberg; the Free State of Bavaria; the Länder Berlin and Brandenburg; the Free Hanseatic City of Bremen and the Länder Lower Saxony and Saxony-Anhalt; the Free and Hanseatic City of Hamburg and the Länder Mecklenburg-Western Pomerania and Schleswig-Holstein; the Land Hesse; the Land North Rhine-Westphalia; the Länder Rhineland-Palatinate and Saarland; the Free States of Saxony and Thuringia. The regional structure has been retained in the Seventh Act amending the Bundesbank Act of 2002. However, the bank has since referred to its Regional Offices by the cities in which they are located, i.e. the Regional Offices in Stuttgart, Munich, Berlin, Hanover, Hamburg, Frankfurt, Düsseldorf, Mainz, and Leipzig respectively. The latter nomenclature is generally used in this study. The Regional Offices are abbreviated by the first three letters of the city of location.

- defined the responsibilities of the Directorate and the Executive Boards of the Landeszentralbanken.[281]

As to the Council's operating procedures, the Bundesbank Act stipulated that it should deliberate under the chairmanship of the president or vice president of the bank, and that it should take its decisions by a simple majority of votes[282]. As a rule, the Council convened every two weeks[283]. Under the Act, the members of the federal cabinet were entitled to attend Council meetings[284]. They had no right to vote, but were allowed to propose motions[285]. In addition, monetary decisions had to be postponed for up to two weeks at the request of the Federal Government[286]. The relevant Council decisions were published at press conferences or in press communiqués, but the details of the deliberations, including particulars on voting by the individual Council members, were not disclosed[287]. Council meetings customarily began with an introductory report by the president or the vice president on the monetary and economic conditions in Germany, followed by comments from the other members of the Directorate on their respective areas of competence[288] and a discussion among the Council members. For the most part, the president and vice president submitted a joint recommendation on how to proceed with policymaking, which was outvoted only on very rare

[281] In specific cases it also issued instructions to the Directorate and the Executive Boards of the Landeszentralbanken. See Paragraph 6 (1), Bundesbank Act, as effective until December 31, 1998.

[282] Further conditions for taking decisions were governed by the Statute of the Deutsche Bundesbank (Bundesanzeiger 1959 No. 7).

[283] The president could convene additional meetings in the case of extraordinary events. Further, meetings could be convened at the request of at least three of the Council's members (Paragraph 1, Statute of the Deutsche Bundesbank).

[284] Paragraph 13 (2), Bundesbank Act, as effective until December 31, 1998. The statute of the bank specified that the ministers for economic affairs and finance had to be invited to each Council meeting. Other members of the federal cabinet could be invited if deemed appropriate by the Council (Paragraph 3 (1), Statute of the Deutsche Bundesbank, as effective until December 31, 1998).

[285] Paragraph 13 (2), Bundesbank Act, as effective until December 31, 1998.

[286] Stern (1998), pp. 186-187. Officially, the right to postponement was never invoked. However, the Bundesbank occasionally took the government's interests into consideration and delayed decisions (Marsh (1992), p. 99).

[287] Minutes of Council meetings and related documents are confidential and classified for at least eighteen years.

[288] The Bundesbank was organised in functional divisions, headed by the responsible member of the Directorate. Most importantly, the internal structure comprised divisions on economics and statistics, communication, international relations, banking and financial supervision, and payment services as well as other departments responsible for the bank's internal organisation.

occasions[289]. Preparatory work by the bank's economics department is understood to have had a decisive influence on the course of discussions on monetary policy[290].

In terms of the organisation of the Bundesbank, the members of the Directorate, including the president and vice president of the bank, ran the headquarters of the bank in Frankfurt. The head office was organised into functional divisions, headed by the responsible member of the Directorate. Most importantly, the internal structure comprised central office departments on economics and statistics, communications, international relations, banking and financial supervision, financial markets, and payment services as well as departments responsible for the bank's internal organisation[291]. The Bundesbank Act further entitled the bank to order and collect the statistical evidence it needed from the banking sector, making it essentially self-sufficient with respect to the information required to fulfil its tasks[292].

The presidents of the nine[293] Landeszentralbanken, on the other hand, presided over organisationally separate bodies, whose primary responsibility was to undertake transactions with the respective Land governments and authorities and transactions with credit institutions in the respective region for which they were responsible[294]. Formally, these tasks were carried out by the Executive Board at each Landeszentralbank, which consisted of the Landeszentralbank president, the vice president and, in exceptional cases, one or two further members[295]. Especially with regard to the presidents' function in the Central Bank Council, each Executive Board was, in practice, supported by specialist divisions, including separate economics departments which prepared the presidents for the two-weekly council meetings in Frankfurt.

Finally, the organisational structure of Bundesbank decision making with respect to monetary policy prior to 1998 also included Advisory Boards located at the

---

[289] Marsh (1992), pp. 100-101.

[290] For a descriptive account of the meetings of the Central Bank Council see Marsh (1992), pp. 95-99. On the importance of the economics department, see pp. 109-110.

[291] Marsh (1992) provides an in-depth description of the internal organisation and procedures at the Bundesbank headquarters. See pp. 106-120.

[292] Collection of statistics: "In order to discharge its duties, the Deutsche Bundesbank is entitled to order and collect statistics in the fields of banking and the monetary system from all credit institutions. [...] The Deutsche Bundesbank may publish these statistics for general purposes. Figures relating to individual institutions may not be disclosed in such publications. [...]", Paragraph 18, Bundesbank Act, as effective until December 31, 1998. The provision was not amended by the 2002 Bundesbank reform.

[293] The number of Landeszentralbanken had been reduced from eleven to nine in the aftermath of German monetary union in 1992.

[294] Paragraph 8 (2), Bundesbank Act, as effective until December 31, 1998.

[295] Paragraph 8 (3), Bundesbank Act, as effective until December 31, 1998. Details were provided in Paragraphs 12 to 15, Statute of the Deutsche Bundesbank, as effective until December 31, 1998.

Landeszentralbanken, which deserve particular attention in the present context. Under the Bundesbank Act, each Landeszentralbank had an Advisory Board that served to confer with the president of the Landeszentralbank on questions of monetary policy and with the Executive Board of the Landeszentralbank on the performance of that board's duties in its area[296]. Each board was composed of up to fourteen members, who were supposed to have special banking expertise. Composition of the boards reflected the broad economic interests in society[297]. The members of the Advisory Boards were nominated by the respective Land governments and, after consultation with the Executive Board of the Landeszentralbank, appointed by the President of the Bundesbank for a term of three years[298]. Meetings of the Advisory Boards were generally held four times a year. The ministers of economics and finance of the respective Land governments had to be invited to the meetings[299].

Overall, monetary decision making prior to 1998 therefore took the form of regular meetings of the decision-making body composed, on the one hand, of the members of the Directorate, who, by virtue of their central position, played an important role in formulating the bank's monetary stance[300], and, on the other, of the presidents of the Landeszentralbanken, who together represented the majority of votes on the Council. In their activities, the decision makers were supported by central and regional staff – amounting end-1998 to 2,606 employees at the Directorate's offices and a total of 13,285 employees in the Landeszentralbanken and their branches. A small fraction of these, mainly experts in economics, monetary economics and statistics, were indirectly involved in formulation of the bank's monetary policy. Landeszentralbank presidents additionally conferred with the private sector via their respective Advisory Boards.

After an interim period extending from the beginning of 1999 to mid-2002, during which the original structure of the Bundesbank was preserved while monetary decision making was already being carried out by the ECB Governing Council, the Bundesbank reform of April 2002 significantly altered the bank's internal organisation and processes. As already pointed out, since Germany joined EMU in 1999 the only person directly involved in monetary decision making has been the president of the Bundesbank, who has an *ex officio* seat on the ECB's Governing Council.

---

[296] Paragraph 9 (1), Bundesbank Act, as effective until December 31, 1998.

[297] Paragraph 9 (2), Bundesbank Act, as effective until December 31, 1998.

[298] Paragraph 9 (3), Bundesbank Act, as effective until December 31, 1998.

[299] Paragraph 16, Statute of the Deutsche Bundesbank, as effective until December 31, 1998.

[300] Marsh (1992) emphasises that the members of the Directorate benefited from the fact that, working together in Frankfurt and meeting once a week for internal sessions, they found it easier to reach common positions on monetary policy and to represent these decisions inside the Central Bank Council. In contrast, the presidents of the Landeszentralbanken met at worst only every two weeks and were then confronted with a joint position by the Directorate (pp. 95-96).

The Executive Board of the Bundesbank, which has replaced the Central Bank Council, does not play a formal role in formulation of the bank's position with respect to monetary policy, unlike its predecessor. It rather

- governs and manages the bank, and
- passes the organisational statutes allocating the responsibilities of the members of the Executive Board and the tasks delegated to the regional offices.

With respect to monetary policy, the members of the Executive Board merely advise the president of the Bundesbank in his capacity as a member of the Governing Council of the ECB[301]. Other than that, the tasks of the members of the Executive Board, with the exception of the bank's president himself, are mainly operational in nature and concerned with the bank's internal organisation. Below the Executive Board level, the organisational structure of the bank's central office departments has essentially remained unchanged. Members of the Federal Government are no longer entitled to observe the meetings of the bank's highest decision-making body, but may still be invited. The right to delay decisions has been repealed[302].

As to the Landeszentralbanken, we have already noted that the federal structure of the Bundesbank has formally been abolished. The Landeszentralbanken have been transformed into Regional Offices of the Bundesbank. Their presidents are no longer political appointees, being selected by the Executive Board, and are no longer formally involved in formulation of the bank's position with respect to monetary policy. Landeszentralbank offices formerly directly involved in the president's preparation for Central Bank Council meetings, i.e. most importantly the regional economics departments, have been abolished. In contrast to the members of the Executive Board, regional office presidents are not formally involved in advisory functions with respect to the bank's position on monetary matters[303].

In the course of the 2002 Bundesbank reform the Landeszentralbank Advisory Boards were retained as advisory bodies to the Regional Offices[304]. However, whereas the Advisory Boards previously conferred mainly with the presidents of the Landeszentralbanken on questions of monetary policy, all they now discuss with the presidents of the Regional Offices is handling of the tasks falling to that area. In other

---

[301] Article 1 (2), Organisational Statute of the Deutsche Bundesbank, as adopted on May 8, 2002.

[302] Deutsche Bundesbank (2002), p. 11.

[303] Deutsche Bundesbank (2002a), pp. 11-12.

[304] Paragraph 9, Bundesbank Act, as effective from April 30, 2002. The Bundesbank itself had made two alternative proposals on how to reform the bank. Neither of the options explicitly involved maintenance of the Advisory Boards. One model, however, included the option of retaining the boards in order to promote the dialogue on the ECB's monetary policy in the regions and with the representatives of the private sector. Deutsche Bundesbank (1999a), p. 13.

words, the Advisory Boards no longer have a formal advisory function with respect to monetary policy[305]. They now meet only twice a year[306].

The extent to which the decision-making and advisory processes for monetary policymaking in Germany were streamlined with adoption of the Seventh Act amending the Bundesbank Act of April 2002 is evident in the comparison of the work flows in charts 9 and 10 below. Federal, pluralistic structures have been replaced by a unitary advisory and decision-making process. The presidents of the Bundesbank Regional Offices and the members of the federal cabinet and the Advisory Boards have no longer been part of the formal policy-shaping process since May 2002, and the process of opinion-building on monetary issues has been concentrated within the Bundesbank's central offices.

Organisation of monetary policy decision making – Bundesbank 1957-1998

Chart 9

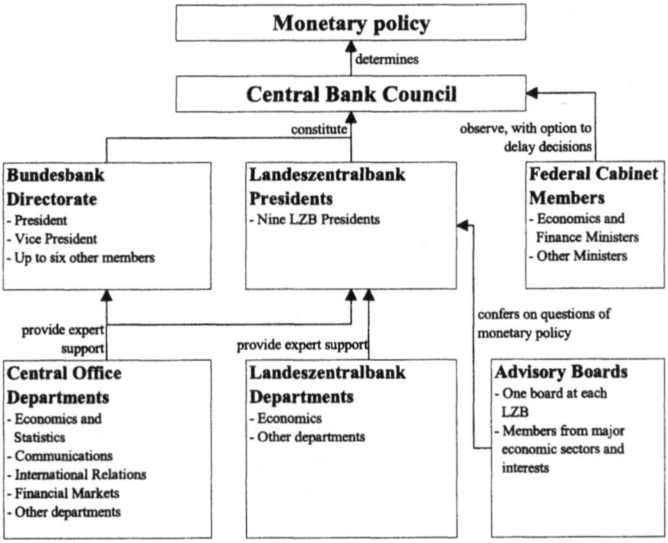

Irrespective of these procedural changes, the Bundesbank's decision-making processes have been characterised throughout by the bank's autonomous status. Once decision-making staff have been appointed, the bank is, for all intents and purposes, self-sufficient in the fulfilment of its tasks. Outside interests do not participate in decision making in the strict sense. Prior to 2002, members of the federal cabinet were entitled

305 Deutsche Bundesbank (2002a), p. 12.

306 Paragraph 9 (2), Bundesbank Act, as effective from April 30, 2002.

to take part in the Council's meetings and even enjoyed postponement powers with respect to monetary decisions. But the overriding status of independence released the Council from any form of intervention by the government and from taking government preferences into consideration when deciding on its policy. Today, invitations to the government to participate in Board meetings are no longer mandatory. In fact, the government itself abandoned the practice of obligatory invitations in its draft of the 2002 law amending the Bundesbank Act[307], suggesting that it was not particularly interested in attending Board meetings. Even in the presence of a representative of the Federal Government and in cognisance of the preferences expressed by the government, the bank is bound only by its objective of maintaining price stability.

Organisation of monetary policy decision making – Bundesbank since 2002

Chart 10

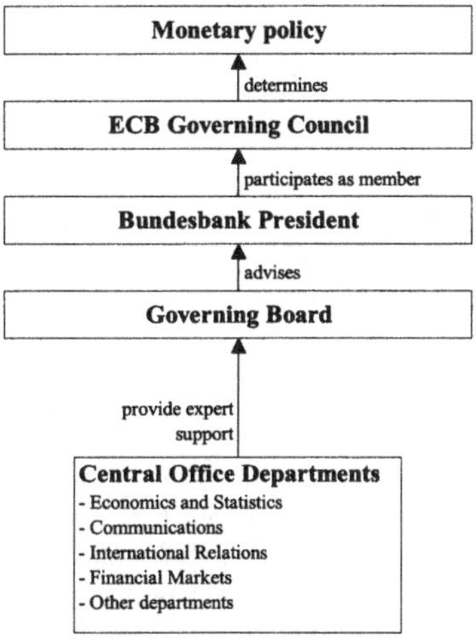

In addition to its decision-making autonomy, the Bundesbank has also been highly self-sufficient in terms of the funding and information-related resources needed to fulfil its mandate. As to material resources, the bank was initially endowed by the Federal Government with capital of DEM 290 m, which was increased to DEM 5 bn or EUR 2.5 bn in 1999. As illustrated in chart 11, the bank has usually generated substantial profits from its activities, which, as already pointed out, are transferred to the government after allowing for reserves and provisions. As to information, its right to collect the statistical information necessary for the conduct of monetary policy has enabled the bank to build up a formidable statistical base, maintained and interpreted

[307] See Seventh Act amending the Bundesbank Act, Cabinet Draft.

by the well-staffed and highly reputed departments for statistics and economics[308]. The Bundesbank has therefore been regarded as a well-informed institution in respect of monetary, financial-market and general economic analysis, and its expertise is valued internationally by central banks, international monetary institutions and academic circles. As a result, the Bundesbank's dependence on resources and information from external sources to support policy makers in their work and provide them with sufficient data and arguments to prevail in political discourse – as frequently observed in the context of parliamentary politics, for example – is extraordinarily low. In practice and as a rule, it is the government, other policy makers and the private sector that tend to receive expertise and information from the Bundesbank, rather than *vice versa*.

Bundesbank financial and staff resources

Chart 11

– Bundesbank profits, EUR bn

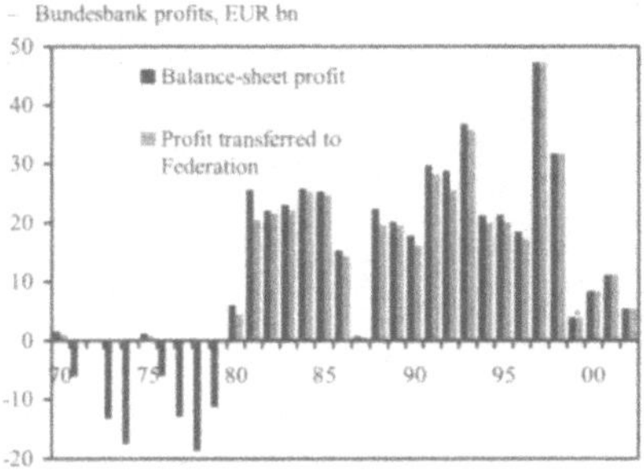

Data source: Deutsche Bundesbank

Chart 12

– Bundesbank staff, numbers, end-2002

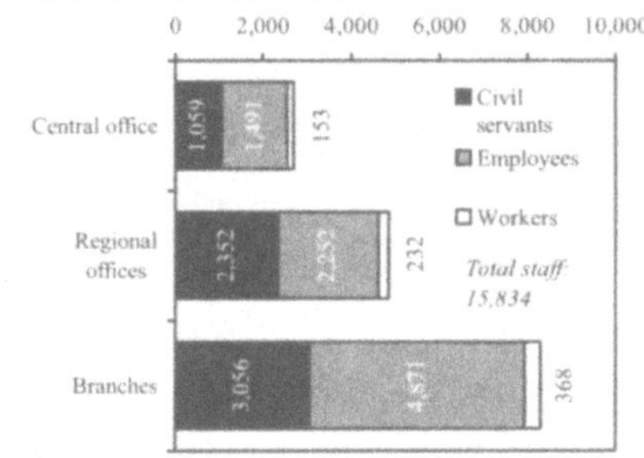

Data source: Deutsche Bundesbank

The logic of Bundesbank independence vis-à-vis the government, being enshrined in law, also reflects on other interest groups, including those from the private sector, which are not referred to in the bank's legal provisions. Their partial concerns are likewise formally irrelevant to monetary decisions. In the light of this, private interests carry much more limited weight in formation of the monetary policy stance on an *ex ante* basis than in other policy fields, where the differential impact on individual sectors or other groups of economic agents represents an explicit element in the formulation of policy objectives and their implementation, as for instance in tax policy or market regulation. Preferences expressed by interest groups or information passed on by them may therefore only enter the policy formation process inasmuch as they

[308] Marsh (1992), pp. 109-110. The total headcount of the Bundesbank amounted to 15,834 end-2002. This included 8,614 employees and 753 workers. However, the staff involved in work most closely associated with monetary policy are the 1,059 civil servants at the bank's central offices in Frankfurt. An overview of the bank's staff structure is provided in chart 12 on page 124.

contain intelligence helping the Board to assess economic and monetary conditions in the economy and to meet its objectives.

This general approach naturally limits the extent to which formal or informal points of access to the overall decision-making process can be used by private-sector interest groups to communicate their preferences with respect to monetary policy on an *ex ante* basis.

With respect to institutional accessibility by formal means, the Bundesbank provides one direct channel of communication between the bank and the private sector in the form of the Advisory Boards at the bank's Regional Offices. As already pointed out, the boards – chaired by the respective Landeszentralbank presidents or their deputies – served to confer with the presidents of the Landeszentralbanken on questions of monetary policy[309]. In consequence, the boards featured close contact with the Landeszentralbank presidents, each of whom was represented on the Central Bank Council and who, together, commanded a majority of votes on the Council in respect of monetary decisions. In addition, the boards provided a forum for meeting the economics or finance ministers of the respective Land governments, who had to be invited to the board meetings under the Bundesbank Act[310]. Furthermore, the chairmen of the boards – the respective Landeszentralbank presidents or their deputies – were entitled to invite expert witnesses to join board sessions[311].

Meetings were generally held four times a year[312]. The frequency of these periodic meetings allowed the members to comment on medium- and long-term monetary developments. Quarterly meetings, however, did not allow for reaction to short-term developments, unless by coincidence they immediately preceded important Central Bank Council meetings. To allow for urgent meetings, the bank's statute provided for additional sessions to be convened by the presidents of the Landeszentralbanken or at the request of at least three of a board's members[313].

As to the composition of the Advisory Boards, each is limited to fourteen members[314], nominated by the respective Land governments and appointed by the President of the Bundesbank for a term of three years following consultation with the Executive Board

---

309 The Boards also conferred with the Executive Board of the Landeszentralbanken on the performance of that board's duties in its area (Paragraph 9 (1), Bundesbank Act, as effective until December 31, 1998).

310 Paragraph 16, Statute of the Deutsche Bundesbank, as effective until December 31, 1998.

311 Paragraph 18, Statute of the Deutsche Bundesbank, as effective until December 31, 1998.

312 Paragraph 16 (1), Statute of the Deutsche Bundesbank, as effective until December 31, 1998.

313 Paragraph 16 (1), Statute of the Deutsche Bundesbank, as effective until December 31, 1998.

314 Each member has a deputy, appointed in the same way, who attends board meetings in the absence of the ordinary member.

of the Landeszentralbank[315]. The three-year term is renewable. Owing to the regional structure of the boards and the nomination and appointment procedures, which were retained after the 2002 Bundesbank reform, they are staffed with members with a regional or local focus. The bank's nine Advisory Boards comprised a total of 122 members at end-2003, 59 of whom (48%) were representatives of local or regional interest associations or the local or regional sections of federal associations. 60 members (49%) were representatives from individual private or public corporations, mainly with a regional or local focus or from regional or local subsidiaries of large corporations, and three (2%) were private individuals[316]. As a result, the structure of neither the Advisory Boards nor their membership promote the formulation or communication of nationally aggregated positions on monetary policy[317]. Rather, the structures favour a regional perspective on monetary affairs[318].

In addition, the great majority of board members over the past three decades have been re-appointed, often several times, so that the overall composition of the Advisory Boards has undergone only gradual change over time[319]. The fact that board members have a term of as long as three years, coupled with the bank's re-appointment practices, suggests considerable continuity in the expertise represented on the Advisory Boards.

In terms of representativeness, the boards reflect a broad range of economic interests, with emphasis on the financial sector. A maximum of half the board members can be chosen from the various areas of banking, while the other members are selected from trade and industry, distribution, the insurance sector, the professions, agriculture, and from among the ranks of wage and salary earners[320]. The boards' sectoral composition

---

[315] Paragraph 9 (3), Bundesbank Act, as effective until December 31, 1998.

[316] The names and functions of the members of the Advisory Boards are published on the Deutsche Bundesbank's internet homepage. The three private individuals comprise one university professor and two representatives from the agricultural sector.

[317] In the negotiations on the Bundesbank Act of 1957, the establishment of a central Advisory Board located at the bank's central offices in Frankfurt and advising the Central Bank Council was rejected both by the Federal Government and the Bundestag Committee on Money and Credit. At the time, it was considered that such a central body would be too large and inoperable. Initially, the Federal Government even intended to abolish the Advisory Boards – which had already existed and advised the Landeszentralbanken at the Bank deutscher Länder. The Bundestag Committee on Money and Credit, however, prevailed with its view that it would be useful to continue the regional Advisory Boards, since "it has proved conducive in the past to cultivate contacts in mutual consultation with all groups of the economy in this way, too." See von Bonin (1979), p. 190.

[318] However, Advisory Board members are not prohibited or explicitly discouraged from communicating views formed with respect to the entire German economy, as e.g. formulated by the federal sections of the interest association they represent.

[319] Prior to the 2002 Bundesbank reform, the Landeszentralbanken published the names and functions of the members of the Advisory Boards in their annual reports, analysis of which allows an insight into the inter-temporal development of board membership.

[320] Paragraph 9 (2), Bundesbank Act, as effective until December 31, 1998.

has been very stable over time. The figures valid at end-2003 therefore present a typical picture of the professional backgrounds represented. 43% of the 122 members of the nine boards were selected from the banking industry, 7% from insurance, 10% from commerce, 16% from trade and industry, 8% from the liberal professions, 7% from agriculture, and 9% represented wage and salary earners (see chart 13). Looking at trade and industry in a wider sense, i.e. including commerce and the liberal professions, as the focus of this study, an average of 34% of Advisory Board members in total came from these sectors end-2003, as shown in chart 14. At 54%, the Advisory Board at the Berlin Regional Office had the highest share of members from trade and industry, while the Leipzig Board had the lowest (21%). Representatives from banking and insurance make up between 57% in Frankfurt and Leipzig and 31% in Berlin, with a total average of 49%. Calibration of the composition is carried out at Landeszentralbank level and is subject to no rules other than those laid down in the Bundesbank Act and Statute.

Composition of Bundesbank regional Advisory Boards

Chart 13

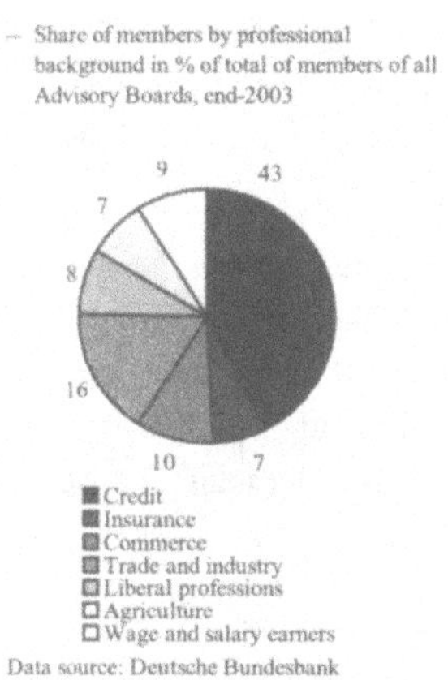

Chart 14

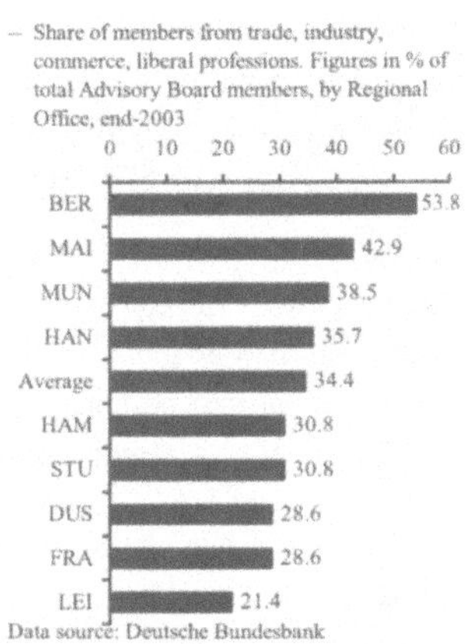

From the angle of interest-group politics, the importance of the Advisory Boards rested on the fact that they provided direct access to decision-makers directly involved in the conduct of monetary policy. This changed after the May 2002 Bundesbank reform came into force. Certainly, the Landeszentralbank Advisory Boards have been retained as advisory bodies to the Regional Offices[321]. However, whereas the Advisory Boards previously conferred primarily with the presidents of the Landeszentralbanken on monetary policy issues, they now merely discuss execution of the tasks falling to that area. In other words, the Advisory Boards no longer have a formal advisory

---

[321] Paragraph 9, Bundesbank Act, as effective from April 30, 2002.

function with regard to monetary policy[322]. Furthermore, the obligation to invite the finance and economics ministers of the relevant Land government to Advisory Board meetings has been repealed[323], further diminishing the bodies' political clout. Moreover, board meetings are no longer required to be held at least four times a year, including provisions for emergency meetings. The new rules call for only two meetings a year[324] as a rule, suggesting less chronological proximity to the monetary decision-making process as well. Given the loss in political significance resulting from the 2002 amendment to the Bundesbank Act, the Bundesbank Executive Board is understood to have decided that, as far as possible, one of its members should be present at each Advisory Board meeting, promoting greater proximity to the bank's decision making body. However, given that the members of the Executive Board other than the president are not immediately involved in the monetary decision-making process and, at best, fulfil advisory functions in that specific context, the political influence of the Advisory Boards has been considerably weakened nonetheless.

In addition to the Advisory Boards, the Bundesbank's legal framework provides for a number of further formal channels of communication, which, however, represent highly indirect ways of communication between the private sector and Bundesbank decision makers, placing the two at a considerable distance. As a result, these formal but indirect channels must be regarded as inefficient when it comes to communicating private-interest preferences with respect to monetary policy.

Most importantly, a number of formal channels of communication result from Bundesbank involvement in Germany's[325] economic and financial politics. This involvement stems, on the one hand, from the bank's obligation – albeit secondary – to support the general economic policies of the Federal Government, which is ongoing even after entry into EMU, as already pointed out. In this sense, the bank also serves

---

322 Deutsche Bundesbank (2002a), p. 12.

323 See Organisational Statute of the Deutsche Bundesbank, as adopted on May 8, 2002.

324 Paragraph 9 (2), Bundesbank Act, as effective from April 30, 2002. Deutsche Bundesbank (2002a), p. 12.

325 The Bundesbank also takes part in a number of international activities, either on its own behalf or on behalf of the German government. At the formal level, the bank participates in the International Monetary Fund, of which the Federal Republic has been a member since 1952. The president of the Bundesbank has an *ex officio* seat on the IMF's highest decision-making body, the Board of Governors (for details see Deutsche Bundesbank (2003a), pp. 14-76, Stern (1998), pp. 177-178). Second, the Bundesbank is a shareholder in the Bank for International Settlements, with a seat in the General Meeting and on the Board of Directors (for details see Deutsche Bundesbank (2003a), pp. 202-214, Stern (1998), p. 178). At an informal level, the Bundesbank also plays a part in the G10 and G7 meetings. Participation in these international forums will not be analysed in the present context, as they are not relevant for domestic private-sector interest groups and their communication with the Bundesbank.

as an important economic advisor to the Federal Government in the pursuit of its policies[326].

With regard to the need to support the government's general economic policies, we have already seen that the government was entitled to attend the meetings of the Central Bank Council as a non-voting observer with the right to delay monetary decisions for up to two weeks. As pointed out, this right has never actually been invoked. In line with the obligatory invitation to the federal economics and finance ministers to attend Central Bank Council meetings, Land economics and finance ministers were invited to attend the sessions of the Advisory Boards on a statutory basis[327]. Both forms of obligatory invitation were repealed in May 2002. As to the Bundesbank's role as an economic adviser to the government, the Bundesbank Act requires the bank to advise the Federal Government on monetary policy issues of major importance and to furnish Berlin with any information requested. Furthermore, the Federal Government is enjoined to invite the president of the Bundesbank to attend its deliberations on important monetary policy issues[328]. Via the EU Council of Ministers, the Federal Government remains involved in monetary and exchange rate policies, so that the Bundesbank's advisory role and participation in the relevant cabinet meetings continue notwithstanding the other institutional changes implemented in 2002. Bundesbank support for the government and the mutual attendance of meetings were seen by the Bundesbank as

> "strengthening the relations between the Federal Government and the Bundesbank and give the latter the opportunity to keep itself informed about the economic aims pursued by the government."[329]

In practice, the possibilities of attending each other's meetings have been used extensively, especially when fundamental questions were discussed[330].

In addition to its immediate relations with the Federal Government, the Bundesbank formally serves as an advisor to four consultative committees at federal level. First, the Bundesbank can be consulted by, and is eligible to present its opinions to the German Council of Economic Experts[331], which regularly advises the Federal Government on

---

[326] Stern (1998), p. 174.

[327] With respect to the Land governments, the Bundesbank had no obligation comparable to that pertaining to support for the Federal Government's general economic policies.

[328] See Paragraph 13, Bundesbank Act.

[329] Deutsche Bundesbank as quoted in Stern (1998), p. 174.

[330] Stern (1998), p. 175. Anecdotal evidence on relations between the Bundesbank and the Federal Government as well as on discussions in the course of Central Bank Council and Cabinet meetings under mutual participation has been presented by Marsh (1992), pp. 222-337.

[331] The German Council of Economic Experts (*Sachverständigenrat zur Begutachtung der gesamtwirtschaftlichen Entwicklung*) is an academic body that advises the German government and

all aspects of economic policy. In particular, the Council examines the sources of current and potential problems and makes recommendations on their resolution[332]. Second, the Bundesbank is entitled to attend the deliberations of the Economic Council for the Public Authorities[333], which advises the Federal Government and supports and coordinates the interests of the Land, regional and local authorities with regard to the Federal Government's economic policies, especially on questions pertaining to public finances, economic provisions and debt policy[334]. Third, the Bundesbank is a permanent member of the Credit Committee of the Public Authorities[335], which participates in the coordination of public debt policy and analyses demand for debt in the public sector and capital market developments[336]. Fourth, the Bundesbank is entitled to attend the meetings of the Council for Fiscal Planning[337] which reports to the Federal Government and issues non-binding recommendations on the coordination of medium term fiscal planning by the federal, Land and local governments. Characteristic of the Bundesbank's role in these bodies is that it serves as an external advisor, acting by virtue of its competence as the country's central bank. As a result, the flow of information runs from the Bundesbank to the respective council or committee. Conversely, discussion of Bundesbank or ECB monetary policy is not intended. With regard to the potential channels of communication between the private sector and the central bank on the bank's monetary policy, these committees can therefore at best be regarded as forums in which issues indirectly related to monetary matters are discussed by policy makers at

---

parliament on economic policy issues. It was set up by law in 1963 with a mandate to periodically assess overall economic developments in Germany. It helps policy makers at all levels to reach informed judgements on economic matters. The Council is independent in respect of its advisory activities. It analyses the economic situation, forecasts economic developments and makes recommendations on how to achieve price stability, high employment, external equilibrium, and economic growth. The Council produces an annual report, published in mid-November, and ad hoc reports addressing particular problems or in response to a government request. The Council consists of five members, nominated by the German government and appointed by the German president for a term of five years. Its members may belong neither to the government nor to any national or regional legislative body and may not be employed by any public authority except as a university lecturer or a co-worker at a research institute of economic or social science. Council members must not be representatives or staff members of any industrial or trade federation, employers' association or trade union.

332 Stern (1998), p. 175.

333 *Konjunkturrat für die Öffentliche Hand.* For details see Stern (1998), p. 175.

334 Stern (1998), p. 175. The Council is composed of the federal ministers for economics and finance, representatives of each Land government and representatives of regional authorities. Its decisions are not binding on the Federal Government.

335 *Ausschuss für Kreditfragen der Öffentlichen Hand.* For details see Stern (1998), p. 176.

336 The committee is composed of representatives from the Federal and Land governments and is chaired by the federal finance minister (Stern (1998), p. 176).

337 *Finanzplanungsrat.* For details see Stern (1998), p. 176.

the federal, Land and regional levels. As channels for the communication of private-sector interests with respect to monetary policy, however, they are of no discernible significance.

At the semi-formal level, not established by law or formal agreements, the Bundesbank invites the chief economists of the major nationally organised interest associations from trade and industry to roundtable[338] discussions at the central office in Frankfurt on a half-yearly basis. The primary aim of these meetings is to communicate Bundesbank and ECB monetary policy. Participants in the roundtable talks are the Head of the Economic Department and other staff members of the Bundesbank[339] and the relevant representatives from the BDI, the BGA, the DIHK, the HDE, the VDA, the VDMA, the WVS, the ZDB, the ZDH, and the ZVEI[340].

Also at the semi-formal level, the Bundesbank holds conferences and workshops focussing on promoting academic research and debate on monetary and exchange rate theory and policy[341]. Lately, these academic activities have been enhanced by the Economic Research Centre founded in 2000, which brings together Bundesbank researchers and visiting scientists from other central banks as well as from scientific institutes[342]. The results of the bank's research activities are published in its monthly reports as working and discussion papers, as well as in other publications.

Informally, there is a wide variety of ways of communicating with Bundesbank decision makers and expert staff. In the first place, the formal and semi-formal activities enumerated above also permit an informal exchange of views. Additionally, although not as publicly present as conventional policy makers, former Central Bank Council and present-day Board members attend conferences, symposia, and other formal and informal events arranged by public, academic or private bodies as guest speakers. Also, Bundesbank decision makers meet colleagues from the private sector individually. Finally, they are understood to be watchful observers of press coverage on Bundesbank activities and of other information and comments forwarded individually to the bank.

---

[338] *Volkswirtekreis*. The Bundesbank also organises a second regular roundtable to which representatives of the financial services industry are invited.

[339] Prior to the 2002 Bundesbank reform, the member of the Directorate in charge of economic affairs participated in the roundtable meetings.

[340] See list of abbreviations, p. 13.

[341] An overview of the activities in this respect is published by the Bundesbank in its annual reports.

[342] Research focuses on issues relating to the monetary transmission process, functioning of the financial systems, including financial markets and financial intermediaries, the transformation process in central and eastern Europe, an analysis of the economic situation and the way in which open economies operate. Details on the Economic Research Centre are published by the Bundesbank on its internet site.

II.1.1.4 Behavioural patterns: monetary decision makers at the Bundesbank

In addition to the institutional and procedural framework of a policy process, theory suggests that the behaviour of the policy makers and administrators involved in shaping policy influences the extent to which interest-group activity bears fruit. In the present context, behavioural patterns are relevant inasmuch as they help answer two central questions emerging from the picture drawn of the Bundesbank so far. First, given the special institutional status the Bundesbank enjoys – especially in respect of its political independence –, the question arises as to how far these legal rights and obligations have been observed by the bank in practice. In other words, we must examine whether the Bundesbank has been as difficult an addressee for interest-group activity as the institutional and procedural framework suggests. Second, with respect to the substance of policymaking, i.e. the bank's duty to ensure price stability, the Bundesbank enjoys considerable discretion, as shown above. Against this background, we must ask how far the bank actually exploits its leeway in practice.

The first question addressed here is prompted by the fact that legal wording necessarily leaves room for interpretation. Most importantly, the legal postulate that the Bundesbank be politically independent *de facto* leaves open whether and to what extent the bank is exposed to outside influences and in how far its policy makers are affected by such influence when it comes to making up their minds on forthcoming monetary policy. This is an important question, and the answer is particularly relevant in the present context, because the Bundesbank's own behaviour on this count may in turn influence the behaviour of private interest groups. If the bank manages to represent in a credible manner that its decisions are, in fact, taken independently from outside political influence, then this might discourage interest groups from actually seeking to influence monetary policy in the first place. After all, why should a specific interest group try to influence the Bundesbank if all the others have already failed to do so? Conversely, an interest group might feel encouraged to start lobbying the Bundesbank if evidence were to suggest that – contrary to the letter of the law – the bank actually did respond to political pressures.

The evidence available on this question so far has two dimensions, a declaratory and an empirical one. At the declaratory level, the Bundesbank itself values its political independence as a cornerstone of its institutional set-up and as a vital precondition for the successful pursuit of price stability[343]. The bank's appreciation of its autonomy has been manifested and is an almost omnipresent element in its publications, reports and the speeches given by its executives. Two examples may be singled out in the present context. In its monograph "The monetary policy of the Bundesbank", first published in 1993 and designed to explain to the public its activities and role in the German

---

[343] Deutsche Bundesbank (1995), p. 8.

economy, the Bundesbank prefaces its remarks by emphasising the importance of its independence:

> "Over the long term, prices have risen less steeply in Germany than in most other industrial countries. At the same time, the Deutsche Mark has appreciated strongly in the foreign exchange markets and developed into the anchor currency of the European Monetary System. The stability of the Deutsche Mark owes a great deal to the monetary policy of the Bundesbank, which has been based on a clear statutory mandate, its independent status and its convincing monetary policy stance. Pursuant to the Bundesbank Act, the Bundesbank's primary function is to safeguard the currency. To ensure that the Bundesbank is able to pursue this target without hindrance, it is independent of instructions from the government. These cornerstones of the German central bank's constitution have meanwhile come to serve as a kind of model for the future European Central Bank."[344]

The Bundesbank subsequently emphasised the significance of the issue by stating that

> "[i]n addition to defining the traditional task of a central bank, namely that of maintaining a properly functioning payment system, the Bundesbank Act [...] lays particular emphasis on the responsibility borne by the Bundesbank for monetary stability. In the interplay between the various economic policy decision-makers – Parliament, the Federal Cabinet, the central bank, both sides of industry – the Bundesbank must always regard its function of being the guardian of the currency, as spelled out in the Act, as being its primary task. That is why the Bundesbank Act has made the central bank independent of instructions from the Federal Cabinet. As a logical consequence, the basic obligation incumbent on the Bundesbank under the Act to support the general economic policy of the Federal Cabinet is explicitly subject to the condition that this does not bring monetary policy makers into insoluble conflict with their primary objective."[345]

The second example of the Bundesbank's own conviction that central bank independence is an essential feature of a well-functioning monetary order is the bank's strategy during the negotiations towards establishing the single European currency and a monetary union in the EU. Both in the Delors Committee[346], which in April 1989

---

[344] Deutsche Bundesbank (1995), p. 8.

[345] Deutsche Bundesbank (1995), p. 22.

[346] The European Council had confirmed the objective of progressive realisation of economic union in June 1988 and mandated a Committee chaired by Jacques Delors, then President of the European Commission, to study and propose concrete stages leading to this union. The Committee members were the governors of the EC national central banks, Alexandre Lamfalussy as the then General Manager of the Bank for International Settlements, Niels Thygesen, Professor of Economics at Copenhagen University, and Miguel Boyer, the then President of the Banco Exterior de España.

issued a report sketching out the plan towards achieving monetary union, and during the negotiations at the Intergovernmental Conference on EMU in 1990, the Bundesbank representatives consistently made the success of the deliberations conditional on the future European central bank's political independence and on this far-reaching autonomy being legally established at Treaty level[347]. In the course of these negotiations the Bundesbank asserted its position and insisted on Bundesbank-style application of the principle of central bank autonomy, even in the face of considerable economic and political reservations among the other European policy makers[348].

A wide range of studies have been conducted on the empirical evidence for the responsiveness of central banks to outside political pressure. Of the studies dealing with the Bundesbank, Maier (2002) has provided a comprehensive overview and comparison. The major results are depicted in table 3[349]. Maier distinguishes in the various analyses available between opportunistic models, partisan models and conflict models. In opportunistic models[350], politicians seek to maximise their popularity and the probability of being re-elected. In partisan models[351], different social parties represent different social constituencies, have different interests and compete for influence on monetary policy. Finally, conflict models[352] focus on periods of tension between government and the central bank. The variables tested include different measures of the supply of money[353], interest rates[354], and inflation.

The resulting Delors Report stipulated that economic and monetary union should be achieved in three discrete but evolutionary steps.

[347] Detailed accounts of the negotiations on EMU can be found in Marshall (1999), pp. 78-97 and Szász (1999), pp. 98-153. Also Marsh (1992), pp. 301-353.

[348] See especially Szász (1999), pp. 147-153.

[349] See p. 135. Maier (2002) uses the term "direct influence" to denote direct correlations between certain measures of political behaviour and the actions on the part of the central bank. "Indirect influence", in contrast, is detected by means of models that measure indirect influence by governments, e.g. when fiscal policy is used in line with some version of the political-business-cycle theory, and the central bank accommodates the subsequent increase in the budget deficit, so that an election cycle may show up in some monetary variables (Maier (2002), pp. 20-29).

[350] The category of opportunistic models includes political business cycle (PBC) and rational political business cycle (RPBC) models. See Maier (2002), p. 10.

[351] Partisan models can again be divided into partisan theory (PT) and rational partisan theory (RPT) models. See Maier (2002), p. 11.

[352] The category of conflict models (CM) also includes party preference theory models (PPT). See Maier (2002), pp. 11-12.

[353] Measures of the supply of money applied in the studies covered by Maier (2002) are the narrow monetary aggregates of central bank money (CBM) and M1 as well as the broad measure M3.

[354] Interest rates tested include the German discount and Lombard rates.

Econometric evidence on direct political influence on the Deutsche Bundesbank

Table 3

Study	Influence	Model	Variables	Result
Basler (1978)	Direct	CM	Inflation	Bundesbank preferences biased during 70s.
Cowart (1978)	Direct	PT	Discount rate	Leftist governments are faced with significantly higher Discount rates.
Frey, Schneider (1981)	Direct	CM	Discount rate	During conflicts, Bundesbank yields to the government.
Baum (1983)	Direct	CM	Discount, Lombard rates	No evidence for Bundesbank adopting government's policy
Berger, Schneider (2000)	Direct	CM	Various	During conflicts, Bundesbank yields to the government.
Soh (1986)	Direct	PBC	Various	Money growth and inflation higher in election years.
Alesina, Roubini (1990, 1992)	Direct	PBC, PT	Inflation	Post-electoral jump in inflation. Inflation higher under leftist governments.
Alesina et al. (1992)	Direct	PBC, PT	M1	Political business cycle in M1, rightist governmnets have higher M1 growth.
Lang, Welzel (1992)	Direct	PBC, RPT	M1, M3, CBM	No evidence for political business cycle, rational partisan behaviour in M3, but not in M1 or Central Bank Money.
Vaubel (1997)	Direct	PT, RPT, PPT	M1	No evidence for partisan theory or rational partisan theory. Evidence for party preference theory.
Berger, Woitek (1997)	Direct	PPT	M1, Discount rate	Rejection of party preference theory and its basic assumptions.
Johnson, Siklos (1994)	Direct	PBC, PT	Interest rate	Political business cycle after Bretton Woods. Partisan theory significant, but wrong sign.
Berger (1997)	Direct	PBC, PPT	Discount rate	Rejection of of political business cycle and party preference theory.
Berger, Woitek (1997)	Direct	RPBC, RPT	VAR	No support for political business cycle. Weak evidence for rational political business cycle.
Lohmann (1998)	Direct	PBC, PT, PPT, CM	CBM	Bundesbank only partially independent. Influence of the Bundesrat significant.
Demopoulos et al. (1987)	Indirect		Monetary base	Accommodation of budget deficits.
Giannaros, Kolluri (1985)	Indirect		M1	No significant impact.
Burdekin (1987)	Indirect		Monetary base	Weak evidence for accommodation.
Missong, Herault (1990)	Indirect		Interest rate	If budget deficit rises, interest rate drops.
Lang, Welzel (1992)	Indirect		M1, M3, CBM	Significant impact of budget deficit.

Source: Maier (2002), pp. 27-29

From his comparative analysis, Maier concludes that there is no clear evidence for political influence on the Bundesbank. Studies testing by single monetary instruments tend to reject any influence on the Bundesbank's monetary decisions from elections or partisan behaviour by policy makers but are found to be technically inappropriate[355]. The models applied in studies concerned with monetary aggregates are judged more useful, but there, too, the evidence is mixed. Studies including more countries than Germany do not yield solid evidence of government influence on monetary

[355] Maier (2002), pp. 29-31.

decisions[356]. In contrast, studies dealing exclusively with the Bundesbank seem to suggest the existence of political pressures and a certain responsiveness on the part of the Bundesbank. Maier, however, points out that a number of the relevant studies actually exhibit substantial deficiencies, suggesting that the results – significant pressure on and responsiveness of the Bundesbank – are not sufficiently reliable. Conflict models are found to be more reliable and actually produce some evidence that – under pressure – the Bundesbank might have yielded to the government. Finally, the hypothesis that government budget deficits are accommodated by the Bundesbank is not well supported by the data[357].

Given the heterogeneity of the empirical evidence in literature and the fact that certain potential sources of political influence had not been covered, Maier supplemented the body of literature by testing additional monetary variables – short-term interest rates and a monetary policy index – and modelled additional sources of controversy over monetary policy by establishing a conflict indicator.

As to the former, no significant evidence can be found to suggest that political business cycles impact on short-term interest rates[358]. Maier further constructs a monetary policy index to include all the possible means a central bank can employ to influence the markets. These include public statements, i.e. rhetoric, which in daily practice seem to be an important instrument by which central banks seek to influence financial market participants' actions. Most remarkably, the tests produce a stable, but twofold, picture. For one thing, analysis of official interest rates as a proxy for actual monetary policy confirms earlier results signalling no significant electoral pressure on the Bundesbank. At the same time, however, analysis of a specifically defined Bundesbank index measuring monetary policy as announced – in contrast to actually implemented – by the Bundesbank yields a robust correlation with electoral pressures. This has been interpreted by Maier as suggesting that the Bundesbank actually responds to electoral pressures at a declaratory level in order to calm down nervous politicians, while in fact leaving its monetary policy and its operations unchanged so as to prevent economic damage[359].

As to the second set of analyses, Maier extends the potential sources of political conflict with the central bank. In all preceding analyses, political pressure was assumed to emanate exclusively from government. Maier employs an indicator of

---

[356] Maier (2002), p. 30. Those studies that do detect political influence are criticised in most cases for not taking institutional and other policy features properly into account.

[357] Maier (2002), p. 31.

[358] Maier (2002), pp. 33-46.

[359] Maier (2002), pp. 47-73.

political pressure stemming from all potential sources, including interest groups[360]. The results of this analysis again confirm that pressure from politicians did not affect German monetary policy[361]. Similarly, pressure from trade and industry interest associations and from trade unions is found to have no impact on Bundesbank policy. However, Maier finds robust evidence that opinions from the financial sector do have a significant impact on monetary decisions[362]. Finally, Maier observes that public opinion on monetary policy has been very mixed, with pressure from one quarter triggering support for the Bundesbank from another. It is suggested that such support partly offsets the pressures brought to bear on the bank[363].

For the analysis of interest-group activity in the field of monetary policy, the latter results raise important issues. They suggest that the Bundesbank responds to pressures from the financial sector, but not to lobbying by the government or the rest of the private sector, notably trade, industry or trade unions, possibly reflecting financial market participants' greater competence of in monetary matters.

This interpretation, however, is far from unproblematic. Given its superior command of information and expertise on monetary policy – going well beyond that existing in the financial services industry – the Bundesbank does not necessarily have a strong incentive to take recourse to advice from the financial sector. This lack of incentive may be reinforced by the fact that the financial services industry itself may be pursuing biased interests, considering that financial market participants benefit most from constantly changing market conditions and less so from a stabilisation of monetary variables. The latter is an important part of the Bundesbank's mandate.

Maier explains the statistical significance of the financial market influence thus:

> "[C]entral bankers have incentives to listen to the financial sector, be it because their utility increases from higher 'popularity' among colleagues, or be it to build up reputation for the central bank and thus ensure independence in the long run."[364]

The first part of this argument assumes that popularity among colleagues in the financial services industry represents a dominant, if not the dominant, objective pursued by Bundesbank policy makers and that this popularity can actually be

---

[360] The indicator was originally designed by Havrilesky and employed to analyse the pressure on the US Federal Reserve Board, suggesting that its policies were, in fact, responsive to pressures expressed through newspaper articles and reports. Havrilesky developed and subsequently extended this approach (see Havrilesky (1988), (1990), (1993), (1994)).

[361] Maier (2002), p. 90.

[362] Maier (2002), pp. 75-96.

[363] Maier (2002), pp. 97-111.

[364] Maier (2002), p. 95.

increased by listening to their recommendations. The second part of the argument assumes that a good central bank reputation can be earned by following recommendations from financial market participants and that such behaviour – if successful – is not observed by the public. Otherwise, both reputation and independence would no longer be credible. None of these assumptions are plausible, as Maier indirectly concedes by subsequently explaining the statistical significance of public support for the Bundesbank:

> "[A] high degree of public support – at least partly – offsets pressures from interest groups. [...] The policy implications of these findings are clear: Public support helps the central bank to concentrate on economic needs and makes it easier to completely ignore political pressure."[365]

In the light of the basic incentives facing the central bank and the financial sector, a systematic responsiveness on the part of the Bundesbank to recommendations from the financial sector seems rather unlikely. An alternative interpretation of the econometric findings would be that the financial sector – given its access to relevant information and its expertise in monetary matters – actually comes to conclusions which are very similar to those at which a central bank arrives. Forecasts and policy recommendations by the financial industry are therefore likely to coincide with those of the central bank. Further econometric analysis of such a potential coincidence may be a promising step[366].

Overall, declaratory and econometric evidence suggests that the legal right and obligation to define and conduct monetary policy independently of outside political pressures is matched in practice by behaviour on the part of decision makers largely consistent with the statutory framework. The Bundesbank and its officials declare their commitment to act independently and defend the bank's independence against potential intrusions or violations. Econometric analysis additionally suggests that there is no unambiguous evidence of any systematic Bundesbank responsiveness to outside pressure. These findings coincide with anecdotal evidence on the *esprit de corps* said to shape the behaviour of incoming decision makers. It has been observed with many central banks, especially independent institutions, that individuals appointed to serve on their decision-making bodies generally adapt to the duties and habits of that institution, irrespective for the most part of the economic or political affiliation that may have promoted their appointment[367]. This process, often referred to as the Becket

---

[365] Maier (2002), pp. 108-109.

[366] Maier (2002) in fact started working in this direction by adding some extra economic state variables – industrial production and the exchange rate – to check whether bank signalling simply picks up the effects of omitted variables, concluding that this was not the case (pp. 93-94).

[367] Marshall (1999), pp. 283-285, Bofinger (2003), p. 4.

effect[368], has been observed in the Bundesbank, where it soon induces decision makers from very different political and regional backgrounds to feel a responsibility for the institution and the currency[369].

The second major behavioural pattern, next to practical adherence to the primacy of political independence, has been the Bundesbank's commitment to its functional objective – maintaining price stability – and the way in which this has been achieved. As observed earlier, the Bundesbank's legal framework provides for a broad definition of its objective, combined with considerable discretion in its interpretation and pursuit. With respect to behavioural patterns, the question arises as to whether and to what extent the Bundesbank has actually exhausted the resultant room for manoeuvre in pursuing its monetary policy and in its position within the ESCB. Relevant behavioural patterns may, over time, influence interest groups in their political activities insofar as discretionary central bank behaviour may be a pre-condition for the success of their activities in the event that they do not agree with a given monetary stance and seek to have it changed. Conversely, if the central bank establishes additional rules for monetary decisions and commits itself to stick to them, then the bank's scope for discretionary decisions diminishes – and so do interest groups' chances of influencing these decisions one way or another. At the same time, interest groups may have greater incentives to criticise such rules should they run significantly counter to the groups' interests.

As a matter of fact, monetary theory and practice suggest that for the pursuit of broadly defined monetary objectives it is useful, if not indeed necessary, to define additional rules on which monetary decisions can be based. Broad monetary objectives, such as the pursuit of price stability in the case of the Bundesbank, can rarely be influenced directly by the central bank due to the complexity of the monetary transmission process and the persistence of time lags between a policy measure and its effect on the final target, as already observed in the theoretical analysis above. As a result, central banks often define targets, intermediary targets as well as operating targets, working towards steering monetary developments as precisely as possible. Besides solving the operational difficulties associated with pursuing monetary objectives, a commitment to such intermediary steps can help increase the credibility

---

368 The term refers to Thomas Becket, Chancellor of King Henry II, who, after he was made Archbishop of Canterbury, opposed the king and became a true adherent of the Church. The effect refers to the presence of an independent dynamic inside central banks that influences outsiders coming into the bank to conform to the bank's norms, beliefs and rituals even if the outsider was not previously part of them (Marshall (1999), p. 284).

369 Bofinger (2003), p. 4. For an anecdotal overview of the effect on different Central Bank Council members see Marsh (1992), pp. 60-64. Also Marshall (1999), pp. 283-288. Theoretical evidence suggests that the effect can be strengthened by increasing the length of office of central bank policy board members relative to the length of the electoral interval (Eijffinger (1997), p. 3).

of the bank and its policies by making its activities more comprehensible and transparent[370].

The monetary policy of the Bundesbank between 1974 and 1998 was characterised by self-imposed rules, which complemented its legal framework, as well as a recognisable determination to retain the option of discretionary monetary measures. As a result, its monetary strategy has been interpreted as a policy of stabilisation with discretionary elements[371]. It is characterised by

- a clear commitment to the primary objective of maintaining the stability of the currency,
- regular announcements of its annual policy targets, including a detailed explanation of past performance as well as of the considerations behind forthcoming targets,
- specification of the conditions under which it was willing to deviate from the pre-announced target, as well as
- stability-orientation in the application of instruments, avoidance of abrupt changes in its policy and a general orientation along the medium-term perspective[372].

Ever since it regained control over the domestic money supply following the abolition of the fixed-exchange rate regime under the Bretton Woods system in 1973, the Bundesbank has made self-binding commitments with respect to its objective and policy targets. It adopted a strategy of money-supply targeting as from December 1974, announcing target values or ranges for the rate of growth in money supply for specified periods of time. As a result, each monetary decision has, in principle, been bound by the rules of this strategy and the need to attain the pre-defined policy targets.

More specifically, the Bundesbank based its strategy on the theoretical and empirical relationship between the price level and the supply of money in circulation, the latter of which a central bank can influence with some accuracy. Given that, in the medium-term, an increase in inflation has been found to be impossible without undue growth in the money stock, the bank has adopted money supply as its monetary target[373]. The

---

[370] Bofinger et al. (1996), pp. 266-269.

[371] Baltensperger (1998), pp. 536-538, and Deutsche Bundesbank (1995), p. 80.

[372] Baltensperger (1998), p. 536.

[373] Between 1974 and 1987, the measure of the money stock targeted by the Bundesbank was Central Bank Money. From 1988 until 1998, the monetary variable chosen was M3 (Deutsche Bundesbank (1995), p. 79). The Central Bank Money stock comprises currency in circulation in the hands of non-banks and the required minimum reserves – other than minimum reserve-carrying bank debt securities – calculated at constant reserve ratios as at January 1974. The money stock components included in Central Bank Money coincide with those included in M3, except for the difference between the two aggregates with respect to the comparatively illiquid block of savings deposits

target value for growth of the money stock is calculated using a basic formula, according to which growth in the money stock[374] equals the sum of the real potential growth rate[375], a medium-term price assumption[376], and the longer-term change in the velocity of circulation of money[377]. Importantly, the Bundesbank's medium-term price assumption included in the equation represents a maximum value for the rate of inflation the Bundesbank is willing to tolerate in the medium term. Implicitly, calculation of the money-supply target therefore also gives an indication as to which maximum rate of inflation the Bundesbank deems consistent with what the Bundesbank Act refers to as safeguarding the currency.

At the behavioural level, the Bundesbank therefore restricted its discretion with a monetary strategy including a set of transparent, publicly available rules. As table 4 shows, these rules had to be considered as comparatively strict. The table depicts an international comparison of monetary targets valid in 1998, including countries that adopted a direct inflation target. Column six contains the rates of underlying normative inflation assumed by central banks with a money supply target, including the Bundesbank. Column five depicts the equivalent inflation targets of central banks pursuing direct inflation targeting. Among the European central banks pursuing monetary targets, the Bundesbank had therefore adopted the most ambitious target.

Besides the practice of monetary targeting and its benefits, as a further rule committing the bank to systematic exercise of the scope granted it by law, the Bundesbank has gained additional credibility by the fact that it has managed to maintain this strategy without interruption since the end of 1974, giving it the longest experience in pursuing monetary targets by international standards, and by the fact that it has made particular efforts throughout to explain its targeting and its policy decisions to the public in a transparent manner[378]. Furthermore, the Bundesbank's policy has set itself apart from

---

with a period of notice between three months and four years and savings bonds with maturities of less than four years. In contrast to Central Bank Money, these are not included in M3 (Deutsche Bundesbank (1995), p. 81). For an extensive rationalisation of the changeover from Central Bank Money to M3 see Deutsche Bundesbank (1995), pp. 81-83. For a discussion of the implications of this step see Baltensperger (1998), pp. 510-511.

374 Defined as the growth in the money stock consistent with the economy's real potential growth rate (Deutsche Bundesbank (1995), p. 81).

375 Expansion of the money stock at the potential growth rate is perceived by the Bundesbank as securing price stability and providing adequate financial scope for the rise in spending needed to absorb available supply (Deutsche Bundesbank (1995), p. 80).

376 The medium-term price assumption represents the maximum inflation rate tolerated by the Bundesbank in the medium term (Deutsche Bundesbank (1995), p. 80).

377 Deutsche Bundesbank (1995), p. 83.

378 Bofinger et al. (1996), pp. 248-249.

that of other central banks not only in terms of its stringency, but also inasmuch as it has been far more geared towards stability, continuity, and consistency than others[379].

Monetary targets in international comparison, 1998

Table 4

Country	Type of target	Target variable	Monetary target (%)	Inflation target (%)	Underlying normative inflation (%)	Intermediate targets
DE	Money supply	M3	3 – 6	...	1.5 – 2	...
ES	Inflation	Genral index of consumer prices	...	2	...	Exchange rate, money stock
FR	Money supply	M3	5	...	2	Exchange rate, money stock, domestic indebtedness
GR	Money supply	M3	6 – 9	...	2,5	Exchange rate, money stock, domestic credit
IT	Money supply	M2	5	...	2	Exchange rate, additional indicators
SE	Inflation	General index of consumer prices	...	2, +/-1	...	...
SF	Inflation	Index of consumer prices	...	2	...	Exchange rate
UK	Inflation	Retail price index	...	2.5	...	Money stock

Source: Deutsche Bundesbank (1998), pp. 38 and 43

As regards the details and performance in pursuing its money-supply target, table 5 below provides an overview of the Bundesbank's record. The table illustrates three important aspects of implementation of the bank's strategy, especially with respect to its attempts at retaining discretion in decision making despite the tight corset of policy rules. First, after four initial years of targeting spot values for Central Bank Money, which the bank consistently failed to meet, it announced target ranges, or corridors designed to give it greater scope in accommodating monetary developments not foreseeable at the time the target was defined[380]. In other words, the Bundesbank restored some of the discretion it had stripped itself of by committing itself to a rule that proved impossible to meet[381]. Second, the fifth column shows that in the early years of targeting corridors the bank chose to narrow down its target in the course of the reporting period, a practice abolished in 1984 so as to give itself the full corridor defined at the beginning of the reporting period as a target range. Third, and most importantly, column eight shows that the bank failed to meet its targets between 1975 and 1998 in eleven out of twenty-four reporting periods, i.e. almost half the time.

379 Baltensperger (1998), p. 537.

380 Baltensperger (1998), p. 488.

381 On the arguments surrounding the Bundesbank's changeover from spot targets to corridors as well as the advantages and disadvantages of this step, see Baltensperger (1998), pp. 488-489.

Bundesbank monetary targets and their implementation

Table 5

		Target growth of the money stock			Actual growth of the money stock		Target achieved
Year	Target	course of year (%)	annual average (%)	more precise definition during the year	course of year (%)	annual average (%)	
1975	CBM	8	...	...	10	...	no
1976	CBM	...	8	...	...	9	no
1977	CBM	...	8	...	...	9	no
1978	CBM	...	8	...	...	11	no
1979	CBM	6 – 9	...	Lower limit	6	...	yes
1980	CBM	5 – 8	...	Lower limit	5	...	yes
1981	CBM	4 – 7	...	Lower half	4	...	yes
1982	CBM	4 – 7	...	Upper half	6	...	yes
1983	CBM	4 – 7	...	Upper half	7	...	yes
1984	CBM	4 – 6	...	...	5	...	yes
1985	CBM	3 – 5	...	...	5	...	yes
1986	CBM	3.5 – 5.5	...	...	8	...	no
1987	CBM	3 – 6	...	...	8	...	no
1988	M3	3 – 6	...	...	7	...	no
1989	M3	about 5	...	...	5	...	yes
1990	M3	4 – 6	...	...	6	...	yes
1991	M3	3 – 5	...	...	5	...	yes
1992	M3	3.5 – 5.5	...	...	9	...	no
1993	M3	4.5 – 6.5	...	...	7	...	no
1994	M3	4 – 6	...	...	6	...	yes
1995	M3	4 – 6	...	...	2	...	no
1996	M3	4 – 7	...	...	8	...	no
1997	M3	3.5 – 6.5	...	...	4	...	yes
1998	M3	5	...	...	5	...	yes

Data sources: Deutsche Bundesbank (1995), p. 79, Bofinger (1996), p. 271, Maier, de Haan (2000), p. 16

Given that the Bundesbank failed to meet its targets in nearly half of the reporting periods, resulting in a positive money supply bias of 1.17 percentage points between 1975 and 1995[382], its targeting policy has been subject to considerable debate. In the course of this it has emerged that the Bundesbank did not strictly adhere to formal targets and that its monetary strategy contained further decision making criteria, i.e. that a meta-rule[383] existed which was not part of the formal targeting process. As the Bundesbank itself conceded,

> "[i]n the short run, the Bundesbank has never regarded the annual targets as the sole guideline for its liquidity and interest rate policy actions, but has also taken domestic and external underlying conditions into account. This

[382] Bofinger et al. (1996), p. 270.

[383] For an analysis of the factors behind this meta-rule see Bofinger et al. (1996), pp. 270-272.

> does not mean, however, that, by doing so, it has also relinquished its medium-term objectives for appropriate monetary growth."[384]

Empirical evidence suggests that this meta-rule encompassed at least two important elements, namely the current rate of inflation and the external value of the Deutsche Mark vis-à-vis the currencies of Germany's most important trading partners. Thus, the overall Bundesbank strategy contained certain elements of direct inflation targeting as well as exchange rate targeting which the central bank deemed conducive to meeting its final objective, i.e. stabilisation of the domestic price level[385]. The bank's liberal handling of its own policy rules, however, did not result in a loss of confidence on the part of the wider public in its commitment and ability to fulfil its duties. The Bundesbank's performance was assessed – both by itself and the public – with reference to its mission to secure price stability, which was achieved satisfactorily by both inter-temporal and international standards. In contrast to the money-supply bias of 1.17% between 1975 and 1995, the bank's inflationary bias, measured against its own benchmark target of underlying normative inflation, was only 0.4% in the same period[386].

Overall, therefore, the Bundesbank's strategy in principle narrowed its room for discretionary monetary decisions by means of self-imposed rules and a clear commitment to meeting its comparatively strict monetary target. In practice, however, the Bundesbank did not submit to these rules in an orthodox manner, taking resort instead to discretionary measures as it deemed useful with respect to keeping inflation close to this implicit target.

II.1.2 Issue context: monetary policy in Germany

According to the analysis framework outlined in the preceding chapters, the salience of a policy issue and the sponsoring it receives from relevant interest groups in society are important determinants of the extent to which formal interest groups and associations are likely to become active and involved with that issue. It has been argued that monetary policy features a number of properties that make it a specific policy issue for interest groups to address. Its diffuse impact and the complexity with which it feeds into the economy make it difficult to form precise and consistent preferences – for individuals, and all the more so across entire groups and sectors in the economy. From a theoretical perspective, interest groups' commitment to the issue of monetary policy has consequently been hypothesised as low, especially when one

---

[384] Deutsche Bundesbank (1995), p. 86.

[385] Bofinger et al. (1996), pp. 271-277.

[386] Bofinger et al. (1996), p. 277.

considers the potentially wide variety of other important economic policy issues with a more immediate and focused impact on private-sector actors.

Given these broad hypotheses, it is the purpose of the following sections to analyse monetary policies in Germany, assessing the importance of the theoretically relevant determinants in this concrete case and highlighting the policy issues raised in the empirical analysis below. They show that interest-group activity on monetary policy in Germany is shaped by four broad stylised trends:

- First, Germany as a whole is characterised by strong anti-inflationary sentiment, which has its origins in negative historical experience.
- Second, monetary policy in the post-war era has been successful and has been perceived as such by the wider public.
- Third, enterprises in trade and industry have little immediate exposure and sensitivity to monetary and exchange rate developments.
- Finally, monetary developments – as a policy issue – are clearly dominated by a wide variety of other economic policy issues, which have been subject to considerable public controversy.

It will be argued that, as a result, major economic and societal interest groups strongly support the basic objectives formerly pursued by the Deutsche Bundesbank, and today by the ECB, as well as the broad policy framework in which monetary policymaking has been embedded. Neither the conduct of monetary policy nor monetary developments are generally regarded as highly salient or critical issues, nor have they found significant sponsorship among German interest groups in trade and industry in the past decades. The historical record suggests that, for most of the past decades, monetary policy has largely been a non-issue on the economic policy agenda.

II.1.2.1 Anti-inflationary sentiment

The most important single determinant of interest-group activity, as argued in chapter I, is the impact of a policy issue on the private sector, how policy makers deal with the issue and whether the private sector agrees with this response. The considerations in chapter II show that in this respect monetary policy represents an intricate field of policymaking which is flanked by a number of economic variables, most importantly inflation, interest rates, and exchange rates. Given the close interdependence of these variables and the limited instruments monetary policy makers have at their disposal to influence them, they can ultimately pursue only one objective at a time, while other aims can at best be taken into consideration at the margin. In practice, contemporary monetary systems resolve this problem by defining rules – establishing central banks equipped with policy objectives – under which the daily business of monetary decision making is conducted on a more or less discretionary basis. As described in the preceding section on the institutional context, the monetary framework in Germany follows this logic with the establishment of the Bundesbank as an independent monetary authority bound by the statutory objective of maintaining stable prices and by further, self-imposed targets limiting the scope for discretionary policy decisions. With respect to the issue context, the question arises to what extent the private sector at large, and enterprises and interest groups in trade and industry in particular, have an incentive to accept, share, or even support the overall policy framework and objectives of the Bundesbank.

One important factor shaping the public perception of monetary policy in Germany has been the country's specific experience with inflation in the past. Since the early twentieth century, the country experienced two severe monetary crises, each leading to a *de facto* collapse of the monetary system, substantial erosion of wealth and major redistributive effects on the economy.

The first of these two currency crises was the period of hyperinflation between August 1922 and November 1923. Starting with a monthly rate of inflation of 64.6% in August 1922, the inflationary process reached a peak in October 1923 with monthly inflation of 32,400%[387]. At the end of November 1923, the value of the Mark to the USD had fallen to one 10^{12}th of its pre-World War I level[388]. The fourteen-month period of inflation severely eroded incomes and wealth in the economy, depriving holders of money and financial assets as well as creditors of the bulk of their wealth. Owners of real assets and debtors, on the other hand, witnessed less dramatic losses or even gained from depreciation of the currency[389]. Further erosion of incomes and wealth was eventually brought to a halt with sweeping monetary reform, in the course of which two additional currencies were introduced and two additional central banks established. In addition to the Reichsbank, which continued to exist and was mandated to stabilise the Mark and later the Reichsmark as the country's legal tender, the Rentenbank and the Golddiskontbank were established. The former was restricted to

---

[387] Bofinger et al. (1996), p. 113. Bofinger provides a detailed analysis of the effects of inflation and hyperinflation on the balance sheet of central banks, illustrated by the example of German hyperinflation in 1922 and 1923 (pp. 113-118).

[388] James (1998), p. 46. An historical account is also provided by Nölling (1993), pp. 21-24.

[389] The redistributive effects of Germany's hyperinflation are discussed by Kindleberger (1993) in a chapter on the social aspects of German inflation (pp. 312-314). Notably and in contrast to intuitive perceptions of the redistributive effects of inflation, Kindleberger observes that in a number of instances the overall distribution of income and wealth was narrowed in Germany as a result of the inflationary period. Thus, the ratio of skilled wages to those of common labour narrowed from 145% in 1913 to 106% in 1923. Similarly, wages of high government officials fell by more than 60% in real terms whereas junior officials lost only about 30%. Nevertheless, midsized businesses and midsized farmers were found to have gained on balance. Incomes from interest and rent fell from roughly 15% of national income in 1913 to less than 3% in 1925 (p. 313).

lending to the public and corporate sectors against the issue of non-legal-tender bank notes, while the latter provided enterprises with hard-currency credit against the issue of gold-based bonds[390].

The second currency crisis was the result of suppressed inflation during World War II and the immediate post-war period[391]. The Nazi war economy massively expanded money supply, with the currency in circulation rising from Reichsmark 5 bn in 1935 to Reichsmark 50 bn in 1945[392]. Bank deposits increased from Reichsmark 30 bn to Reichsmark 150 bn, and government debt – even without allowance for war claims of Reichsmark 350 bn – soared from Reichsmark 15 bn to Reichsmark 400 bn. During the same period, Germany's national real wealth decreased by one-third[393]. The discrepancy between money supply and assets resulted in a substantial monetary overhang, with the supply of money exceeding the amount of goods and services produced in the economy by a factor of six[394]. Open inflation was suppressed[395], however, by an extensive system of price and wage controls and by effectively abolishing the price mechanism in many areas through voucher transactions[396]. This, in turn, led to the development of widespread barter trade and increasing Reichsmark-based black-market activity[397], which made up 10% of overall transactions but 80% of monetary turnover[398]. The bizarre mix of white, grey and black economic activity continued until 1948 and disappeared overnight with the introduction of the Deutsche Mark on June 20, 1948[399]. Again, the inflationary process itself, and the radical monetary reform that stopped it, had immense repercussions on incomes and welfare in society[400].

---

390 Details on the role and activities of the Rentenbank and the Golddiskontbank are provided by Kindleberger (1993), pp. 316-317, and James (1998), pp. 52-63.

391 The monetary and economic development during this second monetary crisis has been documented e.g. by Buchheim (1998), Kindleberger (1993), pp. 393-412, Weimer (1998), pp. 31-55, and Nölling (1993), pp. 25-43.

392 Smith (1994), p. 6, and Weimer (1998), p. 32.

393 Smith (1994), p. 6. See also Kindleberger (1993), pp. 393-394.

394 Nölling (1993), p. 28.

395 Kindleberger (1993), points out that Germany's monetary crisis in the war and post-war years was the most far-reaching instance of suppressed inflation in a disequilibrium system that Europe had ever experienced (p. 394).

396 Weimer (1998), p. 31.

397 Smith (1994), p. 6.

398 Kindleberger (1993), p. 403.

399 On the modalities of the currency reform see Buchheim (1998), pp. 117-136, and Kindleberger (1993), pp. 404-407.

400 For a detailed description as well as a review of the reactions of the German public to the currency reform see Weimer (1998), pp. 48-49.

Despite significant dissimilarities between the two currency crises in historical, economic, political and technical terms[401], their causes and consequences have clearly shaped thinking on monetary issues in large sections of society, including policy makers and entrepreneurs.

- First, the two monetary crises painfully demonstrated the consequences of inflationary policies and their effects on people's welfare. Added to this in the case of hyperinflation in the 1920s were the repercussions on the stability of the social and political system as a whole.
- Second, with regard to the causes of inflationary development it became evident that the lack of a clear and binding mandate and commitment to price stability on the part of monetary policy makers had vitally contributed to monetary derailment. The Reichsbank wilfully abetted spiralling inflation in both periods, even in instances when it was not coerced by the government[402].
- Third, it was evident after the two crises that subservience of the central bank to the government – notably with respect to government demands that it finance budget deficits by printing money – had been major to inflationary tendencies. Inflationary financing of war-, reconstruction- and reparation-related expenses had been an easy way for governments to handle the resulting burdens in the short run. In the long range, though, this came at the expense of the economy as a whole[403].

As a result, by the end of World War II a strong anti-inflationary sentiment, supportive of monetary policy strictly committed to securing stable prices and conducted by an independent central bank, had become firmly entrenched in the perception of the wider German public as a vital precondition for economic stability and social peace[404]. This sentiment has been summarised by Nölling:

---

[401] For a comparison of the two crises with special respect to these differences see Kindleberger (1993), pp. 407-408.

[402] James (1998) identifies five causes of hyperinflation in the twenties. First, in order to finance World War I, the German government suspended important anti-inflationary safeguards in the Reichsbank's legal basis, such as the obligatory backing of German bank notes by gold and restrictions on discounting treasury bills. Second, with increasing war-related demand for finance the government forced the Reichsbank to discount war loans from 1916 onwards. Third, inflationary budget financing continued in the immediate post-World War I period, during which reconstruction and reparation obligations aggravated the budgetary situation. Fourth, the Reichsbank itself cooperated with the government on inflationary financing by discounting an increasing amount of short-term government debt, thereby drastically increasing the supply of money in the economy. Finally, the Reichsbank also discounted private bills, and did so at negative real interest rates. See James (1998), pp. 47-50, and also Kindleberger (1993), pp. 286-293.

[403] See footnote 402 above.

[404] Marsh (1992), pp. 28-32.

> "Regarding the political consequences, especially after the Second World War, the call to protect and safeguard the value of the currency, of incomes and of savings ranks – in my assessment – second among the most eminent duties of the state. Because next to the demand for "No more war!", the call from politicians for "No more inflation!" has assumed great importance. This is extremely forceful and should not be underestimated.
>
> This assessment is widespread, and the consensus in the population, among politicians of all parties [...], and among the leaders of societal groups of all kinds – such as trade unions, entrepreneurs, employers, interest associations as well as the churches – is all-embracing and irrefutable."[405]

Similarly, Marsh notes that

> "Germans are worldwide leaders in announcing and practicing the doctrine of the hard currency. Pursued with zeal and promoted with conviction, this doctrine has developed many meanings: It is the symbol of the country's resurrection after the war and a guarantor of orderly conditions. It provides security at home and inspires respect abroad. Without monetary stability, wealth can neither be generated nor maintained."[406]

This general attitude has, in turn, led to a widespread appreciation of the set-up of the monetary system, i.e. of the Deutsche Bundesbank as an independent institution bound by the objective of securing stable prices[407].

II.1.2.2 Performance of the monetary system

Not only the monetary system as such – its rules, institutions and decision-making procedures – has met with widespread approval, but also the monetary achievements wrought by these tools. From a long-term view and measured against the objective of safeguarding the stability of the currency, the Bundesbank posted a positive track record in the first decades of its existence, as illustrated in chart 15 by international comparison of the purchasing powers of domestic currencies in 1992 compared with their 1948 level. More important for the present purpose than this preliminary long-term view, however, is the detailed development of the major monetary variables in the medium-term past, and the extent to which these variables reached levels that may have been relevant to the performance of enterprises in trade and industry. This section therefore reviews the most important monetary developments in the past three decades and evaluates them with respect to their economic impact. Inflation, interest rate and exchange rate developments will be considered in turn, arguing that monetary policy

---

[405] Nölling (1993), p. 37.

[406] Marsh (1992), p. 39.

[407] Bickerich (1998), p. 159.

over the past decades has presented no serious and urgent challenges to the German economy, to the effect that – viewed in isolation – it was not a serious policy issue for interest groups in trade and industry.

Bundesbank performance on safeguarding stability of prices

Chart 15

– Purchasing powers of domestic currencies in 1992 in % of 1948 levels

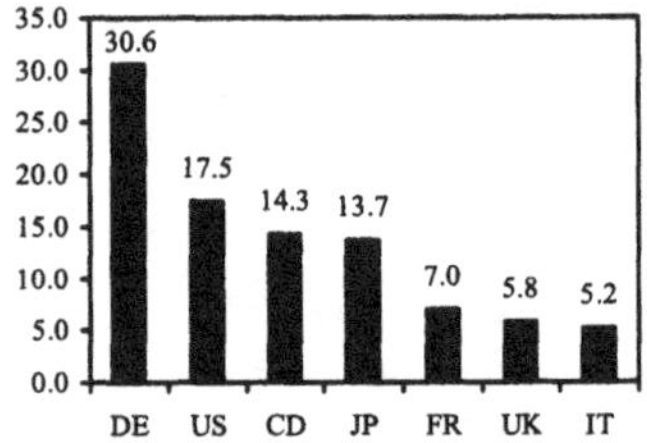

Source: Nölling (1993), p. 41

Chart 16

– Consumer price index, average annual change in % per annum

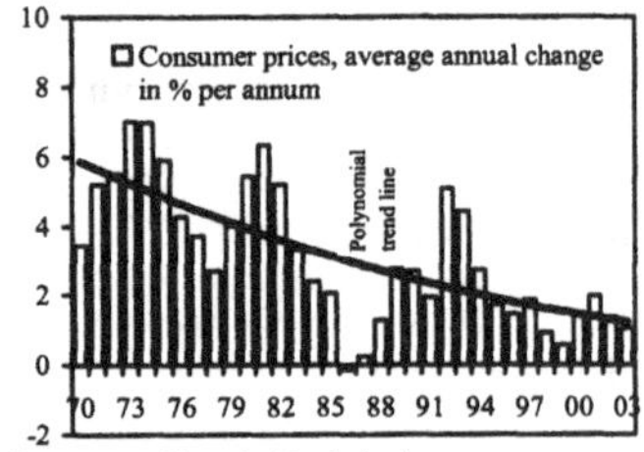

Data source: Deutsche Bundesbank

Given that the overriding monetary objective of providing a stable price level is shared by the majority of German society, the inflationary record of the Bundesbank, and now the ECB, is the single most important criterion by which to judge the performance of monetary policy and its potential impact on the economy. The international comparison presented in chart 15 above already points to good long-term performance in this regard, as the purchasing powers reflect a comparatively low inflationary trend in the years between 1948 and 1992. In more detail, this is confirmed by the development of inflation in the past three decades, as depicted in chart 16. Since 1970 the annual average rate of inflation in Germany has never exceeded 7%. Over the entire period, inflation was as low as 3.2% on average. Most importantly, considering the medium to long-term outlook and formulation of the Bundesbank's monetary strategy, inflation has followed a secular downward trend bringing price changes on average within the range of the bank's latest assumption of underlying normative inflation between 1.5% and 2% and the ECB's recent definition of price stability, i.e. annual price changes of below 2%.

Nonetheless, the development also shows that inflation at times considerably exceeded – and by the same token raised – the long-term average. Thus, inflation climbed to 7% in 1973 and 1974, to 6.3% in 1981 and to 5.1% in 1992. Each of these periods, however, highlights the economic pressures the Bundesbank faced and the inflationary effects it had to counter with its monetary policy. In the early seventies, inflationary pressure grew, first, in response to wage pressures and excess demand in the economy[408]. As from autumn 1973, the first oil crisis substantially aggravated price

[408] Von Hagen (1998), pp. 440-459.

pressures, given Germany's strong dependence on crude-oil imports, and, following a tripling of oil prices in the course of 1973[409], led to a sustained uptrend in domestic price levels[410]. Rising international oil prices, triggering a surge in import prices, were also the reason for the second period of above-average inflation in the late 1970s and early 1980s[411]. The third phase of inflationary pressure in the early 1990s stemmed mainly from German reunification and its economic consequences. Given the low levels of productivity in the new Länder, combined with high wage settlements and substantial fiscal redistribution, domestic wage and price pressure built up, countered by only moderately decreasing import prices[412].

In all three periods monetary policy was not the primary cause of inflationary trends. On the contrary, policymaking worked effectively to cushion and counter exogenous inflationary shocks. This is most clearly evident in the case of the two oil crises, when the Bundesbank managed to contain the inflationary effects of external price pressure such that the country's rate of inflation remained clearly below the levels observed in most other industrialised economies, despite the German economy's comparatively high exposure to international oil markets[413]. In the case of the domestically rooted inflationary phase in the early 1990s, the Bundesbank reined in the effects of continued wage push, especially in the new Länder, bringing about a sustained reduction in inflation. Notwithstanding external shocks, the Bundesbank largely succeeded in realising its objective to establish a medium and long-term trend of low and falling rates of inflation. This trend has continued since the transfer of monetary decision-making powers to the ECB.

This has been achieved by pursuing pre-defined monetary targets. As pointed out in the institutional context, the Bundesbank pursued money supply targets as from 1974, a policy that has essentially been continued by the ECB. Chart 17 below documents the difficulties in meeting these self-imposed targets. Depicting the year-on-year changes in money supply – Central Bank Money and, as from 1988, M3 – as well as inflation – the German consumer price index – on a monthly basis, the lagged correlation between the two variables on which the adoption of money-supply targets is founded becomes evident. The targeted measures of money supply have moved around the target values or outside the corridors announced by the monetary

---

409 Smith (1993), pp. 160-161.

410 Von Hagen (1998), p. 458.

411 Baltensperger (1998), pp. 477-190.

412 Baltensperger (1998), pp. 511-529.

413 Von Hagen (1998), p. 458, and Baltensperger (1998), p. 478.

authorities for considerable periods[414], leading the inflationary surges and contractions over time. From the perspective of the private sector, however, the Bundesbank's performance on meeting the self-imposed monetary targets has been of limited relevance. For one thing, as with the inflation rate itself, the growth in money supply has always remained near the target values despite the deviations observed, never actually reaching levels causing serious concern among policy makers and analysts. Second, the public has been primarily concerned with inflation as such, not so much with the underlying technicalities. As a result, deviations of money supply variables from their targets have aroused only limited public attention or criticism.

Bundesbank and ECB monetary targets

Chart 17

– Money supply, its target values, and inflation, in % per annum

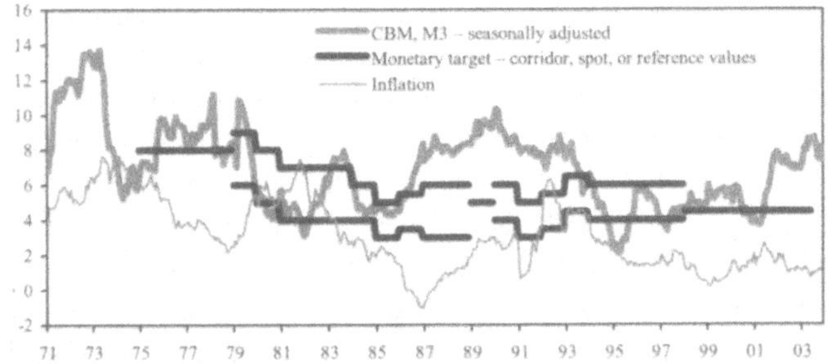

Data source: Deutsche Bundesbank

The achievement of a stable price level and an inflationary environment, which, by both historical and international standards, must be regarded as very moderate, has been consistent with and conducive to the anti-inflationary sentiment generally observed in German society. Deviations from this medium to long-term trend, both in inflation as well as the underlying monetary targets, have been short-lived, and the authorities have generally been able to control them so that monetary policy in this regard has posed no significant problems for the private sector.

Despite the general anti-inflationary attitude, inflation is not the only monetary variable affecting the economy at large and businesses in trade and industry in particular. As the earlier discussion of the process of monetary transmission shows, monetary conditions and monetary policy affect economic activity in a wide-ranging and intricate manner, of which inflation is but one element. Most importantly, interest rates and exchange rates directly affect enterprises in their financing, asset

[414] The chart depicts the money-supply targets of the Bundesbank for the Central Bank Money until 1988 and for M3 until 1998. For the period since 1999, the ECB's reference value for M3 growth is shown, together with the values for changes in M3 in Germany.

management, and foreign trading activities as well as the related corporate decisions. In the short run, changes in these variables can significantly influence the operations of individuals and enterprises alike.

Central bank interest rates in Germany

Chart 18

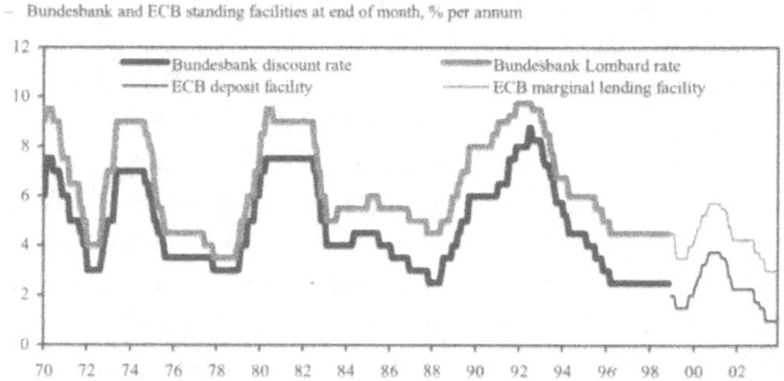

Data source: Deutsche Bundesbank

Chart 18 above shows the major interest rates set by the Bundesbank, the discount and Lombard rates, and by the ECB, the deposit rate and the marginal lending facility, which determine the rates at which the central bank absorbs and gives off liquidity to the commercial banking sector[415]. As reference rates for the banking industry, these parameters form the basis for other interest rates set within the commercial banking sector, both between the banks and between banks and ultimate customers. The chart shows that central bank interest rates have varied considerably over the past three decades, reaching a peak of 8.75% and 9.75% respectively in summer 1992 and a low of 1.00% and 3.00% respectively in summer 2003. Phases of high interest rates, especially the years from 1974 to 1976, 1980 to 1983 and 1991 to 1994, reflect periods of high inflationary pressures and the Bundesbank's counteractive measures curbing liquidity. Conversely, the years 1976 to 1980, 1984 to 1989 and 1996 onward mark the troughs in the economic cycle when inflationary pressures were considered low.

Development in the central bank interest rates shows that, given the spread between peaks and troughs in these rates over time, the interest costs of central bank credit repeatedly more than doubled and, in turn, halved within comparatively short periods of time, i.e. two to four years. In as far as the changes in these reference rates are passed on by commercial banks to their ultimate customers, monetary policy-induced changes in the refinancing and deposit terms can have a significant impact on the

[415] The chart continues the time series after the beginning of 1999 by depicting the equivalent standing facilities maintained by the ECB, the deposit and the marginal lending facilities.

credit costs and returns to capital. The impact is likely to be of particular importance for enterprises needing to borrow during high-interest periods.

From a theoretical perspective, two considerations may mitigate the impression that the interest-rate environment has been subject to considerable inconsistency over time. First, like the development in the rate of inflation, the level and changes of central bank interest rates in Germany have been low by historical and international standards. Second, the impact of changes in the overall level of interest rates may not necessarily be as acute as the above nominal values suggest, since in an inflationary environment the burden of interest payments is partly offset by the fall in the value of money. In other words, the real cost of credit is determined by the real rather than the nominal interest rate[416]. A short-term measure of the real rate of interest – here the annual average of the overnight interest rate on the Frankfurt money market less the seasonally adjusted rate of change in consumer prices – is presented in chart 19, suggesting that changes in real interest rates were far less pronounced over time – even during turbulent periods –, and that the overall level was comparatively moderate, reaching a peak of 6.89% in 1991.

Real short-term interest rates

Chart 19

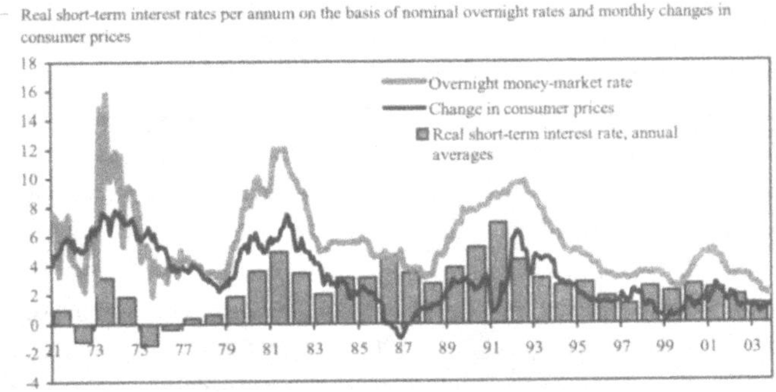

Data source: Deutsche Bundesbank

In practice, however, assessment of the cost of credit by the private sector is based on the determinants immediately affecting it. A comparative view in terms of historical

[416] The Deutsche Bundesbank (2001b) points out that real interest rates have been at an historically low level on a long-term horizon, concluding that this real rate of interest is not an impediment to sustained economic growth in Germany owing to the favourable financing terms for investment. The analysis provides a detailed description of the concept of real interest rates as well as various indicators of that concept. The indicator provided in chart 19, in contrast, is a rather simple illustration of the differences between nominal and real interest rates. Especially with respect to long-term real interest rates, Deutsche Bundesbank (2001b) provides an extensive contemporary evaluation.

trends or the financing terms in other economies is therefore likely to be relevant in the specific case of, say, a financing decision. Similarly, real interest rates are of comparatively little relevance to corporate financial accounting, which is nominal in nature so that the mitigating or amplifying effects of price changes do not become immediately visible. As a result, the higher and more volatile nominal rates of interest are, the more likely they are to dominate the overall appraisal of interest terms by private-sector participants.

The second major monetary variable of concern for the corporate sector is the exchange rate of the domestic currency vis-à-vis the rates of the country's trading partners. As pointed out in the institutional context, German monetary policy operated under various forms of exchange rate regimes for most of the post-war period. After the fixed exchange rate system against the USD under the Bretton Woods agreement was abandoned in 1973, the Deutsche Mark, like most other international currencies, started to float freely on international foreign exchange markets. As a consequence, the 1970s were characterised by substantial exchange rate fluctuation. As this was perceived to be detrimental to international trade and financial market stability, in March 1979 European policy makers adopted the European Monetary System following initial experience with managed exchange rates under the snake-in-the-tunnel arrangement. The Exchange Rate Mechanism of the European Monetary System was designed to stabilise the exchange rates of the participating currencies[417] within a target corridor around a grid of bilaterally fixed parities. The Deutsche Mark served as the *de facto* anchor currency of the system.

Chart 20 shows the development in the major EMU predecessor currencies' exchange rates against the Deutsche Mark, indexed at the irrevocable conversion rates as of January 1, 1999. Most importantly, exchange rate movements between the currencies of the member states participating in EMU were eliminated with their irrevocable fixing as of January 1, 1999 and introduction of the euro. Preceding the fixing of intra-EMU exchange rates, their trend documents the continuous nominal appreciation of the Deutsche Mark against most other European currencies over the past three decades. The depreciation of European partner currencies is most marked in the cases of the Portuguese escudo, the Spanish peseta and the Italian lira, whose nominal value vis-à-vis the Deutsche Mark upon entry into EMU was only a fraction of their values in the early 70s. Within the EMS, this crawling depreciation was accompanied by a total of 18 devaluations between the system's inception and its de facto suspension in

[417] The founding members of the EMS were Belgium, Denmark, France, Germany, Ireland, Italy, Luxembourg, the Netherlands and the United Kingdom. The latter participated in the ERM only as from October 1990. After the ERM was de facto suspended in August 1993, Belgium, Denmark, France, Luxembourg and from 1995 Austria announced their intention to maintain the narrow band of +/- 2.25% around the bilateral parities (Bofinger et al. (1996), pp. 605 and 609).

1993[418]. A similar, albeit less pronounced development has occurred with respect to other important international, non-EMU currencies, notably the US dollar and the British pound, as chart 21 shows[419].

DEM exchange rates, historical

Chart 20

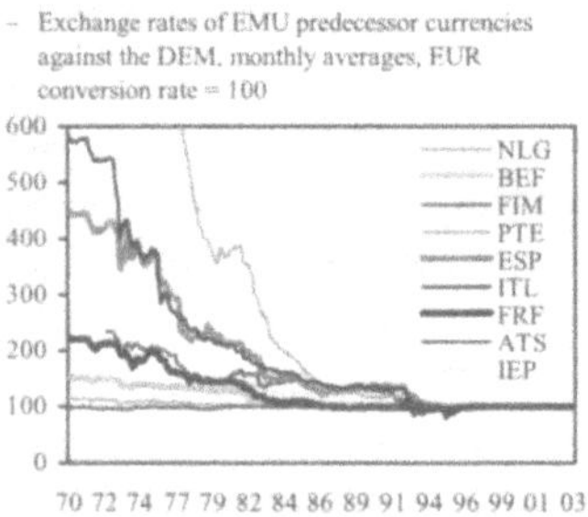

Data source: Deutsche Bundesbank

Chart 21

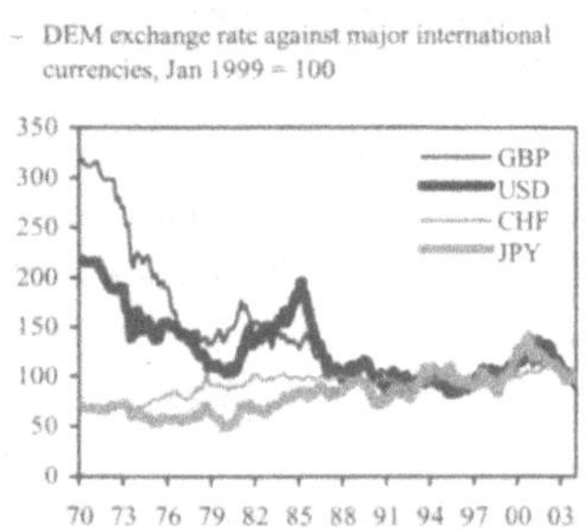

Data source: Deutsche Bundesbank

From an industry perspective, in principle the persistent nominal appreciation of the Deutsche Mark implied *ceteris paribus* a crawling erosion of competitiveness in export business, but also a continuous decline in important prices. However, considering that domestic inflation has been low in comparison to most other industrialised countries, this nominal effect was considerably weakened over time. This becomes evident when comparing nominal exchange rate developments with the Deutsche Mark's real effective exchange rate as measured by an inflation-adjusted weighted basket of the currencies of 19 of Germany's most important trading partners, as in chart 22[420]. In contrast to what the development in nominal exchange rates suggests, the real effective exchange rate of the Deutsche Mark has been extraordinarily stable over the past decades, implying only moderate losses in international competitiveness[421]. Nevertheless, as in the case of real interest rates, this economic logic is not immediately relevant for enterprises in their day-to-day calculations and business planning, as their accounting is based on nominal values. As a result, the development in the external value of the Deutsche Mark has, in practice, given rise to considerable changes in the immediate business environment for enterprises directly or indirectly involved in foreign trade.

[418] Deutsche Bundesbank (1997), p. 123.

[419] DEM exchange rate from 1999 calculated on EUR basis at final conversion rate of EUR 1 = DEM 1.95583.

[420] DEM exchange rate from 1999 calculated on EUR basis at final conversion rate of EUR 1 = DEM 1.95583.

[421] For an opposite view see Weimer (1998), pp. 461-463.

Whether these changes in the business environment are positive or negative for the enterprises concerned essentially depends on two factors.

- First, it hinges on the extent to which individual enterprises or sectors are directly or indirectly exposed to external trade in general and the weight exports and imports have in their turnover. We will look into this question in greater detail in the following section.
- Second, it depends on the intensity and length of the appreciation and depreciation cycles observable within the secular trend of appreciation of the Deutsche Mark, and on individual enterprises' time horizons. Assuming an enterprise takes a medium or long-term outlook, cyclical exchange rate movements may not be perceived as critical, because downward and upward movements may even each other out over time and the real impact of exchange rate changes has been very low in the long-run. For a short-term trade project, however, inter-temporal exchange rate alterations may significantly affect its profitability.

DEM real effective exchange rate

Chart 22

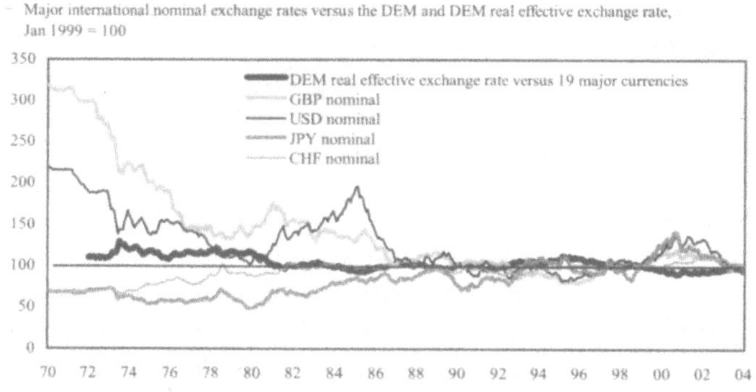

Data source: Deutsche Bundesbank

II.1.2.3 Exposure of trade and industry to monetary policy

The review of major economic variables shows that monetary policy has achieved a stable monetary environment for the German economy over the past three decades. Indeed, there has been a clear long-term downward trend in inflation, nominal and real interest rates and the fluctuation in exchange rates. At the same time, interest and exchange rates in particular naturally continue to move in cycles, at times reaching levels – both peaks and troughs – which enterprises exposed to these variables may perceive as particularly favourable or unfavourable for their operations. Despite the potentially large impact of these variables on the German economy as a whole, the incentives for enterprises and their interest representatives to take political action with regard to monetary policy are even less than the overall picture suggests. This is because the impact of these variables on business activity is rather slight and diffuse, such that the costs and benefits emanating from central bank interest and exchange rates may effectively be viewed as negligible. Given the difficulties associated with tracing the financial impact of monetary policy measures at the individual enterprise level and the lack of representativeness such calculations imply, the following aggregate data are presented as examples illustrating the marginal final impact of monetary policy decisions on the private sector.

Structure of enterprises' external finance in Germany

Chart 23

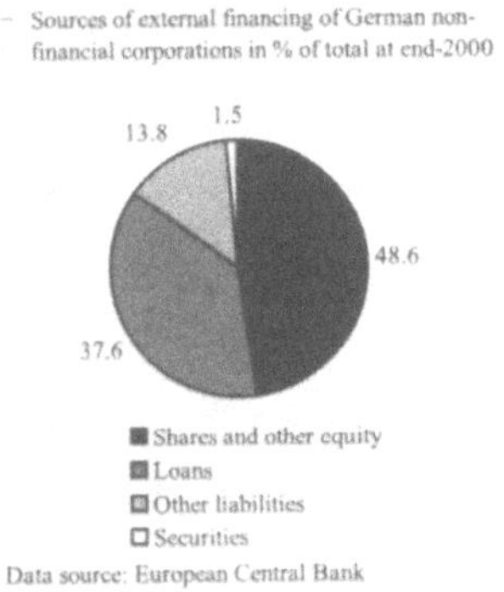

Data source: European Central Bank

Chart 24

Data source: European Central Bank

At first sight, this point looks counterintuitive. For their financing, German enterprises in trade and industry – as chart 23 above suggests[422] – are heavily dependent on commercial bank credit, as opposed to capital-market based financing, notably through bonds or shares[423]. This is especially so for the large number of small and medium-sized enterprises, the segment of Germany's corporate landscape accounting for the highest proportion of aggregate turnover and employment[424]. Given the outstanding and immediate role of banks and bank credit in the transmission of monetary policy, the heavy reliance on bank credit implies rather direct exposure of German enterprises to monetary policy measures.

---

422 Viewed in the long-term, the proportion of credit as the primary source of German non-financial enterprises' financing is structurally higher than depicted in charts 23 and 24, as the data for end-2000 contain a comparatively high weighting of shares and other forms of equity. The latter was particularly high at the reporting date owing to the stock market boom at the time.

423 European Central Bank (2002), pp. 84-86. Also Smith (1993), pp. 354-366, or Franke (1998), pp. 260-263.

424 European Central Bank (2002), pp. 84-86. Also Smith (1993), pp. 419-427.

The structural exposure to bank credit notwithstanding, interest rates have a very small impact on the profit and loss accounts of non-financial corporations in Germany. As chart 25 illustrates, the interest paid by German non-financial corporations in 2001 made up only 1.5% of their total costs, compared to 61.4% spent on materials, 16.6% on labour costs, and 2.7% on taxes.

Components of costs and income of enterprises in Germany

Chart 25

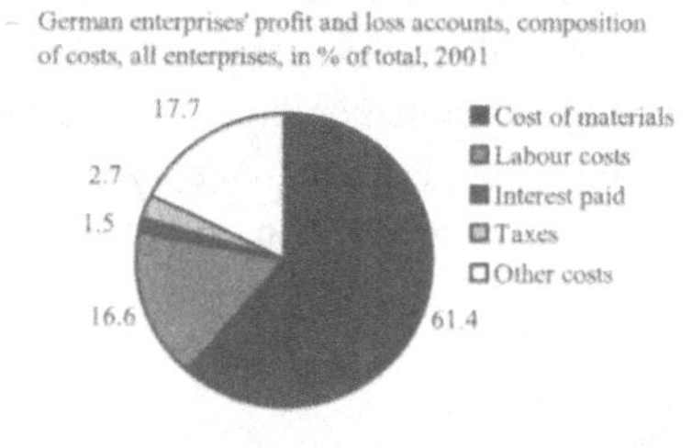

Data source: Deutsche Bundesbank

Chart 26

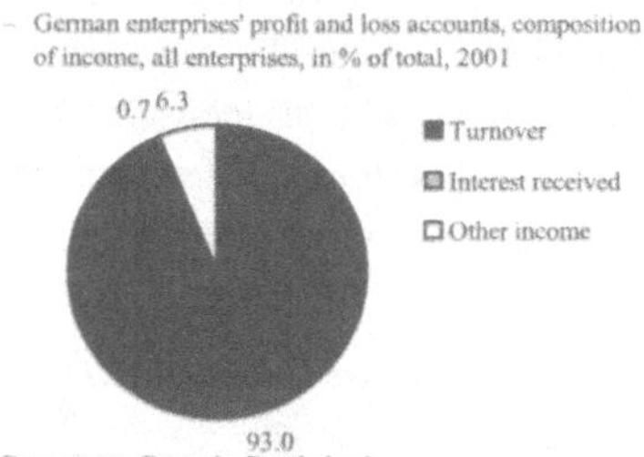

Data source: Deutsche Bundesbank

Over the past three decades, the share of interest-related expenses at non-financial corporations has varied between a minimum of 1.2% in the late 1980s and a maximum of 2.1% in 1974 and again in 1982, as depicted in chart 27[425].

Weighting of enterprises' interest expenditure in Germany

Chart 27

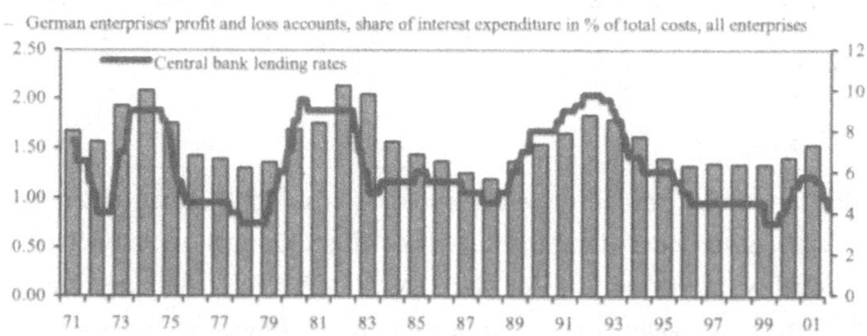

Data source: Deutsche Bundesbank

The cycles of interest expenses broadly followed the movements of central bank interest rates, with a lag of one to two years, as the direct comparison shows. As a result, the share of interest-related costs has not only been comparatively small, but has varied only moderately over time. Even during periods of pronounced rises in central bank interest rates, as in the mid-1970s, the early 1980s and the mid-1990s, the maximum medium-term increase in the share of interest expenses in total costs amounted to only 0.5, 0.8, and 0.6 percentage points respectively.

Insofar as interest-related costs – however small – strain German enterprises' profitability, on average the burden weighs more heavily on small and medium-sized firms than on large enterprises. A breakdown of the corporate sector by legal forms – as presented in chart 28 – shows that the share of interest expenditure is smallest for corporations, slightly higher but still below the total average for partnerships, but twice as high as average for sole proprietorships, i.e. in general the smallest business units. Further, the industry breakdown in chart 29 shows that the burden of interest servicing is greatest for firms in the capital-intensive construction and transport sectors. For firms engaged in wholesale trade, however, the share of interest expenses is 25% below the total average. In industries characterised by large corporations with easier access to alternative forms of external finance, such as manufacturing companies and utilities, the proportion of interest servicing is also comparatively low, despite their capital intensity.

Weight of interest expenses for enterprises in Germany

Chart 28

– German enterprises' profit and loss accounts, share of interest expenditure in % of total costs, by legal form, 2000

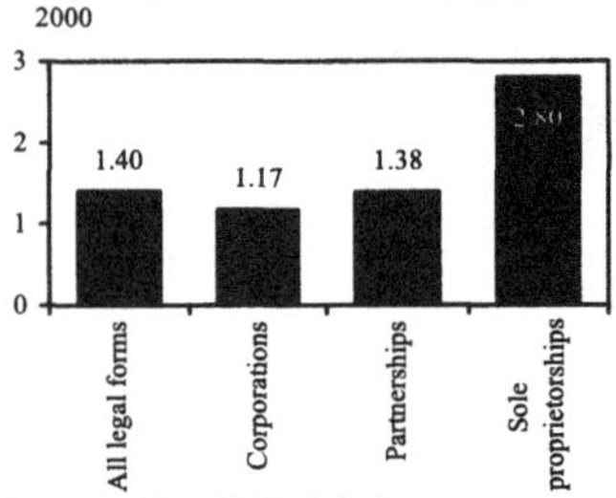

Data source: Deutsche Bundesbank

Chart 29

– German enterprises' profit and loss accounts, share of interest expenditure in % of total costs, by sector, 2000

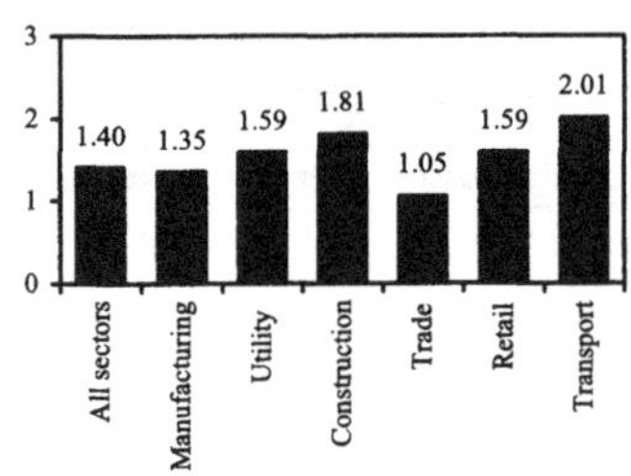

Data source: Deutsche Bundesbank

As a result, the overall burden of interest-related costs on German enterprises is low compared with other cost components. The direct impact of monetary policy – although probably more marked for the large number of small and medium-sized enterprises and for companies in the construction and transport sectors – is relatively small. The impact is even less pronounced on the income side of German enterprises' profit and loss accounts, as the share of interest-related income in total corporate revenues amounts to only 0.7% in the data for 2001[426]. Overall, monetary policy has not had a critical impact on German enterprises' profitability in the recent past.

A second factor weakening the perception of monetary policy as an economic burden on corporate activities is that central bank interest rates are not transmitted directly

[425] The share of German enterprises' interest income is even lower, as shown in chart 26.

[426] See chart 26 on page 159.

into the corporate sector, being channelled instead through the commercial banking system and other segments of the financial markets. This has two intermediary effects on the perception of monetary policy. First, the level of market interest rates on bank lending differs from central bank rates, depending on the pricing behaviour of individual banks. These are driven mainly by considerations of their own profit margins, the credit quality of the borrower and the maturity of the loan.

Interest rates on corporate credit and corporate bond yields

Chart 30

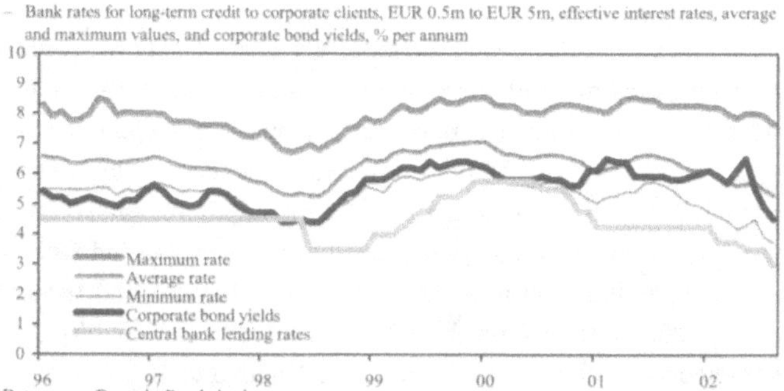

Data source: Deutsche Bundesbank

Chart 30 depicts minimum, average, and maximum rates offered by German commercial banks for long-term corporate lending between EUR 0.5 m and EUR 5 m as registered by the Bundesbank between 1996 and June 2003. The interest rates on corporate credit are generally above central bank lending rates and, most importantly, move within a broad corridor between the minimum and maximum rates observed. On average, lending rates were 1.79% above the central bank rates during the reporting period, with minimum and maximum values for that difference of 0.77% and 2.98% respectively. The spread between the highest and lowest reported lending rates amounted to 2.64% on average, with a minimum of 2.14% and a maximum of 3.99%.

In terms of ultimate customers' perception, this implies that the interest rate terms for corporate loans – although dependent on the overall interest environment created by the central bank – are primarily set by the banking sector, shifting the focus of attention to the latter. This view is accentuated by the fact that the lending rates to ultimate customers set by commercial banks tend to anticipate central bank rate rises, while being slow to follow an easing in overall interest rates. In addition, direct capital market-based financing via corporate bonds can be achieved at comparatively low interest rates, as the level of corporate bond yields in chart 30 suggests. In the case of corporate securities, the average difference to central bank rates amounts to only 1.06%, with a maximum of 3.00% and a minimum of -0.10% during the reporting period.

The second intermediary effect weakening the association of credit costs with central bank policies relates to the maturity of corporate credit. In Germany, lending to corporate borrowers tends to be long-term in nature, i.e. with maturities of more than five years, and mainly on the basis of fixed-rate loan agreements[427]. Changes in the monetary environment therefore tend to have a direct impact on an individual enterprise only when it takes out a new loan or renegotiates an existing contract. Consequently, unless corporations are heavily exposed to short-term or revolving loans, changes in the overall interest environment do not immediately weigh on the cost side.

The immediacy with which changes in the monetary environment are perceived by the private sector is tempered not only in respect of changes in interest rates, but also with regard to exchange rate movements. Again, checks on the perception of the effects of monetary policy do not immediately follow from the basic characteristics of the German economy. After all, the German economy is highly integrated into the global economy, with total receipts from exports, cross-border services and factor income of EUR 877 bn and expenditure on imports, cross-border services and factor income of EUR 783 bn in 2002, as shown in chart 31. Repeatedly, the country has been the world's largest exporting nation, with shipments amounting to 36% of GDP in 2003.

Germany's international trade and capital flows

Chart 31

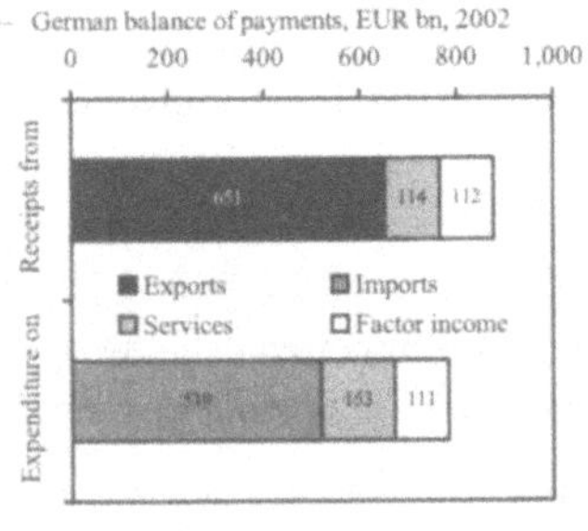

Data source: Deutsche Bundesbank

Chart 32

Data source: Deutsche Bundesbank

Despite this substantial engagement in cross-border trade, however, exchange rate movements are becoming less important to German businesses. As already pointed out, the past decades brought profound stabilisation in the vast majority of exchange rates within the ERM. With the launch of EMU, exchange rate-related costs have been eliminated completely with respect to eleven of Germany's trading partners.

[427] European Central Bank (2002), p. 84. Since the late 1990s, a marked increase in the share of short-term financing has been observed. The stability of this trend has not yet been verified, however.

This trend has been complemented by the patterns of German trade. As chart 32 shows, trade with EMU member states accounts for almost half of Germany's exports and imports. In other words, a large part of German trade has been pursued with countries whose currencies stabilised significantly vis-à-vis the Deutsche Mark over the past years and which in 1999 also joined the single currency. Other important European trading partners not belonging to EMU, such as Denmark, Sweden and the Czech Republic, have also used the Deutsche Mark and subsequently the EUR as an anchor currency, leading to increasing stabilisation of the relevant exchange rates.

At less than 25%, trade with other economies whose currencies have been floating freely against the Deutsche Mark and EUR, i.e. most importantly the US, the UK, Switzerland and Japan, has a modest share in Germany's total external trade. As observed above, these currencies have remained subject to substantial medium-term fluctuation.

An additional aspect weakening involvement with exchange rate-related issues results from the structure of exports and imports across industrial sectors. As charts 33 and 34 show, the four sectors most strongly involved in export business are, at the same time, also the sectors most heavily engaged in imports, albeit in a different order and in different proportions. This overlap reflects, among other things, that – directly or indirectly – the production of finished goods in Germany depends enormously on imports of raw materials or intermediary goods. Insofar as this is the case, the effects of alterations in the exchange rate can cancel each other out along the value chain, limiting possible distortionary effects on exchange rate developments occurring between the purchase of imported raw materials or semi-finished goods and sale of the final product.

German foreign trade by sector

Chart 33

– German exports by sector, in % of total volume (EUR 651.3 bn), 2002

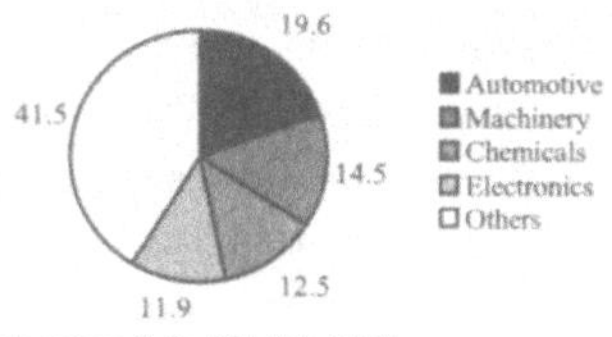

Data source: Federal Statistical Office

Chart 34

– German imports by sector, in % of total volume (EUR 518.5 bn), 2002

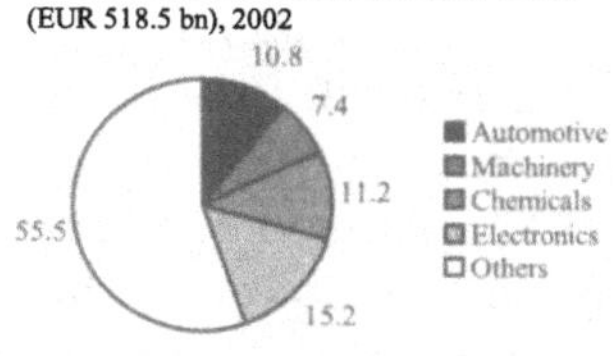

Data source: Federal Statistical Office

A similar picture emerges in the context of Germany's external capital links. Again, German enterprises' commitment is substantial, with a total of EUR 699 bn invested abroad end-2001. 81% of this took the form of foreign direct investment and 19% loans granted by German shareholders in foreign companies, as chart 35 shows. In total, German corporations and individuals hold interests in more than 28,000 enterprises abroad with an aggregate turnover of more than EUR 1 trillion in 2001 and total assets of EUR 4.8 trillion. Again, however, a country breakdown reveals that large proportions of cross-border investment have been realised in countries with stable exchange rate links to the domestic currency.

Germany's foreign capital and direct investment links

Chart 35

– Foreign direct investment by German enterprises abroad, EUR bn, end-2001

Chart 36

– German foreign direct investment by target country, in % of total, end-2001

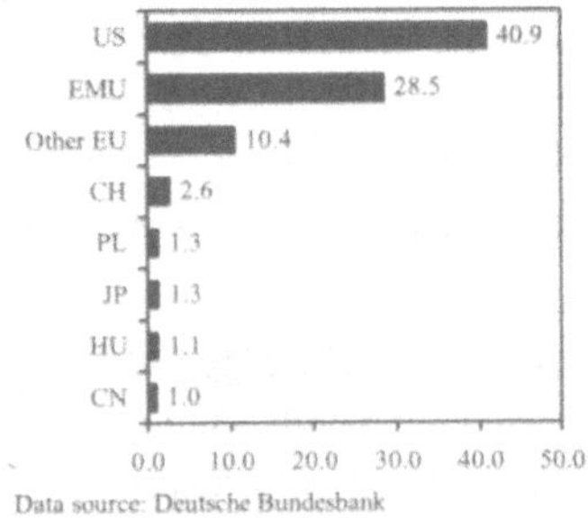

The country breakdown of foreign direct investment nevertheless also shows that cross-border links, especially with the US as the single largest target country for direct investments from Germany, should not be underestimated. The same applies to the share of exports and imports transacted with that country, amounting to 10.5% and 7.8% respectively of the 2002 total. In these cross-border business links, the exchange rate has remained a critical variable, influencing the value of the relevant engagements and the related revenues and expenditures.

One way of looking at these cross-border exposures is to refer to the possibility for trading enterprises to hedge their exchange risks on financial derivatives markets. The importance of these markets for covering trading risks has increased steadily since the 1980s, creating a market segment with an average daily turnover of USD 853 bn in over-the-counter and USD 10 bn in exchange-traded foreign-exchange derivatives[428]. Germany is the fifth-largest market for OTC foreign exchange derivatives with daily turnover of USD 65.2 bn or 5.5% of the world market[429]. In the German market, contracts involving the US dollar capture the largest market share of 44.4%, as chart 37 shows. In April 1998, daily world market turnover in Deutsche Mark foreign exchange contracts with other currencies amounted to USD 218 bn, of which the largest share, namely 76%, were contracts for US dollars, 5% each for Japanese yen

[428] Bank for International Settlements (2002), p. 18. Figures for April 2001.

[429] Bank for International Settlements (2002), p. 21. Figures for April 2001.

and British pounds, and 6.4% for other EMS currencies[430]. With respect to the euro, worldwide derivatives turnover today totals USD 303 bn daily, with USD contracts accounting for 84.5%, JPY contracts 5.9%, and GBP contracts 4.6%[431].

German foreign exchange derivatives market by currency and counterparty

Chart 37

– Daily turnover of OTC foreign exchange derivatives in Germany by currency involved, % of total net turnover, April 2001

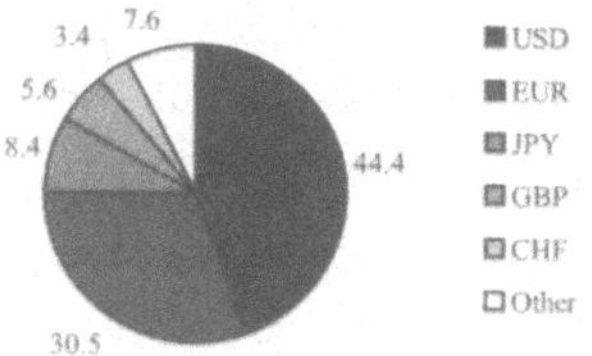

Data source: Bank for International Settlements

Chart 38

– Daily turnover of OTC foreign exchange derivatives in Germany by type of counterparty, % of total net turnover, April 2001

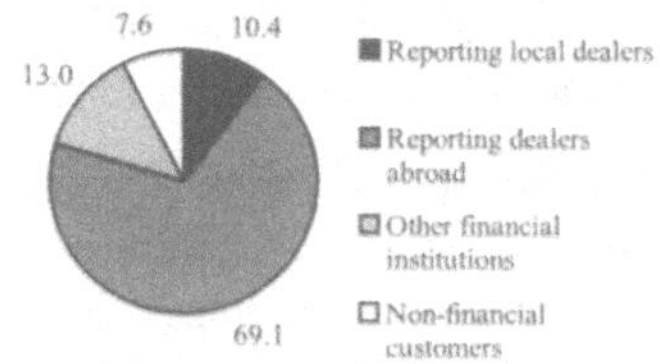

Data source: Bank for International Settlements

Only 7.6% of the daily trading in foreign exchange derivatives on the German market is transacted directly with non-financial customers, suggesting that the large majority of derivatives contracts are concluded among financial market participants, as chart 38 pinpoints. This raises the question as to how far trade and industrial enterprises actually make use of hedging instruments to insure themselves against exchange rate risks. A 1997 survey among 126 non-financial firms in Germany[432] showed as many as 78% used derivative instruments; 96% of these employed exchange rate derivatives as opposed to, say, interest rate or commodity derivatives. Use of derivatives was found to be most extensive in the services and mechanical engineering industries, nearly all of which were engaged in derivatives dealings, followed by the metal, electronics, and chemical industries. Derivatives usage was lowest in the retail and consumer products sectors, where less than 80% of the responding firms reported positively, and in the construction business, with just over 60% of firms participating in derivatives trading[433]. The pattern by sector was found to correspond largely to the respective industries' exposure to foreign trade[434].

Most importantly, however, the survey points to substantial limitations in the use of foreign exchange derivatives. In the main, the survey addressed large corporations

---

[430] Bank for International Settlements (2002), p. 19. Figures for OTC products in April 1998.

[431] Bank for International Settlements (2002), p. 19. Figures for EUR-based OTC products in April 2001.

[432] See Bodnar, Gebhardt (1998). Figures cited here are likely to have changed substantially after the national currencies of the member states participating in EMU were replaced by the euro.

[433] Bodnar, Gebhardt (1998), p. 4.

[434] Bodnar, Gebhardt (1998), pp. 5-6.

with annual turnover of more than EUR 100 m. Within this cohort of large enterprises, the responses showed that company size was the decisive determinant for derivatives usage, with participation ratios ranging from 94% among corporations with turnover between EUR 2.5 bn and EUR 5 bn to only 50% among firms with turnover of less than EUR 250 m. This size effect points to the high fixed costs of hedging programmes that make derivatives usage uneconomical for smaller enterprises[435]. This correlation is corroborated by the responses from businesses not using derivatives, 61% of which cited the lack of sufficient risk exposure as the most important reason for non-usage[436]. As a result, the vast majority of enterprises are unlikely to be in a position in which taking recourse to foreign-exchange hedging is economically viable.

Finally, even enterprises using foreign exchange hedging still face costs from exchange rate fluctuation between the euro and non-EMU currencies, since hedging as such gives rise to trading and transaction costs. In other words, exchange rate hedging merely transforms the potential costs associated with the risk of exchange rate alterations into the more calculable *ex ante* costs of purchasing derivative contracts. Either way, exchange rates and their movements create costs for enterprises. Consequently, fluctuations in the exchange rates of major non-EMU trading partners remain a source of substantial expense for German enterprises.

II.1.2.4 Dominance of competing economic issues

The fourth factor weakening the involvement of stakeholders in trade and industry with monetary policy is the dominance of competing policy issues. As pointed out in chapter I, the resources constraints facing interest associations and their members naturally limit the number of policy issues they can handle at a time, as well as the intensity with which selected policy issues can be addressed. The question arises as to what extent the political agenda is occupied with competing policy issues that are also relevant for interest groups in trade and industry and may outweigh monetary policy in terms of importance for the political activities of these groups.

Issue agendas are different for each stakeholder in the political arena and vary over time, making an all-encompassing view of the agenda of issues competing with monetary policy a resource-intensive undertaking beyond the scope of the present analysis. Nevertheless, in order to achieve a view of the policy agenda on which monetary policy is likely to compete, the economic policy agenda as viewed by the German Council of Economic Experts will be examined here. As noted in the institutional context, the German Council of Economic Experts is an academic body set up in 1963, which advises the German government and parliament on economic

---

[435] Bodnar, Gebhardt (1998), p. 5.

[436] Bodnar, Gebhardt (1998), p. 6.

policy issues. It periodically assesses Germany's economic development and, acting as a body independent in its advisory activities, makes policy recommendations with a view to concurrently ensuring price stability, high employment and external equilibrium, plus steady and adequate economic growth. The Council comprises five economic experts – mainly academics – nominated by the government and appointed by the president for a term of five years.

The Annual Report, which the Council publishes each November and in which it assesses the country's economic development, systematically examines the hurdles on the way towards achieving the four major economic objectives of price stability, high employment, external equilibrium and adequate economic growth. It also submits policy proposals for resolving the problems identified. As such, it represents a useful indicator of the country's economic policy agenda. First, it is primarily concerned with the economic problems of the country as a whole. To that end, it also keeps a sharp watch on the needs of Germany's corporate sector. The latter point is underscored by the close cooperation between the Council and business associations in drafting the report[437]. At the same time, its analysis is not limited to the particular preferences of a single interest group, as the Council has to base its analysis and judgment on the Federation's economic policy objectives, and not on those of particular segments in society. Albeit not perfectly congruent with the views of interest groups in trade and industry, the Council's reports contain valuable hints about the problems besetting Germany's corporate sector. Second, the Annual Reports provide for strong continuity in criteria of issue selection, analysis, and methodology over time, permitting quite a consistent view of the evolution in Germany's economic policy agenda. Finally, the Council concentrates on economically relevant issues. This fades out a number of other politically, socially and otherwise relevant policy issues but allows for a focused comparison of monetary policy with other existing policy issues.

A proxy for the composition and development of the economic policy agenda in Germany can be achieved by listing and comparing the policy issues addressed by the Council in its Annual Report. Although the reports cover the whole range of economic policy-making areas, an indicator of the priorities set by the Council is the foreword in each report, which summarises the main findings and recommendations. Charts 39 and 40 summarise the findings reached by recording the major policy issues identified in the executive summaries of the Council's Annual Reports since 1970.

---

[437] Close cooperation is documented *inter alia* by the Council's acknowledgements in the forewords of its Annual Reports. See German Council of Economic Experts, Annual Report, 1970-2003.

Issue agenda – economic policy issues 1970-2003

Chart 39

– Number of years in which economic policy issues were addressed by the German Council of Economic Experts in its Annual Report, 1970-2003

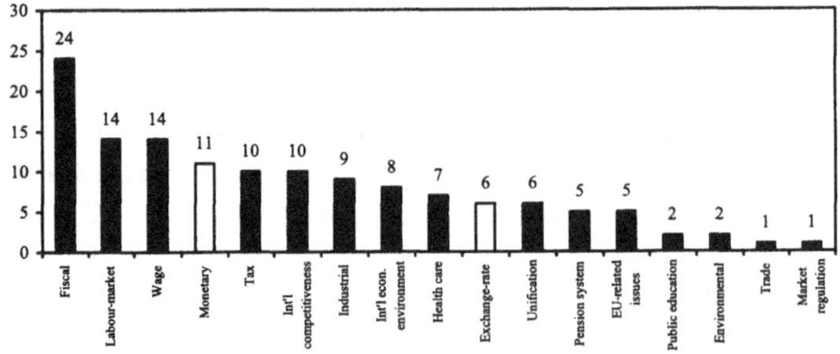

Data source: German Council of Economic Experts, Annual Reports, 1970-2003

As depicted in chart 39, monetary policy is referred to explicitly in eleven of the 34 executive summaries since 1970. Exchange rate developments or policies are referred to in six reports. In addition to these two issues, the reports regularly feature at least 15 other policy areas as relevant to overall achievement of the country's economic objectives. Fiscal policy, together with tax policy, clearly dominates prioritisation by the Council over the past decades, featuring in nearly three-quarters of all reports. Second, labour market and wage policy play an important role in nearly half of the reports respectively. Further important issues include international competitiveness, industrial policy, the international economic environment and the different elements of Germany's welfare state, most importantly the healthcare, pension and unemployment benefit systems. As a result, monetary policy over time has competed with a relatively large number of other important policy issues. The ranking of monetary and exchange rate issues on the economic policy agenda over the past years is illustrated in chart 40.

Issue agenda – density of issues and the role of monetary and exchange rate policy

Chart 40

- Number of major economic policy issues addressed by the German Council of Economic Experts in its Annual Report and indicative ranking of monetary and exchange rate policy according to their priority in the reports' executive summaries

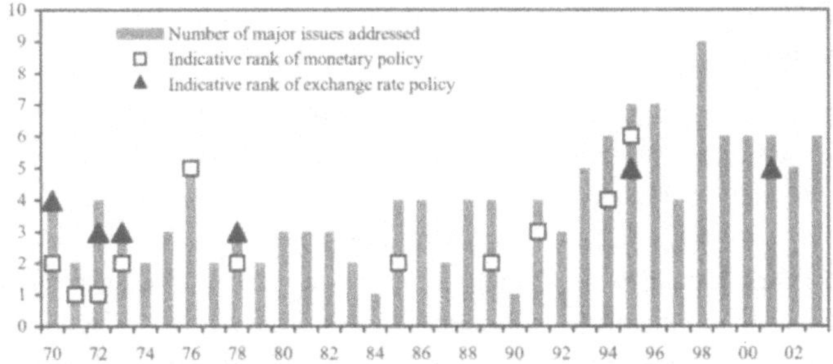

- Average number of major policy issues addressed per year:	3.97
- Average indicative ranking of monetary policy in the relevant years:	2.73
- Average indicative ranking of exchange rate policy in the relevant years:	3.83

Data source: German Council of Economic Experts, Annual Reports, 1970-2003

More detailed examination of the distribution of policy issues over time reveals three important properties of the agenda.

- First, the number of issues on the political agenda has tended to increase over time, most notably during the 1990s. In fact, the Council's analyses and comments suggest that the country's economic problems have become more numerous and more severe over the past three decades.
- Second, in terms of content there has also been a marked shift away from classical macroeconomic issues, such as the balance of payments, exchange rate and monetary policy and income policies, which were dominant throughout most of the 1970s, towards supply-side issues and heightened concern with the level and structure of taxation, the structure of labour markets, wage levels, industrial policy including privatisation, and lately the welfare state and reform of the related benefit and insurance systems.
- Third, monetary and exchange rate policies have entered the list of major issues less and less frequently over time, starting from almost annual references in the early 1970s – i.e. at the time of exchange rate turmoil and accelerating inflation during the first oil crisis – and emerging only occasionally since the 1980s, e.g. in the context of the post-reunification inflationary period or pronounced exchange rate developments in the mid-1990s and since adoption of EMU.
- Fourth, when attempting to rank the issues in each executive summary from the order in which they are mentioned, the space devoted to them and the urgency

attached to individual issues verbally, it becomes clear that – in line with the preceding findings – monetary and exchange rate policies were among the dominant issues, taking first or second rank in a shortlist of policy issues, mainly in the early 1970s and on occasion in the 1980s. Since then, other policy issues have dominated the arena, with monetary issues getting less attention than the growing majority of other issues.

An important case highlighting these four observations is the Council's 2002 report, in which the experts tabled a programme comprising 20 measures they deemed necessary to return Germany to higher employment and economic growth. The 20 measures, listed in table 6, essentially feature supply-side measures typical of the policy debate in the past 15 years related to fiscal and tax policy as well as to reform of the welfare system. Monetary and exchange rate-related issues do not play a role, save for a very indirect reference via the call on the government to meet the conditions of the EU Stability and Growth Pact and thereby contribute to a stability-oriented monetary policy at EU level[438]. This, however, is not addressed to the central bank and monetary decision makers.

On the individual political agendas of business interest groups in trade and industry, the small and diminishing role of monetary policy is accentuated by their specific outlook on the political environment. They are likely to take a less macroeconomic view of the policy agenda, giving priority to the policy issues of immediate relevance to their members, their sector or the region in which they operate. Thus, specific tax provisions, market regulation, industrial policy or sectoral wage developments feature more prominently on individual group agendas. Monetary policy and exchange rates are likely to be regarded as exogenous economic conditions whose impact has been small and has declined in past decades, and which are much harder to influence than other policy issues decided by elected policy makers.

This is indicated by the policy areas interest associations cover. Table 7[439] provides an indicative list of major issue areas addressed by a selection of the leading German interest associations in trade and industry covered in this study[440]. Monetary and exchange rate matters are not explicitly covered by any of these associations. In individual cases, they are subsumed under general economic issues in as far as the latter are dealt with at all.

---

[438] The rise of supply side-related policy issues over the past decades has been analysed in historical perspective by Weimer (1998), pp. 435-467.

[439] See p. 172.

[440] Table 7 is compiled on the basis of lists of topics covered by the relevant interest associations or the titles of their organisational units as published by these associations in brochures, annual

German Council of Economic Experts: Measures for employment and growth

Table 6

- Lowering tax rates further, aiming for integration of income and company taxation
- Rolling back the state in favour of private activity, while at the same time shifting government spending towards public-sector investment
- Reducing public debt, which implies strengthening the forces of growth and easing the burdens on future generations
- Elements of a growth programme for east Germany
- Reducing marginal fiscal charges on labour
- Keeping pay increases below the rate of growth in labour productivity
- Limiting unemployment benefits to 12 months again
- Integrating unemployment benefits into social benefits
- More employment in the low wage sector requires reform of the structure of social welfare benefits
- More flexibility – responsibility of parties to collective pay agreements
- Amendment to statutory regulations in the interests of decentralised wage-setting
- Expanding the possibilities for fixed-term employment contracts – less stringent protection against dismissal
- Allocation of new roles to statutory and private health insurance
- More performance-based fee structures for outpatient doctors
- Liberalisation of pharmaceutical sales
- Freedom of contracting for the statutory health insurance schemes
- No discretionary extension of contributions base
- Shift from income-related contributions to flat-rate capitation charges geared to health costs
- More competition in private health insurance
- Pro-active approach to budget consolidation – adherence to Stability and Growth Pact

Source: German Council of Economic Experts, Annual Report 2002

In summary, the general economic policy agenda and the areas of activity of Germany's major interest associations in trade and industry make it evident that monetary policy is only one of a considerable number of important policy issues and that it has diminished markedly in importance and attention over time, outweighed by other general economic policy issues as well as by individual and specialised associations' sector- and industry-specific concerns.

reports and on their internet pages as per February 12, 2004. Associations and areas of activity are listed in alphabetical order.

German trade and industry associations and major areas of activity

Table 7

Name of association	Sector	Major areas of activity	
Bundesverband des Deutschen Exporthandels e.V., BDEx	Foreign trade	– Export controls – Export counselling – Export credit insurance	– Export finance – Export pricing – Export promotion
Bundesverband der Deutschen Industrie e.V., BDI	Industry	– Central and east European affairs – Economic policy – Energy, telecommunications – Environmental affairs – EU affairs – International markets – Legal affairs, competition	– Public procurement, defence industry – Small and medium-sized enterprises – Taxation, fiscal affairs – Technology, innovation – Trade policy – Transport policy
Bundesverband des Deutschen Groß- und Außenhandels e.V., BGA	Wholesale trade	– Agricultural, environmental policy – Finance and taxation – Legal affairs and competition	– Logistics and transport policy – Trade policy – Wage and social policy
Deutscher Industrie- und Handelskammertag, DIHK	Commerce	– Business location policy – Business services for members – Economic policy – EU affairs – Finance and taxation	– Innovation, environment, energy policy – International affairs – Legal affairs – Services, infrastructure, regional policy – Small and medium-sized enterprises
Hauptverband der Deutschen Bauindustrie e.V., HDB	Construction	– Economic policy – International contracts and relations – Legal, taxation, business affairs	– Social policy – Technology
Hauptverband des Deutschen Einzelhandels, HDE	Retail trade	– Bank cards, customer cards – Business administration, controlling – Business establishment, succession – Business location, transport policy – Consumer policy, non-food products – Economics and statistics – Electronic business – Environmental policy	– Euro, European Monetary Union – Innovation – Labour, social policy – Legal affairs, competition – Postal policy – Taxation – Vocational training
Verband der Chemischen Industrie e.V., VCI	Chemicals	– Chemicals policy – Economic policy, fiscal policy – Environmental affairs, responsible care	– Science and research – Trade policy
Verband der Automibilindustrie e.V., VDA	Automobiles	– Automotive parts and accessories – Environmental affairs – EU affairs – Legal affairs, taxation, insurance – Logistics – Statistics, analysis, forecasts	– Technology – Trade fairs – Trade, commodities, economic policy – Trailers, superstructure, containers – Transport policy
Verband Deutscher Maschinen- und Anlagenbau e.V., VDMA	Mechanical engineering	– Business administration – Economics, statistics – EU affairs – Finance, controlling – Informatics, communication – Legal affairs	– Market information systems – Standards – Taxation – Technology, environment – Trade policy – Transport policy
Zentralverband des Deutschen Handwerks, ZDH	Skilled crafts	– Business services for members – EU affairs – Science and research	– Taxation – Trade fairs – Trade policy
Zentralverband Elektrotechnik- und Elektronikindustrie e.V., ZVEI	Electrical engineering	– Business administration, taxation – Economic, industrial, trade policy – Economics and statistics – Electrical engineering – Environmental policy	– Information technology – Legal affairs, public procurement – Research, vocational training – Sales promotion – Transport policy

Sources: Annual reports, background brochures and internet websites of relevant interest groups

II.1.3 Group context: industry and trade associations in Germany

The third determinant of interest-group activity is the interest group context. Assuming that enterprises and interest groups in trade and industry do indeed have identifiable preferences with respect to monetary policy, the question arises whether and how these preferences are communicated to the relevant policy makers, and what resources the actors mediating these interests can fall back on in their work. This section reviews the interest groups potentially relevant to the communication of trade and industry's monetary policy-related interests in Germany, arguing that the relevant associations are a formidable force in Germany's political arena. But not only is their interest in monetary affairs very low, as argued in the preceding sections; even when interest groups in trade and industry do have preferences on monetary issues that they wish to communicate, the effectiveness of the relevant interest associations' work is, *ceteris paribus,* constrained by certain limitations to the monetary policy-related informational resources and internal coherence necessary for effective representation of such potential preferences.

II.1.3.1 Interest associations in trade and industry

Interests pertaining to monetary and exchange rate policy in Germany are communicated via the country's existing infrastructure of trade and industry interest associations. Specific cause groups dedicated to monetary policy issues do not exist in trade and industry, nor in any other economic or societal stratum in Germany[441].

For interests in trade and industry, this infrastructure essentially centres around five leading interest associations[442]:

---

[441] No relevant entries can be found e.g. in the interest-group registry of the Deutsche Bundestag or in Hoppenstedt (1998). With the Association for the Monetary Union of Europe, AMUE, an interest group existed from 1987 to 2002 dedicated to promoting the establishment of a single currency in Europe. AMUE was a network of European business leaders engaged in formal and informal activities, in the establishment and operation of which German managers and policy makers played a key role. As AMUE was concerned with bringing about a new overall monetary regime for Europe, rather than with influencing operation of the existing system, the association is not covered in the present context. AMUE was dissolved after its objective had been achieved in 2002 with the physical introduction of the euro. For a detailed account see Collignon, Schwarzer (2003).

[442] Other interest associations related to the two sectors in the economy are the Bundesvereinigung Deutscher Arbeitgeberverbände, BDA, representing employers, the Vereinigung Deutscher Elektrizitätswerke e.V., VDEW, and the Bundesverband der Deutschen Gas- und Wasserwirtschaft e.V., representing utilities, and other specialised umbrella associations representing the transport sectors, tourism, cooperative businesses, agriculture and the liberal professions. For a complete list see Hoppenstedt (1999), pp. 76-153. These associations are not covered here on a systematic basis because of their high degree of thematic or sectoral specialisation – rendering activity on monetary issues rather unlikely – and because the majority of enterprises represented by these associations is also directly or indirectly represented by the five leading associations above. This also applies to overarching committees and confederations, such as the Gemeinschaftsausschuss der Deutschen

- *Bundesverband der Deutschen Industrie e.V., BDI*

  The BDI is Germany's top industrial association with 36 sectoral industry associations as its members. In the main these consist of large corporations in the automobile, construction, chemical, media, electronics, commodities, telecommunications, mechanical engineering, steel, tourism, and transport sectors.

- *Deutscher Industrie- und Handelskammertag, DIHK*

  The DIHK is the top-level association of Germany's 81 chambers of industry and commerce. Given that all enterprises in Germany[443] are obliged by law to be a member of one of the chambers of industry or commerce irrespective of their sector or size, the DIHK represents more than three million enterprises and characterises itself as the representative of Germany's trade and industry as a whole[444].

- *Zentralverband des Deutschen Handwerks, ZDH*

  The ZDH is the umbrella organisation of skilled crafts in Germany, uniting 55 craft chambers, membership in which is prescribed by law for craft enterprises, as well as 46 national sectoral confederations, in which craft enterprises can participate voluntarily. Indirectly, these associations represent a total of 840,000 enterprises, especially small and medium-sized.

- *Bundesverband des Groß- und Außenhandels e.V., BGA*

  The BGA is the peak organisation for interest groups associated with wholesale and foreign trade. Its membership comprises 15 Land associations, twelve regional associations as well as 48 national sectoral associations, representing a total of 120,000 enterprises, most of them small and medium-sized.

- *Hauptverband des Deutschen Einzelhandels, HDE*

  The HDE is the peak association of German retail businesses, composed of 15 Land associations, 74 regional associations, and 26 national sectoral associations, representing 430,000 enterprises of all sizes, most of them small or medium-sized.

The work of these five top umbrella associations is complemented by the activities of a large number of sectoral or regional organisations, some of the most important of

---

Gewerblichen Wirtschaft and the Bundesvereinigung Deutscher Handelsverbände, in which the five major peak associations participate on selected issues of joint concern.

[443] Enterprises in the handicraft business, the free professions and agriculture are exempted from this rule (Bundesverband der Deutschen Industrie (2003), p. 4). For a detailed description of the legal and statutory provisions of the German system of business chambers as well as the related funding system see Triesch, Ockenfels (1995), pp. 137-144.

[444] Bundesverband der Deutschen Industrie (2003), p. 4

which are included in table 7 above, and which are either constituents or members of the peak organisations, or associated with them.

The five top associations are well-established in the German political system; most of them, including their sectoral member associations, can look back on a long history of interest representation, often dating back to the nineteenth century[445]. Since their re-establishment between 1945 and 1948[446], the trade and industry associations have become the most important interlocutors for policy makers with trade and industry[447]. Being the formal interest associations of the corporate sector, this is quite natural for the most part. Nevertheless, the importance of these associations has been strengthened by two factors.

- First, German trade and industry is highly organised[448]. As pointed out, enterprises in trade and industry are obliged by law to become part of their local chamber of industry or commerce. Similarly, all crafts businesses are organised in their local craft chambers. The local units are ultimately represented by the DIHK or the ZDH at federal level. In addition, a great number of enterprises are voluntarily organised in specific sectoral interest associations, most of which are, in turn, members of one of the above peak associations, especially the BDI[449].
- Second, the German political system has generally been characterised by a comparatively close relationship between policy makers and organised interests, amounting at certain times to neo-corporatist tendencies[450]. This proximity of politics and organised interests has also extended to the relations between policy

---

[445] For an historical overview see e.g. Verband Deutscher Maschinen- und Anlagenbau (1992), Volume 1, pp. 13-103. Also Weimer (1998), pp. 68-70.

[446] Weimer (1998), pp. 68-70, Verband Deutscher Maschinen- und Anlagenbau (1992), Volume 1, pp. 109-133.

[447] Wilson (1990), p. 95.

[448] Wilson (1990), p. 94.

[449] Wilson (1990) estimates that voluntary associations cover more than 70% of the corporate sector, with only the smallest-scale employers as an exception (p. 94).

[450] Wilson (1990), pp. 88-101. Wilson also elaborates on the changing patterns in these corporatist structures, arguing that the 1960s and 70s saw a brief but marked rise in neo-corporatist relationships between government and business. These relationships, however, failed to become institutionalised in a formal way in the long run. Also, informal neo-corporatist structures weakened in the 1980s. The failure of neo-corporatism to develop fully is traced back to the fact that in many instances neither interest associations nor the Federal Government were able to make binding commitments – the former because of certain shortcomings in their authority over their members, and the latter due to the intricacies of the federal system, in which it relies on the support of the Länder for most decisions relevant to economic policymaking. In addition, Wilson emphasises that the Federal Government is not in command of all areas of economic policymaking. He explicitly refers to monetary policy in this context and to the Bundesbank as one of the central banks "most insulated from political control" (p. 99). Paterson, Southern (1991) emphasise, however, that corporatist or neo-corporatist tendencies have been limited in terms of the policy areas in which they occurred, over time, as well as in intensity (pp. 242-246).

makers and industry. Close formal, semi-formal and informal participation by business associations in the process of federal policymaking has resulted in these associations bringing substantial political weight and influence to bear on the final outcomes of the political process. Historically, this tendency has been most pronounced under conservative governments[451].

In terms of political influence at federal level, therefore, the peak trade and industry associations play an important part in communication of the interests of trade and industry as a whole. Regional and sector-specific associations, in contrast, focus on their specific constituencies' immediate sectional concerns.

In this environment peak associations are likely to play a significant role in communication between business and the Bundesbank. As argued above, monetary policy measures cannot be implemented in a discretionary manner with respect to regions or sectors, say, but necessarily act on the economy as a whole in an indiscriminate manner. By the same token, monetary objectives are formulated with respect to the entirety of the state or economic area to which they apply, and monetary strategy, tactics and measures have to meet these economy-wide objectives and the needs of the economy in its entirety. As a result, monetary policy makers are primarily concerned with aggregate economic developments and, as a corollary, with aggregate economic interests. Regional or sectoral preferences and information are relevant for the central bank only in as far as they help to establish a complete picture of the economic situation. As a result, the wider an association's constituency and the greater its representativeness with respect to the economy in general and economic sectors in particular, the more relevant it is likely to be as a contact for the central bank. In that sense, the above peak associations are the primary interlocutors for the Bundesbank. This is largely reflected in the composition of the roundtable of economists that the Bundesbank invites on a twice-yearly basis, as noted in the institutional context.

This centripetal tendency, however, does not imply that peak associations are the only forms of formal organisation appropriate and able to communicate with the Bundesbank. As the discussion of channels of access to the Bundesbank also shows, the Bundesbank maintains formal contacts with interest groups through the Advisory Boards located at the bank's regional offices, which will be subject to closer examination in part III[452]. In practice, the members of the Advisory Boards have a clear regional background. In the case of representatives of trade and industry the majority are recruited from the regional or local sections of one of the above top-level associations or their member organisations, complemented by a number of members

---

[451] Triesch, Ockenfels (1995), p. 67, Conradt (1989), pp. 103-105, Paterson, Southern (1991), pp. 242-246, Wilson (1990), p. 95.

[452] Especially sub-chapter on the Regional Advisory Boards, p. 302.

from single, mainly local enterprises. Thus, of the 122 members of the nine Advisory Boards, 42 were appointed from trade and industry, 31 of which represented regional or local business associations – i.e. regional or local chambers of trade, commerce or craft, or sectoral business or employers associations – and ten of which represented single enterprises[453]. In as far as they are the main interlocutors in the process of formal communication with the Bundesbank, the regional and sectoral business associations therefore also play an important role in the communication of business interests.

II.1.3.2 Association-specific exposure and issue involvement

The above analysis of the issue context suggests that the overall and directly perceivable impact of monetary and exchange rate policy on German enterprises in trade and industry has been slight in the recent past, thus substantially lowering the incentives for trade and industry groups to become closely involved with monetary affairs as a policy issue. In as far as they do have an impact, however, monetary and exchange rate developments will bear most heavily on enterprises

- which are heavily dependent on bank lending or other forms of debt in their operations, the cost of which responds sensitively to changes in central bank interest rates, i.e. in particular small and medium-sized enterprises and the retail, construction, transport, and utility sectors,
- whose turnover is sensitive to changes in the interest rate environment, e.g. consumption-dependent retail business and, again, the construction sectors,
- which are heavily exposed to exchange rate risk, i.e. through direct or indirect involvement in exports or imports, e.g. the mechanical engineering, chemical and automobile industries.

As an indication, and based on the empirical findings in the issue context above, these exposures can be summarised as in tables 8 and 9 for changes in interest and exchange rates respectively.

---

[453] Figures at end-2003, including commerce and liberal professions.

Business exposure to changes in interest rates

Table 8

Economic exposure		by size of enterprise	by sector
to changes in interest rates	↑ *Higher*	– Large	– Transport – Construction
		– Medium-sized	– Retail – Utility – Manufacturing
	Lower	– Small	– Trade and commerce

Given the structural composition of Germany's peak business associations and their member organisations, the economic exposures at enterprise and sectoral level are likely to be reflected in the aggregated preferences of the peak, sectoral, and regional associations. Thus, the BDI's position on monetary policy may be strongly influenced by the fact that the enterprises in its constituency are, on average, larger than those of the other peak associations such that interest rate-related developments may be relatively less important. At the same time, exchange rate-related developments are likely to be of comparatively high relevance given the marked exposure to foreign trade. In contrast, the DIHK's commitment to the interests of the large number of small and medium-sized enterprises suggests relatively stronger preferences with respect to interest-rate policy, while exchange rate issues may not figure as prominently as in the BDI. The same logic applies, possibly even more so, to the ZDH and HDE, which feature a large proportion of small, domestically oriented enterprises. At the BGA, again, involvement with interest rate-related issues may be comparatively weak, owing to the low weighting of interest expenditure in total costs, but exposure to exchange rate risks may be rather high on average. The sectoral member associations of the umbrella groups representing, for example, the transport, construction and retail sectors are, in turn, likely to be particularly attentive to interest rate trends and less so to exchange rate developments. The opposite should apply to associations in the automotive, mechanical engineering and chemical sectors.

Business exposure to changes in exchange rates

Table 9

Economic exposure		by size of enterprise	by sector
to changes in exchange rates	↑ *Higher*	– Large	– Automotive – Mechanical engineering
		– Medium-sized	– Chemicals – Electronics – Construction
	Lower	– Small	– Other sectors

Despite these general centripetal trends in the potential impact of monetary developments on the aggregate preferences of Germany's large business associations, there is also an important structural element weakening the homogeneity of aggregate preferences and of these entities' overall issue involvement. The wide range of possible interests of affiliated enterprises combined with the large constituencies of the peak associations necessarily result in considerable heterogeneity within each peak association. This is particularly apparent in the case of the DIHK, in which all enterprises – other than the crafts, the liberal professions and agricultural businesses – are indirectly members on a statutory basis. Albeit in a less pronounced manner, this logic also applies to the other peak associations. In as far as interest aggregation within each association results in lowest-common-denominator or median outcomes, the positions reached on monetary or exchange rate issues are likely to be cautious – if, indeed, a common position can be reached at all.

II.1.3.3 Business associations' resource endowment

The resources at the disposal of interest groups are an important determinant of their ability to represent their members' interests forcefully and effectively. As pointed out, this includes financial resources, command of information relevant to communication with policy makers and the ability to apply political or market pressure on policy makers in order to promote their own interests.

With respect to the financial endowment of business associations in Germany, it has been observed that in general German business associations have considerable financial resources at their disposal, drawing on their broad fee-paying membership as well as on substantial additional grants from members and affiliates[454]. Generous financial resources have enabled the associations not only to establish effective lobbying machineries with highly qualified staff working on all political issues of concern to the associations and their members[455], but also to provide far-reaching selective benefits to their members, most importantly legal, business and tax consultancy as well as strategic advice. In principle, therefore, German business associations are in a position to devote substantial resources to the analysis of monetary issues and political work on them.

As to informational resources, German business associations generate a considerable amount of data, statistics, and qualitative information on the economic performance, activities and prospects of their constituencies on a regular basis as well as in the course of individual or irregular fact-finding missions. Generation of information within the associations typically rests on three channels of internal communication:

---

[454] See Triesch, Ockenfels (1995), p. 28. Wilson (1990) describes the BDI's financial resources as lavish (p. 95). Paterson, Southern (1991) find that the member associations of the BDA – which include most peak employers' associations – are extremely well funded (p. 233).

[455] Wilson (1990), p. 95.

- the aggregation of interests and information in the course of the associations' internal decision-making processes via general meetings, committee meetings and working groups,
- the regular or irregular collection of statistical data on the member associations and affiliated enterprises, and
- the regular or irregular conduct of opinion and assessment surveys among the members or affiliates.

The specific value of the information thus produced derives from its industry and sector-specific originality, which in terms of the amount and degree of detail, timely availability, and its often forward-looking nature frequently extends beyond the statistical data collected by official bodies, most importantly the Federal Statistical Office and the Bundesbank itself. As already pointed out, one important question calling for further examination is whether such sector- or region-specific information beyond that already available to the authorities is, in fact, needed when taking the relevant monetary policy decisions.

With respect to the ability to apply political pressure on policy makers, the resources available to private interest groups in Germany are severely restricted by the independent status of the Bundesbank and ECB. As already pointed out in the institutional context, Germany's monetary system has been explicitly designed to limit outside influence on monetary decision making as far as possible. Consequently, there are no direct links enabling private-sector interests to exert pressure on the central bank. Indirectly, influence on the nomination and appointment of Bundesbank decision makers at the governmental and Bundesrat level represents a theoretically possible avenue. The likelihood of its relevance in practice, however, is very slight, given the legal requirements of candidates' qualifications combined with the high degree of competition among candidates and their supporting political factions and the weak incentives for candidates to behave in consistency with their promoters' expectations once they have assumed office. Similarly, monetary policy does not lend itself to pressure from market behaviour by private sector participants.

Overall, therefore, resource endowment presents a varied picture characterised, on the one hand, by the major associations' generally lavish financial and human-capital resources and their potential to contribute – albeit very specific – information to the process of formulating monetary policy and, on the other, the highly limited political and economic leverage on monetary developments and decisions.

II.1.4 Interim conclusions

Analysis of the institutional, issue and group contexts of business interest group activity on monetary policy in Germany shows that the task environment within which trade and industry associations and their members formulate and express their preferences with regard to monetary and exchange rate policy differs considerably from that observed in many other policy areas. The findings can be summarised as follows.

Institutional context

- The conduct of monetary policy in Germany has been embedded in a well-defined institutional and procedural framework, which shapes the communication of interests from the private sector in a number of important respects.
- Communication of interests is facilitated, in principle, by the fact that monetary decisions are isolated from other policy areas and delegated to one single expert institution, the central bank. This also applies to exchange rate policies as long as no exchange rate agreements are concluded at an intergovernmental level.
- Communication of interests is, at the same time, hampered by the Bundesbank's special status as an institution independent of political influence, a principle safeguarded in institutional and personnel respects. This independence largely obstructs indirect influence via the surrounding political framework, especially the government or parliament, and also reflects on potential direct relations with the Bundesbank.
- The Bundesbank is largely self-sufficient in terms of resources, including material, informational and personnel resources. As a result of the high level of experience and expertise, the bank does not in essence rely on external input in the form of policy advice and information.
- Due to its federal structure the Bundesbank, in its former role and today as part of the ESCB, theoretically offers a multitude of institutional points of access for interest groups. Formal and semi-formal access, however, is limited in scope and restricted to an advisory role relatively far removed from the nucleus of decision making. The remoteness of these potential avenues increased with the 2002 Bundesbank reform.
- The insulating properties of the institutional framework also reflect on the behavioural patterns of Bundesbank decision makers, who regard their political independence as an essential condition for the proper pursuit of their primary objective. The latter is the dominating motivation behind their decisions, strengthened by strict, even though not absolute, self-imposed policy rules.

– This institutional framework – as depicted in chart 41 below[456] – may have discouraging effects on interest groups trying to communicate their monetary policy interests.

Channels of direct influence on the Bundesbank

Chart 41

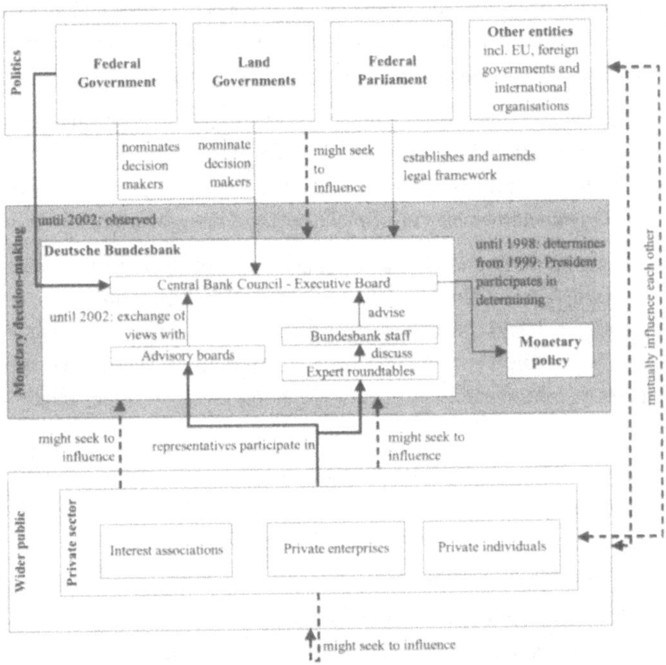

Issue context

– The issue context is dominated by historically rooted anti-inflationary sentiment among the German population as in general, and the business community in particular. This coincides with the Bundesbank's objectives. As to the primary purpose of monetary policy, therefore, there is strong agreement between monetary policy makers and the business sector.

– With respect to this primary purpose, the Bundesbank – and since 1999 the ECB – have delivered a remarkably positive performance, keeping inflation low by

[456] Chart 41 shows the potential direct channels of influence. For the sake of simplicity, indirect channels, especially the media, have not been included. Nevertheless, they may play an important role in mediating, mitigating, or amplifying mutual influence in the policy arena.

historical and international standards and effectively countering surges in wages and prices.

- The transmission of monetary decisions into the economy has been accompanied by significant changes in the interest rate environment for businesses over the past decades. The impact of these changes, however, has on average been small, owing to the small proportion of interest expenses in German enterprises' total costs and income and the low level and stability of real interest rates.
- A similar picture emerges with the impact of exchange rate developments, where the distortionary effects have been weakened by the historical stabilisation and – eventually – elimination of exchange rates with the other EMU member states, Germany's most important trading partners. Stabilisation, although far less pronounced, has also been achieved with respect to the major non-EMU exchange rates.
- Despite these general trends and structures weakening the involvement of business interests with monetary and exchange rate affairs, some sectors are particularly exposed to interest and exchange rate developments. These include the transport, construction, and retail sectors, where corporate financing and demand from end-customers are particularly exposed to interest rates. Similarly, the automotive, mechanical engineering, chemical and electronics sectors are particularly involved in foreign trade. In addition, small and medium-sized enterprises are likely to be more exposed to changes in interest rates and can less easily access derivatives markets to hedge against interest and exchange rate risks.
- Issue involvement is additionally weakened by the fact that monetary and exchange rate related policy issues have, in the past years, been dominated by a whole range of other economic policy issues on the political agenda. Only in periods of strong international and domestic monetary and exchange rate pressures – and increasingly less so since the 1980s – has monetary policy assumed a significant position on the economic policy agenda.

Group context

- Interest aggregation and expression with respect to monetary and exchange rate issues is achieved through the existing infrastructure of business associations and their peak associations. Given its insignificance in terms of impact and urgency, monetary policy has not aroused sufficient attention to provoke the formation of dedicated cause groups.
- Germany's peak business associations feature a wide and heterogeneous membership in terms of both the size of the enterprises represented and their

sectoral affiliation. This heterogeneity hampers the efficient aggregation of interests with regard to monetary and exchange rate policy.

- Downstream interest associations – especially the sector-specific organisations – are likely to find it easier to formulate common positions. Their importance, however, may be severely limited by the Bundesbank's strong economy-wide outlook, in which particular interests are relevant only insofar as they are conducive to reaching conclusions on the monetary conditions in the economy as a whole.
- Given the Bundesbank's strong institutional status and the logic of monetary policy, the scope for exerting political or economic pressure on monetary policy makers is negligible.
- That said, German business associations do have substantial resources at their disposal in terms of both funding and human capital, and they generate a wealth of original information for use in the discourse with policy makers.

II.2 After entry into EMU: a new policy context

By establishing the European Monetary Union and its associated institutions and policy processes, the EU has elevated monetary decision making from the national to the EU level. Accordingly, the member states participating in EMU, i.e. those member states without a derogation or an opt-out as defined in the EC Treaty[457], have surrendered individual monetary sovereignty, handing it over to the EU to be exercised by the newly created institutional superstructure of the ESCB. The ECB, as the repository of the participating member states' monetary sovereignty, determines the single monetary policy for the entire euro area – a larger and more heterogeneous monetary area than existed in any of the constituent member states prior to EMU. This applies not only to macro-level economic development and market structures, but also to the underlying corporate interests in trade and industry. The institutional, issue and group contexts within which corporate interests regarding monetary policy are formulated and articulated by interest groups in Germany have changed as a result. These changes are traced in the following sections, where it will be argued that there are a number of factors complicating the representation of interests, while the potential for disagreement with monetary policy has intensified.

II.2.1 Institutional context

Entry into EMU has fundamentally altered the institutional context of interest-group activity on monetary policy. Even though the new institutional structures and policy processes established in the form of the ECB are largely familiar as such – especially to observers from Germany, since the ECB's set-up and operations resemble those of the Bundesbank in many ways –, the institutional framework within which interest groups articulate their interests is altogether novel. After all, for the first time in decades, the primary addressee of concerns related to monetary issues has changed, as the locus of monetary decision making has been shifted to a new level superimposed on the existing structures. As a result, old channels of access and communication have diminished in importance, while new ones have opened up.

Most importantly, the locus of monetary decision making has shifted to a newly-established institution whose mandate – although similar to that of the Bundesbank – puts it in a stronger position within the constitutional and political system of the EU

[457] Article 122, EC Treaty, provides for the possibility of the Council granting derogation to individual member states, exempting them temporarily from participation in the Third Stage of monetary union and from the relevant Treaty provisions as enlisted in Article 122 (3), EC Treaty. At the time of writing, member states with derogation were Cyprus, the Czech Republic, Estonia, Hungary, Latvia, Lithuania, Malta, Poland, the Slovak Republic, Slovenia, and Sweden. Denmark and the United Kingdom have been granted an opt-out from EMU by way of Protocols 11 and 12 of the Maastricht Treaty. For details on the institutional and procedural provisions see Smits (1997), pp. 134-139.

than that of the Bundesbank in Germany. Most notably, the legal basis of the ECB, including its statutes, is anchored in the EC Treaty, giving it quasi-constitutional status. Apart from the legal implication that it thus enjoys a higher legal status than the Bundesbank, this carries important political implications inasmuch as amendment of the ECB's legal status or any of the provisions in its legal basis requires amendment of the EC Treaty, which in turn presupposes a unanimous decision on the part of all 25 EU member states. Given the difficulty in reaching such consensus, the probability of an alteration in any of the statutory provisions governing the ECB, most particularly essential provisions pertaining to the bank's independence and objectives, is very slight. This specific position renders the position of the ECB within the EU's constitutional and political system stronger than that enjoyed by any other central bank[458].

Like the Bundesbank, the ECB's mandate encompasses the exclusive assignment of tasks related to monetary policy. These include

- definition and implementation of the single monetary policy of the Community,
- the conduct of foreign exchange operations,
- holding and management of the official foreign reserves of the member states, and
- promotion of the smooth operation of payment systems[459], as well as the
- exclusive right to authorise the issue of banknotes within the Community[460] and to approve the volume of coin issuance by the member states[461].
- In addition, the ECB contributes to the work of the authorities charged with the prudential supervision of credit institutions and with ensuring the stability of the financial system[462].
- The ECB also fulfils advisory functions and must therefore be consulted on any act by the Community or the member states in its area of competence[463].

[458] Smits (1997), pp. 168-169.

[459] Article 105 (2), EC Treaty, and Article 3 (1), Protocol on the Statute of the European System of Central Banks and the European Central Bank. For detailed discussion of the relevant legal aspects see Smits (1997), pp. 193-198.

[460] Article 106 (1), EC Treaty.

[461] Article 106 (2), EC Treaty.

[462] Article 105 (5), EC Treaty, and Article 3 (3), Protocol on the Statute of the European System of Central Banks and the European Central Bank. Further to this task, the Council may confer specific tasks upon the ECB concerning policies related to prudential supervision of credit and other financial institutions with the exception of insurance undertakings (Article 105 (6), EC Treaty).

[463] Article 105 (4), EC Treaty, and Article 4 (a), Protocol on the Statute of the European System of Central Banks and the European Central Bank.

Furthermore, the ECB may submit its opinions to Community institutions or bodies or to national authorities on matters in its area of competence[464].

- Further, the ECB participates in international monetary institutions[465], deciding how the ESCB is represented in international cooperation involving its work[466].
- Finally, the ECB and the national central banks are called on in the Statute of the ESCB to collect the statistical information necessary to properly pursue the bank's objectives, either from the relevant Community or member-state bodies or directly from economic agents[467].

In contrast to monetary decisions, the conclusion of formal agreements on exchange rate systems falls not within the sphere of competence of the ECB, but within the Council's remit. On such matters, however, the ECB has the right to table policy initiatives and present them to the Council in the form of recommendations. Further, the Council is obliged to consult the ECB on any measures within this area of policymaking[468]. This also applies to the formulation of general points of reference for exchange rate policy in relation to currencies for which no formal exchange rate arrangements exist[469]. In addition, the ECB needs to be consulted on Community positions at international level concerning issues of particular relevance to economic and monetary union[470].

As in the case of the Bundesbank, the ECB's activities in the field of monetary policy are governed by the principles of political independence and the objective of pursuing price stability. As to independence, the political autonomy of the ECB is explicitly rooted in the text of the Treaty:

> "When exercising the powers and carrying out the tasks and duties conferred upon them by this Treaty and the Statute of the ESCB, neither the ECB, nor a national central bank, nor any member of their decision-making bodies shall seek or take instructions from Community institutions or bodies, from any government of a Member State or from any other body. The Community institutions and bodies and the governments of the Member

---

464 Article 105 (4), EC Treaty, and Article 4 (b), Protocol on the Statute of the European System of Central Banks and the European Central Bank.

465 Article 6 (2), Protocol on the Statute of the European System of Central Banks and the European Central Bank.

466 Article 6 (1), Protocol on the Statute of the European System of Central Banks and the European Central Bank.

467 Article 5, Protocol on the Statute of the European System of Central Banks and the European Central Bank.

468 Article 111 (1), EC Treaty, and Article 111 (3), EC Treaty.

469 Article 111 (2), EC Treaty.

470 Article 111 (4), EC Treaty.

States undertake to respect this principle and not to seek to influence the members of the decision-making bodies of the ECB or of the national central banks in the performance of their tasks."[471]

The provision establishes the principle of central bank autonomy for the ECB going beyond the relevant provisions in the original Bundesbank Act in two important respects. First, it is defined as applying explicitly not only to the government, but to all political bodies at EU and member-state level as well as to any other body. By virtue of the latter provision, the independence of the ECB also implicitly applies to influence from the private sector. Second, ECB independence is defined not only to the extent that monetary decision makers shall not take instructions from these bodies, but also that they shall not seek such instructions in the first place[472]. As already pointed out with respect to the Bundesbank, these strict provisions and their legal status – based on the Treaty requirement that the law of all national central banks be compatible with the provisions in the Treaty itself as well as in the ECB's Statute[473] – also apply to all national central banks. The ECB's particular institutional status is underscored by its position within the EU political system. The ECB is endowed with a legal personality of its own[474] and the most extensive legal capacity enjoyed by legal persons in the member states[475], allowing it to act autonomously without the need to derive its authority and competences from being an organ of the Community[476].

The overall political and operational independence of the ECB has been underpinned by elements securing personnel and financial autonomy. As to independence of the personnel, the members of the ECB's Executive Board have to be of recognised standing and professional experience in monetary or banking matters[477]. They are appointed[478] by common accord of the governments of the member states at the level of Heads of State or Government on a recommendation from the Council after the latter has consulted the European Parliament and the Governing Council of the

---

[471] Article 108, EC Treaty, and Article 7, Protocol on the Statute of the European System of Central Banks and the European Central Bank.

[472] Smits (1997), p. 161.

[473] Article 109, EC Treaty.

[474] Article 107 (2), EC Treaty.

[475] Article 9 (1), Protocol on the Statute of the European System of Central Banks and the European Central Bank.

[476] Smits (1997), p. 162.

[477] Article 112 (2.b.), EC Treaty, and Article 11 (2), Protocol on the Statute of the European System of Central Banks and the European Central Bank. For a detailed discussion see Smits (1997), pp. 162-164.

[478] Chart 42 illustrates the appointment procedure.

ECB[479], for an eight-year, non-renewable term of office. Executive Board members are protected against dismissal on political grounds in as far as removal from office is limited to cases in which a member no longer satisfies the conditions for performance of his duties, or to cases of serious misconduct. In either instance, the decision on compulsory retirement rests with the European Court of Justice, following an application by the ECB's Governing Council or Executive Board[480]. Finally, members of the Executive Board are prohibited from engaging in occupations outside the bank during their term of office, irrespective of whether such activity is gainful or not, unless exemption is expressly granted by the Governing Council[481]. A similar, albeit not as strict, body of rules has been devised for the other members of the Governing Council, i.e. the Governors of the national central banks. Thus, the statute requires a minimum term of office of five years and stipulates that they may be dismissed only for the same strict reasons of health and misconduct that apply to the members of the Executive Board[482]. Decisions to this effect may also be referred to the European Court of Justice[483]. No explicit rules have been established at EU level with respect to the professional background and expertise of the Governors of the national central banks or to possible limitations on the renewal of office and the holding of positions outside the ESCB during their term of office. These details have been left to the national legislators. Nevertheless, the relevant article in the ECB Statute reiterates that national rules need to be in conformity with the provision made in the Treaty and the ECB Statute[484].

The financial independence of the ECB is secured by its endowment with equity as well as the returns it generates on its activities in the financial and foreign exchange markets. The bank's equity, amounting to EUR 5 bn, is owned by the national central banks, who are the sole subscribers and holders[485]. The national central banks'

---

479 Article 112 (2.b.), EC Treaty, and Article 11 (2), Protocol on the Statute of the European System of Central Banks and the European Central Bank.

480 Article 11 (2), Protocol on the Statute of the European System of Central Banks and the European Central Bank.

481 Article 11 (1), Protocol on the Statute of the European System of Central Banks and the European Central Bank. For a discussion, especially with respect to the ability of Board members to take up professional positions after their service at the ECB, see Smits (1997), p. 163-164.

482 Smits (1997), p. 165.

483 Article 14 (2), Protocol on the Statute of the European System of Central Banks and the European Central Bank. The role accorded to the European Court of Justice in this context is unusual, given that the appointment and release of decision makers at national central banks comes within the remit of the member states. For a discussion of the legal implications see Smits (1997), pp. 165-166.

484 Article 14 (1), Protocol on the Statute of the European System of Central Banks and the European Central Bank.

485 Article 28, Protocol on the Statute of the European System of Central Banks and the European Central Bank. The shares of individual national central banks in the ECB's capital are determined

monetary income is redistributed among them at the end of each fiscal year. The net profits of the ECB are allocated to the bank's general reserve fund[486] and to the shareholder national central banks[487].

Overview ECB appointment procedures

Chart 42

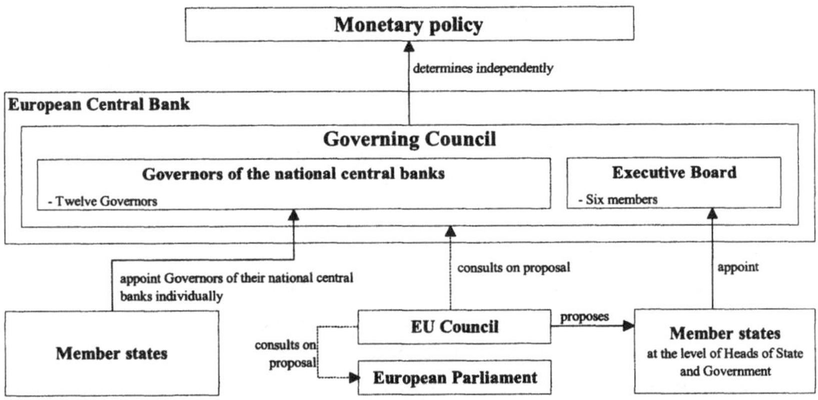

Source: Articles 11 and 12, Protocol on the Statute of the European System of Central Banks and the European Central Bank

Despite its considerable degree of autonomy, the ECB does not operate in political isolation either, but is required by the Treaty to cooperate with the other decision makers at EU level. The obligation to cooperate with the Community institutions is established in four respects: first, the general obligation to support the economic policies in the Community, second, the mutual participation in meetings as provided in the Treaty, third, the fulfilment of Treaty-based information requirements, and, fourth, participation in the Community's economic-policy coordination processes.

With respect to supporting the economic policies in the Community, the Treaty requires the ESCB as a whole – including the ECB and the national central banks – to support these policies with a view to contributing to the achievement of Community

by a key for subscription defined in Article 29 (1), Protocol on the Statute of the European System of Central Banks and the European Central Bank. For details see e.g. Görgens et al. (2001), pp. 66-72.

486 The share of the ECB's net profit allocated to its general reserve fund may not exceed 20% of the net profit (Article 33 (1), Protocol on the Statute of the European System of Central Banks and the European Central Bank).

487 Distribution of the net profit from the ECB among the shareholding national central banks follows the proportions they hold in the ECB's capital (Article 33 (1), Protocol on the Statute of the European System of Central Banks and the European Central Bank). For details see e.g. Görgens et al. (2001), pp. 66-72.

objectives[488]. In addition, the ESCB is required to act in accordance with the principle of an open market economy with free competition, favouring an efficient allocation of resources[489], and in compliance with the principles of ensuring stable prices, sound public finances and monetary conditions and a sustainable balance of payments[490]. The importance of these constraints, however, is limited by two factors. In the first place, the obligation refers to general economic policies and does not extend to single, specific policy measures. This is quite similar to the requirements in the Bundesbank Act. Second, the ECB's obligation to support general economic policies must be considered a comparatively weak legal and political constraint on its actions, as no single general economic policy exists at Community level; there is only a set of national economic policies, whose mutual coordination and consistency the member states are committed by the Treaty to strive for[491]. In economic terms, however, the absence of a single economic policy makes the task of the ECB more difficult in practice, as the impact of its policies varies across the member states because of theirdifferent national economic rules[492].

As to mutual participation in meetings, the Treaty stipulates that the President of the Council and a member of the Commission may participate in the meetings of the ECB's Governing Council. The Council President and the Commissioner are not entitled to vote on the Governing Council, but the President of the Council may submit a motion for deliberation by the Governing Council[493]. A right to call for the postponement of monetary decisions, as was the case with the Bundesbank, has not been written into the Treaty[494]. Conversely, the President of the ECB must be invited to participate in Council meetings when the Council is discussing matters pertaining to the objectives and tasks of the ESCB[495]. Finally, the President of the ECB and the other members of the Executive Board may be heard by the relevant committees of the European Parliament, either at Parliament's request or on the ECB's own initiative[496].

---

488 Article 105 (1), EC Treaty.

489 Article 105 (1), EC Treaty.

490 The principles referred to in Article 105 (1), EC Treaty, are contained in Article 4, EC Treaty. Here especially Article 4 (3), EC Treaty. For an interpretation of the principles of the Community and those underlying EMU, as well as of the implications of these principles for the behaviour of the ECB, see Smits (1997), pp. 190-192.

491 Smits (1997), p. 187.

492 Smits (1997), p. 187. For an extensive discussion of the legal implications and political implications of the ECB's obligation to support the general economic polices in the Community see Smits (1997), pp. 187-192.

493 Article 113 (1), EC Treaty.

494 For details see Smits (1997), pp. 170-171.

495 Article 113 (2), EC Treaty. For details see Smits (1997), pp. 173-174.

496 Article 113 (3), EC Treaty. For details see Smits (1997), p. 174.

In practice, the President of the ECB appears before the European Parliament Committee on Economic and Monetary Affairs on a quarterly basis to report on the bank's monetary policy and answer questions[497].

With respect to reporting requirements, three elements have been established in the Treaty. First, the ECB is required to draw up and publish reports on the activities of the ESCB at least once a quarter. In addition, a consolidated financial statement of the ESCB has to be published each week. Finally, the ECB is required to address an annual report on the activities of the ESCB and on the monetary policy of the previous and current year to the European Parliament, the European Council, the Commission, and the EU Council. All reports and statements in this respect must be made available to the public free of charge.[498]

As regards the interplay of the institutions and actors involved in the various areas of economic policymaking, the EU has responded to the asymmetry between the single European monetary policy and the fact that other major fields of economic policymaking – notably fiscal, structural, and wage and labour-market policies – have remained in the national domain, by strengthening economic-policy coordination among the member states. The relevant policy processes range from single policies, which include the monetary policy of the ECB, to weakly coordinated initiatives among the various decision makers and other parties involved, as shown in table 10. Besides the single monetary policy, the ECB also plays a legally manifested role in formulation of the euro area's single exchange rate policy as well as in the – weakly coordinated – external representation and communication of euro area economic policies. In addition to policy processes established by the Treaty, further processes of economic-policy coordination have been devised, in some of which the ECB plays a part.

Euro area economic policy coordination centres on the Broad Economic Policy Guidelines, which the Council adopts on an annual basis. The aim of the Guidelines is to present broad recommendations for policy actors on macroeconomic and structural policies, and to provide a yardstick for *ex post* assessment in the context of multilateral surveillance[499]. The Guidelines are not legally binding, and compliance is based on peer pressure, which can be reinforced by means of Council recommendations to non-compliant member states[500]. The general guidelines formulated in the course of this

---

497 European Central Bank (2004), p. 69.

498 Article 15, Protocol on the Statute of the European System of Central Banks and the European Central Bank. See also Smits (1997), pp. 174-175.

499 European Commission (2002), p. 5.

500 Recommendations to promote compliance with the Broad Economic Policy Guidelines were issued by the Council for the first time in 2001 (European Commission (2002), p. 5). Ex post surveillance of compliance with the Guidelines is provided by means of annual Implementation Reports.

procedure are complemented by four coordination processes aimed at strengthening overall economic stability and cohesion within the euro area. First, the Stability and Growth Pact provides rules for disciplining fiscal policies in the member states. Second, the Luxembourg Process aims at devising employment guidelines on labour markets in the member states.

Forms of economic-policy coordination in the EU

Table 10

	Policy Area	Policy co-ordination: Form	Policy co-ordination: Mode	Actors involved	Procedures
Single policy	Monetary policy	Single policy, euro area	Single institution	**ECB**	
	Exchange rate policy	Single policy, euro area	Coordination in the Council	Council **ECB** Eurogroup Commission	
	Competition policy	Single policy	Implementation by the Commission	Member states Commission Council	
Close coordination	Budgetary policies, balances	Treaty rules Common rules Common objectives Information exchange Peer review	Coordination in the Council Joint fora	Member states Commission Council Eurogroup	Excessive Deficit Procedure Stability and Growth Pact Broad Economic Policy Guidelines
	Structural policies	Rules Joint decisions Council directives Peer review	Coordination in the Council	Member states Commission Council	
Weak coordination	Policy mix	Dialogue Information exchange	Joint fora	**ECB** Commission Council Eurogroup Social partners	
	Budgetary policies, quality of public finnaces	Commonly agreed objectives	Coordination in the Council	Member states Commission Council Eurogroup	Broad Economic Policy Guidelines Stability and Growth Pact
	Wage developments	Dialogue Information exchange	Joint fora	Social partners Commission Council **ECB**	Macroeconomic dialogue, Cologne Process Broad Economic Policy Guidelines
	Labour market policies	Information exchange Best practices Guidelines Peer reviews	Coordination in the Council	Member states Commission Council Social partners	Employment guidelines, Luxembourg Process Broad Economic Policy Guidelines
	Product and capital market policies	Information exchange Best practices Guidelines Peer reviews	Coordination in the Council	Member states Commission Council	Reports on economic reform, Cardiff Process Broad Economic Policy Guidelines
	External representation and communication	Common understanding	Joint fora	**ECB** Eurogroup Commission	

Source: European Commission (2002), p. 4

Third, the stability and efficient functioning of product and capital markets is subject to economic reforms coordinated in the course of the Cardiff Process. Finally, the Cologne Process aims at improving the interaction of macroeconomic policies and wage developments with a view to supporting non-inflationary growth and employment[501]. The ECB's participation in EU economic policy coordination is – save for informal exchanges of information among policy makers and the social partners in other EU forums not directly related to monetary policy – restricted to the Macroeconomic Dialogue, in the course of which representatives of the Council, the ECB, the Commission and the social partners meet to discuss economic policy and other matters of common interest. Being the ECB's only formal channel of communication with representatives from private interest groups, this dialogue is analysed in more detail below.

Overall, the ECB's independence is thus complemented by a range of instruments designed to ensure cooperation between the various decision makers and consistency of the policy processes at EU level. Most importantly however, none of the provisions may impair the independence of the ECB and its personnel in the pursuit of their tasks. In particular, influence on the ECB's monetary policy may emanate neither from the ECB's obligation to support general economic policies nor from its participation in the Community's economic policy coordination.

Next to political independence, the second major element in the EMU's monetary framework is that the ECB and the national central banks have been committed at Treaty level to the primary objective of maintaining price stability in the euro area[502]. Closely related to the above observations, the provision identifies price stability as the priority objective, while other aims of economic policy – i.e. support for general economic policies in the Community and for the principle of the Community – are strictly subordinate. As in the case of the Bundesbank, the primary objective is not defined in closer detail by the legal framework, giving the bank the authority to establish its own definitions of the concepts and to devise the intermediary targets it deems appropriate for its work[503]. Unlike the case of the Bundesbank, the Treaty clearly refers to internal price stability as the reference value for the ECB's work, so that maintaining stability of the external value of the euro does not fall within the bank's remit[504].

---

501 For a detailed description of the policy processes see European Commission (2002). The processes are illustrated in chart 43 on page 195.

502 Article 105 (1), EC Treaty, and Article 2, Protocol on the Statute of the European System of Central Banks and the European Central Bank.

503 Smits (1997) emphasises the point that no definition of price stability is provided in the Treaty and that the ECB is free to determine for itself what level of price stability it deems acceptable in the context of its overriding objective. With respect to the latter, Smits emphasises that there are no checks on the ECB's auto-interpretation other than the possibility of appeal to the European Court of Justice on the grounds of infringement of Treaty obligations, and the political weight of judgement by the European Parliament, to which the ECB reports (pp. 186-187).

504 Smits (1997), p. 184. Exchange rate developments may nevertheless influence monetary decisions inasmuch as they impact on the internal value of the currency.

Economic policy coordination in EMU

Chart 43

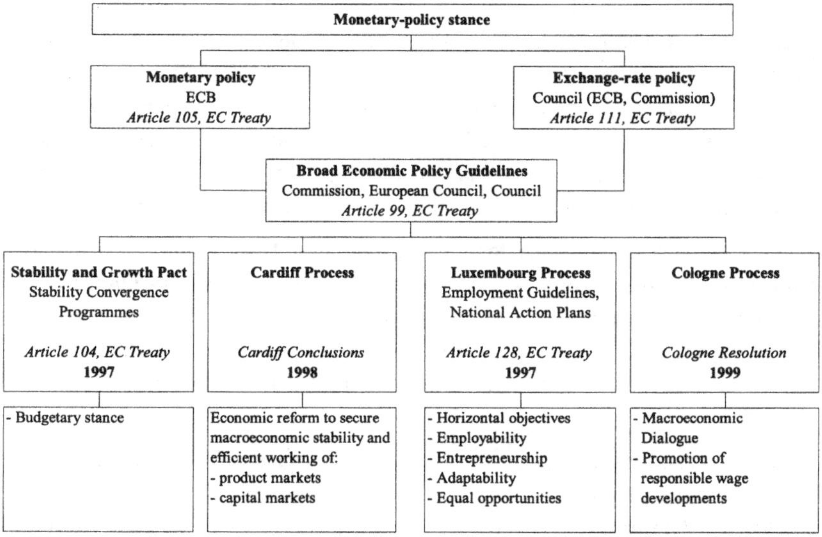

Source: European Commission (2001), p. 5

In order to achieve this objective, the ECB is not only free to define own policy targets, it is also furnished with a wide choice of policy instruments. In dealing with credit institutions, public entities and other market participants[505], the ECB can conduct open-market operations and credit operations, and can decide on other operational methods of monetary control as it sees fit[506]. The general principles governing the use of these instruments are established by the ECB itself[507]. With respect to external operations involving central banks and financial institutions in other countries or international organisations, the ECB may, furthermore, undertake spot and forward foreign exchange transactions in all types of assets, including securities and precious metals, hold and manage these assets, and conduct all types of banking

[505] Article 17, Protocol on the Statute of the European System of Central Banks and the European Central Bank. With respect to operations with public entities, the Statute prohibits overdrafts, the purchase of debt instruments or any other type of credit facility with the ECB or with the national central banks in favour of Community institutions or bodies, central governments, regional local or other public authorities, and any other public authorities (Article 21 (1), Protocol on the Statute of the European System of Central Banks and the European Central Bank).

[506] Article 18 (1), Protocol on the Statute of the European System of Central Banks and the European Central Bank.

[507] Article 18 (2), Protocol on the Statute of the European System of Central Banks and the European Central Bank.

transactions with third countries and international organisations, including borrowing and lending[508].

Overall, the ECB, in conjunction with the national central banks, therefore occupies an eminent position within the EU's constitutional and political system and exercises a great degree of autonomy – with regard to its monetary decision-making, to the targets and to the instruments it applies in the pursuit of its objectives. As a consequence, and in certain respects more so than the Bundesbank prior to EMU, the ECB enjoys wide room for manoeuvre in designing and conducting its policies, making it the central addressee for private-sector interests in the area of monetary and exchange rate policy.

Although the central addressee for monetary policy-related interests, because of its narrowly defined institutional accessibility the ECB offers only very limited avenues for the communication of interests. As in the case of the Bundesbank, low accessibility results from the secluded monetary decision-making process as well as the political, human and material resources that also make the ECB largely self-sufficient in its operation.

Monetary decision making within the ESCB is in the hands of the ECB. Although the Treaty defines monetary policy objectives and tasks for the ESCB as a whole[509], it is up to the ECB to ensure that they are implemented, either by its own activities or through the national central banks[510]. Within the ECB, decisions are taken by its two decision making bodies, the Governing Council and the Executive Board[511]. The former is composed of the presidents of the national central banks and the members of the Executive Board itself, which, in turn, comprises the president and vice president of the ECB and four further members[512]. The Governing Council adopts the guidelines and takes the decisions necessary to ensure performance of the ESCB's duties, including the formulation of Community monetary policy, the adoption of intermediate monetary objectives, the setting of interest rates and management of the ESCB reserves. The Executive Board is in charge of implementing monetary policy, instructs the national central banks, performs other duties delegated to it by the

---

508 Article 23, Protocol on the Statute of the European System of Central Banks and the European Central Bank.

509 For a discussion of the legal background of the allocation of objectives, tasks, and functions to the ESCB as a whole, to the ECB and to the national central banks see Smits (1997), pp. 178-180.

510 Article 9 (2), Protocol on the Statute of the European System of Central Banks and the European Central Bank.

511 Article 9 (3), Protocol on the Statute of the European System of Central Banks and the European Central Bank.

512 Article 11 (1), Protocol on the Statute of the European System of Central Banks and the European Central Bank.

Governing Council, and prepares the meetings of the Governing Council[513]. The national central banks support the ECB in its policies and are subject to the instructions of the Governing Council and the Executive Board[514].

The meetings of the Governing Council at which monetary policy decisions are taken have to be held at least ten times a year by statute[515]. Monetary decisions are taken by a simple majority, with each member of the Council casting one vote[516]. This shall be cast by the members of the Council in a personal capacity only, irrespective of their national origins[517]. The President of the Council and a member of the Commission are, as already mentioned, entitled to attend Governing Council meetings, but are prohibited from voting. The President of the Council may, however, submit a motion for deliberation.

As far as private-sector interest groups are concerned, the monetary decision making process, as summarised in chart 44, is thus largely shielded from external political pressures or influence. Going by the statutory provisions, and save for the optional attendance of Council or Commission representatives[518], monetary decisions are taken exclusively within the ECB and with the support of the national central banks. Formal means of communicating external views, e.g. via an advisory body representing private-sector or academic opinions on monetary policy, have not been devised at Treaty level.

---

513 Article 12 (1) and Article 12 (2), Protocol on the Statute of the European System of Central Banks and the European Central Bank.

514 Article 14 (3), Protocol on the Statute of the European System of Central Banks and the European Central Bank.

515 Article 10 (5), Protocol on the Statute of the European System of Central Banks and the European Central Bank. In practice, the Governing Council meets every two weeks. The first meeting in each month is regarded as particularly relevant for monetary decisions, as it is followed by a press conference held by the president and vice president of the ECB, in which the bank presents its policy-relevant assessment of economic developments to the public (European Central Bank (2004), p. 69).

516 Voting modalities will change once the number of member states participating in EMU exceeds fifteen. While the six members of the Executive Board will retain a permanent voting right, the votes of the Governors of the national central banks will be subject to a rotation system (European Central Bank (2004), p. 12).

517 European Central Bank (2004), p. 12.

518 Smits (1997) rightly points out that the presence of the President of the Council as well as a Commission member has to be understood as a possibility for the two bodies to make their views on economic and monetary conditions freely known to the Governing Council. An exchange of views appears to have been explicitly encouraged by the legislator, as the possibility for the President of the Council to table a motion suggests (pp. 171-172).

Organisation of ECB monetary policy decision making

Chart 44

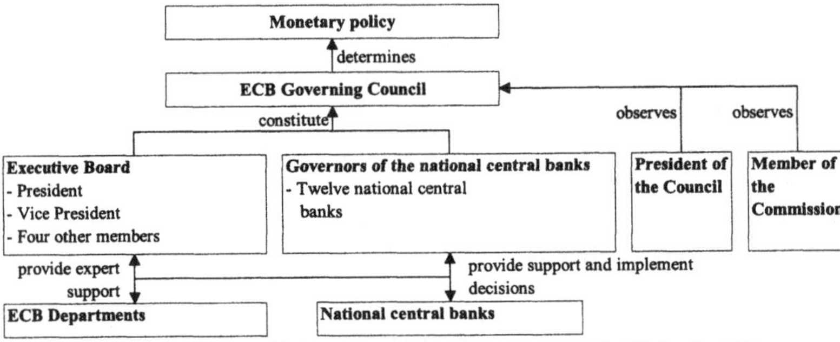

Source: EC Treaty and Protocol on the Statute of the European System of Central Banks and the European Central Bank, various articles

Despite the lack of institutionalised direct communication between the ECB and the private sector as provided in the Treaty, channels for articulating interests nevertheless exist. In the first place, formal forums exist outside the Treaty, in the context of which the ECB discusses its policies with external political players and market participants through the various mechanisms of the Community's economic policy coordination. The ECB's participation in EU economic policy coordination is – save for informal exchanges of information among policy makers and the social partners in other EU forums not directly related to monetary policy – restricted to the Macroeconomic Dialogue. At the same time, the Macroeconomic Dialogue represents the only formal channel of communication between the ECB and representatives of the private sector. The rationale[519] and objectives of the Macroeconomic Dialogue were laid down in the resolutions of the 1999 Cologne Council:

[519] The Council's resolution to set up the Macroeconomic Dialogue goes back to an initiative by the then German Council Presidency, which felt inspired by the concept of Germany's Konzertierte Aktion (European Commission (2002), p. 40). The plan to solve the economic and financial problems besetting the Federal Republic at that time by coordinating the actions of government, representatives of employers and employees and representatives of other economic interest groups was first put into practice on February 14, 1967 and subsequently anchored in the 1967 Law for Stability and Growth. On that basis, it was conceived as an instrument for the Federal Government to formulate broad, non-binding macroeconomic guidelines, whose implementation was sought by means of joint action with the major economic interest groups in society. In practice, the effects of Konzertierte Aktionen remained highly limited. While representing a tool for communicating views and interests, and despite providing important psychological stimuli at a time of economic recession, the dialogue proved ineffective as a means of resolving conflicts of interest among the participants. As a result, disagreement resurfaced once the recession of the late 1960s had been weathered. As from the early 1970s, this led to high wage demands by the trade unions, intransigence on the part of employers and a tightening of the monetary stance by the Bundesbank. Eventually meetings under the heading of Konzertierte Aktionen were discontinued from 1977, after the trade unions had withdrawn their participation. For detailed discussions see e.g. Weimer (1998), pp. 186-189, and Härtel (1999). For a contrasting view, attributing failure of the

sector and the central bank. Given the presence of other policy makers and the group's broad mandate, discussions are not solely destined to get business associations and the ECB talking, but aim at a multilateral exchange of views on a potentially wide variety of issues relevant to the coordination of economic policies between the member states, the Commission, the ECB and the major representatives of labour market participants. In addition, the formulation of the Dialogue's mandate strongly suggests that, in theory at least, interest groups participate in the Dialogue not to represent the overall commercial interests of their members, but are invited as "social partners", i.e. as representatives of the organisation involved at national level in the wage formation process. On an *ex ante* basis, this limits discussions in the context of the Dialogue to issues related to wages and labour market policies, so that the private-sector representatives' general views on monetary and exchange rate developments in a broader sense are not formally part of the discussions under the terms of the mandate. This reflects the fact that the primary purpose of the Dialogue lies in the coordination of economic policies, especially between the Council, the member states, the Commission and the ECB. Representatives of the private sector are invited for the sake of their role in wage determination and their importance with respect to employment policy[525]. *A priori*, exchanges of views between the representatives of EU business associations and the ECB therefore have to be regarded as ancillary effects of a Dialogue with quite different aims.

Next to the ECB's participation in the Macroeconomic Dialogue at Community level, communication via the national central banks represents a further important potential way in which private-sector interests may influence monetary decision making at Community level. The ECB itself assigns an essential role to the national central banks in its communication strategy, emphasising that in a multicultural and multilingual environment the maintenance of close contacts with national and regional audiences represents an important element in communication of the single monetary policy[526].

Thus, private-sector interests can be communicated via the national central banks within the Eurosystem in as far they have direct or indirect avenues of communication with the private sector. As we saw in the above, the Bundesbank – as one example of a central bank within the Eurosystem – has a number of channels through which it can obtain information from the private sector in Germany formally or informally, not least in the form of the Advisory Councils at the Regional Offices and the roundtable

---

[525] For a comprehensive analysis of the political rationale of the Macroeconomic Dialogue, its importance for economic policy coordination among the institutions and bodies of the Community, and its prospects as an effective body for policy coordination see Heise (2002).

[526] European Central Bank (2004), p. 70. The ECB's emphasis admittedly rests on communicating its policies to national and regional audiences, rather than on receiving feedback and reaction from these audiences.

of economists at the Central Office. Even though different in extent and design, the other national central banks within the Eurosystem have their own patterns of communicating with interest groups. Thus, formal bodies in which private-sector representatives discuss monetary policy with the decision makers exist at three further national central banks, i.e. in the Netherlands, in Belgium, and in Austria, as illustrated in table 11 below. In these cases, as well as in those countries where no such formal bodies have been established, additional semi-formal or informal channels of communication are likely to exist, as well as indirect forms of communication, e.g. via the media or other political bodies in the national political system.

The effectiveness of communication via the national central banks in the Eurosystem is, however, severely limited by two important factors. First, the marginal impact of interventions by interest groups with their respective national central banks is greatly diluted by the fact that each central bank is represented on the ECB's Governing Council by one governor, giving each a comparatively small weighting in the voting process. On the basis of twelve member states participating in the third stage of EMU, this implies a share of one in eighteen votes for each national central bank governor. Thus, even if an interest group were able to influence the governor of its national central bank in a significant way, the final effect of doing so on the ECB's monetary decisions would remain highly uncertain. Influencing monetary decisions via the national central banks is further complicated in that the governors of the national institutions are not entitled to represent national interests on the Governing Council, acting instead in an entirely independent, personal capacity and committed to taking a purely euro area view on monetary decisions[527]. To what extent the governors comply with this rule is of course an open question, especially since monetary decisions are confidential and voting behaviour on the Council is not disclosed by the ECB. However, even if Council members did allow their monetary judgments to be guided by national or, for that matter, sectoral or other particular considerations, the degree of the marginal impact of such considerations on the final decision for the entire euro area would be considerably diminished by the process of monetary decision making within the Eurosystem.

[527] European Central Bank (2004), p. 12.

National central banks and interest groups: formal communication

Table 11

National central bank	Advisory body	Function	Membership	Appointment	Meetings	Legal basis
Banca de España	None					- Law of Autonomy of the Banco de España, 13/1994, June 1, 1994.
Banca d'Italia	None					- Statute of the Banca d'Italia, ratified by Presidential Decree on April 24, 1998.
Banco de Portugal	Advisory Board	- The Board issues non-binding opinions on the annual report of the Bank before its release, on the measures taken by the Bank within the scope of its functions, and on the matters referred to by the Governor or by the Board of Directors.	- The governor of the Bank, the vice-governors, the former governors, four persons of recognised competence in economic, financial and business matters, the chairman of the Portuguese Association of Banks, the chairman of the Public Credit Management Institute, one representative each of the Autonomous Regions of the Azores and Madeira to be appointed by the competent self-government bodies, the chairman of the Advisory Board of the Bank.	- The four competent persons are appointed by the Cabinet on a proposal by the finance minister for renewable terms of three years.	- Regular meetings every six months. - Extraordinary meetings upon convention by the governor.	- Banco de Portugal, Organic Law, approved by Law No. 5/98 of 31 January 1998, as amended by Decree-Law No. 118/2001 of 17 April 2001, especially Chapter V and Chapter V, Section V.

National central banks and interest groups: formal communication

Table 11, continued

National central bank	Advisory body	Function	Membership	Appointment	Meetings	Legal basis
Bank of Greece	None					- Statute of the Bank of Greece, Ninth Edition, 2000. An element of interest-representation has been inserted into the bank's decision-making processes with the requirement that at least three of the twelve members of the bank's General Council must be specifically engaged in the fields of industry, commerce and agriculture. The Councillors – other than the Governor, the Deputy Governors and the other members of the Monetary Policy Council – act on an honorary basis and are elected by the General Meeting of Shareholders for renewable three-year terms. The Councillors are required to act in a personal capacity, i.e. not as representatives of their professions. The Council is not formally involved in monetary policy-related tasks.

National central banks and interest groups: formal communication

Table 11, continued

National central bank	Advisory body	Function	Membership	Appointment	Meetings	Legal basis
Banque Centrale du Luxembourg	None					- Law concerning the monetary status and the Central Bank of Luxembourg, December 23, 1998.
Banque de France	None					- Statute of the Banque de France.
Central Bank of Ireland	None					- Central Bank and Financial Services Authority of Ireland Act, 2003, and Central Bank and Financial Services Authority of Ireland, Annual Report 2002.
De Nederlandsche Bank	Bank Council	- The bank's President reports to the Bank Council on general economic and financial developments and discusses with the Bank Council the policy conducted by the bank and any other issue raised by Council members.	- Two members of the bank's Supervisory Board, plus nine to eleven members. - Appointment in such a way as to ensure that the various sections of society are represented.	- Appointment by the Bank Council itself, upon proposal by the Governing Board.	- Not specified.	- Bank Act 1998 and Articles of Association of De Nederlandsche Bank n.v., here especially Article 17.

National central banks and interest groups: formal communication

Table 11, continued

National central bank	Advisory body	Function	Membership	Appointment	Meetings	Legal basis
Deutsche Bundesbank	Advisory Boards at the Regional Offices	- Confers on execution of tasks in the area of the Regional Office. - Formally no longer concerned with monetary questions.	- Not more than 14 members chosen from the banking sector, trade and industry, commerce, the insurance sector, the liberal professions, agriculture and from among wage and salary earners.	- Members are nominated by the governments of the federal states, appointed by the bank's president.	- Advisory Boards meet twice a year.	- Paragraph 9, Bundesbank Act, as effective from April 30, 2002.
Nationale Bank van België	Council of Regency	- On a monthly basis, the Council exchanges views on general questions concerning the Bank, monetary policy and the economic situation of the country and the European Community.	- The Council of Regency is composed of the bank's Governor, its directors and ten regents. - Two regents are chosen on the proposal of the most representative labour organisations, three regents are proposed by the most representative organisations from industry and commerce, from agriculture and from small firms and traders, and five regents are proposed by the Minister of Finance.	- Regents are elected for a three-year, renewable term by the bank's General Meeting.	- Monthly meetings.	- Organic Law of the National Bank of Belgium, February 22, 1998, Articles 20 and Article 23 (3).

National central banks and interest groups: formal communication

Table 11, continued

National central bank	Advisory body	Function	Membership	Appointment	Meetings	Legal basis
Oester-reichische National-bank	General Council	- Advises the Governing Board on the conduct of the Bank's business and in matters of monetary policy.	- Council consists of a President, one Vice President and twelve other members. - Members of the General Council are required to be persons prominent in some business sector or lawyers or economists, and to include representatives of credit institutions, industry, small business and trade, agriculture, and salaried employees and wage-earners.	- President, vice president and six other members of the General Council are appointed by the Federal Government. - The remaining members of the Council are elected by the bank's General Meeting.	- Joint meetings of the General Council and the OeNB's Governing Board take place at least once every quarter.	- National Bank Act, especially Articles 20 through 31.
Suomen Pankki	None					- Act on the Bank of Finland, 214/1998, March 27, 1998.

Finally, beyond formal institutional arrangements, the ECB is also involved in a range of informal contacts with its environment. Thus, the members of the Executive Board and Governing Council are known to take on a large number of public engagements, including appearances and speeches at public events and interviews. They also receive visitors from the general public as well as experts from a variety of institutions. In addition, the ECB describes itself as committed to open dialogue with the academic world.[528]

In addition to the monetary decision makers' mandate and accessibility, EMU is also likely to confront interest-group representatives with behavioural patterns on the part of policy makers varying to some extent from those encountered in the past. As observed above, Bundesbank policy makers' behaviour has been characterised by a strong commitment to the principles manifested in the bank's legal framework, i.e. a strong pledge to institutional and personal independence and to the primary objective of price stability, especially in the form of imposing self-binding policy targets and strategies. Both patterns of behaviour have been observable over several decades of the bank's operations.

The ECB, in contrast, is a very young institution, which means that it is still too early to identify historically rooted behavioural patterns with any degree of certainty. Commitment by ECB policy makers to the bank's fundamental legal principles of independence and the pursuit of price stability are, nevertheless, already evident. As to independence, the specific status of the ECB in the Treaty and within the Community's political system has been consistently stressed by ECB officials as an essential prerequisite for pursuing anti-inflationary monetary policies[529].

Similarly, the ECB has filled out the broad objective of maintaining price stability with intermediary targets and an explicit strategy, limiting its own discretion and making its policy measures more transparent. By and large, the ECB adopted principles for its policymaking similar to those of the Bundesbank's prior to 1999, although in a formally different manner. The ECB's monetary strategy consists of two elements:

- a quantitative definition of the primary objective of the single monetary policy, namely price stability, and
- a two-pillar structure of indicators used to achieve this objective. This assigns a prominent role to the supply of money, including a reference value for growth of the broadly defined monetary target, and features a broadly based assessment of the outlook for future price developments and the risks to price stability in the euro area as a whole.

---

[528] European Central Bank (2004), p. 69.

[529] See e.g. Issing (2000), p. 149.

The ECB defines price stability in quantitative terms as a year-on-year increase in the EU's Harmonised Index of Consumer Prices for the euro area of below 2%[530]. This target value is comparable to the Bundesbank's concept of underlying normative inflation, which was last designated as encompassing a range of 1.5% to 2%. Like the Bundesbank, the ECB takes a forward-looking, medium-range view of price developments and has committed itself to securing price stability – as quantitatively defined – in the medium term[531].

In contrast to the Bundesbank's strategy, the ECB's two-pillar architecture explicitly states that the ECB takes a wide range of indicators into consideration when making its policy decisions, of which the supply of money is one, albeit prominent, variable. Unlike the Bundesbank, the ECB initially refrained from formulating an explicit target or corridor for money growth, specifying instead a quantitative reference value of 4.5% of annual M3 growth, derived from three elements: the quantitative definition of price stability – below 2% – plus the trend in real gross domestic product growth – estimated as being within a range of 2% to 2.5% – plus a medium-term decline in the velocity of circulation of M3 in the range of 0.5% to 1% per annum. At the same time, the ECB conceded that monetary data, on their own, do not constitute a complete summary of all the information about the economy required to set an appropriate monetary policy. Consequently, as a second pillar of its strategy the bank chose to have a broadly based assessment of the outlook on price developments and the major risks to price stability in the euro area play a major role in its policy decisions. This includes such factors as wages, the exchange rate, bond prices and the yield curve, various measures of real activity, fiscal policy indicators, price and cost indices, and business and consumer surveys[532].

Compared with that of the Bundesbank, the ECB's strategy and the self-binding rules applied are less stringent, affording it more discretion in its policy decisions. In fact, the two-pillar approach not only allows for a wide range of variables to shape monetary decisions, but also explicitly mentions information from market participants, e.g. from business and consumer surveys, which may potentially be taken into account. Discretion was expanded in May 2003 when the ECB effectively abandoned its quantitative monetary reference value for M3 by announcing that the Governing Council no longer reviews it on an annual basis[533]. Nevertheless, the monetary pillar and the reference value have been retained as a benchmark for analysing the

---

[530] European Central Bank (1999), pp. 45-46. For a comprehensive explanation of the ECB's monetary strategy and its components see European Central Bank (2001).

[531] European Central Bank (1999), p. 47.

[532] European Central Bank (1999), p. 49.

[533] European Central Bank (2003), p. 91.

information content of monetary developments and – according to the ECB – as a medium to long-term quantitative benchmark for assessing monetary developments[534].

In addition to the ECB's commitment to the principles laid down in its legal framework, one further aspect may potentially shape ECB policy makers' behavioural patternsf. Being a young institution, the ECB naturally cannot look back on a long record of accomplished anti-inflationary policy and defence of its independence as manifested in the Treaty. At the same time, it has been emphasised that credibility in these two respects has to be built up by the ECB over time: the legal framework alone cannot guarantee successful anti-inflationary policy, nor can credibility in terms of anti-inflationary reputation and institutional and personal independence be inherited entirely from the predecessor institutions[535]. In addition, as discussed in greater detail below, conducting monetary policy successfully in the euro area is a more difficult task than the ECB's predecessor central banks faced, given that a monetary stance has to be established for an economically more heterogeneous area than the constituent economic areas the national central banks were dealing with prior to 1999. Consequently, the ECB has an uphill task in its early years, putting considerable pressure on it to make the single currency work and to make a success of EMU, as an historically unique political venture. Since the success of the undertaking will ultimately be measured primarily against the overriding objective of maintaining stable prices and stable monetary conditions in the entire euro area, this pressure is likely to influence ECB decision makers' behavioural patterns to the effect that they will be less prepared to let themselves in for looser monetary conditions than in a routine environment.

Finally, the institutional context has not changed in terms of the shift in monetary decision making powers to the Community level. As important as this primary political restructuring are two important secondary effects that have occurred in response to the single currency at the national level and affect communication between monetary decision makers and interest-group representatives. First, monetary union has led to a marked shift in the national central banks' remit and functions. From a position of autonomy in determining the monetary stance for the national economies, national central banks have moved to become part of the ESCB and the Eurosystem. Instead of being in charge of monetary policy in their member states, they now merely participate in the monetary decision making process on the Governing Council of the ECB. Beyond that, it is now the task of the national authorities to implement the

---

[534] European Central Bank (2003), p. 91.

[535] Szász (2000), pp. 1-4.

monetary and other decisions taken by the ECB. In doing so, they are strictly subordinated to the guidelines and instructions given by the ECB[536].

Second, and in response to the national central banks' new role, most member states have reformed their national monetary authorities with the aim of adjusting their legal basis to the requirements of the Treaty under Article 14 (1) of the ESCB Statute and of streamlining the national institutions in line with their narrower mandate. As observed with the Bundesbank, the 2002 institutional reform led to a substantial reduction in the number of members on the bank's decision making body, marked simplification of appointment and decision making procedures and the definition of a more efficient internal structure, in the course of which the Regional Offices were deprived of their political status within the Bundesbank. Not least, streamlining also implied that the Advisory Boards at the Regional Offices formally lost their role as advisors on monetary issues. This vividly illustrates the erosion of political power at the Bundesbank and the bodies associated with it. At the end of the day, EMU and establishment of the ECB therefore necessarily result in a weakening of the input into monetary policy formation achieved via the existing channels of communication between the national central banks and the private sector.

Based on the agreement between the EU leaders on the Treaty establishing a Constitution for Europe of June 17 and 18, 2004, the institutional set-up of the ECB and the economic policy framework of EMU was expected to remain essentially unchanged in the course of the constitutional reform of the Union as envisaged at the time[537].

Most importantly, price stability would remain as the primary objective of the ECB, the ESCB[538] and the EU[539]. Further, the three features on which the ECB's *sui generis* status within the Treaty framework is based, namely the bank's independence, its legal personality and its regulatory powers, was to be maintained[540]. The term Eurosystem

---

[536] Article 14 (3), Protocol on the Statute of the European System of Central Banks and the European Central Bank.

[537] The manuscript of this study was completed before a potential ratification and entry into force of the European Constitution. All references made here apply to the Treaty establishing a European Constitution in the text version agreed upon by the Heads of State or Government during their meeting on June 17 and 18, 2004 in Brussels.

[538] Article I-29 (2). For a detailed discussion see ECB (2004), p. 58.

[539] Article I-3 (3). For a detailed discussion see ECB (2004), p. 58.

[540] ECB (2004), p. 61. The ECB's independence was manifested in Article I-29 (3) of the draft Constitution. Compared with the Treaty provisions currently in force, the Constitution would, in fact, reinforce the bank's independence by recognising its financial independence for the first time. The ECB's legal personality was to be confirmed in Article I-29 (3). The bank's regulatory powers would remain unchanged. The Statute of the ECB and the ESCB would remain in force – annexed to and an integral part of the Constitution (ECB (2004), p. 61). The bank's *sui generis* status was to

would be introduced at Treaty level for the first time, conferring constitutional status on the concept referring to the ECB and the national central banks of the member states that have adopted the euro. Amendments to the Treaty framework were to be minor and would apply to selection of the ECB Executive Board – the decisions on which would then be taken by a qualified majority vote in the European Council rather than by common accord, as is the current practice[541] –, the procedures for revising certain provisions under Part III of the Constitution[542], and certain provisions concerning the international role of the euro[543]. In addition, minor changes were to be made to the procedure for amending the Statute of the ECB and the ESCB in the areas of statistics collection and the bank's capital[544]. Changes to the economic policy framework of EMU, too, would be minor. Thus, the euro group – the group of finance ministers of the member states that have adopted the euro plus representatives from the ECB and the European Commission – would be recognised in primary law for the first time[545]. In addition, the Constitution would clarify that decisions on non-compliance by a member state of the euro area with the broad economic policy guidelines or the excessive deficit rules were to be taken only by euro area member states[546]. With respect to the institutional and procedural provisions relevant in the context of analysing interest group relations with the ECB, however, the planned European Constitution had provided for no changes.

In summary, EMU has changed the operational environment of interest groups with respect to monetary affairs in a number of respects. From the viewpoint of interest groups in Germany, this renders the effective communication of private-sector

---

be underlined by classification of the ECB as one of the "other Institutions and bodies" of the EU and the explicit differentiation of the ECB from the Institutions listed under Article I-18, namely the European Parliament, the European Council, the Council of Ministers, the European Commission, and the Court of Justice of the European Union (ECB (2004), p. 61).

[541] ECB (2004), p. 62.

[542] Under the simplified revision procedure of Article IV-7b, provisions in Part III of the Constitution could be revised by a unanimous decision of the European Council without convening an Inter-Governmental Conference. Ratification by all member states, though, would still be required, as would be the prior consultation of Parliament and the Commission, as well as of the ECB in the event of institutional changes in the monetary area (ECB (2004), p. 62).

[543] According to Article III-90, euro-area member states could adopt decisions in Council that establish common positions and ensure unified representation within international financial institutions and conferences. In this context the ECB observed that its exclusive competence for the monetary policy of the euro area and thus the right to determine the position on monetary policy would remain anchored in the provisions of the Constitution (ECB (2004), pp. 62-63).

[544] According to Article I-24 (2), decisions or regulations in these areas which were not initiated by the European Commission, but e.g. by the ECB itself would be subject to qualified majority voting in Council more rigidly defined than otherwise. For details, see ECB (2004), p. 63.

[545] ECB (2004), p. 56.

[546] ECB (2004), p. 56.

preferences even more difficult than in the national pre-1999 context. The major factors contributing to this conclusion are:

- Monetary decision-making has been elevated to a supra-national level, widening the distance between interest groups and policy makers.
- The ECB enjoys a broad legal mandate and extensive discretion in pursuing its objectives, complemented by an unmatched degree of political independence vis-à-vis all public and private bodies at Community and member state level.
- Institutional accessibility is severely restricted by the secluded process of monetary decision-making and the absence of formal channels of direct communication with the private sector at Community level.
- Stronger channels of communication may continue to exist at member state level. Their final impact on ECB-level decision making, however, is limited by the low weighting of the votes of individual governors on the ECB Governing Council and their obligation to act in a personal capacity on behalf of the euro area as a whole, and not as representatives of their member states.
- General commitment to the legal principles governing monetary policy at Community level as well as the pressure to steer euro area monetary policy successfully, especially in the early days of monetary union, are important factors conditioning the behavioural patterns of decision makers at the ECB and the national central banks.
- The input into monetary policy formation achieved via the channels of communication between the national central banks and the private sector is weakened by the diminished role of the national authorities and the advisory bodies associated with them.

II.2.2 Issue context

With the shift in the locus of monetary decision making to the Community level, the issue context in which interest groups work with respect to monetary affairs has also changed. In the first place, the ECB has to conduct a monetary policy suitable for the entire euro area. As the euro area is economically more heterogeneous than each of the constituent member states, determining an optimal policy stance is more difficult than in the member states prior to 1999. And second, monetary policy has developed from a national to a Community issue, changing the political agenda of the interest groups involved. Taken together, these factors alter the issue context from the vantage point of interest groups, forcing them to adjust their activities in this policy field.

As to the first factor, the single monetary policy of the Community needs to establish an optimal policy stance for the euro area as a whole. However, compared with smaller economic areas – such as the member states prior to 1999 – the EMU single monetary area exhibits greater heterogeneity of economic cycles and structures. These differences make it more difficult to formulate an appropriate monetary stance for the euro area as a whole than for more homogenous monetary areas. Thus, the national economies of the euro area continue to exhibit substantial differentials with respect to their domestic growth and inflation rates. In 2003, the spread between the countries with the highest and lowest growth performance amounted to 5.6 percentage points, while the difference between the highest and lowest inflation performance was as much as 3 percentage points, as illustrated in charts 45 and 46. At the same time, rates of unemployment ranged from 3.7% to as much as 11.3%, as depicted in chart 47.

Euro area differentials in GDP growth and inflation

Chart 45

– GDP growth rate at constant prices (1995=100), 2003

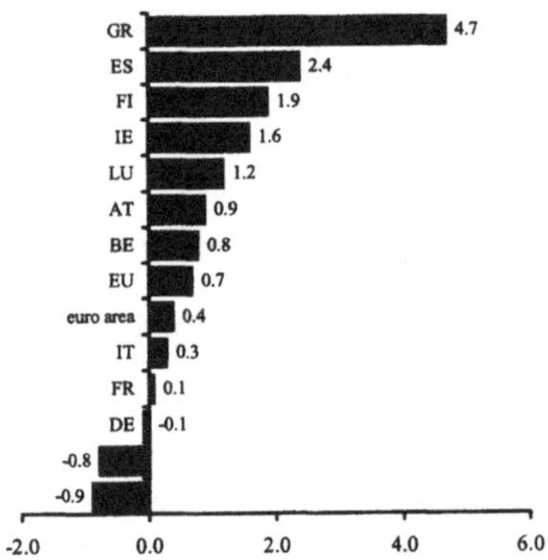

Data source: Eurostat

Chart 46

– Annual average rate of change in Harmonised Indices of Consumer Prices (HICPs), 2003

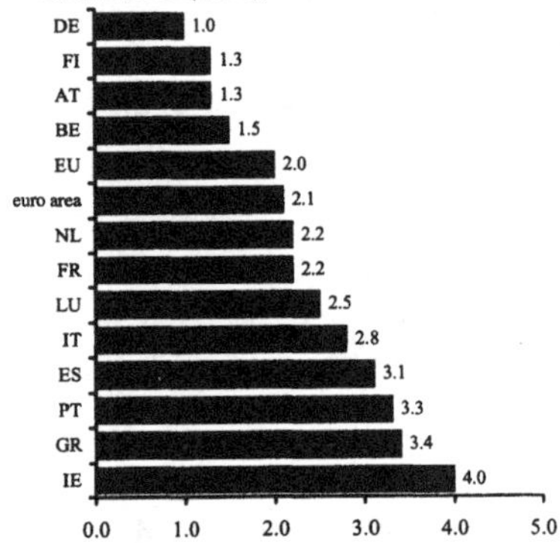

Data source: Eurostat

Ceteris paribus, the differences in cyclical variables reflect disparities in economic structures and differing degrees of economic development in the various member states. Growth rates tend to be higher in those member states in the process of catching up with the wealthier economies. As chart 48 shows, these structural income differentials are still substantial within the euro area in marginal cases, despite great homogeneity among the majority of member states.

Euro area differentials in unemployment rates and per capita income

Chart 47

– Unemployment rates, 2003

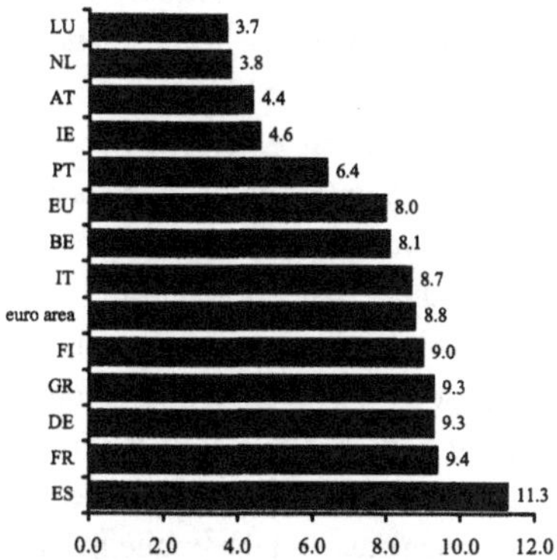

Data source: Eurostat

Chart 48

– GDP per capita in purchasing power standards, EU=100, 2003

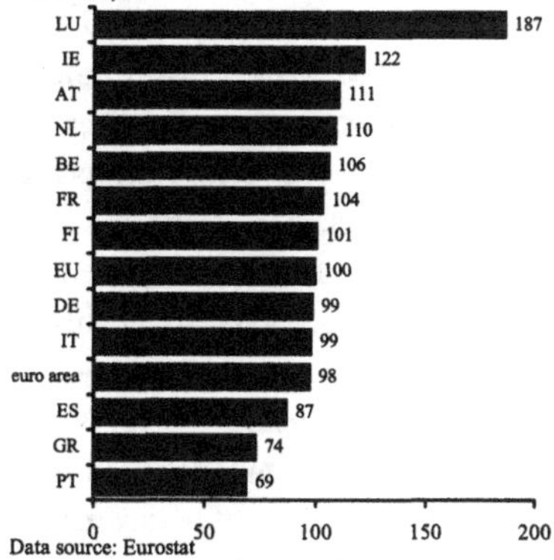

Data source: Eurostat

Similarly, cyclical and structural indicators of the member states' fiscal positions – which influence the level of interest rates in the member states as well as for the euro area as a whole – point to considerable differences in the underlying economic conditions among EMU participants, with budget balances ranging from deficits of 3.5% to surpluses of 4.2% and consolidated public debt between 5.7% and 106.7% of GDP in 2002, as depicted in charts 49 and 50, respectively.

Despite considerable convergence over the past decades, economic heterogeneity between the member states persists. In principle, this makes finding an optimal monetary policy for the euro area as a whole more complicated. Most importantly in the current context, it implies that an optimal euro area-wide monetary policy can depart from the monetary stance deemed appropriate for each individual member economy[547]. From the perspective of an economy exhibiting structurally low growth and inflation rates, such as Germany for example, a single monetary policy dovetailed to the entire euro area will therefore probably tend to be tighter than a policy stance geared to that economy in isolation. Given the strong concurrence of interest groups in Germany with monetary policy prior to 1999, in principle structural deviations between a tailor-made monetary policy for the domestic economy and a one-size-fits-

547 The question as to whether and how an optimal monetary policy can be achieved for an economic area the size of the euro area has accompanied the political process of creating a monetary union in the Community all along, inspiring a great deal of controversy and literature on the subject. A systematic analysis of the effects of economic heterogeneity on the conduct of monetary policy in Europe as well as a discussion of EMU in the light of the theory of optimal currency areas has been provided by De Grauwe (1994), especially pp. 5-59.

all stance within the euro area have the potential for greater or more frequent interest group disagreement with the monetary policy of the ECB.

Second, the status of monetary policy on political agendas at both the national and the EU level has changed with the third stage of EMU. At the national level, monetary policy continues to compete with other economic policy issues. Although monetary decisions are now taken at Community level, their impact on enterprises remains structurally unchanged, and channels of communicating interests with regard to monetary policy retain a strong domestic dimension given the role of the national central banks within the Eurosystem, as observed above. In addition, the most important areas of economic policymaking, most notably taxation, fiscal and labour market issues as well as social policy, which in the past have proved dominant on the domestic economic agenda, remain within the realm of policymaking at member state level. As a result, economic policy in general has retained a strong national dimension. The overall domestic bias of policy makers, market participants and the public at large, as manifested not least in the fact that much of the reporting and analysis of monetary developments still focuses on the domestic economies, has further contributed to the circumstance that monetary policy is still largely discussed in a national context.

At the same time, the Union's single monetary policy, determined exclusively at Community level by a separate, dedicated EU body, has turned monetary policy into a unique EU issue. As such, it is a novelty on the EU policy agenda. To be sure, EMU as the political and economic process leading up to creation of the single currency and establishment of the institutional framework within which the single monetary policy for the euro area is determined, has been an item on the EU's political agenda for some time, going back to the first proposals on monetary unification in the Werner Plan. In the discussions and work towards reaching the third stage of EMU, private sector interest groups played a key role[548]. Once EMU had been achieved, however, the day-to-day conduct of monetary policy in the euro area and the formation and articulation of private-sector interests in monetary policy was a new issue on the policy agenda of interest groups at EU level.

548 For a comprehensive description and analysis of interest-group activity with respect to establishing and shaping EMU and its institutional framework see Collignon, Schwarzer (2003).

Euro area differentials in public deficits and public debt

Chart 49

– Net public balance of consolidated general government sector as a percentage of GDP, 2002

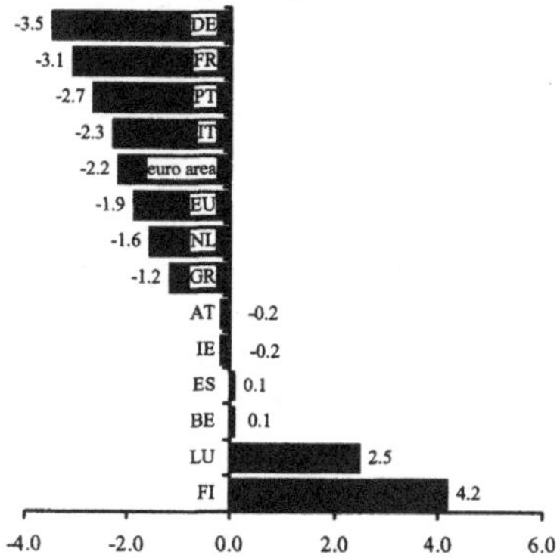

Data source: Eurostat

Chart 50

– General government consolidated gross debt as a percentage of GDP, 2002

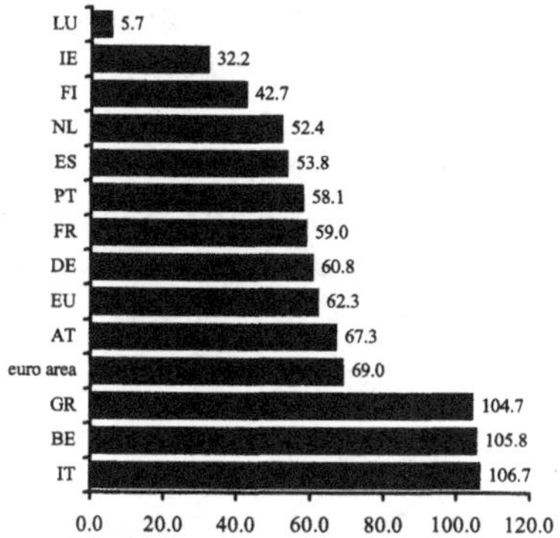

Data source: Eurostat

As a result, ECB policies compete on the EU political agenda with the major economic policies pursued exclusively or concurrently at EU level, including establishment and maintenance of the internal market, the common agricultural policy, competition policy, employment policy, commercial policies, industrial policy, structural policies, and economic-policy coordination.

In structural terms, this constellation of economic policy issues at EU and member state level features an important asymmetry in as far as the issues with which the single monetary policy competes at EU level are only loosely related to monetary policy, with the notable exception of economic-policy coordination. More closely related policy areas, such as fiscal and labour market policies, are almost exclusively part of the national economic policy agendas, where monetary policy, in turn, has lost political momentum after entry into the third stage of EMU. This asymmetry of the EU and domestic policy agendas reflects the more general asymmetry in the allocation of powers and duties between the national and the Community level within the EU in the context of economic policies, where the single currency has led to exclusively supranational policymaking on monetary policy, while a number of important policy areas still fall within the competence of the member states. Like the political level, where attempts have been made to bridge this asymmetry by calling for intensified coordination of national economic policies, the fragmented allocation of competencies between the EU and the member states makes specific demands of interest groups and their activities in this policy field. Irrespective of the individual consequences interest groups draw from this for their work, the distribution of policy competencies complicates the localisation of monetary issues on the economic policy agenda, both at the member state and the EU level.

Finally, the urgency of exchange rate related issues has *ceteris paribus* declined for enterprises engaged in intra-euro area trade since introduction of the single currency. As pointed out above, exchange rate exposure for transactions between the member states in the euro area has been eliminated as a result of the irrevocable fixing of exchange rates and the replacement of national currencies by the euro. Consequently, the related costs and risks have been reduced to zero in the euro area, eliminating them for most of enterprises' foreign transactions within that area, as illustrated by charts 51 and 52 in the instance of Germany.

German trade by region

Chart 51

– German exports by target region, in % of total exports, 2003

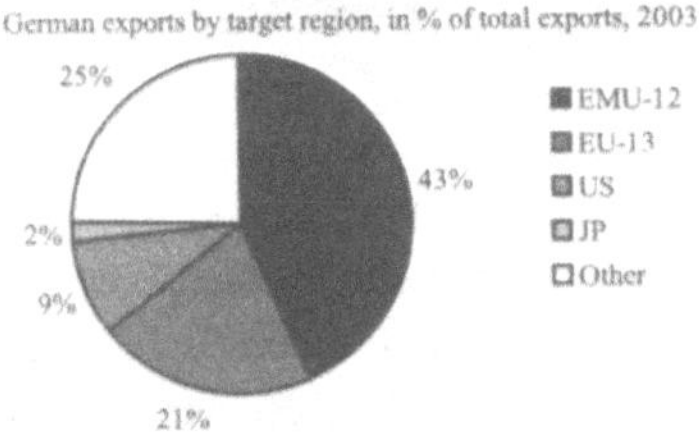

Data source: Statistisches Bundesamt

Chart 52

– German imports by region of origin, in % of total imports, 2003

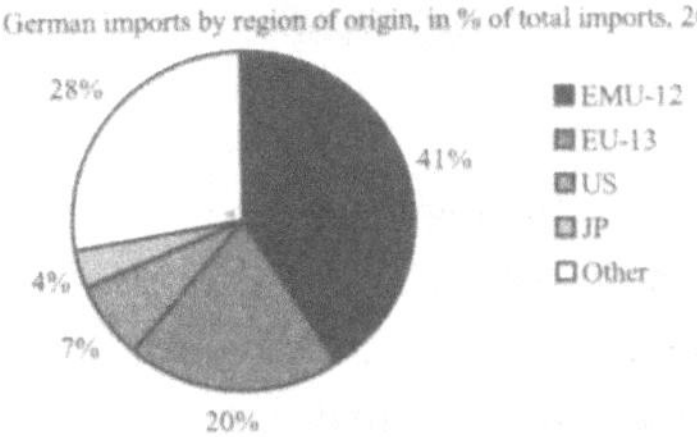

Data source: Statistisches Bundesamt

II.2.3 Group context

Together with the institutional and issue contexts, the interest group context within which views on monetary issues are aggregated and represented differs markedly today from that prior to introduction of the single currency. In the first place, monetary policy is now on the political agendas of an additional level of interest representation, namely interest groups operating on an EU-wide basis. Second, the number of interest groups concerned with monetary decisions today is a multiple of that observed in each individual economy when these decisions were still in the hands of national authorities, now encompassing general and sectoral groups at regional, national and EU level. Third, the heterogeneity of interests represented by these groups within the euro area as a whole is greater than that observed in each individual member state.

Competition among private-sector interests with respect to monetary policy in the euro area is tighter today than in the individual member states when monetary decisions were still in the hands of national authorities, owing to the much higher number of interested parties within the political arena, which, in turn, represent a far more heterogeneous array of interests. In contrast to the national central banks pre-1999, which essentially dealt with the interest groups operating within the respective member states when conducting their policies, the ECB and the national central banks of the Eurosystem today face a multitude of interest groups at various levels of the political system. With monetary policy as a Community issue since entry into the third stage of EMU, EU-level peak interest associations now represent the natural interest group counterparts of the ECB at the Community level. At the same time, national and regional interest groups continue to work towards influencing ECB monetary policy by targeting their respective national central banks. Thus, the arena of interest groups potentially involved in articulating interests on monetary issues in the euro area encompasses the relevant peak, sectoral, and regional business associations in the twelve participating member states as well as their counterparts at the EU level. The wider scope of interests involved also applies to all other potential stakeholders, such as governments, parliaments, other political bodies at member state and EU level, think tanks and academic institutions. The result is a large and potentially crowded arena of stakeholders latently interested and active in the field of monetary policymaking in the euro area.

As in the case of Germany, no dedicated cause group exists at EU level which is exclusively concerned with monetary issues. Rather, interests with respect to monetary policy are aggregated and represented through the existing infrastructure of business associations. Despite the Community's infancy compared with the polities of the member states, this infrastructure is well-established, with the major industry federations dating back to the early 1950s, when interest representation at trans-national level arose in response to the creation of the European Coal and Steel Community[549]. EU-level business associations are officially registered with the Commission and are generally regarded as preferred interlocutors by the relevant Community policy makers, with a number of the peak associations enjoying a privileged status within the Community's policy processes[550].

For interests in the area of trade and industry, this infrastructure essentially centres around three peak interest associations:

- *Union of Industrial and Employers' Confederations of Europe, UNICE*

  Founded in 1958, UNICE is the peak industrial association at EU level, representing 34 national industry federations from 27 countries.

- *Association of European Chambers of Commerce and Industry, Eurochambres*

  Founded in 1958, Eurochambres represents 41 national associations of chambers of commerce and industry, a European network of 2,000 regional and local chambers with more than 17 million member enterprises in Europe.

---

549 Mazey, Richardson (1993), p. 192.

550 Mazey, Richardson (1993), p. 193.

- *Eurocommerce*

  Founded in 1993, Eurocommerce represents more than 100 European and national associations of enterprises in retail, wholesale, and international trade in 29 countries.

These cross-sectoral peak business associations are complemented by a number of specialised sectoral interest associations, whose membership in turn consists of the major national sectoral business associations.

As to association-specific exposure and issue involvement, the patterns are similar to those observed in the case of German business associations. However, the variety of enterprises ultimately represented by peak EU associations in terms of their size, dependence on foreign capital and their exposure to national or regional economic cycles and movements in interest and inflation rates and to extra-euro area exchange rate risks is necessarily greater than within national associations. The heterogeneity of interests with respect to monetary policy represented within peak EU business associations is therefore greater than within their national counterparts, to the effect that the views represented at EU level are highly aggregated and naturally reflect a comparatively low common denominator.

The position of EU business associations is also similar to that of their national counterparts, e.g. in Germany, in terms of their endowment with resources. Financially, business associations in Brussels are generally well-equipped by their constituent groups in the member states. Access to information and data is also secured by the national member associations, making most EU business groups providers of unique, aggregated EU-wide information on their specific area of activity. Thus, both UNICE and Eurochambres publish EU-wide surveys among enterprises in their constituencies, providing information on the economic situation in their sectors, as well as assessments of overall economic conditions. Since introduction of the single currency, these surveys have been extended to encompass assessments on monetary and exchange rate conditions, indicating that information relevant to monetary affairs exists or is being generated and that these associations have, in fact, picked up on the issue and the views articulated by their members. Considering that they can generally draw on years of experience in analysing the EU economy as a whole, EU business associations have in fact enjoyed a certain informational lead over the ECB, whose own work on analysing European monetary, financial, and general economic conditions began only in mid-1998. Although supported by the resources provided by the national central banks as well as the preliminary work undertaken by the European

Monetary Institute[551], the ECB has been dealing with an entirely new policy problem – i.e. of devising a single monetary policy for an economic area whose composition was decided only months before the bank's operations started – relying on new, largely untested statistical and analytical groundwork. At least in the initial period, EU-level business associations have therefore benefited from a certain routine in collecting and analysing EU-wide evidence, which the ECB as such did not itself possess.

With respect to political resources, on the other hand, EU-level business associations are as limited as their national counterparts in Germany prior to 1999. As argued above, monetary decisions are taken by means of a closed process with very few points of access. Given the set-up of the monetary system of EMU and the appointment, monetary decision making and implementation procedures of the Eurosystem, no practical ways of exerting political pressure on monetary decision makers exist.

II.2.4 Interim conclusions

With entry into EMU, the participant member states shifted the locus of monetary and exchange rate decision making to the EU level, thereby significantly moving the institutional, issue, and group goalposts for business interest group activity. More so than in the case of Germany and the Bundesbank, the task environment within which trade and industry associations deal with monetary and exchange rate policy differs considerably from the environments in other areas of policymaking at EU level. The findings can be summarised as follows:

Institutional context

- The institutional framework of monetary policy at EU level mirrors that previously operated in Germany in important respects, providing a well-defined institutional and procedural framework, isolating monetary decisions from other policy areas and delegating it to one single expert institution, the ECB.
- In many respects the institutional independence of the ECB is more pronounced than that of the Deutsche Bundesbank, given enshrinement of the principle of central bank independence in the Treaty and the ECB's position within the institutional framework of the EU as the only single independent decision-making body. This suggests that direct and indirect influence by interest groups via the surrounding political framework, especially via the EU's executive and legislative

[551] The European Monetary Institute (EMI) was established on January 1, 1994 as the predecessor institution to the ECB, preparing the upcoming central bank's work in terms of coordination of the national central banks' monetary policies, strengthening their cooperation, technical preparation of the ECB's work – including setting up a payment system, designing policy instruments and preparing the physical currency changeover – and supervision of the European Monetary System. For a comprehensive analysis of the EMI's role and work see Mehnert-Meland (1995), pp. 53-69.

institutions, is even more limited than in many national jurisdictions. Institutional independence is further strengthened by the ECB's own substantial material, informational and personnel resources, coupled with those of the national central banks within the ESCB.

- Owing to their pyramid structure, in principle the ECB and ESCB offer a multitude of institutional points of access for interest groups. In practice, though, direct formal access to the ECB by interest groups is limited: The twice-yearly Macroeconomic Dialogue, as the only formal point of contact with interest groups, does not even fulfil an advisory function as far as the ECB is concerned.

Issue context

- The single monetary policy is a relatively new issue on the EU policy agenda, building on a multitude of diverse inflationary developments and policy approaches in the respective member states that belong to EMU. Within the single currency area, economic conditions differ substantially in structural as well as cyclical terms, pointing up a relatively high degree of heterogeneity of interests associated with monetary and exchange rate issues across the currency area.
- With respect to this primary purpose, the ECB has delivered a remarkably positive performance, keeping inflation low by historical and international standards and countering surges in wages and prices effectively while maintaining a largely stable interest rate environment. At the same time, there have been substantial swings in the external value of the euro versus the US dollar, while exchange rate movements between the participating member states were eliminated with entry into EMU. As a result, monetary and exchange rate related policy issues have largely remained in the background of policy debate, with the exception of the euro exchange rate.
- At the national level, numerous sectors nevertheless remain specifically exposed to interest and exchange rate developments, including the transport, construction and retail sectors, the automotive, mechanical engineering, chemical and electronics industries, and interest rate-sensitive small and medium-sized enterprises.
- Issue involvement at the EU level is weakened by the fact that monetary and exchange rate-related policy issues are relatively new on the policy agenda. For practical purposes, this means that many policy makers and interest groups are being systematically exposed to monetary issues for the first time. More so than at national level, EU economic policy debate was dominated by a whole range of other economic policy issues on the past political agenda, mainly focusing on improving the structural competitiveness of the EU economies, including completion of the single market and pursuit of the Lisbon Agenda. In view of this,

monetary policy has remained detached from overall economic policy debate at EU level.

Group context

- With EMU, monetary policy is now on the agendas of an additional level of interest representation, i.e. interest groups operating on an EU-wide basis. Interest aggregation and expression with respect to monetary and exchange rate issues are achieved through the existing infrastructure of EU-level business associations and their peak organisations. Given its insignificance in terms of impact and urgency, monetary policy has not aroused sufficient attention to provoke the formation of dedicated cause groups.
- With national central banks as important parts of the ESCB and ECB communication strategy, avenues of interest communication at the national level have not become obsolete. Interest mediation can thus be sought through both traditional regional and national channels and through new channels at EU level.
- Not only does a greater spectrum of interests exist within the euro area, but also a great number of interest groups at all levels of policymaking are competing for influence. This makes the group landscape more fragmented. Peak interest organisations at EU level have the task of aggregating a more heterogeneous set of interests among a large number of diverse constituent or associated groups in the member states, complicating the emergence of strong policy positions on monetary and exchange rate-related issues.

Part III Empirical analysis

III.1 Research design

In chapters I.1 and I.2, a theoretical framework was devised to assess whether and to what extent private-sector interest groups are likely to seek political influence on monetary policy makers and which channels they use to communicate their interests. Chapter II.1 provided preliminary evidence on the institutional, issue, and group contexts within which interest groups operate in Germany.

The key propositions identified at the end of chapter I.2 are tested against the reality of relations between private-sector interest groups and central banks in chapter III.2, analysing interest group relations with the central bank in the case of Germany and the impact of institutional, issue and group contexts on the behaviour of major trade and industry associations in Germany with respect to monetary issues and the Bundesbank. The research design applied in testing the propositions is presented below.

III.1.1 Analysis of interest group behaviour in Germany and at EU level

Developments and policies, decision-making structures and processes in monetary affairs differ considerably across countries. The same applies in many cases to interest group structures, strategies and activities in general. If the theoretical observations made earlier are correct, then the extent to which interest-group activity can be observed is likely to differ, depending on which country or economic area is examined. Ideally, a comprehensive analysis should seek to assess as great a number of countries as possible to produce maximum evidence and insight into the behaviour of interest groups in this policy area. By the same logic, it is desirable to examine as many players, i.e. interest groups and policy makers and their representatives, as possible. For the sake of practicability, however, it is necessary to stake out the scope of analysis and limit the set of respondents. Accordingly, the following analysis will be limited in a number of dimensions to ensure relevance and focus.

First, the empirical evaluation will be concerned primarily with interest groups in Germany and their behaviour towards the German central bank, i.e. the Bundesbank. This choice is based on three considerations.

First, for most of the post-World War II period the Bundesbank was one of the most important central banks in the world, second only to the Federal Reserve System in the United States and on eye level with the Bank of Japan.

Second, until 1999 it was the leading central bank in Europe and *de facto* the anchor of the Exchange Rate Mechanism of the European Monetary System[552], making it the

[552] Bofinger et al. (1996), p. 608.

benchmark for monetary policies in the participating member states during the past two decades.

This latter point is of pivotal importance for the present analysis. As discussed above, central banks obliged to operate within a certain exchange rate regime and to maintain a certain exchange rate parity are not in a position to pursue an autonomous monetary policy. The extent of their autonomy depends on the limitations the regime imposes. In such circumstances potential public debate necessarily focuses on the appropriateness of the exchange rate regime as such, the band in operation or the targeted central parity. Since monetary policy in the narrow sense does not exist where exchange rate regimes are in operation, an analysis of private-sector reactions to monetary policy under such circumstances is likely to produce very specific results, which in the present context are not looked for. In contrast, a public debate on monetary policy as under examination here can only be observed in the context of autonomous monetary policymaking, unconstrained by exogenously determined exchange rate targets.

The Bundesbank is a suitable object of analysis because it was able to pursue monetary policies largely unaffected by formal exchange rate arrangements after abolition of the Bretton Woods System in March 1973[553] and, in contrast to most other EU central banks, even during the existence of the European Monetary System, whose Exchange Rate Mechanism provided for exchange rate bands[554] and bilateral commitments to intervene in defence of the agreed currency parities. Monetary policy for the Deutsche Mark, as the *de facto* anchor currency, was pursued by the Bundesbank more or less autonomously, while the remaining ERM members worked towards keeping their currencies within the agreed exchange rate bands. As a result, the Bundesbank was not only the leading central bank in the EU, but also the only one to consistently pursue an autonomous monetary policy. For interest groups in Germany, this implied that there was, in fact, an autonomous monetary policy to discuss. Conversely, an empirical examination of interest group behaviour in other ERM member states would be limited in the above-mentioned sense. Consequently, Germany is, taking the pre-EMU era into

---

[553] On the functioning of the Bretton Woods System see Bofinger et al. (1996), pp. 607-608.

[554] From its establishment in 1979 the EMS provided for a standard narrow exchange rate band of +/- 2.25%, which was adhered to by the EMS founder members Belgium, Denmark, Germany, France, Ireland, Italy, Luxembourg and the Netherlands. Italy operated under the optional, wider band of +/- 6%. The United Kingdom joined the Exchange Rate Mechanism of the EMS in October 1990 at +/- 2.25%. Following the exchange rate turmoil in autumn 1992 and spring 1993, the exchange rate band was widened to +/- 15% in August 1993, by which the ERM was de facto suspended. Continuation of the narrow band on a bilateral basis was agreed only for the Dutch Guilder and the Deutsche Mark (Bofinger et al. (1996), pp. 605-609).

account, the only EU country[555] for which the present analysis in its narrow focus can be appropriately pursued.

Third, the Deutsche Bundesbank has been portrayed as the institutional and, moreover, the behavioural role model for the ECB. The overall monetary objectives and most of the institutional and procedural features of the Bundesbank were used as a blueprint for the ECB during the negotiations on the statutes of the European System of Central Banks and the ECB. Bundesbank monetary policy decisions and operations are still seen as setting an example for the ECB's actions even today. Selecting Germany as an exemplary study consequently offers the additional advantage that empirical evidence may allow for subsequent conclusions on the ECB's potential present and future behaviour.

In this sense, the Bundesbank also represents a suitable substitute for the ECB as an object of analysis. Since taking over monetary decision making in the euro area from the participating national central banks in 1999, the ECB represents the most interesting study case in Europe. National central banks in the member states of that area, including the Bundesbank, are still part of decision making structures but today no longer possess autonomous decision-making powers in the field of monetary policies.

However, despite the relevance of the ECB for studies on monetary policymaking, it does not lend itself as the primary object of analysis in the present context. After only few years of operation, structures of communication with the private sector are still in the process of development, just as the ECB and the national central banks of the Eurosystem have remained concerned with adapting to the new political landscape: Thus, the ECB revised its monetary policy strategy after the first years of operation[556] in spring 2003, while the Bundesbank put an extensive internal structural reform into place in summer 2002[557]. Similarly, just a few years into the euro era, interest associations are equally unlikely to have reached equilibrium in their activities pertaining to monetary policy and central banks. A final judgement on the relations between EU interest groups and the ECB may therefore be premature at the current juncture.

In addition, focusing on the Bundesbank as the primary object of analysis is justified on the grounds that much of the contact between central banks and the private sector in the euro area is likely to remain associated with the national central banks, which are

---

555 With respect to the criteria applied here, the United Kingdom also represents a suitable, but not as important a test case as Germany, given Germany's central role in the EMS.

556 For details on the results of the ECB's evaluation of its monetary policy strategy see European Central Bank (2003a).

557 For details on the structural reform of the Bundesbank see Deutsche Bundesbank (2003a).

not only responsible for the operations of the Eurosystem in the member states, but also for communication of the ECB's monetary policy in the respective constituent countries of the euro area. Besides the potential exemplary role that the relations between national central banks and the private sector prior to the delegation of monetary policy to the ECB may play for communication by the ECB with interest groups, relations at the national level may still be important for the formulation of monetary policy at the European level today through the influence national central banks have on euro area monetary decisions inside the ECB Governing Council.

In the light of these considerations, focusing the following empirical analysis on Germany and the relations between interest groups and the Bundesbank seems a promising way to proceed. This will be done in chapter III.2

The shift of monetary sovereignty to the ECB nevertheless needs to be taken into account. Not only has it transferred the locus of monetary decision making to a new superstructure above the existing national central banks and thereby diminished the political weight of each of the latter institutions in their national policy arenas, it has also triggered far-reaching measures by the member states aimed at streamlining the national central banks. Both developments are likely to alter communication between the national central banks and the interest groups in their constituencies. In order to capture the potential impact of this important systemic break, monetary policymaking at the euro-area level will be analysed, concentrating on how the shift of monetary decisions to the European level in 1999 has impacted interest group behaviour, and to what extent and how business interests are communicated at the European level with respect to monetary issues.

III.1.2 Qualitative and quantitative approach

The objective of the empirical analysis in chapters III.2 and III.3 below is to answer – for the specific cases of Germany and the euro area – the three general questions identified at the outset, namely:

- Do interest groups seek to influence monetary policy decision making?
- What are the factors contributing to the decision whether to express interests with respect to monetary policy, and to what extent?
- If influence on monetary decisions is sought, how are interests articulated by the relevant groups?

To that end, it seeks to compare the propositions established in chapter I.2[558] with the reality of interest group activities and monetary policy practices.

---

[558] See list of propositions on pp. 88 to 89.

In order to gain a picture of the motivations and behaviour of German interest groups with regard to monetary affairs, empirical evidence has been collected through interviews with decision makers and experts from interest associations as well as from the Bundesbank and the ECB, investigating their perception of monetary and exchange rate developments and policies as well as the factors promoting or hampering political activity. The approach rests on semi-structured, focused interviews with experts and decision makers in the policy field along a catalogue of questions designed to operationalise the key propositions. A set of core questions was identified and worded so that it could be put forward to all interviewees, i.e. to respondents from central banks, on the one hand, and corporations or interest associations, on the other.

Additional questions were raised on a case-by-case basis to allow for detailed follow-up discussions and a more focused approach towards individual experts' or decision makers' specific perceptions. All questions were formulated as open questions, allowing respondents to answer freely and individually and to elaborate where deemed appropriate. Furthermore, questions were drafted[559] and interviews conducted[560] in line with the present standards in qualitative social science research.

Following collection and transcription[561] of the interviews, a combined qualitative and quantitative approach[562] was adopted to evaluate responses. Answers to core questions were compared among all respondents and coded according to the method proposed by Schmidt (2000), i.e. in a first step coding categories were identified for each question. Subsequently, individual answers were coded and the resulting quantification processed, evaluated and appropriately displayed. Coding and quantification result exclusively from evaluation of the qualitative answers. Interviewees were not asked to give their own quantitative assessments. Throughout the study, these quantitative results complement the qualitative material in the form of quotations from

---

559 Questions were designed to satisfy contemporary scientific standards to a maximum degree, including brevity, comprehensibility and precision. Ingratiation, double negations, normative concepts, suggestive questions and multiple dimensions were excluded. Indirect questions were avoided as far as possible. For a list of criteria for qualitative interviews see Dieckmann (1997), pp. 410-414. The qualitative methods applied here are based on the techniques presented in Flick et al. (2000), pp. 224-587, and Schnell et al. (1999).

560 See Hopf (2000), Hermanns (2000), Dieckmann (1997), pp. 410-418.

561 The methods applied in transcribing interviews were based on Kowal, O'Connell (2000).

562 Combining qualitative surveys with quantitative evaluation methods has been advanced as one way of improving evaluative objectivity in social science research (Dieckmann (1997), pp. 451-455, also Kelle, Erzberger (2000)). However, there is a risk of blurring results at the interface between the two approaches, namely when translating qualitative items for use in quantitative analysis by means of coding (Schmidt (2000)).

interviewees[563] or insights from other sources, such as related literature or archival material.

This inherently qualitative approach to analysing interest group behaviour towards monetary policy stands in some contrast to the almost exclusively quantitative methods applied in the existing literature, which is concerned with the closely related analysis of influence on monetary policy decisions by governments and party politics. In this latter field of study, scholarly attention has so far focused on the degree to which monetary policy decisions are in fact influenced by electoral politics. To this end, econometric models have been applied, relating monetary developments to the occurrence of elections, elected policy makers' party affiliations or the existence of conflicts between monetary decision makers and elected politicians[564]. By regressing indicators of these potential sources of political influence on observed monetary developments, these models yield important insights into the correlation between monetary decision making and electoral politics.[565]

Similar approaches have been applied to private-sector interests, even though attention to this issue has at best been marginal, as already pointed out. Most importantly, Havrilesky[566] examined banking and other private sector influences on monetary policy in the US by regressing directives from the Federal Advisory Council, a body composed of private-sector representatives advising the Federal Reserve Board, on the central bank's Federal Funds Rate. Havrilesky also tested the impact of business surveys[567]. More recently, Maier et al.[568] and Maier[569] picked up on a method Havrilesky had used in a different context[570] and tested the responsiveness of monetary indicators to private-sector statements on monetary policy as reflected in newspaper articles in the case of Germany.

What characterises the above-mentioned studies is their common objective of determining the final influence of interested parties – be they located in electoral

563 All interviews were conducted on a confidential basis. Any quotations are reproduced anonymously.

564 A comprehensive overview of existing studies on political business cycles and the models applied in the field of study is provided by Maier (2002), pp. 10-12.

565 Maier (2002) contains a review of the major results yielded by applying econometric models in this context (pp. 15-31).

566 Havrilesky (1993), pp. 251-285.

567 Here the quarterly survey of the National Association of Business Economists. See Havrilesky (1993), pp. 271-272.

568 Maier, Sturm, de Haan (2000).

569 Maier (2002), pp. 87-96.

570 Havrilesky had initially constructed his SAFER index in order to measure public statements by politicians in the executive branch in the US and their effects on monetary policy (original study see Havrilesky (1988), later refined in Havrilesky (1993), pp. 29-80).

politics or in the private sector – on monetary developments or decisions. To that end, it is appropriate to measure statistically the dependence of monetary variables on the behavioural variables associated with interest group activity.

In contrast, the focus of the present study lies on quite different aspects. It tries to look into the black box of interest representation, which is taken as given in the above-mentioned studies, and seeks to examine the incentives groups face when they decide in the first place whether or not to take political action on monetary policy. Secondly, it sets out to describe the means by which interest groups seek to exert political influence on monetary policy decisions once they have decided to do so. Both of these issues, as well as the questions and propositions derived, essentially touch upon the perception of a policy issue and the related variables and upon the decisions and behaviour based on these perceptions. With respect to their empirical evaluation, such perceptual and behavioural patterns clearly do not lend themselves to a purely econometric analysis. Thus, the sensitivity of interest groups and their members towards the economic effects of monetary developments on their businesses and operations cannot be read off directly from readily available statistics. The same problem applies to the role of institutional or behavioural hurdles, which might discourage interest groups from approaching decision makers on monetary affairs. Similarly, the channels interest groups use if they do approach monetary policy makers are not plainly evident.

The qualitative approach aims to open up these difficult perceptual and behavioural issues to empirical analysis. First of all, it enables research into issues in a way that provides a comprehensive picture of the policy issue and policy arena, and of how the relevant actors operate within it. In as far as these insights generate comparable answers, their contents can, where appropriate, be quantified and prepared for statistical analysis[571]. In addition, by using focused but open interview methods in contrast to standardised questionnaires, it is possible to capture the subjective views of those actors who effectively shape political communication between the private sector and monetary policy makers. Furthermore, this technique leaves room for arguments that cannot be anticipated from a purely theoretical discussion on which the instruments of research, i.e. propositions and questions, are based[572].

---

[571] Dieckmann (1997), pp. 453-455. Also Kelle, Erzberger (2000).

[572] For a discussion of the benefits of qualitative research methods in social sciences see Dieckmann (1997), pp. 443-445. Dieckmann points to a third benefit of qualitative methods, namely that they allow the observation of interviewees in "day-to-day situations" as opposed to the "artificiality of interview situations", which may be generated by standardised questionnaires or laboratory-based quantitative social science research. The latter are, in practice, not viable as research instruments in discourse with high-ranking experts or policy makers.

In order to maximise the benefits of qualitative interviews and to anticipate their limitations as a research instrument in the present context, it is also useful to look into the problems associated with this method. Three major sources of difficulty have been identified in literature[573]. First, the results of qualitative methods are likely to depend very much on the choice of interviewees. Qualitative interviews are generally designed so as to produce detailed and comprehensive information through intensive and lengthy conversations with the interviewees selected, aimed at a better and deeper understanding of the reality under consideration. This often needs to be achieved at the cost of rather small samples of interviewees, compared with standardised mass questionnaires. All else being equal, this reduces the representativeness of the research results[574] and may amplify the problems associated with selection biases[575]. As discussed in more detail below, this problem arises only to a very limited extent in the present context, and corrective measures have been taken by addressing all relevant peak interest groups within the domain of trade and industry in Germany and at the EU level[576].

Second, conducting and evaluating qualitative interviews can be more problematic than with their quantitative counterparts, i.e. in the context of standardised mass questionnaires, inasmuch as the advantage of qualitative techniques in terms of more individual, focused and detailed investigation of a certain issue can come at the cost of lower comparability of individual responses. This may result from less uniform conduct of individual interviews in terms of application, phrasing or sequencing of questions, or from the challenge of ensuring an objective evaluation of the resulting responses[577]. In order to minimise the problems associated with the conduct and evaluation of qualitative interviews, the present analysis is based on the rules commonly devised for ensuring objectivity, reliability and validity in social science research[578] as far as applicable and realistic in the present context. In addition, maximum comparability was sought, as described above, by devising a set of core questions, which were put forward consistently to all interviewees, ensuring the existence of a set of questions and responses largely satisfying quality criteria

On the benefits of qualitative research methods in social sciences, see also Flick, von Kardoff, Steinke (2000). With respect to the theory of qualitative social science research see Dieckmann (1997), pp. 375-381, von Kardoff (2000) on qualitative evaluation research and Flick (2000) on the design and process of qualitative research.

573 For an overview see Dieckmann (1997), pp. 451-455.

574 Dieckmann (1997), p. 326.

575 Dieckmann (1997), pp. 326-329.

576 Sectoral interest groups were selected on the basis of their importance in economic terms, i.e. with a view to the shares of the output of their members in GDP and in external trade.

577 Dieckmann (1997), p. 453.

578 Dieckmann (1997), pp. 216-227.

observed in quantitative studies. Furthermore, comparable responses were systematically coded and statistically evaluated, ensuring that the core of empirical evidence was founded on quantitative findings backed up with additional qualitative insights from interviews, literature and archival material where appropriate.[579]

Finally, the quality of the empirical results critically depends on the precision and truthfulness of the replies obtained from interviewees. As explicitly intended by such an approach, qualitative methods primarily capture subjective views, impressions and opinions, rather than measuring objective states of the world. Subjective replies may be imprecise, not well founded or even untruthful.

In order to minimise the potentially distortionary effects of this problem, the interview-based study below was conducted exclusively with well-informed decision makers and experts. Information obtained in the course of the interviews that was either formulated imprecisely, speculative in nature or otherwise inappropriate for the present purpose was not included in the evaluation. In addition, given the sensitivity of the majority of issues discussed during interviews, all interviewees were assured that the contents of the conversations would remain confidential. In most instances, confidentiality was a precondition for the interview as such as well as for the unconstrained disclosure of information and personal views. As a result, the information obtained in the course of the interviews is presented below in an anonymized manner without explicit reference to the names of individual interviewees. This also extends to the names of the organisations the interviewees represented.

---

[579] The sensitivity of qualitative methods to the potential problems cited above has given rise to doubts over the scientific value of studies based on such methods. Some researchers working on social science methodology have argued that qualitative approaches are less suitable for testing hypotheses precisely because they are said to perform less well than quantitative methods in terms of the comparability of individual responses. See Dieckmann (1997), pp. 444-445. In fact, adherents of qualitative methods have themselves rejected the testing of hypotheses as a field of application for qualitative techniques, arguing that the formulation of hypotheses on an *ex ante* basis as such was inadequate because it represented, at best, prior knowledge and, at worst, a systematic bias on the part of the researcher. This may distort subsequent research results from the very outset. According to this view, research should be guided by maximum openness with respect to statements, interpretations and the setting of priorities by the actors under scrutiny. The formulation of theories and hypotheses should be the result of empirical work rather than preceding it. See Meinefeld (2000), pp. 266-269.

The present analysis seeks neither to follow nor to contribute to this academic debate. Rather, a pragmatic approach is taken with the objective of describing and exploring a specific field of policymaking. It is based on sound theoretical foundations, the theoretical and empirical validity of which has been tested and confirmed elsewhere, and applies the most suitable empirical method, i.e. a qualitative proceeding. Potential weaknesses are minimised by incorporating alternative, quantitative approaches, as specified above.

III.1.2.1 Sample

With respect to the sample of decision makers and experts asked to provide information on the relations between interest groups and central banks, selection was made both with respect to the relevant institutions and actors as well as to the types of decision makers and experts addressed inside each institution.

As to the types of institutions and actors under scrutiny, empirical evidence was collected among both central banks and interest groups. In the case of Germany, evidence on the central bank view of the problem was gathered from representatives of the Bundesbank, including the Bundesbank headquarters in Frankfurt/Main as well as its constituent regional central banks, i.e. the Hauptverwaltungen or Landeszentralbanken[580].

Among private-sector interest groups, the analysis focuses on the major German peak business associations in industry and trade. By looking at these peak business associations, the study seeks to capture a picture of interest groups which, in principle,

- are representative of the private-sector economy at large in terms of exposure to monetary developments and the related policy decisions,
- are exposed to monetary or exchange rate developments in a significant way,
- are sufficiently resourced to actually have sufficient means for conveying their interests to policy makers, provided such interests exist and are deemed worthy of pursuit,
- exhibit some degree of homogeneity in purpose, exposure, and interests so as to make motivations and activities relating to monetary affairs directly comparable,
- reflect the views of those associations, groups, and individuals involved in formal and semi-formal contacts with the monetary authorities.

As defined in the introduction, interest groups in trade and industry fulfil these criteria most appropriately and therefore represent the primary focus of the present analysis. By the same token, certain sectors and sub-sectors of the economy are not covered here explicitly. As explained in the introduction, these include agriculture, finance, employer and employee organisations.

---

[580] Until the Bundesbank's April 2002 institutional reform, regional central banks were known as Landeszentralbanken, i.e. state central banks. In the course of the reform, the legal and institutional status of these regional entities was altered. Since May 2002, these entities have been referred to as Hauptverwaltungen, i.e. main administrative units.

Specialised sectoral or regional business associations have been included in the fieldwork selectively, based on two criteria. Sectoral or regional groups or their representatives were addressed[581]

- if they were represented on a formal or semi-formal advisory body to the central bank or to a relevant policy committee – i.e. on one of the Bundesbank's Advisory Councils, or on its roundtable of economists – or
- if their constituencies were economically particularly exposed to monetary or exchange rate developments.

Other sectoral or regional interest associations in trade and industry are not included in the analysis. In terms of contents, this is unlikely to result in significant omissions, as the perceptions on the part of these associations are likely to be proxied by the views expressed by those representatives interviewed. On average, the responses gained from representatives of regional or sectoral groups, e.g. sitting on a Bundesbank Advisory Council, should not deviate systematically from their equivalents not represented on such bodies[582]. In addition, all relevant regional or sectoral interest groups in trade and industry are constituents, members, or associates of the peak cross-sectoral associations covered in the analysis.

At the euro area level, background interviews were conducted with representatives at the ECB and peak EU industry and trade associations. The sample of central bank and interest group representatives was selected with reference to the same criteria as in the case of Germany. National central banks in other euro area member states and interest associations operative at the national level in euro area member states other than Germany were not included in the analysis.

In line with the overall qualitative approach and in order to obtain responses with a great degree of detail and validity, the empirical work presented here focuses on interviews with working-level experts as well as with decision makers. Based on the above selection criteria, a total of 180 decision makers and experts were identified as holding positions or possessing substantial knowledge relevant to the present topic in the entities specified above. Identification of the target group was based on the evaluation of organisation charts, direct requests for appropriate contacts and explicit recommendations by experts or decision makers. 84, or 47% of that group, were

---

[581] Further details are presented in chapters III.2 and III.3.

[582] The only substantial exception to this assumption are views expressed with respect to the channels of communication used by interest groups to mediate their interests with respect to monetary policy. The criteria for selection of interest groups applied here necessarily produce a selection bias in favour of groups with either formal or semi-formal contacts with central banks, or with substantial exposure to monetary or exchange rate developments. This bias is taken into consideration in the analysis.

identified as being of particular relevance to the current study owing to their involvement in communication between central banks and interest groups and were approached for background interviews. 27, or 32%, of these requests were not answered or turned down with reference to the confidentiality of the issue, the insignificance of private-sector activity for monetary policy, lack of evidence, or other constraints.

The total sample of experts and decision makers therefore consisted of 57 respondents, who were interviewed between November 2002 and August 2003. Two additional respondents – one high-ranking official at the EU Commission close to the Macroeconomic Dialogue, and one academic – were consulted, and their insights entered the study as background information but were not included in the quantitative evaluation.

Composition of sample of interviewees

Table 12

	Business associations from trade and industry					
	DE			EU		DE, EU
	Federal peak associations	Regional level, Advisory Board	DE total	EU peak associations	EU total	Sample total
Number	12	12	24	9	9	33
% of total	*50.0*	*50.0*	*100.0*	*100.0*	*100.0*	
% of total			*72.7*		*27.3*	*100.0*

	Central bank					
	DE			EU		DE, EU
	Bundesbank, Central Office	Bundesbank, Regional Offices	DE total	ECB, Central Office	EU total	Sample total
Number	7	15	22	2	2	24
% of total	*31.8*	*68.2*	*100.0*	*100.0*	*100.0*	
% of total			*91.7*		*8.3*	*100.0*

Memorandum items

	All respondents		
	Decision makers	**Experts**	Sample total
Number	25	32	57
% of total	*43.9*	*56.1*	*100.0*
	Acting	**Retired**	Sample total
Number	49	8	57
% of total	*86.0*	*14.0*	*100.0*

A detailed breakdown of the sample is provided in table 12 above. Of the 57 interviewees, 33 came from interest groups and 24 from central banks. The former can be decomposed into 24 respondents reporting on interest group activity in Germany and nine at EU level. The sample of German interest group representatives was evenly distributed among respondents from peak federal associations and members of the Bundesbank's regional Advisory Boards. Among the 24 respondents at central banks, 22 came from the Bundesbank and two from the ECB. The Bundesbank sample included seven respondents from the bank's Central Office and 15 from its Regional Offices.

In total, the sample of interviewees comprised 25 decision makers, i.e. high-ranking central bank officials including acting board members and retired members of the Bundesbank's central bank council, and 32 experts working as economists, personal assistants or communications specialists involved in the preparation of monetary policy decisions and in maintaining and preparing external contacts. 49 respondents were acting decision makers or experts, while eight were retired at the time of interviewing.

Overall, the sample of 57 respondents covers a large number of the relevant experts and decision makers in the specified entities, or their designated representatives, providing a strong empirical basis for the analysis presented below.

III.1.2.2 Evaluation

Following collection and transcription[583] of the interviews, a combined qualitative and quantitative approach[584] was adopted to evaluate responses. Answers to core questions were compared among all respondents and coded according to the method proposed by Schmidt[585]:

- In an initial step, coding categories were identified for each question.
- Second, the answer categories were complemented by a scale of numerical values to enable quantification of the answers given by respondents.
- Subsequently, individual answers were coded and scaled on that basis.
- The resulting quantification was processed and evaluated mathematically.
- Where useful, insights gained from quantification were complemented by quotations or other qualitative elements from the interviews, with the aim of either explaining or elaborating on numerical results, or to identify behavioural or perceptional aspects that could not be explored by quantitative means.

Evaluation encompassed the aggregation of numerical values and calculation of statistical averages across the key strata of the samples, i.e. for interest group and

[583] The methods applied in transcribing interviews were based on Kowal, O'Connell (2000).

[584] Combining qualitative surveys with quantitative evaluation methods has been propagated as one means of improving evaluative objectivity in social science research (Dieckmann (1997), pp. 451-455, also Kelle, Erzberger (2000)). However, there is a risk of blurring results at the interface between the two approaches, namely when translating qualitative items for use in quantitative analysis by means of coding (Schmidt (2000)).

[585] Schmidt (2000).

central bank respondents as well as for regional or federal level responses in the case of Germany.

Calculation of arithmetic averages was selected as the most important indicator for aggregate responses, reflecting the total of all observations in the sample or its subsets. In addition, median responses were calculated, providing evidence on the typical responses delivered by interviewees. The median is considered a particularly robust indicator useful for evaluating small samples ranked along ordinary scales, especially in cases where single, extreme observations tend to have a substantial impact on the arithmetic average[586]. Median values are referred to in the above analysis in cases where substantial aberrations from the arithmetic average were observed.

Beyond these fundamental calculations, the response set does not lend itself to further statistical and econometric evaluation due to the small size of the sample – i.e. the limited number of respondents available in this policy area – and the relatively small number of individual statistical items collected in the course of the qualitative fieldwork as a result. Most importantly, regressions and the values yielded for correlation coefficients to identify interdependencies between the different institutional, issue, or group determinants tested here were found to lack statistical robustness. This lack of robustness, however, is primarily the result of the small size of the sample, which does not allow for meaningful sophisticated statistical analysis. It does not imply that no correlations exist between the different variables, for example, or that such correlation could be detected if the sample included a sufficient number of items.

To compensate for the fact that a meaningful sophisticated statistical analysis was discouraged by the small number of statistical items available, qualitative remarks made by the respondents and recorded in the course of the interviews are used in the above analysis to explain, illustrate, and compare the basic statistical evidence.

In addition, the responses on propositions 3 and 15 are analysed in qualitative terms only. In practice, the majority of responses were found to be highly differentiated, tempering and qualifying the overall reaction, so that an unambiguous allocation of reactions to a set of categories of answers and to a corresponding scale of numerical values was found to be inappropriate, potentially not doing justice to the level of differentiation of the responses.

Similarly, the respondents' reactions to the follow-up questions pertaining to the ways and means of communicating interests in practice, i.e. the channels used for articulating interests in the area of monetary policy, are captured above in qualitative

---

[586] For comprehensive discussions of the various measures of the centres of distribution, see e.g. Wonnacott (1990), pp. 32-39, and Dieckmann (1997), pp. 555-663.

terms only. Again, a majority of responses were highly differentiated, discouraging quantification in a meaningful way and rendering qualitative analysis the superior tool for investigation.

Coding and quantification are exclusively the result of evaluation of the qualitative answers. Interviewees were not asked to give their own quantitative assessments. Throughout the study, these quantitative results complement the qualitative material in the form of quotations from interviewees or insights form other sources, such as related literature or archival material.

III.1.2.3 Time horizon

Private-sector attitudes and activities with respect to monetary policy not only differ across countries but are also likely to change over time in each individual economy. In an inter-temporal perspective, relations between the private sector and monetary institutions and decision makers are likely to be characterised by both structural and cyclical elements. Structural relations in the current context would encompass any kind of contact, formal or informal, which the two sides maintain on a continuous basis, irrespective of whether the private sector agrees with the course of monetary policy, and aimed at securing a long-term exchange of views between the two sides. Cyclical activity, in contrast, would be in response to particular, acute developments in monetary policy which in terms of salience and urgency of the issue compel interest groups to take concrete action.

In the present context, structural and cyclical elements are of equal interest. Both elements together constitute interest groups' political activities with respect to monetary policy, and measuring the extent to which such activities are pursued is one aim of this study. In addition, the intensity with which relations are maintained in both respects can, in as far as cyclical activity is an indicator of the acuteness of an issue, give additional hints as to the intensity of preferences in trade and industry vis-à-vis monetary policy.

In terms of the time horizon under consideration, this implies that empirical evidence has to be collected in two dimensions. First, in order to identify structural patterns hypotheses with respect to interest-group behaviour need to be tested against political practices in general, irrespective of acute monetary developments. Considering that structural patterns, too, can change over time, research in this regard focused on recent and present-day patterns and was primarily addressed to acting experts and decision makers.[587] Second, in order to gain an impression of the cyclical variance in interest-

---

[587] Empirical evidence in the form of background interviews was collected between October 2002 and October 2003.

group activity with respect to monetary policy, acting as well as retired respondents were asked about past experiences in this policy field, with responses concentrated on the 1990s but some also reaching back into earlier decades.

III.2 Private-sector interest groups and the Deutsche Bundesbank

Following the analytical approach outlined above, the analysis proceeds in two steps. The first part of this chapter examines and describes the environment in which interest group preferences with respect to monetary policy are formed and communicated. Along the lines of the broad analytical framework outlined above, the following sections are concerned with the Bundesbank and other policy makers relevant to the institutional context in which interest groups operate. Further, the issue context – monetary policy in Germany – is analysed with respect to the historical development of major monetary variables as well as the record of policy decision making in the past. Finally, a section is dedicated to the group context, looking at the specific exposure of industry and trade to monetary developments as well as the interest-group infrastructure through which policy preferences can be aggregated and communicated.

Examining these three contexts in some detail helps to interpret the empirical findings presented in the second part of this chapter. The findings are structured around the three policy contexts. The questions aimed at verifying or rejecting the core propositions above and the responses collected in the background interviews with experts and decision makers are presented and discussed in turn. This is followed by a comparative analysis of the results as well as a set of interim conclusions.

Against the background of the framework conditions under which the formation, aggregation, and representation of interests among German enterprises in trade and industry takes place with respect to monetary policy, decision makers and experts from business associations, individual enterprises and the Bundesbank and ECB were interviewed with the aim of identifying the factors promoting or hampering the expression of interests in practice.

Following an outline of the specific sample of decision makers and experts whose contributions are evaluated in this chapter, the analysis commences with the results from the respondents' assessment of the level and kind of interest group activity in monetary affairs, followed by detailed analyses of the views expressed on the institutional, issue, and group contexts in which interest representatives operate. The chapter is then wound up with interim conclusions on the evidence from Germany.

III.2.1 Sub-sample of decision makers and experts in Germany

The sample of interviewees was composed of decision makers and experts from

- the peak German business associations in trade and industry, including industry[588], chambers of commerce[589], wholesale and foreign trade[590], retail trade[591], and skilled crafts[592],

---

[588] Bundesverband der Deutschen Industrie e.V., BDI.

- interest associations from those sectors in the German economy identified above as being particularly exposed to interest and exchange rate developments, including the export[593], construction[594], automotive[595], chemical[596], mechanical engineering[597], and electronics[598] sectors,
- those associations represented on the roundtable of economic experts at the Bundesbank Central Office[599], as well as those represented on the Advisory Boards of the Bundesbank Regional Offices[600],
- the Bundesbank Central Office as well as its Regional Offices. Interviewees from the Central Office included current members of the Executive Board, former members of the Central Bank Council and former Bundesbank presidents, as well as expert staff from the bank's economics and communications departments. Respondents from the Regional Offices included acting presidents of the Regional Offices as well as former presidents of the Landeszentralbanken, or experts speaking on their behalf[601].

---

589 Deutscher Industrie- und Handelskammertag, DIHK.

590 Bundesverband des Deutschen Groß- und Außenhandels e.V., BGA.

591 Hauptverband des Deutschen Einzelhandels, HDE.

592 Zentralverband des Deutschen Handwerks, ZDH.

593 Bundesverband des Deutschen Exporthandels e.V., BDEx.

594 Hauptverband der Deutschen Bauindustrie e.V., HDB.

595 Verband der Automobilindustrie e.V., VDA.

596 Verband der Chemischen Industrie e.V., VCI.

597 Verband Deutscher Maschinen- und Anlagenbau e.V., VDMA.

598 Zentralverband Elektrotechnik- und Elektronikindustrie e.V., ZVEI.

599 The roundtable is composed of external representatives from the BDI, BGA, DIHK, HDE, VDA, VDMA, WVS, ZDB, ZDH, and the ZVEI.

600 The sample included representatives of regional business associations sitting on the Advisory Boards of the Bundesbank's Regional Offices in Berlin, Düsseldorf, Frankfurt, Hamburg, Hanover, Leipzig, Mainz, and Munich. The Advisory Board members interviewed were representatives – mainly presidents – of regional chambers of commerce, trade, and crafts as well as of regional industry associations or individual enterprises. Three Advisory Board members were represented by their staff.

601 In total, the sample included acting or former decision makers or experts from the Bundesbank's Regional Offices in Berlin, Düsseldorf, Frankfurt, Hamburg, Leipzig, Mainz, Munich and Stuttgart and from the former Landeszentralbank in Bremen.

Interviewees at German business associations and the Deutsche Bundesbank

Chart 53

– Composition of sample of interviewees at German interest associations.

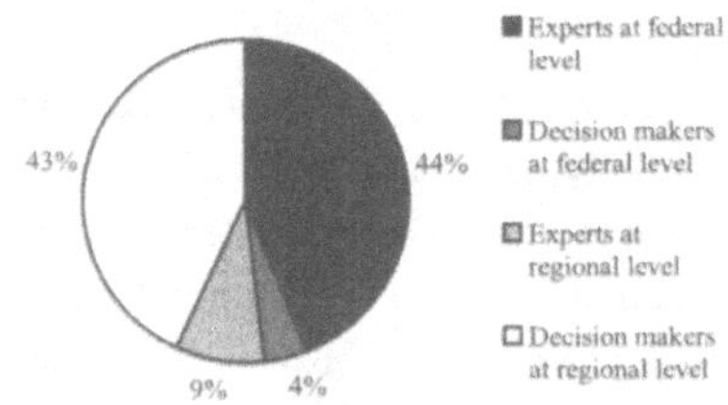

– Total number: 24

Chart 54

– Composition of sample of interviewees at the Deutsche Bundesbank.

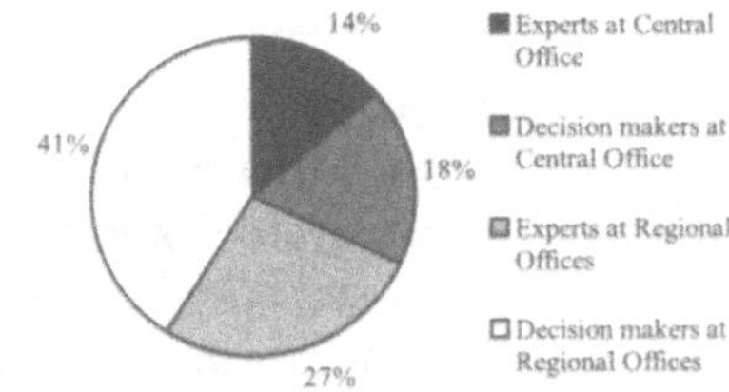

– Total number: 22

The number of decision makers and experts interviewed in Germany between November 2002 and January 2004 totalled 46, 24 of whom were representatives of business associations and 22 representatives from the Bundesbank. Twelve of the 24 business representatives were selected from federal business associations, including peak associations as well as sectoral organisations. Twelve business representatives came from regional or local organisations represented on one of the Bundesbank's nine Advisory Boards. As chart 53 shows, the majority of respondents at federal peak associations were expert staff working at the headquarters of these associations, while the majority of representatives of regional interest associations were decision makers. Representatives from regional associations were approached for their membership in one of the Bundesbank's Advisory Boards. Interviews were conducted directly with these members, who, in general, hold the position of presidents of the relevant regional association. Overall, more than one quarter of all 42 Advisory Board members from trade and industry were interviewed.

On the Bundesbank side, seven respondents were interviewed at the Central Office and 15 at the Regional Offices. As chart 54 above shows, respondents at the bank's Central Office were evenly distributed between decision-maker and expert status. At the regional level, the number of interviewees at decision-making level outnumbered that of expert-level interviewees, reflecting the comparatively large number of former Landeszentralbank presidents who – as *ex officio* members of the former Central Bank Council – were directly involved in monetary decision making prior to 1999[602]. In total, the number of retired Bundesbank staff amounted to eight – two former decision makers at the bank's Directorate and six former Landeszentralbank presidents.

The sample consequently captures the major stakeholders in the monetary policy field as well as a large number of the key individuals involved at decision-making and

[602] Acting presidents of the Regional Offices who are no longer directly involved in monetary decision-making have been categorised as experts rather than decision makers.

expert levels in policymaking at present and in the recent past. In so far, the sample can be regarded as ample and highly representative of the relevant policy community[603].

III.2.2 Interest-group activity on monetary policy in Germany

The most fundamental question to be answered at the outset in the present context is whether and to what extent interest groups actually undertake political action on monetary policy. From a lobbying angle, the answer to this question is interesting in its own right, but it may also carry important implications in terms of empirical findings on the influence of private interests on monetary policy established in literature examining the pressures on monetary policy. It may be recalled from the discussion in the institutional context that empirical evaluations of the impact of interest-group statements as reflected in newspaper coverage on monetary policy in Germany show that the effects of such public utterances is minimal at best.

However, this does not necessarily mean that no influence on monetary policy is sought at all. Interest groups may seek to influence monetary decisions by means other than public statements vis-à-vis the media. If this were the case, then analyses based exclusively on indices of interest group positions as reflected in the media – valuable as such indices are as an indicator – may miss out on signals from interest groups to monetary policy makers relevant for the assessment of pressure on decision makers at central banks. Given the broad behavioural patterns of monetary policy makers at the Bundesbank discussed earlier, the possibility cannot be ruled out that the Bundesbank may prefer a confidential style of communication outside the public arena, considering that policy recommendations in public may signify impairment of the bank's independent status and of its reputation as the expert institution on monetary issues. In addition, public comments on monetary policy by an interest group may not entirely reflect that group's position, especially in terms of its intensity, as interest groups themselves have incentives to support the Bundesbank publicly, given a certain commitment to monetary stability and central bank independence on their own part.

In line with the propositions derived from the theoretical discussion, interviewees were therefore asked about the extent to which monetary policy and the Bundesbank are subject to interest group lobbying and about the channels used by group representatives to influence monetary decision making.

---

[603] All quantitative data presented below, including coding and quantification of responses, are derived exclusively from evaluation of the qualitative answers. Interviewees were not asked to give their own quantitative assessments. Cases in which no or an inconclusive answer was obtained are not included in the calculations and illustrations. The same applies to cases in which a given question was not asked to individual respondents due to time constraints during the interview. For the sake of transparency, all graphical illustrations cite the number of responses included in the quantification.

Proposition 1	Question	Categories	Scale
In general, interests with respect to monetary or exchange rate policy are not communicated very intensively to the relevant decision makers.	*As addressed to interest groups:* "Do you or the organisation you represent, in general, mediate interests with respect to monetary or exchange rate policy?" *As addressed to central banks:* "Do interest associations, in general, mediate interests with respect to monetary or exchange rate policy?"	"Very intensively"	1
		"Intensively"	2
		"Moderately"	3
		"Very moderately"	4
		"No"	5

The general assessment by the decision makers and experts questioned shows that monetary policy is, in fact, a policy field in which the communication of business interests is almost negligible. 35% of all respondents stated that such interests were, in general not communicated at all. Another 41% perceived the communication of interests as very moderate. 20% of respondents considered interest group activity moderate, and only 4% thought that such activity could be described as intensive, as illustrated in chart 55. In other words, more than three quarters of all respondents considered lobbying on monetary policy as very moderate or non-existent. The numerical average of the responses amounted to 4.07, indicating that, on average, interest group activity was judged very moderate[604].

However, perception of the intensity of interest-group activity differs markedly between interest group and central bank representatives, i.e. between the senders and recipients. As chart 56 shows, the average numerical values for the two sides – 4.21 and 3.91 respectively – suggest that interest group representatives considered their individual activities to be less intensive than their addressees. This discrepancy is particularly visible at the federal level, i.e. comparing the responses by representatives of peak federal associations – 4.42 on average[605] – with those of Bundesbank staff at the Central Office – 3.57 on average –, implying that monetary policy makers perceived significantly stronger activity on the part of interest groups than the latter said they were taking.

---

[604] The corresponding median value was 4.00, indicating that the typical response lay very close to the average.

[605] For respondents of regional interest groups represented on the Advisory Boards, the average value was 4.00, while the median result was 5.00, suggesting that the typical answer among these respondents was tilted even more towards a more pessimistic assessment of interest group activity in this policy field.

These numerical results are underscored by the structure of replies from the two sides, as shown in charts 57 and 58. Most strikingly, 67% of replies from federal-level peak associations considered that virtually no systematic communication of business interests with respect to monetary policy existed. In contrast, the majority of members of Bundesbank Advisory Boards at regional level perceived their activities as slightly more intensive, albeit as still very moderate. At the Bundesbank, more than three-quarters of respondents rated interest intermediation moderate or very moderate, with less than one-quarter of replies suggesting practically no interest group activity. The latter were made exclusively by respondents at the bank's Regional Offices, where interest-group politics was seen as less intensive – 4.07 on average – than by their colleagues at the Central Office – 3.57 on average.

Interest group activity on monetary policy

Chart 55

– All respondents, in % of total responses

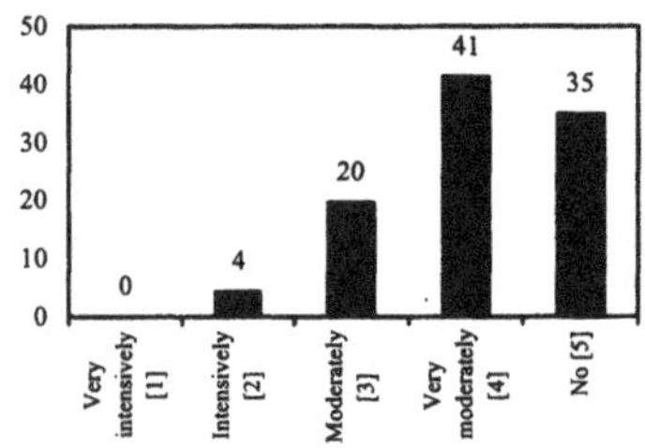

– Number of responses: 46
– Average value of responses: 4.07

Chart 56

– Average values of responses by level

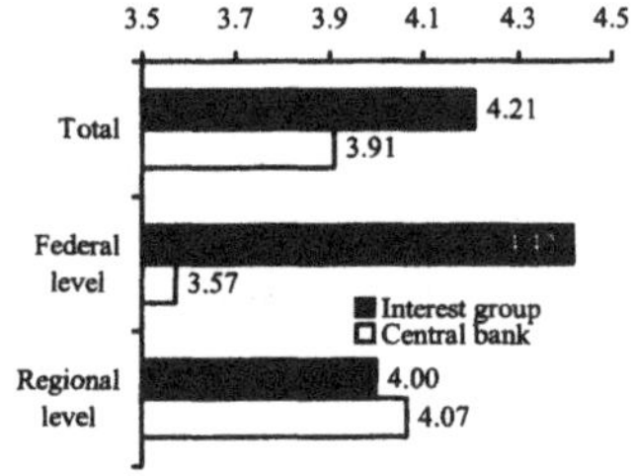

– Number of responses: 46

Chart 57

– Respondents from interest groups, in %

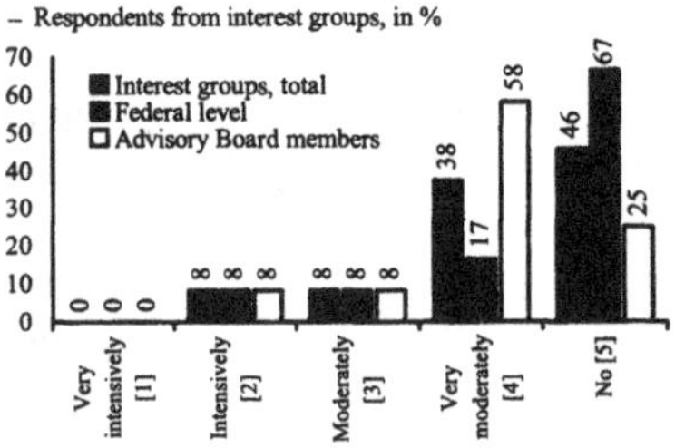

– Number of responses: 24

Chart 58

– Respondents from Deutsche Bundesbank, in %

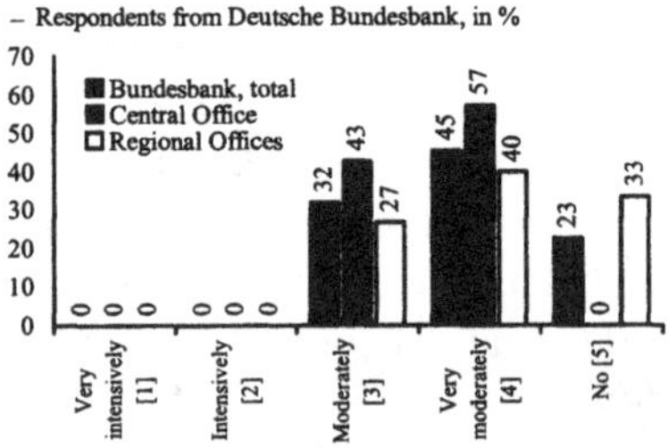

– Number of responses: 22

In summary, therefore, lobbying by private business associations on monetary policy – viewed in isolation and without regard for potential distortion from competing dominant issues – is very moderate, a view shared by a great majority of policy makers and experts on both the association as well as the central bank side. Central bankers, however, consider interest group activity markedly higher than their counterparts in the private sector, which together with replies from the Regional Offices suggests that the Central Office is slightly more exposed to interest group activity than the Hauptverwaltungen.

Proposition 2	Question	Categories	Scale
In general, communication of interests with respect to monetary or exchange rate policy is significantly lower than in other policy fields.	*As addressed to interest groups:* "Do you or the organisation you represent, in general, mediate interests with respect to monetary or exchange rate policy to the same extent as with respect to other policy fields?" *As addressed to central banks:* "Do interest associations, in general, mediate interests with respect to monetary or exchange rate policy to the same extent as with respect to other policy fields?"	"Much more intensively"	1
		"More intensively"	2
		"As intensively"	3
		"Less intensively"	4
		"Much less intensively"	5

The findings on proposition 1 are confirmed by the results yielded after adding a comparative dimension to the assessment, i.e. interest group activity with respect to monetary policy is not just low by itself but it is lower than that observed in other areas of economic policymaking, e.g. with respect to fiscal and tax policy, regulatory policy, or labour market and wage policies. Adding this comparative dimension is useful in two respects. First, it provides an anchor for assessing the intensity of interest intermediation. The question as to how much lobbying is being undertaken naturally triggers the counter-question: By which standards? Comparison with other policy areas is the most relevant yardstick to be applied in the current context. Second, it is of assistance in interpreting the findings on the first proposition in as far as it helps explain the particular insignificance of interest representation with respect to monetary policy detected by the majority of peak business associations.

First, the responses to this proposition confirm and accentuate the evidence on the first proposition. Asked to what extent communication of interests with respect to monetary policy was comparable to activities in other policy areas, 27% of all respondents stated that activity was less intensive and 70% stated that it was much less intensive than in other policy areas[606]. At 4.67, the numerical average of total responses was close to the maximum possible. This result is accentuated by the median value, which is 5.00 for

[606] See chart 59.

all respondents as well as for almost all sub-sets[607] of the sample, suggesting that activities were generally regarded as much less intensive than in other policy areas. Only one respondent – from a federal business association with a focus on trade interests – considered the communication of interests with respect to monetary and exchange rate issues comparable to other activities.

Second, the distribution among interest group and Bundesbank representatives, as depicted in charts 61 and 62, suggests that interest associations at federal level regard their work on monetary policy as particularly less intensive when compared to other policy issues. Almost all respondents stated that monetary affairs-related political activity was much less extensive than activities in other policy areas. Compared with the non-comparative assessment of interest group activity under the first proposition, this result strongly suggests that the large federal business associations in particular are involved in a greater number of policy issues, with monetary policy clearly being of lesser priority. Central bankers, in contrast, are almost exclusively concerned with monetary policy and confronted with the views expressed by a wide variety of associations, so that interest group activity on aggregate is perceived as more intensive, explaining the difference in answers between the two sides on the non-comparative and comparative propositions.

This interpretation is supported by the comments of the majority of respondents, pointing – especially at federal level – to major policy areas such as taxation, industry regulation, labour market and wage policy, and social security provisions as the fields in which the major business associations take an interest, formulate and express strong positions and seek to influence policy makers actively and on a continuous basis.

Most regional and local-level business representatives drew attention to the wide variety of taxation, regulation and public procurement-related issues discussed at Land or community level, on which they concentrated their lobbying activities. A large number of respondents stated that monetary and exchange rate issues were, by their nature, federal – and since 1999 EMU-wide – concerns which did not fall within the scope of their activities in the strict sense. In this sense, membership on the Advisory Boards at the Bundesbank Regional Offices was characterised by many members as an anomaly compared to their conventional activities, which were mainly restricted to policy issues with a regional dimension.

---

[607] Bundesbank staff at the Central Office produce a median reply of 4.50.

Interest group activity on monetary policy compared with other policy fields

Chart 59

– All respondents, in %

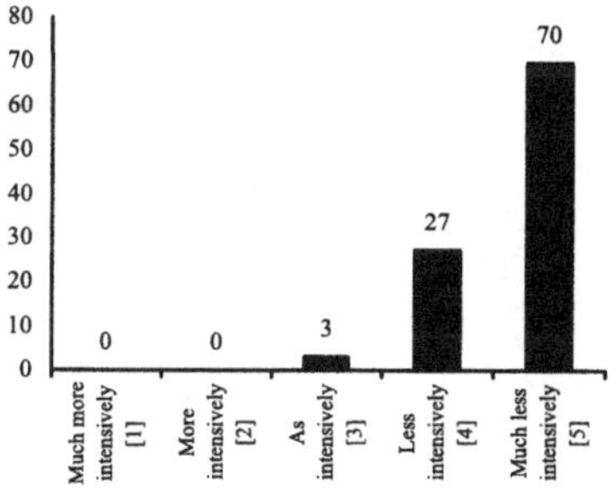

– Number of responses: 33
– Average value of responses: 4.67

Chart 60

– Average values of responses by level

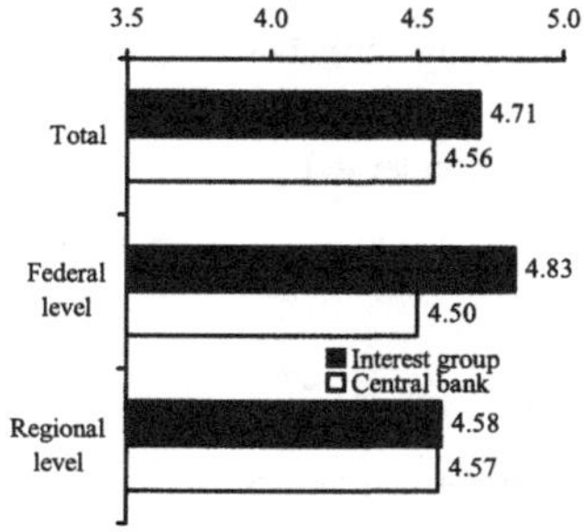

– Number of responses: 33

Chart 61

– Respondents from interest groups, in %

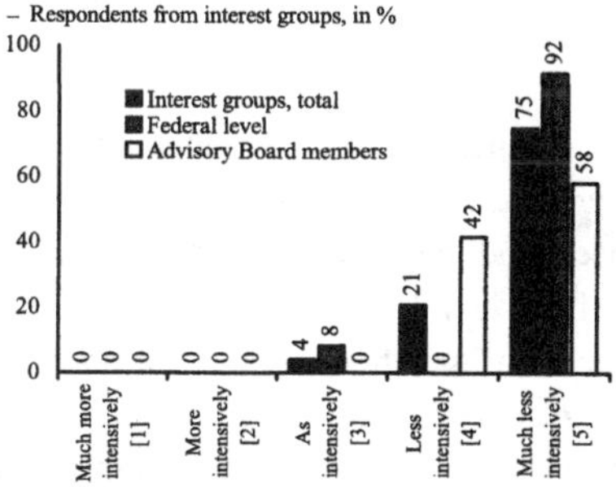

– Number of responses: 24

Chart 62

– Respondents from Deutsche Bundesbank, in %

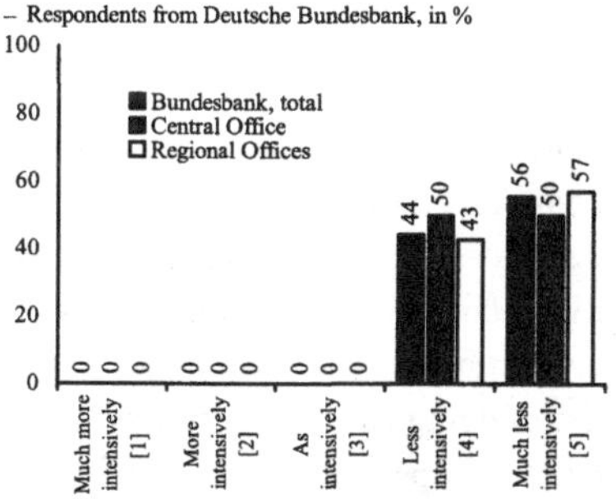

– Number of responses: 9

A number of respondents pointed out in this context that in practice the intensity of activity in the various policy areas differed markedly over time, depending on the salience of each individual issue, as analysed in greater detail below. None of the respondents commenting on this point reported instances in which action on monetary or exchange rate policy had clearly dominated interest group activity. A number of respondents observed instances of intensified work in this policy area relative to other policy fields, including

- the period of monetary and exchange rate instability during the early and mid-1970s,
- exchange rate fluctuations in the mid-1980s,
- the high-interest period in the first half of the 1990s and the tensions within the EMS of 1992 and 1993, and

- backing of the plan to establish a monetary union within the EU in the late 1980s and early 1990s and the subsequent promotion of the EMU project.

Respondents emphasised that at any given moment in recent history, other economic policy issues, especially taxation, industry regulation and welfare policy, took clear preference over monetary and exchange rate issues in terms of lobbying activity by the interest groups concerned.

Proposition 3	Question	Categories[608] Scale
Mediating interests with respect to monetary or exchange rate policy does not yield sufficient benefits relative to the associated costs.	"Do you, in principle, consider mediating interests with respect to monetary or exchange rate policy to be worthwhile pursuing?"	None
		None
		None
		None

The third general proposition derived from the theoretical discussion is that mediating interests with respect to monetary policy does not yield sufficient benefits relative to the associated costs. Assuming that enterprises and their interest representatives essentially compare the potential costs and benefits when deciding on whether to take political action on a certain policy issue, it has been hypothesised that the potential benefits of doing so are particularly low and the related costs particularly high – given the specific properties of the issue, institutional, and group contexts in which lobbying activities on monetary issues would occur.

In order to examine whether this logic applies in practice, interest group representatives were asked whether in principle they considered mediating interests with respect to monetary policy worthwhile. The responses to this question produced three major insights. Most importantly, all respondents agreed that a meaningful cost-benefit analysis of whether and to what extent action should be taken on monetary or exchange rate issues was not feasible. Acknowledging that it was generally difficult to weigh up the costs and benefits of interest-group activities, the potential material benefits from influencing monetary policy were considered particularly hard to capture, either in a qualitative or quantitative manner. A number of respondents

608 Responses to this proposition are analysed in qualitative terms only. In practice, the majority of responses were found to be highly differentiated, qualifying the overall response, so that an unambiguous allocation of reactions to a set of categories of answers and a corresponding scale of numerical values was found to be inappropriate, potentially not doing justice to the level of differentiation of the responses.

pointed to the complexity of the monetary impulse transmission mechanism, combined with the differences in their members' exposure to interest, exchange and inflation rates as the most important source of uncertainty in the calculus.

In addition, a majority of respondents observed that lobbying central bank decision makers was considered more resource-consuming than lobbying conventional politicians and policy makers, given their independent status and expertise. In order to reach a reasonable level of communication with monetary policy makers, substantial resources were considered necessary, presupposing additional investment in the issue.

Second, and subject to the predominant view that a meaningful cost-benefit analysis of political action was particularly difficult in the area of monetary and exchange rate policy, responses to proposition 3 exhibited a discernible, albeit non-quantifiable tilt towards pessimistic assessment of the net benefits of political action in this area. Systematic interest group activity on monetary policy was not considered worthwhile by a large majority of respondents, with roughly two-thirds of the 24 interest group representatives who gave an assessment on this question positing that systematic lobbying on monetary policy was rather or even very worthless. Only about one-third of the respondents considered it worthwhile to some extent, mentioning potential benefits from becoming engaged.

Almost all of the sceptical respondents argued that there was no reason to lobby in the first place. Monetary policy is generally perceived as working effectively and largely in consistency with the general interests of the business sector. In addition, many respondents argued that changes in monetary and exchange rate variables were a part of the economy's cyclical development, which had to be taken as largely exogenous. In line with this reasoning, one respondent from a peak industry association stated that

> "[c]hanges in interest and exchange rates over time are a natural thing. Complaining about their movements is like objecting to the weather."

Another characteristic reaction, by a federal sectoral industry association, was that

> "[i]nfluencing monetary or exchange rate decisions would be unrealistic at best. The financial and reputational costs of targeting the Bundesbank would be astronomical – only to find out that the Bundesbank does not actually have very much of a choice when making its policy decisions owing to the pressures from international financial markets."

Further, many also referred to the Bundesbank's economy-wide outlook, in the context of which individual positions on the policy stance were considered irrelevant, and to the bank's independence and the difficulties this implied for influencing its policies. A number of respondents held that central banks, including the Bundesbank, had no realistic chance of intervening effectively on exchange rates, even if they wanted to. It was pointed out that central banks' abilities to influence interest rates, inflation and other monetary variables, were rather limited.

According to a less sceptical interpretation, if preferences existed on the state of the economy and the course of monetary policy, then mediating and explaining these interests could do no harm. These respondents maintained that arriving at a moderately informed opinion on monetary policy was not particularly resource-consuming for interest groups.

Third, as in the case of propositions regarding the intensity of interest-group activity, respondents at federal level were on average particularly sceptical about the usefulness of political action in this policy area, with about half of them conjecturing that it was very worthless to operate in this field. Again, the reservations at this level are likely to be closely associated with the density of political issues covered at federal level, suggesting that from a comparative perspective the expected pay-offs from work in other, more pressing policy areas were deemed higher than from activities associated with monetary policy. Here too, a number of representatives from business associations pointed out that the major policy challenges and the greatest material impact of economic policies on their constituents were expected from tax and regulatory policies. The economic impact of the latter was considered comparatively straightforward to qualify and quantify, while policy makers in these areas were considered much easier to approach than monetary decision makers.

III.2.3 Institutional context

Monetary policy decisions are taken within an institutional context differing markedly from other policy areas, especially from political decisions taken in a parliamentary context. In the final analysis, the theoretical considerations and the basic patterns of decision making in Germany discussed above suggest that these institutional specificities are likely to constrain interest representation by private interest groups. The feedback by interest group and central bank representatives shows that in practice the institutional framework strongly conditions the way in which the two sides communicate. The hurdles to accessibility in the form of the Bundesbank's independence and certain behavioural patterns by monetary decision makers are, however, not fundamentally criticised, being respected by the majority of interest representatives as largely unavoidable.

The central question arising in this context is whether institutional hurdles existed impeding interest group representatives' access to monetary decision makers, and to what extent the associated difficulties in mediating private-sector interests contributed to the low level of such activity observed above. To answer this question, the interviewees in trade and industry and the Bundesbank were first asked whether the

Bundesbank was actually perceived as particularly inaccessible, compared to other political institutions and policy makers. Evidence on the most important explanatory variables identified theoretically – i.e. the Bundesbank status of independence within the political system, its independence from political support from the private sector, the bank's superior provision with information and expertise in its area of policymaking and certain behavioural patterns on the part of Bundesbank policy makers – is presented in the subsequent sections.

Proposition 4	Question	Categories	Scale
Central banks are perceived as inaccessible to interests from the private sector, compared to other political bodies.	"Is the central bank – compared to other political bodies – viewed as accessible to interests from the corporate sector?"	"Very accessible"	1
		"Rather accessible"	2
		"Rather inaccessible"	3
		"Very inaccessible"	4

Asked whether the Bundesbank was perceived – in general terms – as accessible for interest groups trying to communicate their interests in monetary policy, a relative majority of 49% of all respondents considered the bank to be either very or rather accessible, with 44% tending to the latter. In contrast, 51% characterised the bank as either rather inaccessible or very inaccessible, as shown in chart 63. At 2.63, the average numerical value of the replies was slightly below the median answer[609] of 3.00 so that the overall picture is one of inaccessibility. On average, accessibility was deemed slightly greater by central bank respondents, while interest-group representatives were considerably more sceptical about the Bundesbank's accessibility, as the comparison in chart 64 suggests. Respondents from peak federal associations and the Bundesbank Central Office, in turn, perceived accessibility to be greater than their regional counterparts, suggesting that the bank's Regional Offices are less accessible than the Central Office[610].

---

[609] On this proposition, average and median responses did not differ systematically.

[610] Interviewees were asked to give an assessment based on their experience with the levels with which they were primarily concerned, i.e. either the bank's Central Office or the Regional Offices. The replies obtained on this proposition can, therefore, also be used to draw conclusions about the difference in accessibility for the two levels.

Institutional accessibility of the Bundesbank

Chart 63

– All respondents, in %

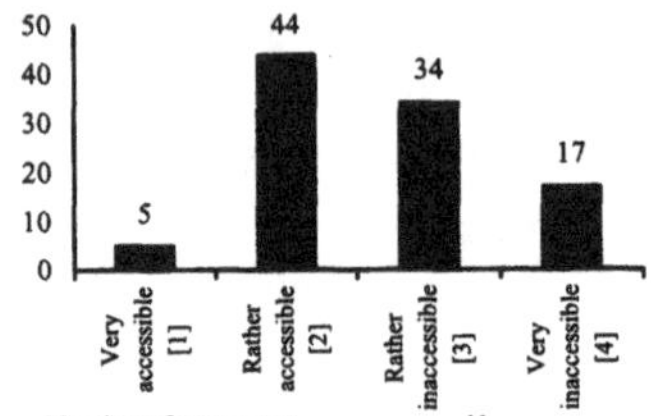

– Number of responses: 41
– Average value of responses: 2.63

Chart 64

– Average values of responses by level

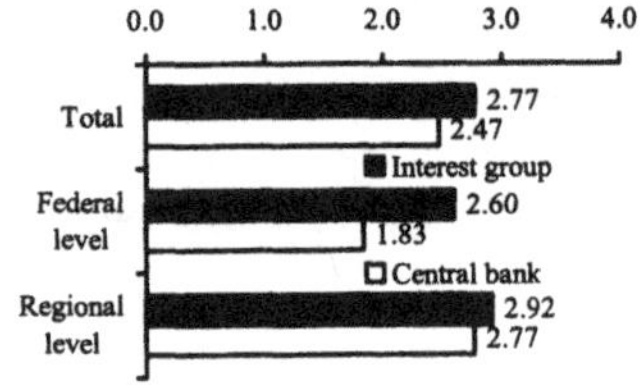

– Number of responses: 41

Chart 65

– Respondents from interest groups, in %

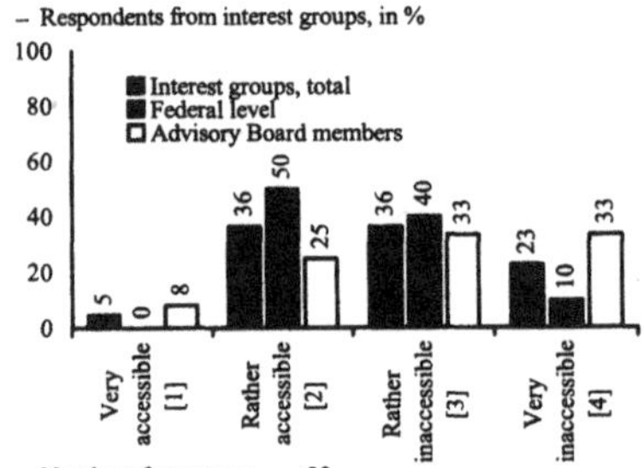

– Number of responses: 22

Chart 66

– Respondents from Deutsche Bundesbank, in %

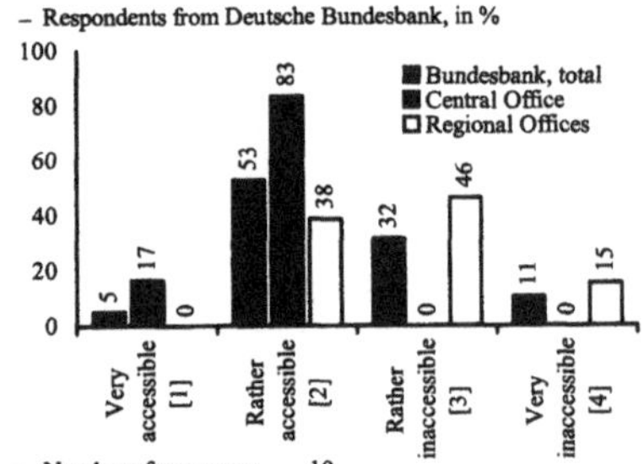

– Number of responses: 19

A detailed view on the quantified replies, as provided in charts 65 and 66, points up three important properties of the distribution of answers. First, the majority of Advisory Board members, 66% in total, considered the Bundesbank either rather or very inaccessible. Only one quarter of respondents characterised the bank as rather accessible. This assessment differs markedly from that of interest group respondents at the federal level, as reflected in the corresponding numerical averages of 2.92 and 2.60 respectively. The remarks made by respondents at both levels suggest that the relative and – after entry into EMU and the recent institutional reform – increasing remoteness of the Bundesbank's Regional Offices and the adjacent Advisory Boards from monetary decision making is the most important factor explaining this difference. In addition, verdicts in the case of Advisory Board members that the Bundesbank was considered very inaccessible may be influenced by their assessment of the specific behaviour of individual presidents of the respective Regional Offices, some of whom were reported to have displayed particular seclusion or disinterest during Advisory Board meetings. Finally, for almost all Advisory Board members, the board represents the only channel of communication with the Bundesbank, reducing their contacts with the relevant experts and decision makers to the now half-yearly board meetings.

Conversely, the large number of respondents from peak federal associations considering the Bundesbank a rather accessible institution can be traced back to the fact that, if at all, federal-level interest representatives maintained relations with the Bundesbank's Central Office and thus enjoyed greater proximity to the bank's decision making bodies. Further, a majority of the respondents perceiving greater accessibility relative to their peers also reported that they maintained more than one point of contact to the Bundesbank, e.g. membership in the roundtable of economists plus informal or personal contacts with Bundesbank experts or decision makers.

Third, the marked difference in assessment between interest group and central bank representatives results primarily from the responses given by decision makers and experts at the bank's Central Office, all of whom considered the Bundesbank to be either very or rather accessible. This contrasts with 61% of the representatives at the Regional Offices, who stated that the bank was either rather or very inaccessible. Detailed responses by representatives at the Regional Offices suggest that much of this critical assessment reflects reservations as to their own position in the policymaking process. Certain doubts as to the influence of the presidents of the Landeszentralbanken on monetary decision making at the time were articulated by a number of retired LZB presidents, suggesting that – although formally provided with an equal vote on the Central Bank Council – individual views from the Regional Offices did not have the same weight as for example a policy position prepared by the Central Office-based Bundesbank Directorate. This distribution of influence was subsequently accentuated by entry into EMU and the bank's recent structural reform, as a result of which it is now only the president of the Bundesbank who formally participates in monetary decision making at the ECB level. The above empirical results therefore pay tribute to the fact that the presidents of the Regional Offices and the other members of the bank's Board are no longer formally involved.

Finally, detailed remarks by interest group respondents suggest that, comparatively speaking, Bundesbank policy makers are perceived as less accessible – although not fundamentally so – than policy makers in other policy fields, especially governmental or parliamentary functions at federal or Land level:

- Their independence of political support was mentioned as the single most important factor limiting comparative accessibility.
- Second, a majority of interest group respondents refer to the superior expertise of the Bundesbank and its officials in their field of policymaking as a factor rendering intervention on their part obsolete or difficult, setting communication with the Bundesbank clearly apart from that with other political bodies.
- Finally, a number of respondents, both at the federal and regional level, pointed out that it was more difficult to establish regular contacts with Bundesbank

officials than with other policy makers because the Bundesbank, being located in Frankfurt, was geographically detached from the country's political centre, Berlin, and from the Land capitals.

Overall, this quantification shows that interest group representatives, especially those operating at the regional level, perceive the Bundesbank as not very accessible on average. Nevertheless, these initial results do not lend strong support to the proposition that inaccessibility is a dominant explanation for the low level of interest group activity in monetary policymaking. The structure of assessments is rather heterogeneous, though, suggesting that the criteria or the experiences on which the positions are based differ considerably among the respondents. As the following dissection of the determinants of institutional accessibility shows, the differences in perception are likely to originate from the varied experiences with policy makers' behavioural patterns. In contrast, the impact of the bank's political independence and resource-related autonomy on interest groups' ability to influence monetary policy decisions is perceived as strong quite homogeneously across the sample of interest group interviewees.

III.2.3.1 Institutional mandate and accessibility

The concentration of decision-making powers in one single institution separate and largely independent of the surrounding political system is the central feature distinguishing monetary policy from most other instances of political decision making. In the case of the Bundesbank, a comparatively high level of independence was established, accompanied by a clear assignment of tasks, broadly defined single objectives and far-reaching discretion with respect to the strategies, tactics and instruments applied to meet its objectives. While the clear assignment of tasks can facilitate interest group activity in as far as it implies that one single interlocutor exists for private-sector concerns, the independence of the Bundesbank may be perceived as an obstacle to effective interest representation, as it limits the channels of communication, especially the indirect communication of interests via the government and other political bodies, and potentially constrains the responsiveness of Bundesbank decision making to private-sector preferences. As to the institutional mandate, the respondents were therefore asked to give their assessment of the impact of central bank independence on communication between the Bundesbank and private-sector interest groups.

Proposition 5	Question	Categories	Scale
Political independence is an obstacle for private interests in mediating their interests to the central bank.	"Is political independence of the central bank perceived as an obstacle to mediating corporate interests?"	"Strong obstacle"	1
		"Obstacle"	2
		"Weak obstacle"	3
		"No obstacle"	4

In practice, the Bundesbank's independence is assessed differently by the actors involved. Asked whether they perceived the Bundesbank's political autonomy as an obstacle to mediating private-sector interests, 47% of all respondents said it did represent an obstacle, or even a strong obstacle, while 54% considered it to be a weak obstacle or did not perceive it as an impediment to interest group politics at all, as illustrated in chart 67. The numerical average of the total responses works out at 2.70, i.e. slightly below the median of 3.00, suggesting that overall independence is perceived as a rather weak impediment. Although, at 2.79 and 2.63 respectively, central bank and interest group respondents arrived at a similar assessment of this issue on average, interest group representatives interestingly considered political independence to be less of an obstacle than their counterparts at the Bundesbank. This picture is confirmed by the median responses for the sub-sets, which show that interest group respondents typically considered independence a weak obstacle, while Bundesbank respondents typically viewed it as an obstacle, or even a strong obstacle in the case of the respondents at the Central Office. This discrepancy is confirmed by average numerical values, as chart 68 suggests.

The differences in perception become more apparent in the breakdown of responses according to the respondents' background, as in charts 69 and 70. More than half of all interest group respondents state that independence is, in fact, an obstacle or even a strong obstacle to interest communication, with no significant differences between the responses from federal and regional-level interest representatives. More than two-thirds of all Bundesbank representatives at the Central Office, in contrast, consider independence to be no significant obstacle to communication with the private sector. Respondents from the bank's Regional Office adopted no dominant stance on this issue.

Impact of institutional independence

Chart 67

– All respondents, in %

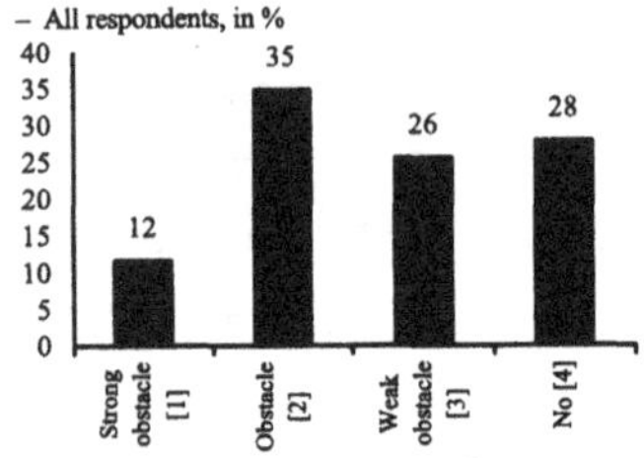

– Number of responses: 43
– Average value of responses: 2.70

Chart 68

– Average values of responses by level

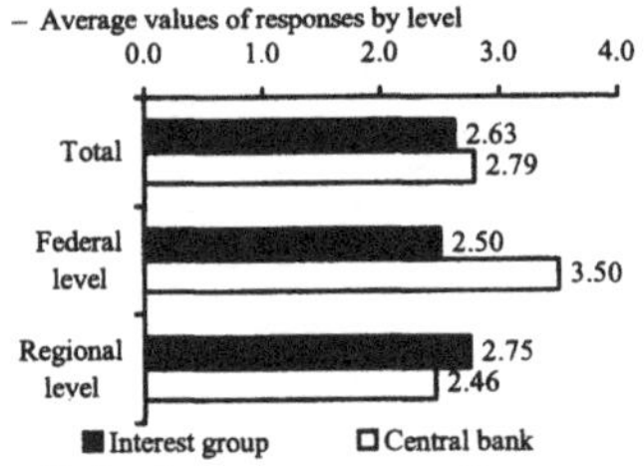

– Number of responses: 43

Chart 69

– Respondents from interest groups, in %

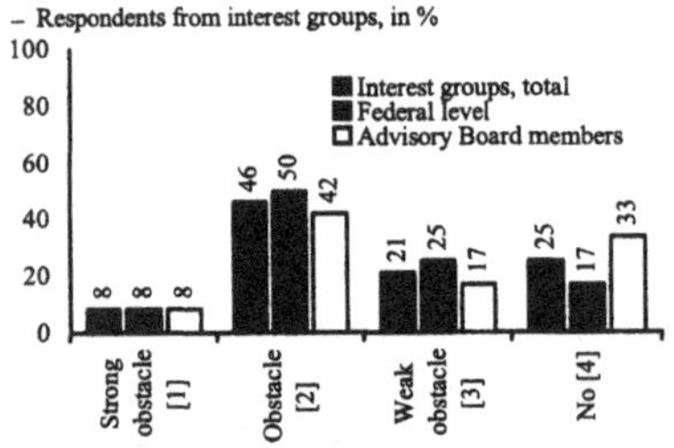

– Number of responses: 24

Chart 70

– Respondents from Deutsche Bundesbank, in %

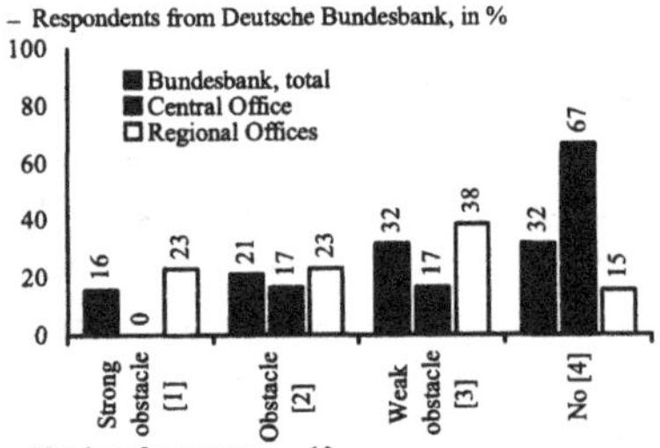

– Number of responses: 19

The reactions captured in this quantitative evaluation give the initial responses to the question concerning the impact of independence and are therefore likely to reflect the respondents' intuitive views. A more differentiated picture on the structure of responses can be obtained by taking into account the more detailed comments made, especially on the interest group side.

First of all, in-depth analysis of the responses reveals a close qualitative correlation between the assessments of accessibility, as examined under proposition 4, and of political independence, as examined here. In general, respondents critical of the Bundesbank's accessibility also referred to its independence as a serious obstacle to mediating interests, and *vice versa*. Conversely, those interest group representatives who perceived the Bundesbank as rather accessible also rejected political independence as a significant hurdle to political communication.

Second, most commentators point out that they prefer to distinguish between

– political independence in the strict sense, i.e. the legal bar on orders being issued to the central bank by government or other political bodies in the constitutional system, and

– political independence in a wider sense, i.e. that the central bank should not be subject to political or otherwise motivated external influence.

Without exception, all commentators agree that political independence in the strict sense is an important, if not necessary precondition for monetary stability and a highly desirable feature of the country's monetary system. Accordingly, political institutions, i.e. government, parliament, or other national and international political institutions, should be prohibited from actively influencing monetary policy or from seeking such influence. As emphasised by a number of respondents, this naturally extends to the private sector, which by its very nature does not possess instruments of direct influence on central bank decision making.

In contrast, political independence in the wider sense is a more controversial issue in Germany. Particularly as far as those respondents are concerned for whom independence does represent an obstacle to the communication of interests, for either of the following two reasons the logic of independence from politics also spills over into the private sector with regard to the expression of group-specific preferences on monetary policy. First, monetary policy should exclusively serve the common good and should therefore be conducted and based on an economy-wide view rather than on particular interests. In this sense, interest group activity is not considered legitimate, even by a considerable number of interest group representatives. Second, interference with the Bundesbank in its monetary decision making – especially in public – is considered counterproductive in as far as interest groups demand that the central bank be politically independent on the one hand, while simultaneously seeking to influence its policy decisions on the other. For a number of interest group respondents, claiming non-interference from political institutions while at the same time having the private sector attempt to influence monetary decisions would be inconsistent and damaging to the group's credibility. As a result, interest group representatives emphasising these arguments tended to see political independence as a constraining factor – also on the private sector.

On the other hand, a large number of respondents stressed that political autonomy was to be understood in the narrow sense only, and that in the wider context of interest group politics no limitation applied to the communication of interests. In these respondents' view, central bank independence serves to prevent monetary measures becoming instrumentalised by electoral politics. In as far as the private sector has no direct influence on the Bundesbank and its decisions, mediating group interests in this policy area is, in principle, a legitimate expression of private interests. Being independent, the Bundesbank can decide for itself whether and to what extent it chooses to take these interests into consideration when adopting its monetary decisions. Nevertheless, even among the respondents arguing along this line, a great majority emphasised that the Bundesbank's specific status necessitated a much more moderate way of communication than in other areas of policymaking.

Both strands of argument were also reflected in the replies from Bundesbank representatives. In general, Bundesbank respondents emphasised that political independence was a fact, placing the bank in a position to take autonomous decisions on monetary questions. This applied to the Bundesbank's own monetary policy prior to 1999 as well as to formulation of the monetary stance the bank's president defends on the ECB Governing Council. In the light of this, the great majority of Bundesbank decision makers did not perceive the expression and communication of private-sector interests as interfering with the bank's activities or its independence, provided such claims were not aimed at limiting the Bundesbank's independence as such.

Calls for the latter from the business sector have reportedly never been registered in the bank's history. Quite the contrary, the business community is perceived as having been one of the most reliable, if not the most reliable, supporters of the Bundesbank whenever its institutional independence was at stake in the past. Bundesbank and interest group representatives cited as two recent examples calls in 1998 and 1999 by the then finance minister Oscar Lafontaine for a more lenient monetary policy and the attempt by finance minister Theo Waigel in 1997 to revalue the Bundesbank's gold reserves with the aim of paying down part of the national debt. In both cases, the major business associations were said to have supported the Bundesbank, arguing that the government's plans marked illegitimate encroachment on the bank's exclusive rights and obligations.

Overall, therefore, Bundesbank independence is largely considered a factor constraining, or at least moderating, the communication of private-sector interests to a greater or lesser extent and for differing reasons. It is nonetheless seen as a vital precondition for a well-functioning monetary regime.

Proposition 6	Question	Categories	Scale
Given their institutional, material, and expertise-based resources, central banks are not dependent on external political support in order to fulfil their tasks in the field of monetary or exchange rate policy.	"Does the central bank depend on external political support in order to fulfil its tasks in the field of monetary or exchange rate policy?"	"Strong dependence"	1
		"Moderate dependence"	2
		"Weak dependence"	3
		"No dependence"	4

The legal guarantee of political independence places the Bundesbank in a strong position. Legally manifested independence as such, however, does not necessarily mean that monetary decisions are taken in political isolation. On the contrary, analysis of the institutional framework of monetary decision making shows that a number of points of contact exist between the Bundesbank and politics and private-sector interests, ranging from appointment procedures through mutual participation in Central Bank Council and Cabinet meetings to mutual advisory functions. Thus, the Bundesbank is likely to be exposed to political interests and pressures. In view of this, the question was raised as to what extent the bank depended on external political support from the private sector.

The reactions to this proposition strongly confirm that the Bundesbank's specific institutional status is acknowledged by both Bundesbank and private-sector respondents as promoting a high degree of political independence. More than half the interviewees see no need for external political support for the Bundesbank. Another quarter perceive political dependence as weak. Only 16% see a moderate degree of dependence on external political support, as illustrated in chart 71. Chart 72 shows that this overall assessment is shared in largely the same way across the federal and regional level, and by central bankers and interest group representatives alike.

The share of respondents perceiving no dependence at all, however, is markedly higher among interest representatives than among the respondents at the Bundesbank. Interest group respondents typically see no dependence on political support at all, as indicated by a median response of 4.00 for the sub-set. Central bank respondents, in contrast, typically see weak dependence. This result is underpinned by the comparison of charts 73 and 74 below. Most importantly, more than a quarter of the respondents at the bank's Central Office consider the need for external political support to be of moderate importance to the bank.

Bundesbank dependence on external political support

Chart 71

– All respondents, in %

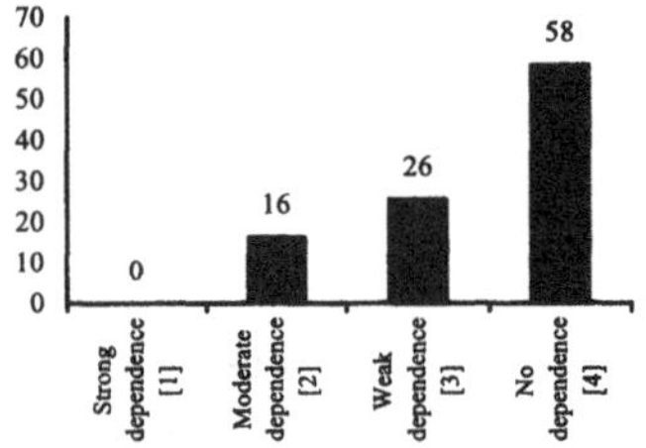

– Number of responses: 43

– Average value of responses: 3.42

Chart 72

– Average values of responses by level

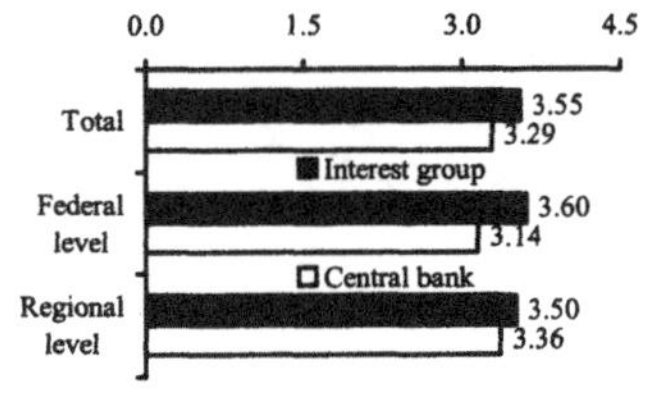

– Number of responses: 43

Chart 73

– Respondents from interest groups, in %

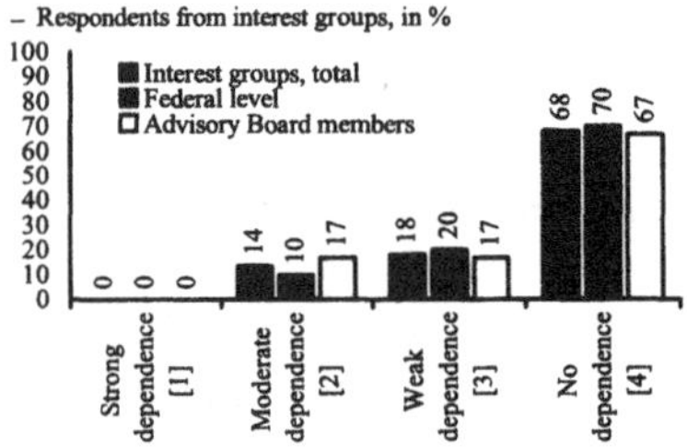

– Number of responses: 22

Chart 74

– Respondents from Deutsche Bundesbank, in %

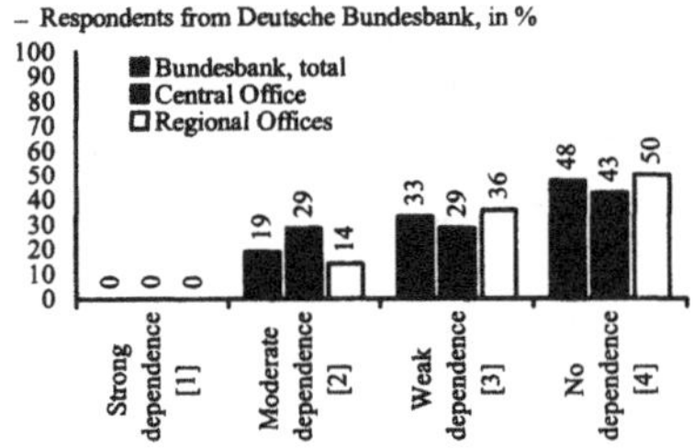

– Number of responses: 21

In essence, this difference can be traced back to the role of public opinion and the importance allocated to that role by Bundesbank staff, especially at the Central Office. Rather than a short-term need for political backing on certain monetary decisions, respondents at the Bundesbank emphasised the importance of the wider public's general attitude towards the central bank and its policies. By this reasoning, long-term support from the wider public – as documented for instance in opinion polls, media coverage, expert analyses or interest group positions – is perceived to be important because it reflects public approval and indirectly strengthens the bank's own institutional position within the political system. As one of the most important decision-making bodies in economic policy, the lack of direct democratic legitimacy is pointed out by a number of central bank respondents as a potential source of criticism – especially from politicians at times when they deem monetary stimuli to economic growth useful in the electoral cycle. Public approval for its policies, in this sense, is seen as an important pillar on which the Bundesbank's political independence rests in the long run.

Anecdotal evidence from interviews with interest group representatives in turn suggests that not just the bank's autonomy but the entire institutional set-up and the bank's past achievements are widely appreciated by the private sector. Asked for their assessment of the Bundesbank's institutional framework and its policy performance over the past decades, interest-group representatives consistently approved of the existing arrangements and welcomed the adoption of a similar design at EU level for the institutional arrangement of the ESCB. Typical of the overall assessment by business representatives was the remark made by an Advisory Council member, who stated that

> "[o]ver the past forty years, the Bundesbank has been the only institution in Germany's political system – maybe with the exception of the Constitutional Court – which has functioned well, fulfilled its duties, and consistently worked for the benefits of the entire country."

At the same time, many interest-group respondents observed that they saw a close relationship between the Bundesbank's success over time and the fact that it relied very little on external political support, including backing from politics or interest groups. Again, one typical reaction may be quoted, given by a representative from a peak business association, who observed that

> "[m]any of the problems the German economy faces today can, in aggregate, be traced back to the overload of interest group demands on the state, and the fact that policy makers gave in to these demands. I dare not think how monetary policy would have developed had Bundesbank policy makers been exposed to similar demands, and had they reacted in the same way as their colleagues in Bonn and Berlin have done in the past. Viewed in this light, the Bundesbank's institutional framework and its policies cannot be valued highly enough."

Conversely, respondents from interest associations see a strong causal link between the effects of central bank independence on the communication of private sector interests and the Bundesbank's lack of need for external political support. Almost all respondents attesting a constraining impact of political independence on interest group activities trace this back to the perceived fact that the Bundesbank does not rely on, and does not respond to, external political support of any kind in its operations.

Proposition 7	Question	Categories	Scale
Given their focus on aggregated economic indicators and their access to the relevant statistical resources, central banks are not dependent on external information with respect to monetary or exchange rate conditions and developments in order to fulfil their tasks in the field of monetary or exchange rate policy.	"Does the central bank depend on external information in order to fulfil its tasks in the field of monetary or exchange rate policy?"	"Strong dependence"	1
		"Moderate dependence"	2
		"Weak dependence"	3
		"No dependence"	4

Next to political support, policy makers may also depend on external resources to perform their tasks. Expertise in the relevant policy field and information concerning the object of policy measures constitute the most important resources private-sector interest groups can contribute to the policymaking process. With respect to central banks in general, and the Bundesbank in particular, it has been observed that the specific and exclusive assignment of monetary policy-related responsibilities as well as ample endowment with financial resources has promoted the establishment of a profound bedrock of expertise and information inside the monetary authority, including command over the statistical and scientific resources necessary to perform its tasks. Given the information and expertise-related lead central banks have in comparison to other stakeholders – including business associations, but also research institutions and think tanks –, the latter are less likely to be able to contribute significantly to the process of monetary policy formation than they usually are in other fields of policymaking.

This proposition was tested by asking stakeholders how dependent they considered the Bundesbank on information and expertise from the private sector for the fulfilment of its monetary policy tasks. As with the results on external political support, more than three-quarters of all respondents consider the Bundesbank's dependence on external information to be either weak or non-existent. Only 18% believe that there is a moderate degree of dependence in this regard, as depicted in chart 75. The numerical average of all replies, at 3.41, is well above the median value and nearly as high as that obtained on the preceding proposition.

Again, responses were relatively homogenous across levels of decision-making as well as between interest group and central bank respondents, as chart 76 shows. The maximum deviation from the average occurs in the responses from central bank representatives, as also reflected in the detailed illustration of responses in charts 77 and 78. As with proposition 6 and the related question of central bank dependence on political support, interest group respondents were more sceptical as to central bank dependence on external information than their counterparts at the Bundesbank: the average numerical value for the former set is 3.58, while the latter average was 3.20. The corresponding median values of 4.00 and 3.00 respectively support this conclusion.

Bundesbank dependence on external information

Chart 75

– All respondents, in %

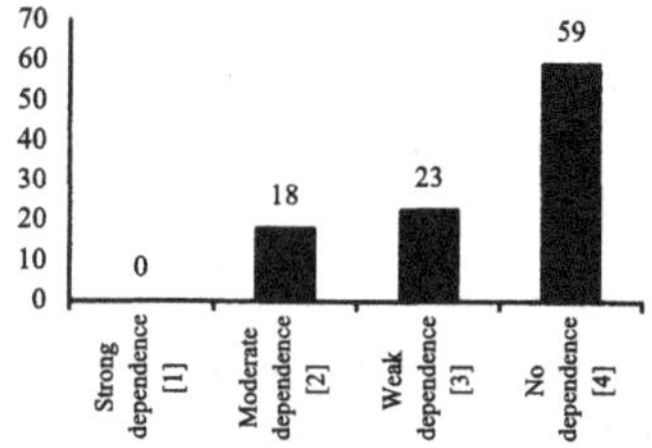

– Number of responses: 44
– Average value of responses: 3.41

Chart 76

– Average values of responses by level

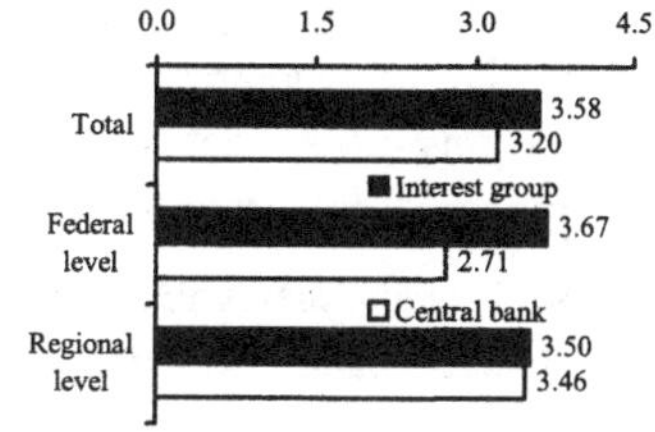

– Number of responses: 44

Chart 77

– Respondents from interest groups, in %

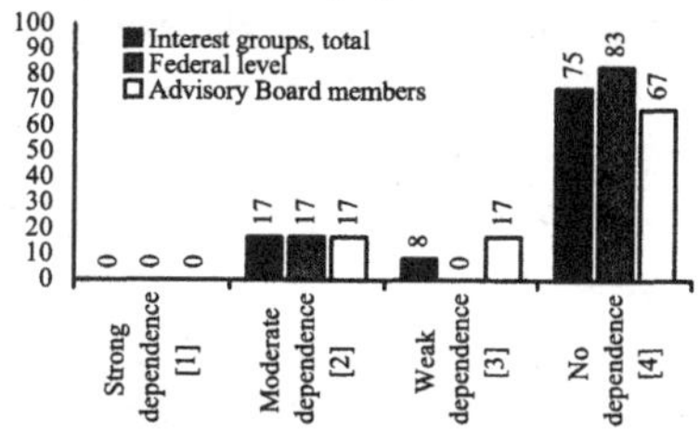

– Number of responses: 24

Chart 78

– Respondents from Deutsche Bundesbank, in %

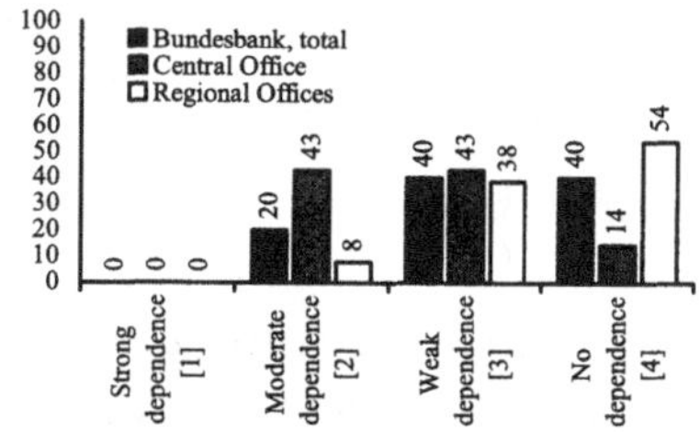

– Number of responses: 20

Once again, the replies from central bank representatives were significantly more varied than those from the interest groups consulted. Respondents at the bank's Central Office presented a more open picture of the bank than suggested by theory and perceived by their counterparts in the private sector, reporting moderate or weak dependence on external information in 86% of the interviews conducted. Only 14% of the respondents at the Central Office reported no dependence on external sources of information, against 54% at the Regional Offices, where the need for input from outside the central bank is perceived to be significantly lower.

Detailed comments from the interest group representatives show the vast majority stressing the high level of expertise and abundant supply of statistical data at the Bundesbank's disposal as the primary reasons leading them to conclude that the bank does not need to take recourse to information from the private sector. In this view, the

Bundesbank is not only largely self-sufficient with respect to information and expertise; a great majority of respondents emphasised that in practice information flows in the opposite direction, i.e. from the Bundesbank to the private sector. Thus, most interest groups use publicly available Bundesbank statistics and analyses for their own work. In addition, the Bundesbank's assessments of economic and monetary developments in Germany are regarded by most interest representatives as a benchmark for the formation of their own opinions. Finally, the Bundesbank's explanations of monetary policy decisions, most importantly through its monthly reports, are generally regarded by business association experts as useful information for an understanding of economic and monetary developments and policy positions. For the most part this assessment has been carried over to the period since 1999 and the transfer of monetary authority to the ECB.

The Bundesbank broadly shares this view, also pointing to the existing expertise and data resources. Central bank respondents agree that in principle these resources suffice to reach appropriate monetary judgements. At the same time, however, a number of decision makers and experts pointed out that additional information, which is obtained directly from market participants and other sources and not collected by the Bundesbank itself, can be useful in two respects:

- First, additional information on regional and sectoral economic developments can help establish as complete a picture of the state of the economy as possible. Particularly with regard to sectoral developments, business associations can contribute insights which would not otherwise have been readily available to the bank.
- Second, and most importantly, it was pointed out that the usefulness of statistical data is naturally limited when it comes to forming expectations of future economic developments. The backward-looking nature of most statistical analyses can partly be compensated by examining economic variables containing information on future developments – mainly by capturing market participants' expectations – such as the term structure of interest rates and financial futures and options market valuations. Obtaining information on the expectations and planned activities of major actors in the economy – for example with respect to investment, consumption, pricing and wage formation – is nevertheless regarded as useful for rounding off the picture generated by conventional statistical and econometric means.

Given these two factors, the sectoral and regional information provided by external sources, including business associations, as well as by scientific institutions, think tanks or international organisations, is considered useful by Bundesbank respondents for obtaining a comprehensive view of present and future economic developments.

The Bundesbank's ultimate reliance on such external information, however, is still perceived as very low, since the information is generally considered non-essential to the bank's work, serving primarily as a backup complementing the bank's own findings, and as a way of verifying its own economic assessments.

III.2.3.2 Behavioural patterns of Bundesbank policy makers

Next to the Bundesbank's political independence and the strength of its resources of expertise and information, monetary policy makers' behavioural patterns represent a third possible institutional explanation for the low level of interest group activity on monetary polices. As discussed above, the specific institutional provisions governing the Bundesbank are largely matched by the behaviour of its policy makers, who are committed to maintaining a high level of personal independence as well as to the bank's policy objectives, backed up by additional rules working as a self-constraint on policy makers' discretion. For the present purpose, this essentially shows that – beyond the institutional safeguards towards securing a stability-oriented monetary policy – policy makers are personally committed to fulfilling the bank's objective, not least by shielding the institution and themselves against influences which may run counter to this objective. With respect to the factors influencing the incentives for interest groups to articulate their preferences on monetary policy, the question arises whether policy makers are actually perceived to be interested in the views of the private sector, or whether such views are considered irrelevant by monetary decision makers.

Proposition 8	Question	Categories	Scale
Given the independence of central banks in terms of political, material, and expertise-related resources as well as their focus on aggregated economic indicators, central bank policy makers are not interested in the views of private-sector interest groups on monetary or exchange rate policy.	"Are central bank representatives interested in the preferences of the corporate sector regarding monetary or exchange rate policy?"	"Highly interested"	1
		"Interested"	2
		"Slightly interested"	3
		"Not interested"	4

Asked whether they perceived the Bundesbank and its policy makers to be interested in the positions of private-sector interest groups on monetary developments and monetary decisions, more than half the total respondents stated that they considered monetary policy makers to be either highly or moderately interested, as depicted in chart 79. More than one quarter of respondents considered central bankers slightly interested, while 19% thought that the bank was not interested at all. In comparison, interest group representatives considered the Bundesbank less interested than Bundesbank officials perceived themselves to be. This difference was, again, most pronounced at the federal level, as chart 80 shows, and is confirmed by the typical response as measured by the statistical median of 3.00 for interest group and 2.00 for central bank respondents.

Once more, the structure of replies reveals a certain heterogeneity in the assessment by interest group representatives, of whom more than a quarter considered Bundesbank staff to be interested, more than a third considered them slightly interested, and one-fifth deemed them not interested at all, as illustrated in chart 81. Only one Advisory Board member perceived bank staff to be highly interested. In contrast, the great majority of Bundesbank staff, as shown in chart 82, said they were interested or even highly interested in interest groups' views on the bank's monetary policy, namely 59% and 9% respectively. Only 14% considered interest group views slightly interesting for Bundesbank staff. Another 14% stated that Bundesbank staff were not interested at all.

Like the comments made in the context of the role of private-sector information, respondents rather critical of the Bundesbank's interest in private-sector interest groups' opinions of its policies primarily emphasised the bank's expertise and its command of scientific and statistical resources as the reason for limited interest. Furthermore, most respondents referred to the fact that monetary policy was, by nature, aimed at the economy as a whole, making regional or sector-specific views largely irrelevant for the central bank's own assessment of monetary conditions. In close relation to this, it was pointed out by many respondents that owing to the bank's obligation towards the general good it would, as matter of principle, be wrong for monetary policy makers to take particular interests into consideration. As a consequence, they should not be exposed to particular preferences and should not therefore be interested in them in the first place.

Respondents rating Bundesbank policy makers rather interested in interest group views, on the other hand, referred to the additional information on the impact of monetary developments on the private sector and expectations as to the future course of monetary variables, future policy measures and forthcoming market activities, especially with respect to pricing and wage bargaining behaviour, that may emerge from interest groups' views and be potentially useful for the bank's opinion formation. Second, an exchange of views is considered by some respondents as a measure necessary for the central bank to underscore its legitimacy, being an institution largely unaccountable to the political environment. This argument, so the respondents emphasised, applied irrespective of whether policy makers ultimately take the opinions and information thus gathered into consideration when making their policy judgements.

Bundesbank interest in private-sector views

Chart 79

– All respondents, in %

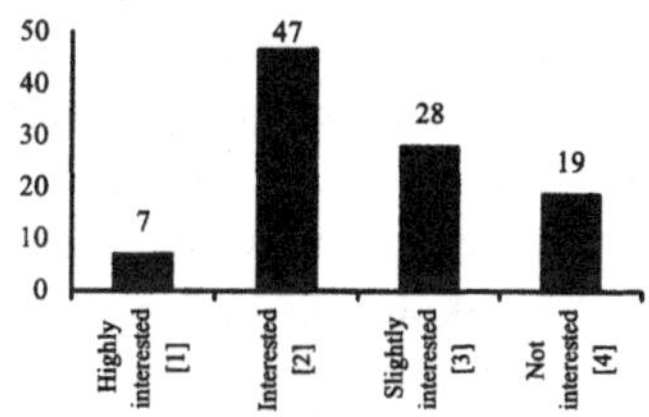

– Number of responses: 43
– Average value of responses: 2.58

Chart 80

– Average values of responses by level

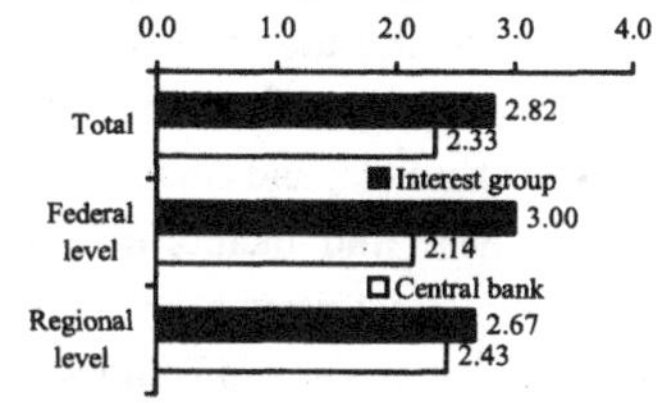

– Number of responses: 43

Chart 81

– Respondents from interest groups, in %

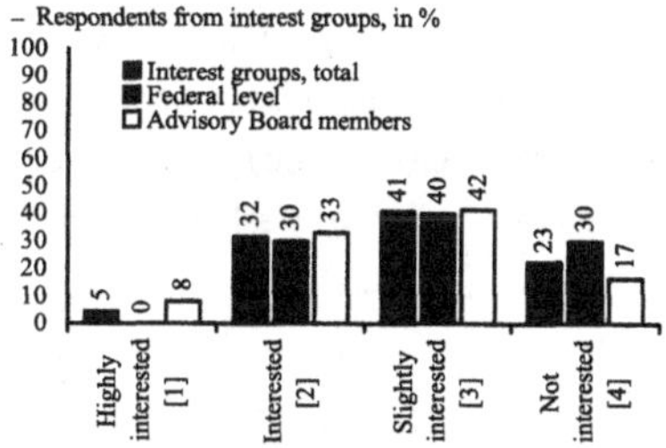

– Number of responses: 22

Chart 82

– Respondents from Deutsche Bundesbank, in %

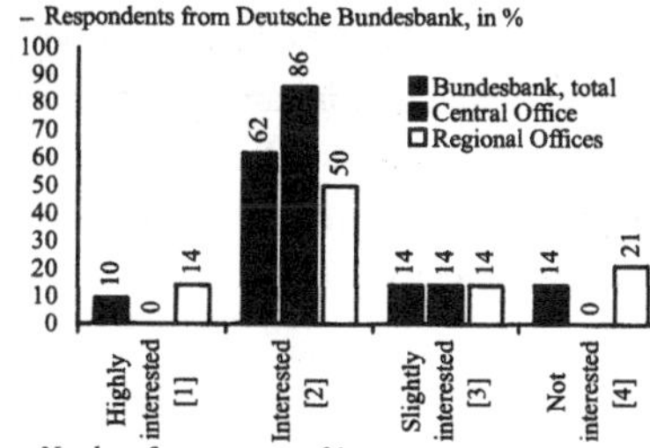

– Number of responses: 21

Finally, the responses from interest group representatives suggest that behavioural patterns contain a strong individual element and vary greatly. Thus, a large majority of respondents stressed that interest in the assessment of business associations, openness towards interest group views and the readiness to discuss the bank's policies vitally depended on the attitudes of individual policy makers. This element was particularly emphasised by members of the bank's Advisory Boards with respect to their relationship with the presidents of the Regional Offices. In practice, the exchange of views with the Bundesbank was said to be severely limited by the lack of interest and willingness on the part of individual officials to discuss the bank's policies. At the same time, some Bundesbank decision makers were explicitly pointed out as comparatively open to discourse with interest group representatives. As a result, many interest-group representatives cited the personal accessibility of Bundesbank policy makers as a very important determinant for their own ability to present their views to the bank.

III.2.4 Issue context

Next to the institutional context, theory suggests that the specific issue context may be the second broad factor explaining the low level of interest group activity on monetary affairs. With respect to monetary policy in Germany, it has already been observed that, first, there is broad agreement with the overall objectives set for the conduct of monetary policy; second, the immediate economic impact of monetary policy on the business sector is very low; third, the effects of monetary policy are diffuse and work through complex channels; and finally, the political agenda business associations work on is very full. These four factors diminish the importance of monetary policy as a political issue for interest groups – a tendency powerfully confirmed by the responses obtained from interest group and Bundesbank officials.

III.2.4.1 Agreement with monetary policy objectives

The preceding section showed that the institutional framework within which monetary policy in Germany is embedded is strongly supported by the German business sector. By the same token, the interest group representatives addressed expressed very strong agreement with the Bundesbank's and – since 1999 – the ECB's primary objective of maintaining price stability as well as with the central banks' overall approach to reaching that objective.

Proposition 9	Question	Categories	Scale
Individual firms or interest associations agree with the objectives and the overall conduct of monetary or exchange rate policy.	"Do interest groups, in general, disagree with the overall objectives and the conduct of monetary or exchange rate policy?"	"Agree strongly"	1
		"Agree"	2
		"Disagree"	3
		"Disagree strongly"	4

Asked whether interest groups in business agreed with the established central bank objectives and the overall conduct of monetary policy by the Bundesbank and the ECB, 47% of the respondents stated that they agreed with the conduct of monetary policy. Another 53% even professed strong agreement, as depicted in chart 83. None of the interviewees considered the business sector in general or a discernible segment of it as being in disagreement with the primary aims of monetary policy. As the comparison of the average numerical values on this question in chart 84 illustrates, agreement on the part of interest group representatives – irrespective of whether they work at federal or regional level – is, in fact, even stronger than their central bank counterparts believed.

As one senior expert at a large federal, cross-sector industry association typically observed:

> "A stability-oriented monetary policy is of elementary importance for a business location like Germany. The quality of a location is primarily determined by its economic stability. A stable, inflation-free monetary environment is an important part of the latter, and a necessary precondition for good economic development."

A former member of the of Bundesbank's Central Bank Council maintained that

> "[f]or industry, monetary stability is everything. It was – and in my perception still is – something like a fetish."

As to the reasons for their agreement with the given monetary policy objectives, business representatives emphasise the importance of stable prices for the proper functioning of the market economy in general and for investment and planning certainty at individual enterprises in particular. Also, Germany's experience with inflation in the inter-war and post-war period was cited as an important historical factor shaping the perception of the great majority of actors in the business sector. Finally, all interest group respondents considered the constitutional manifestation of price stability as the primary objective of monetary policy an important element, stressing that it was considered sensible to commit policy makers as strongly as possible to this end and to avoid any inroads for inflationary policies.

In conformity with the strong overall agreement on the objective of price stability throughout the business sector, interest group respondents described anti-inflationary policies as the most important by far of their own monetary policy preferences. At the same time, interest group respondents' reactions show that price stability is not the only objective they associate with monetary policy. Thus, a large majority of respondents stated that low nominal and real interest rates were conducive to their business environment. In particular, interest associations representing small and medium-sized businesses expressed a strong preference for low interest rates, referring to their members' heavy dependence on external capital. In the same vein, most respondents argued in favour of export-friendly exchange rate policies, saying that their members had perceived past periods of weakening exchange rates for the Deutsche Mark and the euro as mitigating the generally high level of production costs in Germany, helping enterprises exposed to international competition to strengthen their competitive positions, albeit only temporarily. Finally, a large number of respondents stressed the importance of stability of the major relevant monetary variables as another key priority among businesses. By this reckoning, it is not only specific levels of interest rates or exchange rates that enterprises perceive as a burden, but also the frequency and magnitude of changes in these variables. High variability was pointed out as a significant factor aggravating enterprises' investment and planning activities. Continuity in the movement of financial variables was considered by many as an important objective of monetary policy.

Interest group agreement with Bundesbank objectives

Chart 83

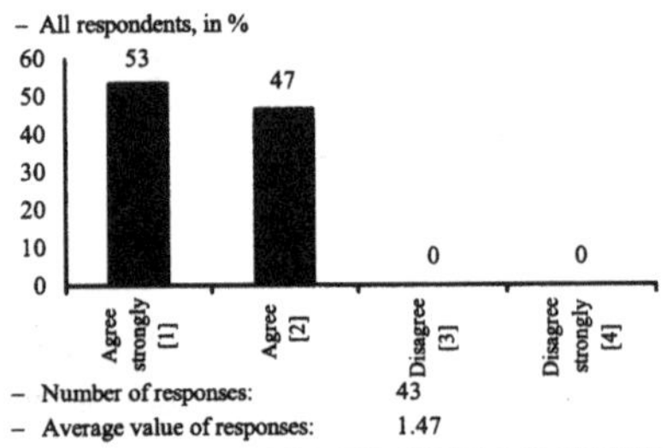

Chart 84

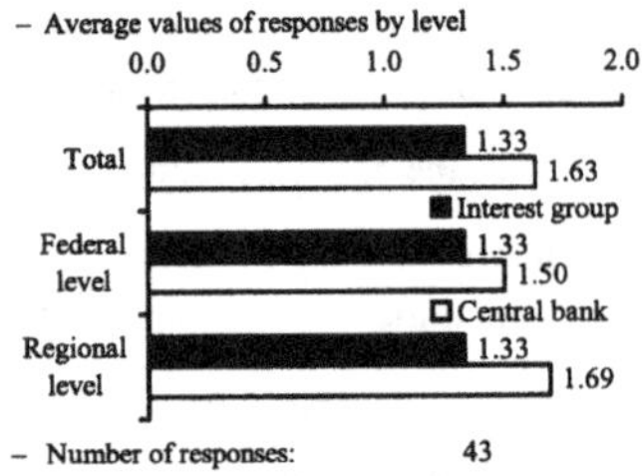

Given these multiple, not necessarily consistent preferences, the question arises as to how interest groups assess the monetary policymaking record over time. As we saw from the above analysis of the issue context, the German economy has been confronted with considerable movement in inflation, interest and exchange rates, moderate as they may be by international or historical standards. In particular, the Bundesbank adopted restrictive monetary stances in order to counter inflationary pressures, often accompanied with phases of rising and high interest rates as well as a strengthening of the external value of the currency. *Ceteris paribus*, such restrictive policy measures increase domestic enterprises' financing costs and can hurt their international competitiveness. As a result, it is conceivable that enterprises disagree with monetary policy decisions at certain points in time when the economic effects of monetary developments are perceived to be particularly painful, even if, in principle, they support the objectives the central bank pursues.

Proposition 10	Question	Categories	Scale
Interest groups rarely disagree with the monetary or exchange rate policy decisions of the central bank.	"Have interest groups encountered situations in the past in which they urgently disagreed with the conduct of monetary or exchange rate policy?"	"Very frequently"	1
		"Frequently"	2
		"Rarely"	3
		"Very rarely"	4
		"Never"	5

Evidence from the interviews held with experts and decision makers from business associations and the Bundesbank shows that disagreement with individual monetary policy decisions is very rare. Asked whether there had been situations in which German business strongly disagreed with the monetary policy decisions of the Bundesbank or the ECB, more than 31% of all respondents stated that business had never strongly disagreed with the course of monetary policy, as shown in chart 85. Among interest group representatives, this figure was as high as 46%. Another 50% reported that disagreement had been rare or very rare. Notably, only one respondent representing a largely export-oriented constituency expressed frequent dissatisfaction with monetary decisions, pointing to the financial burden to the members of his association originating from exchange rate movements and their desire for further stabilisation of external currency value. On average, agreement as expressed by interest group representatives was significantly higher than central bank officials expected it to be (see chart 86), with a particularly high average level of agreement among Advisory Board members at the regional level.

In their comments, the vast majority of interest group representatives reported that disagreement with monetary policy decisions very rarely centred on the direction of interest rate adjustments. Most respondents emphasised that they had very rarely disagreed with the central banks' overall assessment of monetary and economic conditions. In contrast, in the rare cases that disagreement was reported to have occurred, it focused principally on the timing and magnitude of monetary measures. Thus, a large number of interest group representatives stated that monetary authorities tended to react very early in the economic cycle to signs of inflationary pressure with a tightening of their monetary stance. At times, such early reactions were judged premature by some respondents. In the same vein, the relaxation of monetary conditions was perceived as taking place comparatively late in the economic cycle, leading some commentators to conclude that monetary stimuli should be given more early when economic downturns are immediately foreseeable.

As a former member of the Bundesbank Central Bank Council said:

> "Certainly, there have been controversial discussions at times. But these were without exception concerned with the details – the timing and size of monetary measures – and never led to outright controversy. The real fights were with the Federal Government."

One federal-level sectoral industry representative characteristically observed that

> "[t]here can be no question that – as a capital intensive industry – we strictly prefer low interest rates to high ones, and – as an export-oriented sector – a weak exchange rate to a tight one. But whatever the preferences, our basic belief is in the expertise and wisdom of the Bundesbank. Thus, we usually refrain from commenting on its monetary decisions, and most times there is no reason to complain in the first place."

Disagreement with course of monetary policy

Chart 85

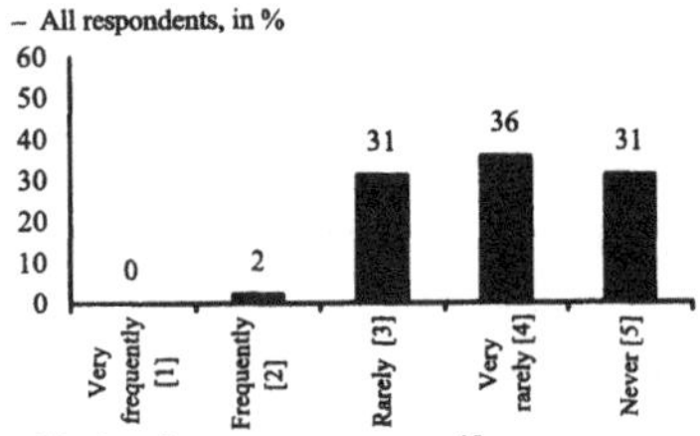

– Number of responses: 45
– Average value of responses: 3.96

Chart 86

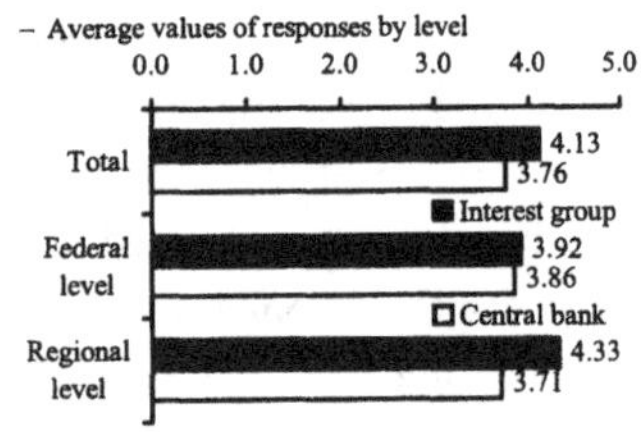

– Number of responses: 45

Chart 87

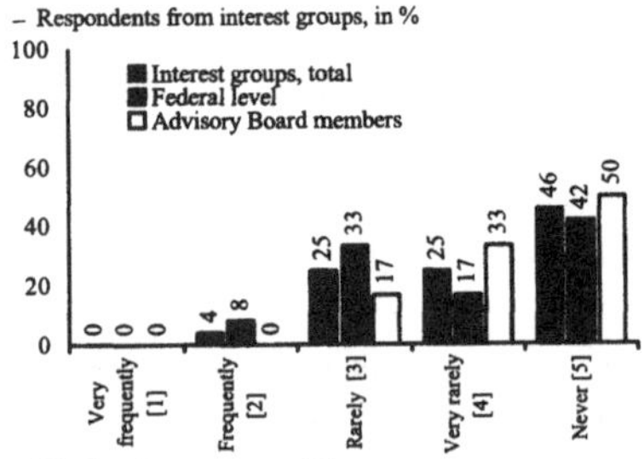

– Number of responses: 24

Chart 88

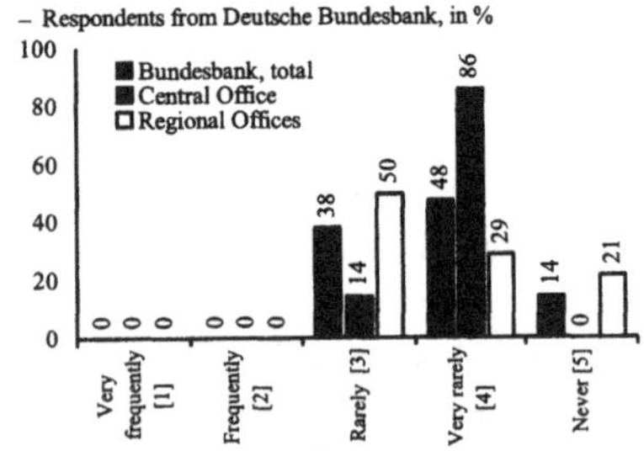

– Number of responses: 21

Interest group representatives deemed the scale of monetary policy responses to movements in the economic cycle problematic even less frequently. In this regard, most respondents emphasised that they trusted the Bundesbank and the ECB to find an appropriate response development in the overall monetary environment. Some respondents, however, pointed out that in certain instances the Bundesbank was perceived as having been too restrictive in its reactions to inflationary pressures. This referred mainly to the mid-1990s, when monetary tightening was considered too harsh and too prolonged by some. Some respondents also cited the monetary tightening in the early '80s as an example of too rigorous a monetary hardening by the Bundesbank.

The breakdown in charts 87 and 88 shows that the overall assessment on the interest group side is largely shared by their counterparts at the Bundesbank, albeit in a more heterogeneous manner. While almost nine out of ten officials at the bank's Central Office considered disagreement by interest groups to occur very rarely, only one-third of their colleagues at the Regional Offices shared this view. Two-thirds of the latter had more varied views on the question, with half of them reporting rare disagreement and another fifth never observing disagreement at all. As a consequence, at 3.50 the median answer among respondents at the Regional Offices was lower than the rest of the sample, suggesting that dissatisfaction with the course of monetary policy – inasmuch as it exists at all – is slightly more frequently articulated at the regional than the federal level.

Given the respondents' occasional disagreement with the *de facto* conduct of monetary policy in the past – as rarely as this may have occurred –, none of the respondents naturally ruled out the possibility of objections to monetary decisions in the future, as well as political action by interest groups in response to such objections. As one representative of a large, cross-sectoral federal industry association typically remarked:

> "We have not encountered extreme monetary situations over the past decades. Occasionally, conditions got tenser, compelling us to ask monetary policy makers to use the scope and discretion at their disposal – in both directions, depending on the circumstances. In difficult times, the pain that industry can take naturally decreases. But in general, the threshold for interest group action in the policy area remains an abstract one. The trigger only becomes evident in each concrete case. Either way, there can be no doubt that in difficult circumstances, well-known and recognised fundamentals of our policy positions may need to be revised, and we and our members may become very nervous."

III.2.4.2 Size and urgency of impact of monetary policy

A result of earlier consideration has been that, owing to the complexity with which it affects the economy at large and individual enterprises in particular, and given the comparably small immediate economic impact it has on businesses, the perceived need for political action on monetary policy is further lessened. This tenet is largely confirmed by the reactions from the decision makers and experts consulted.

Proposition 11	Question	Categories	Scale
Monetary or exchange rate policy is not perceived to have a significant effect on individual firms or interest associations.	"Is monetary or exchange rate policy perceived by the private sector to have an economic impact on individual corporations or interest groups?"	"Strong"	1
		"Moderate"	2
		"Weak"	3
		"Negligible"	4

Asked about the perceived impact of monetary policy measures or the absence of such measures, only 17% of all respondents considered there was a moderate impact on trade and industry, while 69% observed only a weak impact and 12% described the economic impact as negligible, as shown in chart 89. The average values of the answers, as illustrated in chart 90, show interest group representatives reporting a slightly weaker perceived impact than their counterparts at the Bundesbank. A median value of 3.00 for all respondents as well as all sub-sets, however, suggests that respondents typically reacted in a homogenous way.

A detailed examination of the responses, as presented in charts 91 and 92, reveals no significant differences in the assessments of the perceived policy impact between the federal and regional levels. Interestingly, no discernible patterns existed with respect to the type of enterprises the interest group respondents represented. In other words, neither the associations representing small and medium-sized enterprises, nor those representing the export sector or large industrial corporations reported a particularly strong or weak perceived impact of monetary policy on their members. As a result, monetary policy is generally regarded as weak in its economic impact on the operations of German enterprises in trade and industry.

This perception was typically reflected in the statements made by interest-group respondents with respect to both monetary and exchange rate developments, as the following quotations exemplify:

> "The share of interest-related costs in total corporate expenses is very low. Thus, a movement in central bank interest rates does not make much of a difference. Psychologically, such movements may well accumulate over time. But the impact of this effect – via consumption and investment behaviour – is too indirect and difficult to account for to be a driving factor for enterprises' behaviour."[611]

> "The impact of monetary policy on the average enterprise in Germany is minimal, especially when compared to other sources of risk. This is linked to the share of interest-related costs in companies' total expenses.

[611] Quote by a senior expert at a large federal cross-sectoral industry association.

> Considering that on average interest expenditure makes up between 0.5% and 1.5% of total operating costs, while wage costs are around 25% to 30%, it becomes clear that managers have more urgent things to do than complain about the monetary environment."[612]
>
> "The danger to the German economy from exchange rates is very low. Exchange rates were stabilised after the launch of the EMS at the end of the 1970s. With the advent of the euro, 90% of our members' trade is either transacted within the euro area or denominated in euro. For the rest, effective insurance is in principle possible through exchange rate hedging. So even a difficult period such as 2003, when we had three appreciations of 10% each a week, does not seriously endanger our trading activities."[613]
>
> "Interest expenses have never been of great concern to German industry. In fact, our exposure has consistently declined over the past years. Financially, monetary tightening is hardly noticeable for an average business. Marginal as the impact may be, though, we would always prefer low refinancing conditions to high ones."[614]

Insofar as monetary policy was conceded by interest-group representatives as having a significant effect on enterprises, respondents strongly confirmed the above findings on the exposure of sectors and groups of enterprises. From the respondents' comments, particular exposure to monetary policy is given in the following cases:

- Small and medium-sized enterprises, owing to the high average rate of debt financing and their dependence on bank credit in this regard.
- Capital-intensive industries whose investment decisions are influenced by debt financing costs, making them relatively interest rate-sensitive, such as the mechanical engineering, chemical and construction sectors.
- Sectors whose products are subject to interest rate-sensitive demand patterns in consumption and investment, such as the retail and wholesale trade and construction.
- Enterprises heavily exposed to export or import activities, especially large industrial corporations in the automobile, chemical and mechanical engineering businesses.

---

612 Quote by a senior Bundesbank official.

613 Quote by a representative of a federal-level group specialising in trade issues. The view that exchange rate risks can be countered effectively by hedging transactions was challenged by a number of other respondents who pointed out that hedging instruments were largely inappropriate for use by small and medium-sized enterprises owing to the small trading volumes. Also, it was emphasised that hedging was a very costly way for a company to protect itself against exchange rate and interest rate exposure.

Perception of economic effects of monetary policy on enterprises

Chart 89

– All respondents, in %

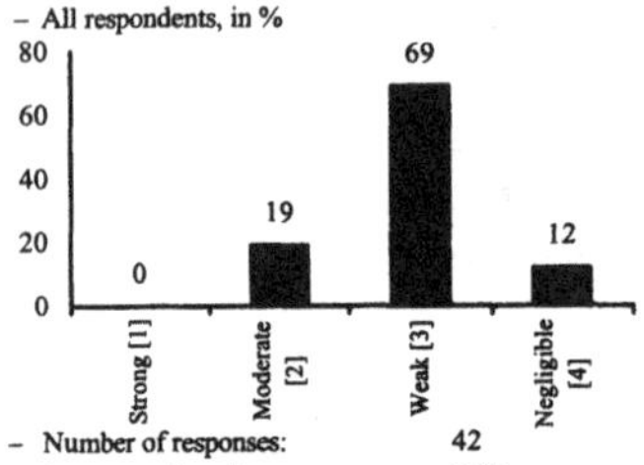

– Number of responses: 42
– Average value of responses: 2.93

Chart 90

– Average values of responses by level

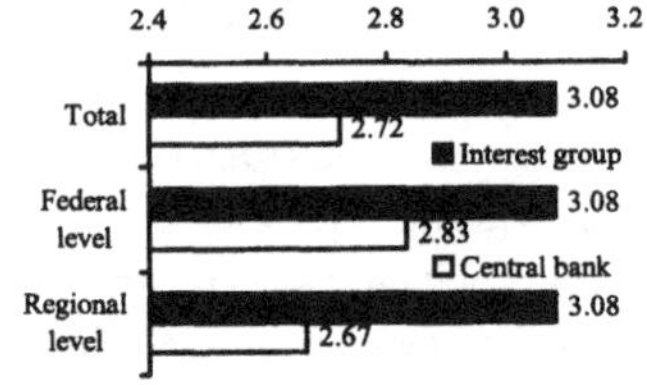

– Number of responses: 42

Chart 91

– Respondents from interest groups, in %

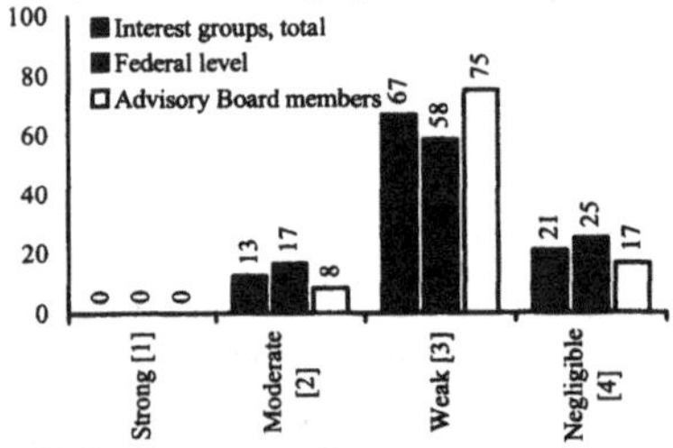

– Number of responses: 24

Chart 92

– Respondents from Deutsche Bundesbank, in %

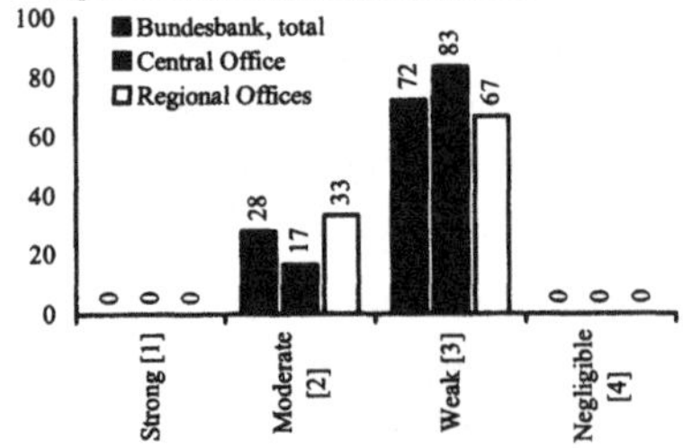

– Number of responses: 18

Despite these patterns of interest and exchange rate exposure, none of the respondents representing enterprises in any of the above sectors regarded the impact of monetary policy on their constituencies as strong. The fact that specific patterns of exposure are not directly reflected in the immediate responses to this question by decision makers and experts can be traced back to three arguments that were contained to varying degrees in the vast majority of responses and broadly confirm a number of observations made on the issue context earlier on.

First, inflation, interest and exchange rate related costs were said to be only one factor in corporate expenses, and a very minor one at that. This was also said to apply to expenses on interest or exchange rate hedging for enterprises in a position to insure themselves against the associated risks on derivatives markets. Compared with the costs of changes in monetary variables, without exception the respondents found other corporate expenses a much greater burden. The most important cost factor for German firms, as seen by a large majority of respondents, is wage and labour costs, including non-wage social security contributions. In addition, expenses on material and commodity factor inputs were cited as an important cost component. Finally, the

614 Quote by a representative of a regional industry group.

burden of corporate taxation was stressed. Next to these direct cost components, many respondents pointed out that even the impact of economic policy measures weighing indirectly on the profitability of German enterprises, such as economy-wide or sector-specific regulation and indirect taxes influencing corporations' investment behaviour and their customers' consumption and investment patterns, were considered to have a greater impact on the corporate sector than monetary policy.

Second, the perception of the impact of monetary policy was said to be narrowed by the cyclicality of monetary developments and the periodicity of monetary policy decisions. Thus, many respondents pointed out that even at times of rising or high interest rates, enterprises could be sure that, owing to the cyclicality of monetary policy, they would eventually return to lower levels again. In this respect it was stressed that monetary policy differed fundamentally from other policy areas and that the burden of taxation, for example, had in the past trended almost exclusively upward. Tax rates were rarely seen to fall. In contrast, the fact that enterprises could be certain that – however high interest rates rose at any given point in time – they would sooner or later come down again greatly diminished the overall impact of monetary policy as perceived by business. This logic, it was pointed out, certainly also applied to the reverse constellation, i.e. corporations were realistic and understood that low interest rates in one period were sure to be followed by rising interest rates in a subsequent period. As a result, the majority of respondents characterised the cyclicality of monetary policy as a quasi-natural phenomenon[615] in the face of which it was up to businesses to optimise their finance and asset management behaviour so as to keep corporate costs as low as possible. In essence, this view was also said to apply to exchange rate developments.

Accordingly, the effective magnitude of the impact of monetary policy on the corporate sector is determined by the level of inflation, interest and exchange rates at any given moment in time, the length of the prevailing business cycle and the duration of periods of rising and high as well as falling and low levels of the major monetary variables. The duration of cycles has been emphasised by respondents representing export-oriented enterprises as particularly important for the impact of exchange rate developments on firms exposed to international competition. Thus, even critical appreciations of the domestic currency were reported to be manageable by the majority of export-oriented firms as long as they were of limited duration. Prolonged phases of exchange rate appreciation, in contrast, were considered harmful to international exporting firms' competitiveness. The Deutsche Mark's appreciation against the

---

[615] This logic essentially forms the basis of the views reported in the quotation on page 251, suggesting that it was pointless trying to influence monetary policy.

US Dollar and many European currencies throughout the 1990s was repeatedly referred to as an example of a difficult period for export-oriented firms.

As to the periodicity of monetary decision making, some respondents stated that central banks' step-by-step approach, with monetary decisions taken every two to four weeks and often evolving in a sequence of small, quarter percentage-point steps at a time, made it difficult to assess the aggregate effect of monetary policy over time. Equally, however, the respondents emphasised that this evolutionary approach was considered useful and necessary insofar as it promoted continuity in the development of the target variables and thereby helped maintain an overall stable monetary environment.

As one industry representative typically noted:

> "Monetary decisions usually come in small, incremental steps. Of course, we observe these developments over time and are therefore aware of the aggregate impact of a sequence of monetary measures over the political cycle. But there can be no doubt that the visibility of monetary policy and the major private-sector actors' awareness is, in practice, constrained by the incremental nature of monetary decision making. If central bank verdicts came as one big bang once a year, private-sector reactions would certainly be different from those observed in current practice."

Third, almost all experts and decision makers pointed out that a precise determination or quantification of the effects of monetary policy on the business sector – a factor to be discussed in detail below – was rendered difficult by the complexity of the monetary transmission process and the wide variety of different channels through which policy measures fed into the economy. In contrast to most other policy areas, and notably with respect to taxation, wage settlements, social security contributions and even regulation, where the impact of policy measures was almost comprehensively calculable, the economic impact of monetary developments and monetary policy measures was considered diffuse and difficult to aggregate.

Proposition 12	Question	Categories	Scale
The magnitude of the impact of monetary or exchange rate policy on individual firms or interest associations is difficult to determine.	"Is it possible for individual enterprises or interest groups to determine the magnitude of the impact of monetary or exchange rate developments on them?"	"Very precisely"	1
		"Rather precisely"	2
		"Rather vaguely"	3
		"Very vaguely"	4
		"No"	5

Derived from the above qualitative feedback, only 13% of all respondents stated that the economic impact of monetary developments and policy decisions on individual enterprises and interest groups could be determined rather precisely, as shown in chart 93. More than 55%, in contrast, reported that monetary effects could be determined only rather or very vaguely. Almost one-third of respondents even held that no sensible quantification was possible. The problem of identifying monetary policy effects was considered particularly acute by interest group respondents, with a numerical value of 3.96 compared to the total average of 3.84 and an average for central bank responses of 3.64. Interest group representatives at the regional level were most critical of their ability to assess the magnitude of the effects of monetary policy, with a numerical average of 4.00, as illustrated in chart 94.

On the basis of the detailed reactions, three sources of imprecision can be identified, rendering determination of the magnitude of the impact from monetary policy decisions particularly difficult.

- First, the multitude of channels through which monetary policy is transmitted to private sector enterprises makes a comprehensive calculation difficult.
- Second, monetary policy does not work directly on enterprises, but indirectly through intermediaries and financial markets. As a result, it is impossible for enterprises to distinguish which changes in the conditions for corporate financing and asset management are actually the result of monetary policy measures or their omission, and which changes are caused by the behaviour of financial intermediaries and market participants. In addition, time lags in the effects of monetary policy measures resulting from the indirectness of transmission were said to complicate accurate assessment.

  Although in principle true for all major financial variables such as bond-market yields, equity prices or exchange rates, a large number of respondents, especially those representing small and medium-sized enterprises, pointed to the banking sector as the major source of irritation in this respect. Given the high degree of dependence on bank credit, particularly by small businesses, respondents emphasised that banks were generally considered reluctant to pass on interest rate cuts to their ultimate clients, resulting in considerable time lags in transmission and substantial mark-ups in the lending rates quoted to enterprises compared to equivalent bond-market rates. In addition, it was pointed out by interest representatives that at times the problem as viewed by enterprises was not the rates at which credit was available, but rather whether and how much credit banks were willing to grant to individual firms. In periods of weak corporate returns and liquidity, banks' reluctance to extend loans in conjunction with high interest rate mark-ups was reported as a critical factor for the profitability and, indeed, in marginal cases the existence of individual firms.

Indirectness of transmission not only makes it difficult to trace potential changes in financial variables back to their source and to identify the potential role of monetary policy as one possible cause, it also complicates identification of the appropriate addressee for political action by interest groups. In terms of interest rates on corporate credit, enterprises therefore primarily consider individual banks or the banking sector at large as the most important determinant of lending terms. The part played by the underlying monetary conditions is said rarely to be taken sufficiently into consideration. Much of the criticism of corporate financing terms by the business sector therefore concentrates on the banking sector as the primary addressee and rarely reaches the central bank.

- Third, enterprises' individual exposure to changes in inflation, interest and exchange rates proved varied even within specific regions or sectors. As a result, interest group representatives maintained that an aggregation of the effects of monetary policy on enterprises in specific sectors, regions or the economy at large would either yield very limited results or be extremely costly.

In these respects, a vast majority of respondents confirmed the hypothesis that monetary and exchange rate policy was more difficult to assess than other policy issues. The effects of taxation and regulation were cited as the most important examples of policy areas where the effects on industry were more immediate and easier to assess in terms of their qualitative and quantitative impact. However, the difference between monetary and exchange rate developments on the one hand and other policy issues on the other is not considered a qualitative one. Policy measures in the form of taxation or industry regulation were recognised as difficult to account for in their long-term effects and in quantitative terms. Similarly, substantial differences in exposure on the part of individual interest group members were also observed in other policy areas. Nonetheless, monetary and exchange rate developments were broadly regarded as clearly harder to account for.

Size of economic impact of monetary policy

Chart 93

– All respondents, in %

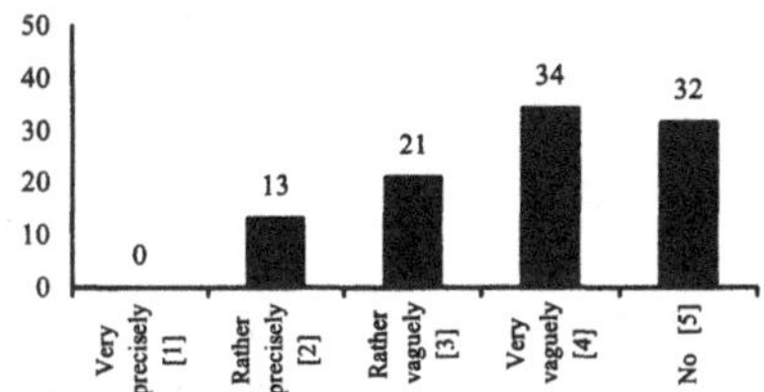

– Number of responses: 38
– Average value of responses: 3.84

Chart 94

– Average values of responses by level

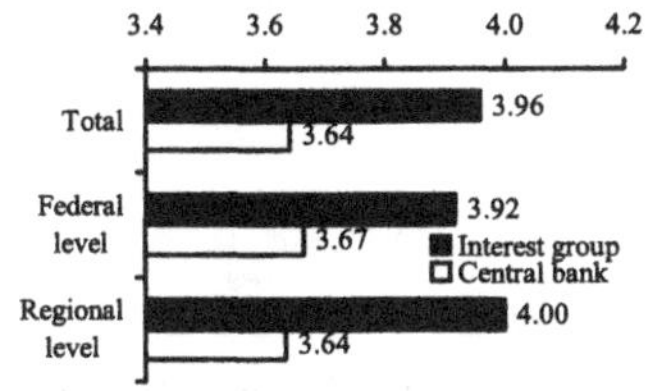

– Number of responses: 38

Chart 95

– Respondents from interest groups, in %

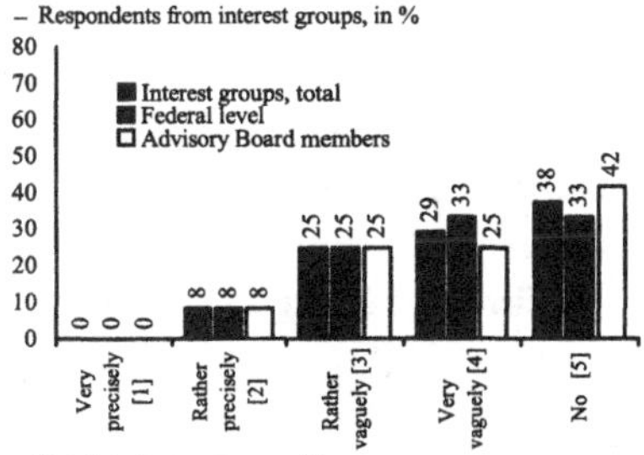

– Number of responses: 24

Chart 96

– Respondents from Deutsche Bundesbank, in %

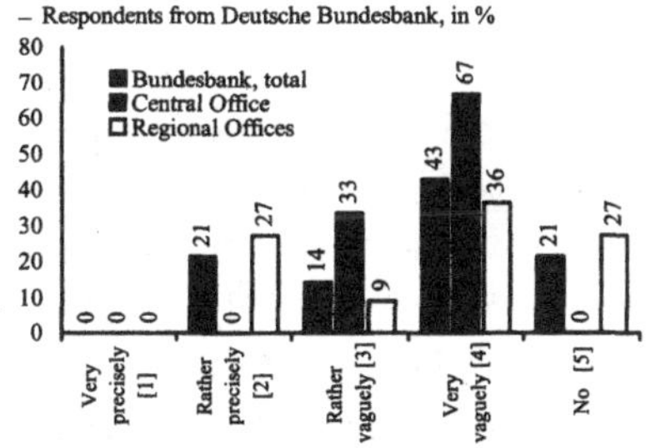

– Number of responses: 14

As a result, the diffuse transmission of monetary policy, the indirectness of channels of transmission and the differential impact on individual enterprises and sectors were firmly corroborated by interest group representatives as the most important reasons for the difficulties in determining the magnitude of the economic impact of monetary policy on Germany's business community.

Proposition 13	Question	Categories	Scale
Owing to the comparatively low and varied impact of monetary or exchange rate policy on individual enterprises, interest associations find it difficult to form strong preferences with respect to the day-to-day conduct of monetary or exchange rate policy.	"Do interest groups have strong preferences with respect to the conduct of monetary or exchange rate policy?"	"Very strong"	1
		"Rather strong"	2
		"Rather weak"	3
		"Very weak"	4

Given the perception that monetary policy has a rather varied impact on individual enterprises and sectors, the question arises to what extent it is possible for interest associations to form strong preferences with respect to this policy issue, the latter being an important precondition for effective interest representation vis-à-vis policy makers.

Asked whether interest associations in fact had strong preferences on how monetary policy is conducted, a majority of respondents referred back to the general priorities in the form of stable prices, low interest rates, export-friendly exchange rates and an overall stable monetary environment, as discussed above[616]. With respect to these general priorities, interest-group preferences were confirmed as strong on average.

In contrast, with respect to the day-to-day conduct of monetary policy interest group preferences were perceived as comparatively weak. Very much like the responses to the initial question on the intensity of interest group activity in the field of monetary policymaking, 90% of all respondents considered interest group preferences over time as either rather or very weak, as illustrated in chart 97. Only four respondents, including one former Bundesbank official and two experts from federal business associations primarily representing enterprises in the construction and machinery sectors, considered interest group preference rather strong on a continuous basis. On average, central bank representatives perceived interest group preferences with respect to the conduct of monetary policy as slightly stronger than reported by interest group representatives themselves (see chart 98). The latter typically described their preferences as rather to very weak, with a median response value of 3.50, against 3.00 for the total and the remaining sub-sets of respondents.

One sophisticated response was that

> "[t]he final impact of monetary measures is inscrutable. We cannot see what exactly happens down the line of the transmission mechanism, and it is impossible to follow their impact over time. Nor can we account for the

[616] See page 271.

> impact on individual enterprises, especially the dynamic effects. This is not least because most companies look at the issue from different perspectives all at the same time – as borrowers and investors, as exporters and importers. Sure, we can easily calculate the impact of an interest rate hike on a company's forthcoming financing conditions. But that is only a very small part of the complete story."[617]

This was complemented by a point from a respondent at a federal-level, sectoral industry association, who added:

> "Especially in our sector, the electronics trade, the structure of interests with respect to external trade becomes even more complex. By the time a final product is completed in our industry, it and its constituent parts have travelled several times around the world. It is therefore impossible in this sector to tell exports from imports, and *vice versa*. Against that background, drawing conclusions on our exchange rate policy preferences becomes an almost futile task."

In line with earlier findings on the intensity of interest group activity, periods when preferences were considered to have been strong include the early to mid-1990s and the early '80s, during which interest rates were comparatively high, both in nominal and real terms. Some respondents also pointed to interest and exchange rate developments during the early to mid-'70s, which were described as having triggered strong criticism from individual interest associations.

Finally, the responses suggest that in terms of preference formation, too, monetary and exchange rate policy represents a particularly delicate policy area for interest groups when compared with other fields. In line with the view expressed in the context of the economic impact of monetary and exchange rate developments, interest group representatives largely confirmed that producing stable and forceful positions in this policy area was more difficult than, say, on taxation, labour and welfare legislation or industry regulation, owing to the hardly discernible impact of monetary and exchange rate developments as well as the varied interests within their constituencies.

---

[617] Quote by a regional industry representative.

Strength of preferences on monetary policy

Chart 97

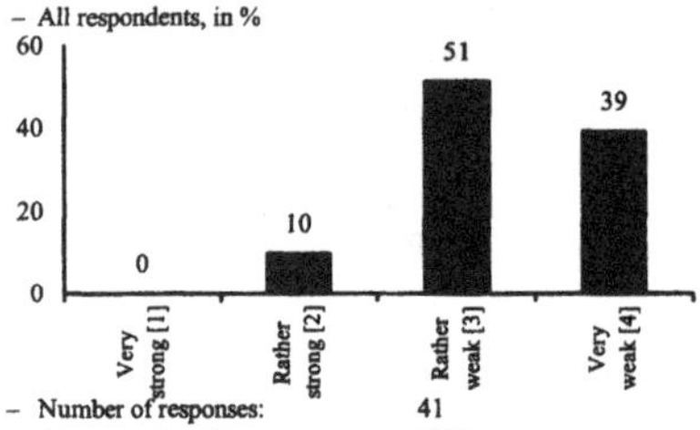

- Number of responses: 41
- Average value of responses: 3.29

Chart 98

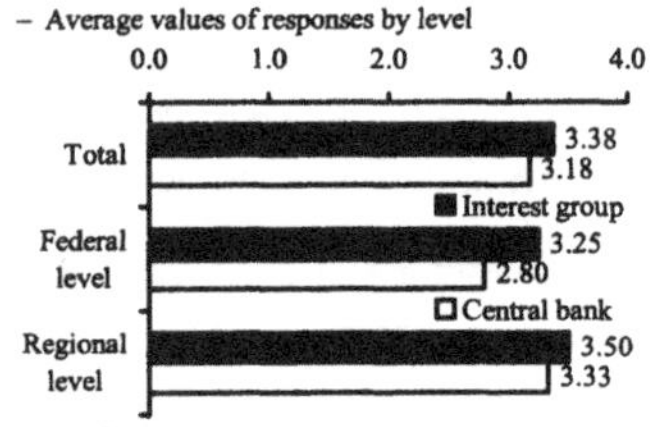

- Number of responses: 41

Chart 99

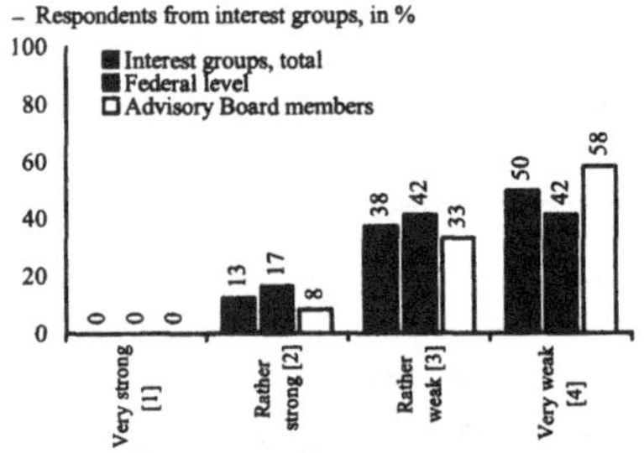

- Number of responses: 24

Chart 100

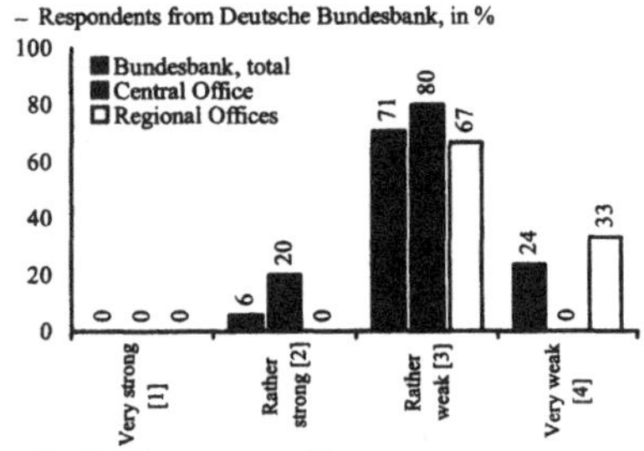

- Number of responses: 17

III.2.4.3 Monetary policy on the economic policy agenda

In the light of strong agreement with central bank policy, the low and diffuse impact of monetary developments and the comparatively weak preferences of German business associations from trade and industry, the question arises as to what extent monetary policy can compete as a policy issue on the overall economic policy agenda. Considering the great number of competing issues and the need for interest associations to prioritise their activities, monetary policy theoretically plays no prominent role in the overall economic policy discourse. This hypothesis was strongly confirmed by business and central bank respondents.

Proposition 14	Question	Categories	Scale
Given the low perceived impact of monetary or exchange rate developments and the importance of other policy fields, monetary or exchange rate policy is not perceived by interest groups as a priority issue on the economic policy agenda.	"Compared with other policy issues on the political and economic agenda, how significant an issue in general is monetary or exchange rate policy as far as interest groups and their members are concerned?"	"Highly significant"	1
		"Significant"	2
		"Insignificant"	3
		"Highly insignificant"	4

Asked how significant an economic policy issue monetary policy was assessed as being, more than half of all respondents stated that it was regarded as a highly insignificant issue[618] (see chart 101). Another 36% regarded it as insignificant. Four respondents, one with a strong export-oriented constituency and three representing primarily small and medium-sized businesses at regional level, considered monetary and exchange rate issues significant. At 3.45, the average numerical value of all replies shows that monetary issues are, in general, regarded as unimportant compared to other topics on the economic-policy agenda. This view is shared homogeneously by the respondents from interest groups and the Bundesbank and irrespective of whether respondents were active at federal or regional level, as illustrated in chart 102. The overall picture is confirmed by the median responses delivered on this question, which amounted to 4.00 for all respondents as well as the sub-sets[619], suggesting that monetary and exchange rate policy was typically assessed as being a highly insignificant policy issue. Compared with the responses on the perceived economic impact of monetary policy[620], the comparative assessment presented here underlines the importance of the former and suggests that – given the salience of other policy issues – monetary matters appear to be even less relevant for the work of the interest groups consulted.

618 The share of respondents considering monetary affairs highly insignificant was even higher when looking at interest group respondents alone, namely 58% in total and 67% among respondents at federal level.

619 The median response for the entirety of respondents as well as the sub-sets totalled 4.00, except for respondents from the Bundesbank, whose median response was 3.50.

620 See p. 276.

Monetary issues on the economic-policy agenda

Chart 101

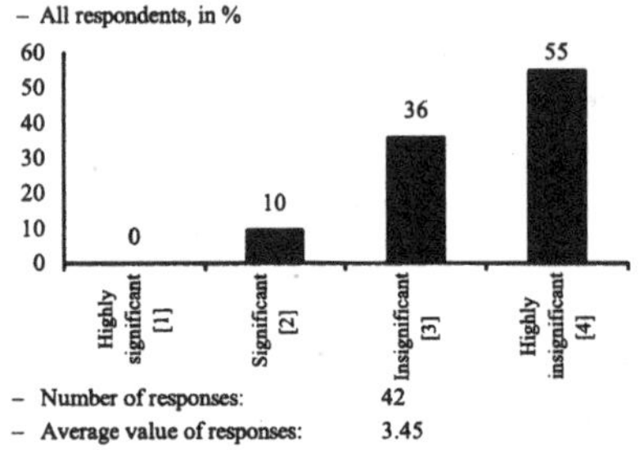

Chart 102

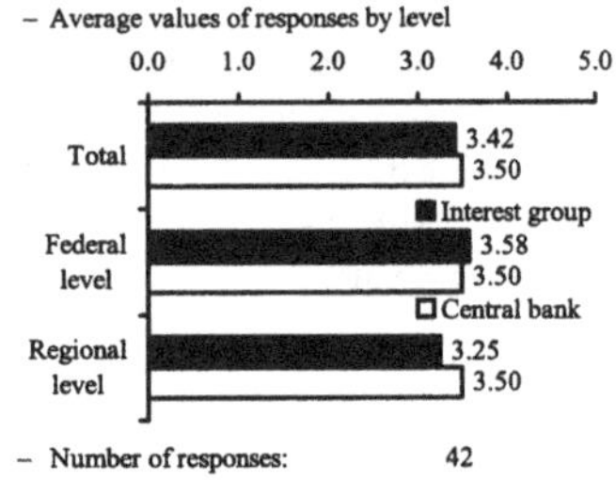

Typically, one expert from a large sectoral association at federal level stated that he could

> "[...] easily name a hundred policy issues which are more important to this association than monetary or exchange rate matters. Monetary policy is a non-issue compared with other policy fields, and this is true for most of the time".

Other respondents from a regional chamber of commerce maintained that

> "[c]ertainly, there are times when monetary and exchange rate decisions received greater public attention. However, monetary developments consistently range far behind other economic policy topics, first and foremost tax and fiscal policies, wage developments, non-wage contributions and industry regulation."

> "Even at times of extraordinarily high interest rates – by historical as well as international standards – other, more pressing economic problems kept us preoccupied. In the past half decade, at any rate, we have been operating in a very benign monetary environment, so that monetary issues were completely outside of our attention."

> "To us, interest and exchange rates are non-market framework conditions. No need and no use for lobbying. As a consequence, we save our resources for more important issues."

In line with the above list of economic policy issues derived from the annual reports of the German Council of Economic Experts, the priority issues on the political agendas of the interest representatives addressed can be summarised as follows:

- level and structure of taxation, especially corporate taxes,
- fiscal policy, government spending, subsidies,
- wage settlements and labour market structures,

- non-wage social security contributions and the structure of the welfare system,
- economy-wide or sector-specific market regulation,
- industrial policy, especially with respect to small and medium-sized enterprises,
- credit policy.

The last point on this list illustrates the relevance of the earlier finding that with respect to financing terms for German enterprises it is not monetary policy but the lending policies in the banking sector that are considered the primary source of controversy, especially since the late 1990s. The importance of this issue reportedly stems from two sources. In the first place, small and medium-sized enterprises have come under increasing pressure with respect to their financing patterns since the second half of the 1990s, when a number of German banks began to optimise their loan portfolios. Banks have tried to reduce their individual value at risk, wound up non-performing loans and pruned the share of high-risk, low-return commitments. This has reduced the availability and affordability of credit to small and medium-sized businesses in recent years, as many respondents pointed out. In addition, German enterprises were said to have been particularly concerned about the progress of deliberations on the reform of international capital adequacy standards for commercial banks in the context of the Basel II negotiations. The majority of respondents feared risk-adequate credit pricing would substantially push up the cost of credit for small and medium-sized firms. Against the backdrop of these two developments, the German commercial banking sector's lending policy has become a relatively important issue for a number of interest associations in trade and industry. Monetary conditions, in contrast, are not subject to political activity by the relevant interest groups in this context.

III.2.5 Group context

In addition to the limited accessibility of the central bank as an independent policy maker and the low and diffuse impact of monetary policy, limitations on the interest associations' ability effectively to represent the interests of their members have been identified as a third potential factor behind the low level of interest group activity on monetary policy. There can be no doubt that the associations from trade and industry under consideration in the present context generally represent strong and effective lobbying organisations. At the same time, we have seen that business associations may have difficulties in arriving at strong common policy positions on monetary issues and are likely to lack the political and information-related resources necessary to make a strong case. These propositions are largely supported by the feedback from decision makers and experts active in this field of policymaking.

III.2.5.1 Heterogeneity of preferences within interest associations

As observed above, a majority of respondents said they did not perceive interest group policy positions on day-to-day monetary policy decisions as strong. Although a solid consensus was reported with regard to the broad monetary priorities, i.e. stable prices, low interest rates and export-friendly exchange rates as well as a stable monetary environment, interest associations' and their members' preferences on individual monetary policy decisions over time were considered rather weak. Given the difficulties encountered in identifying monetary policy impacts and the varied exposures observed among enterprises and different sectors of the economy, the question arises whether this weakness in preferences can be traced back to a lack of homogeneity in interest associations' policy preferences.

Proposition 15	Question	Categories[621] Scale
Heterogeneity of interests related to monetary or exchange rate affairs within existing interest groups weakens the formation of strong policy positions in the business sector.	"To what extent does the heterogeneity of interests related to monetary or exchange rate affairs within existing interest groups weaken the formation of strong policy positions in the business sector?"	None
		None
		None
		None

First, in practice heterogeneous preferences on monetary policy within individual interest associations have a very subtle, non-decisive impact on their activities, as interest group representatives' reactions to this proposition show. Three general trends can be deduced from their responses:

- In line with the above findings on the strength of policy positions, all interest group respondents reported homogeneous and strong commitment by their associations and members to the objective of maintaining price stability. Equally, no significant internal frictions were reported on secondary preferences, i.e. with respect to low interest rates and export-friendly exchange rates. With regard to general policy objectives, therefore, heterogeneity of preferences was not considered a significant problem.

[621] Responses to this proposition are analysed in qualitative terms only. In practice, the majority of responses were found to be highly differentiated, qualifying the overall response, so that an unambiguous allocation of reactions to a set of categories of answers and a corresponding scale of numerical values was found to be inappropriate, potentially not doing justice to the level of differentiation of the responses.

- Accordingly, in the absence of major policy conflicts – of which there are very few, as borne out in the replies to the question on whether there had been instances of urgent disagreement with central bank policies in the past – interest associations and their members were said not to take up explicit policy positions. This in itself reflected not a lack of consensus, but rather the strong common perception that nothing needed to be done.
- In cases of conflict between these primary and secondary objectives, e.g. when interest rates were raised sharply by the central bank to counter inflationary pressures, most respondents reported a generally strong consensus on the fundamental assessment of the state of the economy. The rare debates that ensued were concerned primarily with whether and when the interest association should adopt certain measures and how emphatic the action should be.
- This basic homogeneity of preferences with respect to monetary policy was essentially observed across the whole range of interest associations, irrespective of whether they were federally or regionally organised, and regardless of their size and the sector under consideration.
- However, representatives from large, federal, cross-sectoral interest associations did tend to emphasise the existence of differing interests – especially along sectoral lines and with respect to the average sizes of the enterprises represented – within their organisations more strongly than those from sectoral or regional organisations. Nevertheless, none of the representatives inferred systematic disagreement or frictions from these differences.
- Internal differences in the assessment of monetary conditions, if observed, were said either to lead to a delay in the association's reaction or were resolved by toning down policy messages.
- Many respondents emphasised that strong policy messages on which no consensus could be found at peak association level could still be approved and disseminated via the regional or sectoral organisations, where agreement was found easier to reach.
- Finally, it was pointed out that the coverage of broad economic policy issues was characterised by an implicit division of labour aimed at establishing and representing policy positions on such issues – including monetary policy – at the peak level, i.e. primarily via the federal cross-sectoral associations of the BDI and DIHK, which enjoy the greatest degree of interest coverage. Specific concerns with regard to monetary policy at sectoral or regional level could be voiced via the dedicated associations. The latter, however, generally reported that they did not regard monetary policy as a primary field of activity, but rather relied on their

peak associations to take care of this issue. Failure to act because of unclear responsibilities within this implicit arrangement was not observed by any of the respondents, who pointed out that coverage of all issues considered vital was secured by means of appropriate communication between the various actors.

As a result, the responses by interest group representatives suggest that heterogeneity of preferences does not constitute a significant explanation for the low level of interest group activity on monetary developments and policy. On the contrary, the existing association infrastructure was stressed as being effective in aggregating and communicating common preferences, also in the monetary area.

Homogeneity of interests and coverage of interests by interest associations

Chart 103

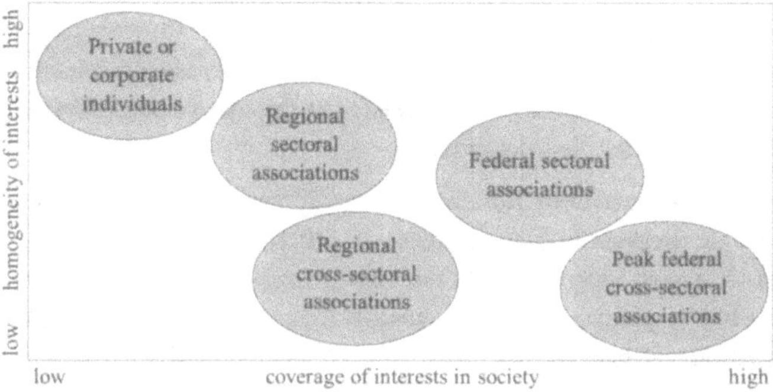

Second, interest group responses suggest that there is an indirect trade-off between the homogeneity of preferences by interest associations and their coverage of interests in society at large, which becomes particularly relevant in the context of monetary policy. Homogeneity of preferences tends to increase, the smaller and more focused an association is. At the same time, the larger the association, the broader its membership and therefore its coverage of interests in society. This trade-off can be illustrated diagrammatically as in chart 103. When mediating interests with respect to monetary policymaking, the disseminating organisation's representativeness plays an important role, as policy makers necessarily take an economy-wide view in the context of their policy objective and mindful that their instrument cannot be applied in a discriminate manner. Peak cross-sectoral associations have therefore been described by interest group representatives as particularly suitable for mediating interests with respect to monetary policy. This view was shared by a number of respondents at the Bundesbank.

III.2.5.2 Political and information-related resources

Despite having substantial financial and personnel resources at their disposal, theory suggests that interest associations in trade and industry may not be in a position to apply political pressure or contribute appropriate information or expertise on monetary affairs. Responses to the propositions on the dependence of the Bundesbank and the ECB already showed that central banks were deemed well-equipped with political independence and expertise and information-related resources in their area of operation. To complete the picture, we still have to investigate whether and to what extent interest groups consider themselves endowed with the political and informational resources enabling them to exert influence on monetary policy makers.

Proposition 16	Question	Categories	Scale
Interest associations and their members do not possess means of exerting economic or political pressure on the central bank.	"Do interest groups or their members possess means of exerting pressure on monetary policy makers?"	"Significant potential pressure"	1
		"Moderate potential pressure"	2
		"Insignificant potential pressure"	3
		"No potential pressure"	4

Tallying with the results obtained on the institutional context, interest group and Bundesbank representatives strongly confirmed the propositions that interest groups did not possess means of exerting economic or political pressure on the central bank. Asked whether sources of economic or political pressure were available to interest associations and their members, 84% of all respondents stated that no such means existed. Another 16% considered potential political pressure to be insignificant, as shown in chart 104. Chart 105 illustrates that this assessment was homogeneously shared by interest group and Bundesbank representatives at all levels. Even more distinctly than this, the median values, at 4.00 for all responses as well as all sub-sets, suggest the typical view is that interest groups cannot exert any systematic economic or political pressure at all.

On average, interest group representatives were slightly more sceptical of their own ability to exert political or economic pressure on the monetary authorities, with only two respondents reporting insignificant potential pressure. Among their Bundesbank counterparts, five respondents considered pressure possible, albeit insignificant. All other interviewees did not see any way in which interest associations could exert pressure on the authorities, as detailed in charts 106 and 107.

In principle, this verdict extended to all conceivable forms of political pressure. Without exception, respondents referred to the special institutional status of the Bundesbank and ECB, which rendered attempts to exert pressure either futile or self-defeating:

- No respondent reported involvement in or interference with the appointment of central bank officials. This was deemed ineffective owing to the Beckett effect. In addition, most interest group representatives asked said the selection of Bundesbank and ECB decision-making staff was generally satisfactory, so that no interference had been regarded as necessary in the past.
- Indirect pressure via other political institutions in the central bank environment, i.e. especially via government or parliament, was generally rated counterproductive, since these political institutions were the primary subject of central bank independence and therefore not an effective channel of communication.
- If any potential for political pressure – however insignificant – was identified, then this was related to business associations' importance for the formation of public opinion at large, primarily through the multiplication of views within their organisations and through positions adopted in public, e.g. via the media. Public opinion, in turn, was regarded by the Bundesbank as an important element in support of its own independent position. At the same time, interest group respondents reported that they did not consider the wider public an appropriate avenue through which to exert indirect influence on monetary decision makers, both for idealistic reasons and in terms of practicability: Systematic pressure via public opinion was perceived as undermining the bank's independence, which the business sector, in turn, regarded as an essential part of the monetary order, and the ability to influence public opinion on a highly specific issue such as monetary policy was seen as very limited.

Means of exerting political pressure

Chart 104

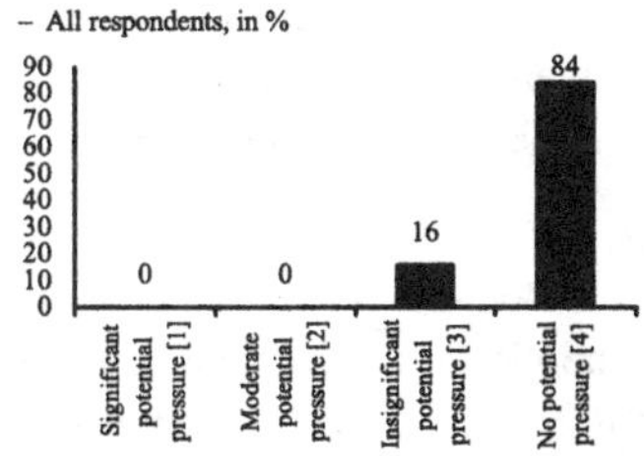

– Number of responses: 44
– Average value of responses: 3.42

Chart 105

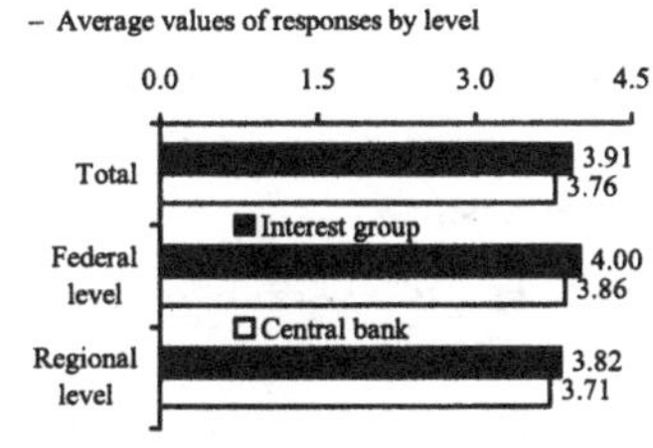

– Number of responses: 44

Chart 106

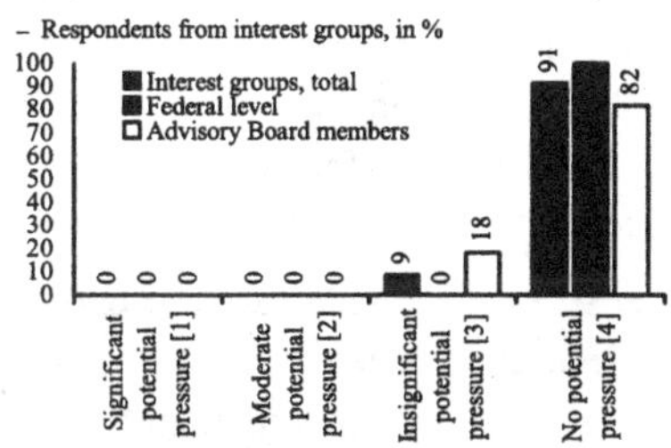

– Number of responses: 23

Chart 107

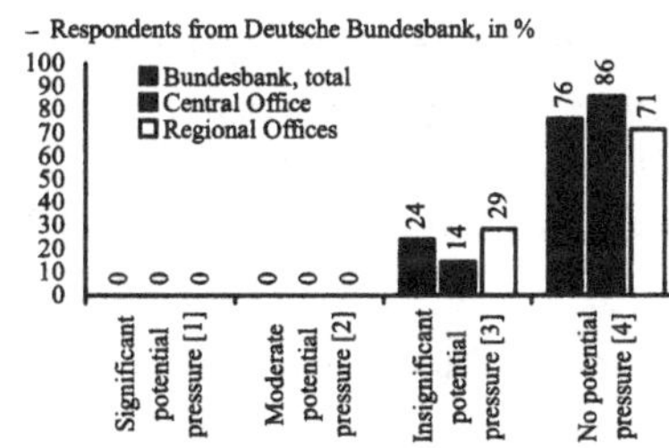

– Number of responses: 21

With regard to economic pressure, a number of interviewees from both the interest group and the central bank side acknowledged the interdependence of central banks and the private sector, first of all through the formation of market prices and wages, which directly determine the primary policy objective of the Bundesbank and the ECB. In addition, the central bank's ability to influence major monetary variables, such as interest and exchange rates, depends on the behaviour of financial intermediaries and other financial market participants playing a part in the monetary transmission process.

However, it was stressed that the ability of actors in trade and industry to exert pressure on monetary policy makers through their market behaviour was highly limited.

– First, the role of businesses in trade and industry is limited to the process of price and wage formation. Their part in the transmission of monetary stimuli, in contrast, was basically rated non-existent and mainly passive in nature, i.e. enterprises are the final link in the monetary transmission chain.

– Most importantly, however, neither wage formation and price setting nor financial market activity were regarded by any of the respondents as a means of exerting pressure on policy makers. Although conditioning monetary policy makers' decisions, respondents saw no way in which market behaviour could in fact coerce a central bank into policy measures it actually rejected. Moreover, meaningful pressure from market activity, e.g. with respect to price setting, presupposes a certain critical amount of collective action on the part of market participants, which was deemed highly unlikely given the existing level of competition in most product markets.

In this regard, too, a majority of respondents saw monetary policy as differing markedly from other policy areas. Even though not applied on a continuous basis, conventional fields of policymaking were said to offer ways of exerting political or economic pressure that could be used as a last resort in the course of policy formation. One typical example cited was the threat that costs from higher taxation or tighter regulation could be passed on to final customers or might be translated into lower employment. While elected politicians generally tended to be responsive to such arguments, the only yardstick non-elected central bank policy makers were measured by was their ability to maintain price stability. The latter, again, can be achieved irrespective of market participants' immediate reaction.

Almost as clearly as they rejected the possibility of exerting political or economic pressure on the Bundesbank or the ECB, so the respondents doubted whether interest associations were able to contribute expertise or information that, in turn, might enable them to influence monetary policy decision making.

Proposition 17	Question	Categories	Scale
Individual firms or interest associations do not possess relevant information exclusively available to them alone, which they can contribute to the discourse with the central bank.	"Can interest groups provide central banks with expertise or information of relevance to the conduct of monetary or exchange rate policy?"	"Contribute greatly"	1
		"Contribute"	2
		"Contribute slightly"	3
		"Cannot contribute"	4

Asked whether interest groups were able to contribute expertise or information of relevance to the monetary decision-making process, three-quarters of all respondents stated that interest groups could contribute only slightly or not at all. Only one-quarter thought they could contribute moderately or greatly, as illustrated in chart 108. On average, interest group representatives again proved slightly more critical of their own capabilities than perceived by their central bank counterparts, especially at the federal level[622]. More than half of all interest group representatives had the impression they could not contribute at all. Another 35% considered their potential to contribute minimal. Overall, the structure of responses closely correlates with those outlined above in respect of the monetary authorities' dependence on external expertise and information[623].

Information-related interest group resources

Chart 108

– All respondents, in %

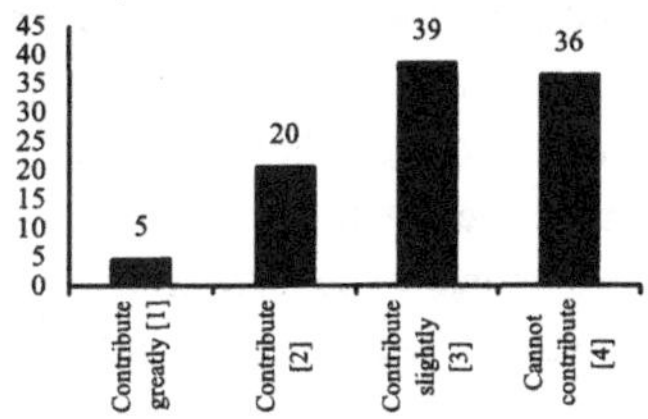

– Number of responses: 44
– Average value of responses: 3.42

Chart 109

– Average values of responses by level

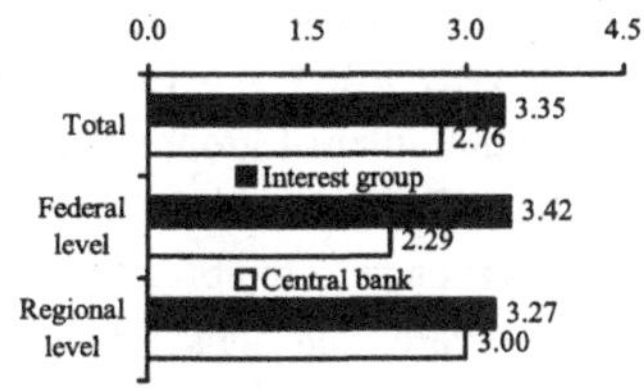

– Number of responses: 44

Chart 110

– Respondents from interest groups, in %

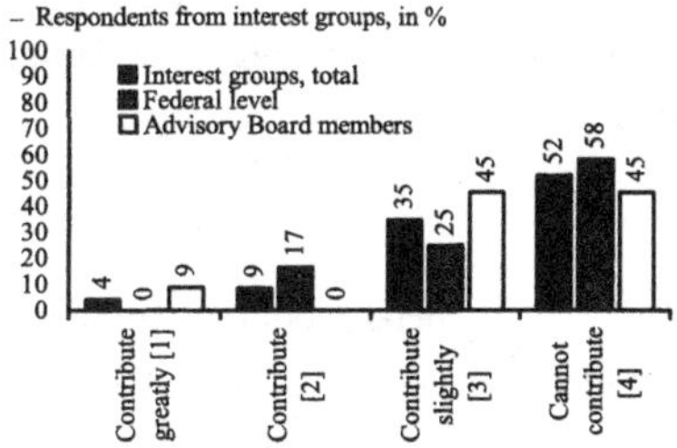

– Number of responses: 23

Chart 111

– Respondents from Deutsche Bundesbank, in %

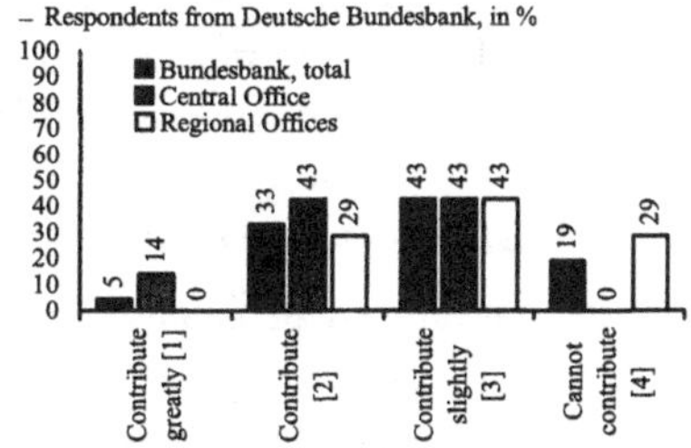

– Number of responses: 21

Also in line with the evidence on central bank dependence on external expertise and information, interest group representatives view their abilities as more limited than do their counterparts at the Bundesbank. This is illustrated in charts 110 and 111 as well as by the median values attained for the sub-set responses. More than half the interest group respondents rated their potential to contribute expertise or information non-existent, another third as very low. The typical response by interest group respondents overall, as well as the federal and regional sub-sets, was 4.00, i.e. indicating no capacity to contribute at all. Among central bankers, in contrast, one-third stated that interest groups could, in principle, contribute. 5% even considered that potential to be

[622] See chart 109.

[623] See page 264.

great[624]. Only 43% deemed the information potential low, and another 19% non-existent. Median answers by Bundesbank respondents – 3.00 for the total sub-set, 3.00 for respondents at the Regional Offices, and 2.00 at the Central Office – show that interest groups' ability to contribute valuable information was typically considered greater than by interest group representatives themselves.

III.2.6 Secondary evidence on communication of interests in practice

Confirming the central hypothesis of this study, evidence from interviews with decision makers and experts from German trade and industry associations shows that interest group activity with respect to monetary policy is very low. At the same time, it becomes evident that interest groups are neither indifferent nor altogether silent on this policy issue. Specific interests do exist, and they are articulated via the existing association infrastructure. Two broad questions therefore remain to be answered. First, it needs to be determined what triggers interest group activity – especially the articulation of specific views vis-à-vis monetary policy makers – over time. In other words, given that most of the time monetary policy works to the satisfaction of the business sector but that there are also periods when interest groups become concerned over the effects of monetary developments on their members, how is the decision on articulation of the resulting preferences taken? Second, how do interest associations actually communicate their interests once they deem political action necessary?

III.2.6.1 Group-internal decision making

Against the background of empirical findings so far, monetary policy provides a particularly illustrative example of the general problem in interest group analysis of how a certain policy issue is elevated to priority status on an association's agenda. In other words, the above evidence suggests that monetary policy is, for most of the time, a non-issue or, at best, a latent issue. At times of growing impact and urgency of monetary developments and decisions, the monetary policy issue naturally moves to the forefront. Eventually, albeit rarely, business representatives adopt strong positions on monetary policy and articulate their members' related interests vis-à-vis policy makers or in public. One important question emerging from the analysis so far is how monetary policy gets pushed up the political agenda, rising from latency to urgency.

Very much like other policy issues, the prioritisation of monetary policy on the associations' policy agendas is determined by two sources of input into their internal decision making processes: first, by the assessment at association level, and second, by

---

[624] 14% of respondents based at the bank's Central Office consider interest groups' ability to deliver valuable information great.

the views voiced by their members. In the case of monetary policy, evidence suggests that the first element is particularly strong.

All peak federal-level associations, whether cross-sectoral or sectoral, maintain economics departments concerned with analysing the relevant economic and political developments. Almost all peak associations dedicate some part of this expertise to the regular monitoring and evaluation of monetary or exchange rate developments. These dedicated resources usually take the form of one economic expert – in the case of individual peak cross-sectoral associations sometimes two experts – whose portfolio of responsibilities also includes monetary and exchange rate matters among what is generally a large number of other issues as well. This includes monitoring the development of major monetary variables, as well as the collection and review of information and statistics in this field. An association's view on monetary developments and policy measures is essentially formulated by these experts and subsequently communicated to monetary policy makers directly or indirectly by them or by other association officials.

With opinion formation primarily undertaken at the associations' central offices, bottom-up communication of preferences from member enterprises on monetary issues proves to play a moderately complementary role. In principle, monetary policy-related preferences can be communicated to associations through the conventional channels of group-internal communication, i.e. membership assemblies, committees and informal communication. Selected peak associations were even said to maintain specific working groups or committees on money and credit issues, in which monetary and exchange rate issues could in principle be communicated. However, none of the respondents found that bottom-up communication from member or constituent regional sections or from member enterprises had in the past yielded strong systematic impetus to the associations' monetary policy-related activities, being regarded mainly as complementary anecdotal evidence in addition to the associations' existing views, expertise and information.

III.2.6.2 Fundamental characteristics of communication

Interest group activity on monetary policy is not only low but also differs in quality from activities in other policy fields. A central finding from the conversations with decision makers and experts from interest organisations in trade and industry is that none of the actors characterised their activities in the monetary arena as lobbying in the strict sense. The concept was almost exclusively regarded as inappropriate as a precise description of the activities in this field of policymaking.

On the basis of the comments from the respondents, communication with the Bundesbank and the ECB can – more so than in other policy areas – best be characterised as an exchange of views and information, or as an informed dialogue, differing in quantity or quality from conventional lobbying activities in at least four respects:

- *Focus on general welfare*

  Respondents from the major interest associations stressed their awareness of the Bundesbank's and ECB's commitment to the primary objective of maintaining price stability. Neither bank is mandated to give in to particular interests from whatever side, nor would it be appropriate for them to do so. Information from the private sector can only be taken into consideration by monetary policy makers inasmuch as it is relevant in obtaining a comprehensive picture of the state of the economy. Interest group representatives stated that as a result they did not consider pushing narrow particular interests helpful in the context of monetary affairs.

- *Contents of policy messages*

  With a view to respecting the independence of the Bundesbank and ECB, many respondents considered *ex ante* monetary policy recommendations and demands or *ex post* criticism of monetary decisions in public to be counterproductive. Most associations were said to resort primarily to cautious *ex post* assessments of policy decisions.

- *Rhetoric*

  A large majority of respondents stated that they adjusted their rhetoric to the specific circumstances in discourse with monetary policy makers. Statements were generally aimed at providing factual, expertise-based information on the potential effects of monetary conditions and decisions on their constituencies in a non-confrontational manner.

- *No pressure*

  Pressure – political, economic, or rhetorical in nature – is regarded as ineffective and an inappropriate means of mediating interest group positions in monetary and exchange rate policy.

- *Direction of flow of information*

  Given the asymmetry in monetary expertise and the Bundesbank's and ECB's informational lead in this area, a great amount of information was reported as actually flowing from the monetary authorities to the private sector, and not *vice versa*. This appears to be particularly so with respect to regional-level communication, i.e. at the Advisory Boards; but it also applies to the roundtable of economic experts at the bank's Central Office and to Bundesbank and ECB communication in general, where both interest group and central bank respondents perceived explanation of the course of monetary policy and individual policy decisions as the primary purpose of communication.

Despite the differences in communication versus other policy areas, this characterisation should not be misinterpreted as implying that wherever monetary policy is concerned business associations act as impartial promoters of the common interest. Most interest group representatives left no doubt that communication with the central bank had the primary purpose of furthering their members' interests. Rather, the above characteristics bear witness to the fact that

- disagreement with the central bank, should it occur at all, is hardly ever perceived as so acute that a demanding or confrontational posture needs to be taken, and that
- interest groups are careful to adopt a rhetoric which they deem appropriate in discourse with an institution they generally hold in high esteem and which would not, anyway respond to explicit demands, even were they tabled.

Finally, it became evident that the equilibrium in communication between the interest associations and the central bank critically depends on the coincidence of priorities on both sides and on interest groups' overall concurrence with the implementation of these priorities by the Bundesbank and the ECB. A number of interest group respondents pointed out that if systematic disagreement on objectives and priorities were ever to arise, political activities by interest associations – whatever form these would then take – would possibly be stepped up significantly, and that communication might become less conciliatory in tone in such a hypothetical circumstance.

III.2.6.3 Channels of communication

If interest groups take an interest in monetary affairs, these interests are communicated via the conventional channels, even though the relative importance of these instruments for effectively communicating preferences may differ marginally from conventional policy areas[625].

Most importantly, the interest group representatives addressed expressed a clear preference for direct communication with the Bundesbank. This generally works through three major channels:

---

[625] As described above, the interviewees addressed in the course of the field work were selected on the basis of their involvement with monetary affairs. The regional interest group representatives in particular were all selected on the strength of their membership on the Bundesbank's regional Advisory Councils. Consequently, a selection bias cannot be ruled out with respect to the priority the respondents assigned to certain channels of communication, especially as regards direct formal ways of communication. The analysis therefore refrains from weighting the importance of the different channels of influence or from quantifying the views expressed by the respondents.

- First, via the only formal consultative channel enshrined in the Bundesbank Act, namely the Advisory Boards at the bank's nine Regional Offices,
- second, via the semi-formal channel established with the roundtable of economists from trade and industry and,
- third, via informal direct contacts between the decision makers or experts from the Bundesbank on the one hand and interest associations on the other.
- Indirect channels, in contrast, are said to play a negligible role, with the exception of the media.

III.2.6.3.1 Regional Advisory Boards

The Advisory Boards at its nine Regional Offices represent the only formal channel of communication between the Bundesbank and the private sector, as outlined above. As such, the Boards theoretically assume a key role in the transmission of private-sector interests. In practice, they are highly appreciated by their members as a forum for exchanging views, even though their effectiveness as a channel of communicating interest, expertise and information has reportedly remained limited and is expected to have declined following the recent organisational reform of the bank.

As to the purpose of the Advisory Board, it has already been pointed out that prior to the 2002 institutional reform this was defined as conferring with the presidents of the Land Central Banks on questions of monetary policy. Up to then the LZB presidents were members of the Bundesbank's Central Bank Council, which determined the country's monetary policy until Germany joined EMU in 1999. Since 2002, the task of the Advisory Boards has been defined as discussing with the presidents of the Regional Offices execution of the tasks falling to that area. From a statutory perspective, monetary policy is therefore no longer the subject of the Boards' work. Meetings used to be held four times a year, a frequency which has now been reduced to two.

In practice, participants in Board meetings, i.e. the presidents of the Regional Offices, their members and the finance or economics ministers in the relevant regions, gather at the respective Regional Offices for two to three-hour meetings. Depending on the conventions at the different Regional Offices, the formal sessions are often followed by an informal part, usually in the form of a joint lunch or dinner. The sessions begin with an introductory presentation by the president of the Regional Office or one of the office's experts, analysing the monetary and wider economic conditions and explaining the Bundesbank's, and since 1999 the ECB's, monetary policy decisions. This introduction is followed by a general discussion, in some cases preceded by a *tour de table*, allowing each Board member the opportunity to give an initial reaction to the bank's remarks. Sometimes, experts or decision makers from inside or outside the Bundesbank are invited to Board meetings to give presentations on selected policy issues. Meetings and the contents of the discussions are confidential. Minutes of each session are prepared by the President's office, circulated among the members and subsequently archived at the Regional Office[626].

In principle, the discussions at Advisory Board meetings were reported to focus on monetary policy, but in many cases they also moved on to other topics of general economic relevance. While monetary policy took centre stage in the Bundesbank's introductory remarks, the presence of the regional finance or economics ministers was said to be viewed by most Board members as an opportunity to discuss more pressing issues, such as fiscal, labour market or regulatory affairs, with the political representatives. Some Board members said this opportunity was one of the most important reasons for their participation.

Asked for an assessment of the importance and effectiveness of the Advisory Boards, the relevant respondents emphasised that the meetings were deemed an important forum for exchanging views with policy makers. Only a very small minority of individual Board members considered attendance at the meetings purely a matter of duty. In general, seven elements can be identified in the Boards' overall appreciation:

- The vast majority of Board members appreciated the meetings as an important channel of communication with monetary policy makers and representatives of the Land governments.
- The primary benefit of the meetings, as viewed by Board members from trade and industry, lay in the easy and regular access to first-hand information on monetary policy and the state of economic affairs in Germany.
- The primary benefit of the meetings, as viewed by Bundesbank respondents, lay in explanation of the bank's and subsequently the ECB's monetary policy. Board members were considered important multipliers in the process of informing the wider public of the bank's activities.
- Board meetings were, in principle, considered to be a forum for articulating private-sector interests with respect to monetary policy. Assessments on the Boards' effectiveness as a channel of communication were inconclusive, with views ranging from great effectiveness – emphasising the immediacy of access and the interest on the part of Bundesbank officials – to very low effectiveness – referring to the bank's independence and the lack of interest on the part of Bundesbank officials. A large majority of interest group respondents emphasised

---

[626] Like other confidential Bundesbank documents, Advisory Board minutes are classified for thirty years.

that they were not aware of the impact of deliberations during Board meetings on opinion formation within the Bundesbank.

- A significant constraint on the effective articulation of interests appears to be that Advisory Boards were composed of regional or local interest group representatives who did not possess the monetary policy expertise and information that their counterparts at peak federal associations commanded, and whose political weight in terms of representativeness was clearly limited.
- Many Board members pointed out that overall appreciation of the Advisory Boards considerably varied, depending on the approach taken by individual Regional Office presidents. Accordingly, openness for discussion and interest in private-sector views was said to differ strongly.
- All participants valued the meetings for their confidentiality. In many cases, a great degree of openness in the discussions was said to result from this confidentiality. Confidentiality and openness were perceived as promoting a frank exchange of views, firstly between the Board members and Bundesbank representatives, secondly between the members and regional ministers, and finally also among interest group representatives themselves. As to the latter effect, some interest group representatives emphasised that the Board represented a forum in which employers and trade union representatives were able to discuss wage and labour market policies outside the conventional ideological constraints.

The institutional reform implemented in mid-2002 diminished the statutory role of the Advisory Boards, as observed above. This is mainly because of the new mandate, which no longer foresees an advisory function on monetary policy; decreasing proximity to the decision-making process since the presidents of the Regional Offices are no longer involved in monetary decision making; removal of the obligation to invite the relevant ministers of finance or economics; and the lesser frequency of Board meetings which, at twice a year, narrows the scope for near-time comments on individual monetary decisions. At the same time, the Bundesbank has tried to preserve some political weight for the Boards by deciding that each Board meeting should be attended by one member of the bank's Governing Board, even though its constituents – save for the Bank's president – are not formally involved in monetary decision making either.

Consequently, the future role of the Advisory Boards is viewed critically by a majority of the members addressed. Most respondents expected the Boards to lose political importance as a result of the organisational changes, making them less attractive as a channel for communicating private-sector interests. Some respondents consider the Boards now completely ineffective in this regard, calling future participation into question, at least inasmuch as this participation may not necessarily be exercised by a top-level representative. Many respondents, on the other hand, stated that participation remained interesting in principle, provided that comprehensive information continued to be given on monetary decisions and the Bundesbank's assessment of the state of the economy, or that the economics or finance ministers continued to attend.

III.2.6.3.2 Roundtable of economists

At the semi-formal level, not established by law or formal agreements, on a half-yearly basis the Bundesbank invites the chief economists of the major nationally organised interest associations from trade and industry to the central office in Frankfurt for an economists' roundtable. As pointed out above, the primary aim of these meetings is to communicate Bundesbank and ECB monetary policy. Participants in the roundtable talks are the Head of the Economic Department and other staff members of the Bundesbank and the relevant representatives from the BDI, the BGA, the DIHK, the HDE, the VDA, the VDMA, the WVS, the ZDB, the ZDH, and the ZVEI. Like Advisory Board proceedings, meetings of the economists' roundtable begin with an introductory presentation on monetary developments and the Bundesbank's assessment of the general economic environment and major financial market developments. These introductory remarks are followed by a *tour de table* allowing each participant the opportunity to give an initial reaction to the bank's remarks, and a general discussion.

Discussions in the context of the economists' roundtable were reported as very focused on monetary policy, complemented by detailed discussions of credit and financial market developments and policies. General economic policy was said to be of secondary importance.

In general, the economists' roundtable is appreciated by interest group and central bank representatives as a confidential, expert-level forum for exchanging views on monetary and financial market affairs. As to its effectiveness as a means of communicating private-sector interests, respondents stated that they considered the direct exchange of views with the Bundesbank's top-level experts and decision makers very useful. But they also emphasised the factual, non-political nature of the discussion, which was intended as an expert-level exchange of economic assessments rather than the communication of particular interests, and was respected as such. Some respondents pointed out that the frequency of meetings, at two a year, was too little to react to individual policy measures and articulate views on them.

III.2.6.3.3 Informal communication with the Bundesbank

Informal communication between the private sector and the Bundesbank takes two major forms, namely personal contacts and the dissemination of specific information by interest associations to the Bundesbank beyond the articulation of views in the formal or semi-formal contexts.

Informal personal contacts were reported to exist, even though interest group respondents generally judged them far less intensive than those with other policymakers. Personal contacts are mainly horizontal in nature, between monetary policy makers on the one hand and high-level interest-group representatives on the other, as well as among experts at the federal or the regional levels. They range from individual meetings dedicated to discussing certain issues of common concern, through mutual invitations to academic or social events, to chance meetings. Although important for maintaining contacts between the two sides, such informal personal meetings were generally not considered relevant to particular monetary policy measures.

Especially for peak cross-sectoral or sectoral associations, publications containing policy studies, opinion polls, regular assessments of general economic and individual sector-specific conditions, and statistical releases were seen by both sides as important instruments of mutual information, not least because some of these publications regularly documented interest associations' assessment of monetary conditions, including potential policy recommendations.

III.2.6.3.4 Indirect communication

The most important indirect means of communicating monetary policy-related views, particularly from the viewpoint of top-level business associations, is the dissemination of views and information via the media. The public release of economic reports and studies was described by the peak associations in particular as an opportunity to portray the impact of monetary and exchange rate developments on their constituencies and, if deemed appropriate, to publicise how they would like monetary policy to develop, moving forward.

Media relations are, however, approached with considerable caution by the interest groups investigated. Most importantly, detailed responses by experts and decision makers show that statements on monetary and exchange rate policy are much less frequently communicated to the media than in other fields of policymaking. In line with the earlier findings on issue salience and interest groups' self-assessment of their ability to influence monetary decisions, respondents pointed out that their ability to introduce policy positions into the public arena was limited. Given the far greater importance of taxation, welfare reform, industry regulation or trade issues, for example, the majority of respondents typically considered monetary and exchange rate issues unattractive for communication though the media. In addition, those respondents whose organisations had communicated their views on monetary issues to the media in the past emphasised that in this area particular care was devoted to the way in which policy messages were communicated. Many respondents emphasised that explicit and systematic policy recommendations to the relevant decision makers, as are frequently proposed in other policy areas, are not considered an effective means of communicating monetary policy related interests.

This qualitative finding confirms quantitative results reached earlier by Maier[627], who investigated a segment of media work by interest groups on monetary policy. Maier examined the statements made by different stakeholders in three important German daily newspapers[628] between January 1960 and December 1998, producing a comprehensive overview of interest group comments on monetary policy over almost four decades. Interest groups investigated in that analysis included organisations from the financial sector and export-based and domestically oriented employers' organisations[629]. For each sector, Maier calculates the number of observations, i.e. the number of newspaper articles found in the reporting period, the sum of all observations[630], and a ratio denoting the percentage of articles demanding tighter monetary policy over the total number of articles[631]. The calculations suggest four important conclusions, which the qualitative findings of the present research corroborate:

- Trade and industry take recourse to the media relatively seldom – here specifically the press – to mediate their views on monetary issues. In the course of 39 years, Maier counted 527 relevant articles in the three newspapers under investigation. Only 10.4% of the statements made there came from employers' organisations outside the financial sector[632]. In total, only 23 statements by domestically oriented organisations were counted. Considering that some public statements by the organisations under review are likely to have been reported simultaneously by all three newspapers examined, the effective number of times these organisations actually turned to the media may, in fact, be much lower. Looking at the three

---

[627] Maier (2002), pp. 75-96.

[628] The dailies analysed by Maier were the *Frankfurter Allgemeine Zeitung*, *Die Welt*, and *Handelsblatt* (Maier (2002), p. 80).

[629] Further stakeholders analysed were the government, trade unions and other sources (Maier (2002), p. 84).

[630] To indicate the policy message conveyed by the relevant interest group in each article, Maier counts articles demanding higher interest rates as +1 and articles calling for monetary relaxation as -1, and subsequently adds up all correspondingly labelled observations (Maier (2002), p. 80).

[631] By this classification, a ratio of +100% would denote a state in which all articles found called for monetary tightening. A ratio of -100%, in contrast, would indicate a case in which all articles called for monetary relaxation. Maier's main results are reproduced in table 13 on p. 309.

[632] Government accounted for 16.1%, the financial sector for 26.6%, trade unions for 13.1%, and other sources for 20.9%.

press sources in isolation, it becomes evident that domestically oriented interest organisations were cited only on seven, 13, and three occasions respectively over the nearly four decades under scrutiny.

- Most of the statements from employers' organisations – almost 60% – originated from export-oriented organisations, suggesting either that export-focused organisations were more prone to work via the media, or that exchange rate-related issues were debated more controversially than monetary policy in the narrow sense. The latter interpretation is supported by the -94% ratio of calls for monetary relaxation to total observations, suggesting that the vast majority of export-oriented interest group interventions were critical of a monetary policy perceived as too tight. Further, the latter interpretation seems warranted in the light of the findings on the impact of monetary and exchange rate policy and the evolution of the issue agenda as reported above.
- Even in the rare cases when domestically oriented organisations did turn to the press, on average their interventions aimed at tightening rather than easing the monetary stance, as the ratio of +4% shows. Indeed, the ratio for one of the three newspapers was +23%, indicating that on average the relevant organisations were supportive of raising interest rates. This picture bears out the theory suggested by a majority of respondents in this study that industry associations actually tended to back the Bundesbank – informally as well as publicly – in its stability-oriented monetary policy.
- The analysis of press reports is also consistent with the findings reported here on the intensity of the political work by industry associations as opposed to other groups. The figures show that in the period under review organisations from the financial sector and trade unions were significantly more active than employers' organisations. In addition, Maier finds that interest groups' overall lobbying on monetary policy is far lower than, for example, in the US[633].

In as far as press relations give an indication of industry associations' general approach to the media in the current context, these findings confirm the general thrust of the answers we observed.

---

[633] Maier (2002), p. 80.

Survey of mediation of interests via the media

Table 13

Pressure from	**Frankfurter Allgemeine Zeitung**	**Handelsblatt**	**Die Welt**	***Total***
Government				
Number of observations	36	30	19	*85*
Sum	-32	-26	-13	*-42*
Ratio	-89%	-87%	-69%	*-49%*
Financial sector				
Number of observations	39	58	43	*140*
Sum	-29	-26	-23	*-58*
Ratio	-74%	-45%	-43%	*-41%*
Employers' organisations: export-oriented				
Number of observations	9	14	9	*32*
Sum	-9	-12	-9	*-30*
Ratio	-100%	-86%	-100%	*-94%*
Employers' organisations: domestic-oriented				
Number of observations	7	13	3	*23*
Sum	-1	3	-1	*1*
Ratio	-14%	23%	-33%	*4%*
Trade unions				
Number of observations	16	42	11	*69*
Sum	-16	-42	-11	*-69*
Ratio	-100%	-100%	-100%	*-100%*
Other sources				
Number of observations	25	67	18	*110*
Sum	-17	-47	-8	*-72*
Ratio	-68%	-70%	-44%	*-65%*
Total				
Number of observations	*153*	*254*	*120*	*527*
Sum	*-111*	*-158*	*-70*	*-339*
Ratio	*-73%*	*-62%*	*-58%*	*-64%*

Source: Maier (2002), p. 84

Other channels of indirect communication were said to exist, but generally regarded as comparatively unimportant for the communication of monetary policy-related preferences. These include testimonials before expert councils not directly related to monetary policy, including the German Council of Economic Experts, as well as participation in public opinion polls. Similarly, individual enterprises' responses to surveys, including the Ifo-index on economic expectations established by the Munich-based Ifo Institute for Economic Research, which is widely recognised as the most important indicator of business expectations in Germany, or economic surveys on business expectations carried out by the European Commission, are considered to be important economic indicators through which individual enterprises' business sentiment can be conveyed, but they are not regarded by business associations as instruments of communicating concrete monetary policy-related interests. Respondents pointed out that these surveys and indicators did not contain detailed information on monetary conditions and did not transmit identifiable and co-ordinated interests and expectations. Similarly, international organisations regularly commenting on Germany's economic policies, such as the OECD or the IMF, were not used by interest associations as indirect ways of articulating monetary policy-related interests.

Finally and most importantly, almost all respondents emphasised that a number of indirect channels often used in other policy areas were not viable in the context of monetary affairs. In particular, political institutions, especially government and parliament, were unavailable for indirect lobbying on monetary policy, as noted above. Not only was the independence of the Bundesbank and ECB perceived as an effective hurdle to influence on monetary policy from the political arena, but demands on monetary decision makers from the political side were also widely perceived as counterproductive – often provoking monetary authorities not to follow precisely those claims staked out by politicians. As well as being counterproductive, instrumentalising politicians in this regard was considered inconsistent with the general call by Germany's business associations for central bank independence. In practice, business associations have repeatedly found themselves supporting the Bundesbank in its policies and defending it against intrusion by policy makers, as already noted.

III.2.7 Comparative analysis

Given these results, we need to establish whether they add up to a coherent picture in terms of the theoretical thoughts enumerated at the outset of this study. It was hypothesised that interest group activity on monetary and exchange rate policy was likely to be low by the standards of other major economic policy areas owing to the specific framework conditions governing the institutional, issue, and group environments encountered in this policy arena.

Most importantly, the overall explanatory approach has been confirmed by a consistent set of empirical findings, none of which squarely rejected the underlying propositions. No contradictions have been identified between the responses on the core propositions. An overview of the propositions and the general results achieved so far is presented in table 14 below.

Central propositions and empirical support, summary table

Table 14

Proposition		**Empirical support**
	General context	
Proposition 1	In general, interests with respect to monetary or exchange rate policy are not communicated very intensively to the relevant decision makers.	**strong**
Proposition 2	In general, communication of interests with respect to monetary or exchange rate policy is significantly lower than in other policy fields.	**very strong**
Proposition 3	Mediating interests with respect to monetary or exchange rate policy does not yield sufficient benefits relative to the associated costs.	**strong**
	Institutional context	
Proposition 4	Central banks are perceived as inaccessible to interests from the private sector, compared to other political bodies.	**strong**
Proposition 5	Political independence is an obstacle for private interests in mediating their interests to the central bank.	**strong**
Proposition 6	Given their institutional, material, and expertise-based resources, central banks are not dependent on external political support in order to fulfil their tasks in the field of monetary or exchange rate policy.	**very strong**
Proposition 7	Given their focus on aggregated economic indicators and their access to the relevant statistical resources, central banks are not dependent on external information with respect to monetary or exchange rate conditions and developments in order to fulfil their tasks in the field of monetary or exchange rate policy.	**very strong**
Proposition 8	Given the independence of central banks in terms of political, material, and expertise-related resources as well as their focus on aggregated economic indicators, central bank policy makers are not interested in the views of private-sector interest groups on monetary or exchange rate policy.	**moderate**

Central propositions and empirical support, summary table

Table 14, continued

Proposition		**Empirical support**
	Issue context	
Proposition 9	Individual firms or interest associations agree with the objectives and the overall conduct of monetary or exchange rate policy.	**very strong**
Proposition 10	Interest groups rarely disagree with the monetary or exchange rate policy decisions of the central bank.	**strong**
Proposition 11	Monetary or exchange rate policy is not perceived to have a significant effect on individual firms or interest associations.	**strong**
Proposition 12	The magnitude of the impact of monetary or exchange rate policy on individual firms or interest associations is difficult to determine.	**strong**
Proposition 13	Owing to the comparatively low and varied impact of monetary or exchange rate policy on individual enterprises, interest associations find it difficult to form strong preferences with respect to the day-to-day conduct of monetary or exchange rate policy.	**moderate**
Proposition 14	Given the low perceived impact of monetary or exchange rate developments and the importance of other policy fields, monetary or exchange rate policy is not perceived by interest groups as a priority issue on the economic policy agenda.	**very strong**
	Group context	
Proposition 15	Heterogeneity of interests related to monetary or exchange rate affairs within existing interest groups weakens the formation of strong policy positions in the business sector.	**moderate**
Proposition 16	Interest associations and their members do not possess means of exerting economic or political pressure on the central bank.	**very strong**
Proposition 17	Individual firms or interest associations do not possess relevant information exclusively available to them alone, which they can contribute to the discourse with the central bank.	**very strong**

This inherent consistency notwithstanding, it is necessary to discuss the detailed results with respect to their implications for the central questions addressed in this study. This discussion takes account of four dimensions of interdependence between the dependent and independent variables identified here, i.e. on the one hand the extent to which interest group activity in this policy area can be identified, and on the other the issue, institutional, and group contexts. These four dimensions are:

- the extent to which the independent variables – the three contexts – can in fact explain the dependent variable – the amount of political activity,

- the extent to which the propositions within the institutional, issue, and group contexts respectively are consistent,
- the extent to which individual propositions across the three contexts are consistent, and
- the extent to which responses across individual propositions yield a coherent and plausible picture.

As to the causal relation between the amount of political activity on the one hand and the three specific policy contexts on the other, the above analysis suggests that institutional, issue, and group framework conditions provide a plausible account of interest groups' political activity with regard to monetary and exchange rate policy in Germany. Taken together, the three contexts explain the decisive driving – and braking – forces behind the low level of lobbying encountered in this policy area, with an emphasis on the issue-related properties of the matter as the main moderating factors. Even though the institutional environment and specific group capabilities in this field of monetary policymaking certainly also discourage political work in this regard, the issue context – i.e. broad agreement with central bank objectives, low perceived policy impact, and weak preferences – are found to be the most important brake on lobbying. In other words, the analysis shows that owing to the issue environment, most of the time there is no significant reason for lobbying in the first place, and therefore no identifiable demand for political activity. Institutional and group conditions add to the disincentives to taking political action on the supply side, as interest groups' abilities to contribute to the central bank's policy-making process in terms of political support and information are limited, and their ability effectively to mediate these interests within the existing institutional framework is rather restricted. In addition, none of the responses suggested that factors existed, other than those identified in the core propositions, which they considered instrumental for their political activities and their decision to operate with respect to monetary and exchange rate issues as they do. In this sense, the list of independent variables worked out here can be considered exhaustive.

Second, the consistency of responses within each of the contexts can also be regarded as high. As to the extent of interest group activity as the dependent variable, responses show that both in isolation and from a comparative angle, interest group attention to monetary issues is broadly regarded as very moderate, based on a relatively homogeneous set of responses. In the same vein, the expected pay-off of measures in this policy area is considered relatively slight, again in quite a homogeneous manner. Differences in assessment occur in nuances inasmuch as interest group activity is rated even less intensive when compared with activities in other policy fields than when viewed in isolation.

With respect to the institutional context, overall accessibility is considered rather low, even though the dispersion of views is slightly wider than on other propositions. This understanding is based mainly on the Bundesbank's perceived independence from external political support and information, underlining the bank's autonomy in terms of political power as well as material and immaterial resources. Political autonomy is generally prized as a precious good worth defending. This is suggested by the reference made by a number of respondents to the fact that they repeatedly feel compelled to defend the bank's decisions and status against occasional intrusions from the political level. This may at first sight seem to be a contradiction, but it is explained when the respondents make it clear that they regard the societal consensus in support of central bank independence as stable and violations of the bank's status as exceptional and non-existential. Backing for the bank from interest groups, if and when it is given, can therefore be viewed as precautionary rather than a matter of immediate necessity. Surprisingly, political independence as such is not generally regarded as an immediate or onerous burden on interest groups' relations with the Bundesbank. This protective measure is – in the eyes of many interest group respondents – designed with politicians in mind rather than interest groups. Even if interest group representatives do feel affected in principle, they nevertheless deem interest group activity legitimate, given that the bank cannot be coerced into following the advice from the private sector and is free to choose how to react to private-sector views. All the same, interest groups perceive very little demand for political and informational resources by the central bank. By the same token, they find central bank interest in interest group views on monetary decisions moderate at best.

As to the issue context, a high degree of consistency can be detected between the key propositions and the responses yielded. The very strong overall support for the general objectives of monetary and exchange rate policy is underscored by strong confirmation of the proposition that interest groups rarely disagree with day-to-day policy decisions. In conformity with this picture, monetary and exchange rate developments are generally perceived to have a low impact on the interest groups consulted and their constituents compared with other policy issues. At the same time, though, interest groups find it hard to assess the precise magnitude of that impact. The question naturally arises as to how respondents can maintain that monetary developments have a very low impact even though they are uncertain of its precise magnitude owing to the complexity of the way monetary stimuli work on the economy. What at first sight appears contradictory is most likely shedding light on the subjectivity and narrowness of enterprises' and their interest associations' perception of the related economic developments. Judging from the detailed responses, the latter assess monetary and exchange rate developments by their immediate impact on corporate operations and financing, i.e. on interest rates, lending terms, asset management, imports and exports.

This impact can, in principle, be calculated with some precision, and – given that it is small compared to enterprises' other cost and income components – it is generally viewed as negligible. At that point already, however, varying and rivalling exposures – i.e. being debtor and creditor or importer and exporter at the same time – render a formal assessment difficult. Things become even more complicated once indirect channels of transmission and second-round effects are taken into consideration. This complexity, however, seems to be largely faded out by individual enterprises for lack of immediacy and relevance, considering that the initial impact is in itself considered minimal. This sequence of events, in turn, explains the conundrum addressed at the outset of this study. While overall effects of monetary measures on the economy and general welfare at large are substantial in statistical terms and comparable to the effects of measures in other economic policy areas, the immediate, calculable impact as perceived by enterprises and their interest associations is very small in comparison. From this focused perspective, low interest group activity is not an omission but rather a rational response given the existence of other, more pressing and more concrete problems. Finally, the issue-related picture is complemented by the finding that interest groups do not therefore easily form string preferences with respect to day-to-day policy decisions and that, compared with other policy issues, monetary and exchange rate matters are not perceived as priority issues on their political agendas.

As to the group context, interest group representatives clearly declare that there is precious little they believe they can contribute to policy formation, perceiving their political and informational resources as inadequate for shaping policy debates as they are accustomed to do in other policy areas. This is complemented by the view that the heterogeneity of interests within the interest groups consulted weakens the formation of strong policy positions on the issue, albeit not very substantially.

Third, the individual responses yield an overall complementary and coherent picture. Most importantly, there is a strong correlation in responses between the institution-related propositions that the Bundesbank does not depend on external political support, on the one hand, or external information, on the other. Naturally, information and political support were considered closely related by most respondents in as far as they were ultimately granted with the aim of furthering the aims of the respective interest group. At the receiving end, the Bundesbank's autonomy in both regards was regarded as a manifestation of the idea of institutional independence. Given the Bundesbank's endowment with both expertise and political autonomy, a consistent set of responses was obtained. Both together represent the most important drivers behind scepticism as to the bank's accessibility, whereas political independence as an immediate obstacle and a lack of interest in private-sector views can be considered secondary in importance. As already pointed out, the fact that political independence was not regarded as a very strong immediate obstacle to interest group activity, while the bank was viewed as independent of external political support, should not be interpreted as a contradiction. Rather, the former was seen as applying primarily to electoral and government politics. Insofar as government respects and safeguards political independence in practice, the bank is in no immediate need of political support from the private sector for most of the time. The views on interest associations' ability to contribute political support and information to the policymaking process presented in the group context are strongly in line with the results on the corresponding questions in the institutional context. Similarly, the results on agreement with central bank objectives, the lack of disagreement with day-to-day policy decisions, their immediate effects on enterprises and interest groups and the prioritisation of monetary and exchange rate affairs on the political agenda add up to a consistent picture.

Interestingly, groups' perceived issue-related weakness in forming strong preferences for day-to-day monetary policy decisions does not prevent them from actually adopting strong policy positions at group level where necessary, i.e. when certain – albeit apparently unquantifiable – critical thresholds of sensitivity towards monetary and exchange rate developments are transgressed by policy makers. Once more, the solution to the apparent contradiction seems to lie in the time horizon applied: interest groups obviously find it more difficult to assess and respond to short-term, incremental developments, as investigated in the issue context, than to form general policy positions as addressed in the group context.

Finally, responses across the spectrum yield a consistent picture with two important exceptions. First, responses at the regional level differ repeatedly – although not substantially – from those at the federal level. Thus, regional representatives are more critical of the Bundesbank's institutional accessibility, perceive less interest in private-sector views by the bank, agree less rarely with monetary policy measures, and perceive the impact of monetary developments to be stronger than their counterparts at the federal level. The discussion above, however, indicates that these differences do not reveal systematically different attitudes towards the issue at large, but rather reflect their particular position within the economic and institutional environment. For one thing, the more critical view of institutional accessibility reflects the increasing remoteness of the Advisory Bodies from the locus of monetary decision making following the changeover to the euro and the recent institutional reform of the Bundesbank. Further, detailed answers by the relevant respondents suggest that the lower degree of interest as perceived at the regional level also bears witness to these institutional changes, as well as to the specific behaviour of individual presidents of the Regional Offices chairing the sessions of the regional Advisory Boards. Finally, the responses on the impact of monetary policy and the greater dissatisfaction with monetary decisions appear to be related to the fact that Advisory Board members generally represent small and medium-sized enterprises whose exposure to bank credit, and hence to monetary conditions, is greater than that of larger companies. With financing conditions in general having become tighter between the mid-1990s and early 2000s for small and medium-sized enterprises, the perception of monetary affairs has become more critical in these circles. However, this result has to be qualified by the recognition that most detailed responses showed respondents failing to differentiate strictly in their comments on financing conditions between the changing patterns of bank lending originating from the behaviour of commercial banks and the effects on lending conditions that can actually be traced back to monetary decision making. Considering that central bank-controlled monetary conditions progressively eased in that period, it must be doubted whether the criticism voiced by respondents at the regional level in the present context can, in fact, be ascribed wholly or partially to central bank decision making[634].

More important, however, is the rift in the perceptions between interest group respondents and central bankers. Compared to their interest group counterparts, central bank policy makers and experts perceive

- interest group activity to be more intensive,
- themselves as more accessible,
- political independence as less of an obstacle to communication with the private sector,
- their reliance on external political support and information as more intensive,
- themselves as more interested in private-sector views,
- interest groups as more critical of the Bundesbank's objectives, and more often in disagreement with its policies,
- the impact of their actions on enterprises to be more substantive, and
- interest groups' information-related resources with respect to monetary and exchange rate affairs as more substantial.

These discrepancies can partly be explained by central banks' subjective self-perception of their activities and their relevance for the economy, as pointed out earlier. Interest group views may be perceived as relatively more intensive, since the central bank is the intended addressee. Accessibility may be considered greater by central banks than by interest groups, whose benchmarks may suggest that greater openness is exercised by other institutions. Similarly, political independence may look much less of an obstacle to the central bank than to an interest group seeking to

[634] When attention was drawn to this difference in the course of the relevant interviews, respondents generally revised their responses wholly or partially. Even though the empirical evaluation was adjusted for this effect, it is likely to have influenced the final results presented here.

overcome that hurdle. By the same token, monetary policy makers are likely to perceive themselves as much more reliant on and open to outside information than outsiders themselves may believe. Finally, their specialised insight into the subject matter may enable central bankers to have a broader view of the impact of their actions on the corporate sector than individual entrepreneurs or managers.

Subjectivity may, however, be only one element in an explanation of these systematic deviations. The responses obtained offered no indication that the deviations did not also reflect unique differences in the approaches to certain issues. Thus, the bank may not be as indifferent to private-sector views as the latter perceive it to be, implying greater scope for private-sector central bank communication than realised so far. Even though the bank and its representatives did not report concrete attempts to intensify mutual interaction, a number of respondents stated that they appreciated the exchange of information with the private sector and welcomed direct or indirect contributions to the policy debate.

To be sure, if the Bundesbank desired greater input from the private sector it could invite interest groups or enterprises to become more active, formally or informally. Invitations for exchanges of views beyond the formal and informal channels examined so far have not been issued in recent history, though[635]. In the same vein, it is worth noting that there is no indication that the Bundesbank or members of the Advisory Boards have made use of the option to convene extraordinary board meetings during the period reviewed in this study. This suggests three possible conclusions. First, there is disagreement among Bundesbank decision makers as to the benefits of more far-reaching consultation, with the consequence that no decisions are taken in that direction. In fact, feedback from high-level decision makers within the bank suggests that such disagreement may exist, as interest in private-sector views varied considerably at that level. Second, interest in private-sector attitudes towards monetary policy may only be declaratory in nature, blurring the reactions obtained from the relevant respondents. Most likely, however, there is no immediate contradiction in the strong declarative interest by bank representatives and the fact that nothing has been done so far to intensify the dialogue with the private sector. A broad majority of respondents at both regional and federal level inside the Bundesbank said they felt existing arrangements were largely appropriate and sufficiently flexible to allow the bank to access additional information from the private sector on an *ad hoc* basis as necessary, e.g. through extraordinary meetings of Advisory Boards or the roundtable of economists, or by means of informal communication.

---

[635] More intensive consultation with the private sector has repeatedly been sought by the Bundesbank on an *ad hoc* basis. Exchanges of views in that sense, however, occurred with respect to topics not

III.2.8 Interim conclusions

The results of the survey among 46 decision makers and experts on monetary and exchange rate affairs from German business associations and the Bundesbank confirm the major propositions of this study.

- Interest group activity in the field of monetary and exchange rate affairs is low, especially when compared with other policy areas, owing to the fact that the expected benefits do not justify the costs associated with more intensive activity.
- Institutional accessibility is one of two major explanatory variables for low interest group activity. Political independence and ample endowment with material resources and expertise in its field of policymaking contribute greatly to the fact that the Bundesbank does not need to rely on political support or information from the private sector, effectively insulating the bank from external influence. This is recognised by interest group representatives and enters their cost-benefit analysis of action in this policy field.
- The second major explanatory variable is the coincidence of major policy objectives between the private sector on the one hand and the Bundesbank and ECB on the other, coupled with a great degree of agreement with the monetary authorities' policies in general. Most of the time, monetary policy thus becomes a non-issue as perceived by trade and industry associations.
- Even if monetary and exchange rate developments do become more urgent across economic cycles, their direct and indirect impact – if at all identifiable – is regarded as very low compared with that of other economic policies. As a consequence, preferences with respect to monetary and exchange rate policies are comparatively low in intensity. Despite the considerable impact of monetary policy on the economy as a whole, it is not a priority issue on the political agenda of business associations.

Two additional findings deserve emphasis:

- Heterogeneity of interests does not seem to play as great a role in inhibiting interest group activity on monetary affairs as theory might suggest. Preferences are perceived in a general manner, and in most cases they are not necessarily considered contradictory.
- Interest group and central bank perceptions differ systematically in as far as Bundesbank respondents consider themselves more interested in private-sector information and views and less exposed to external dependencies, and monetary

related to monetary or exchange rate policy, e.g. technical implementation of the changeover to the euro, Basel II, or payment systems.

policy plays a more significant role for enterprises than perceived by respondents in the private sector. These systematic deviations point up room for improvement in communication as a whole.

Finally, the specific institutional, issue and group contexts condition the way the two sides communicate with each other:

- Most importantly, interest groups do not lobby monetary policy makers in entirely the same way as they approach decision makers in other conventional policy areas. The style of communication is rather un-political, factual, and non-prescriptive, tending to take the form of an informed, expertise-oriented dialogue geared towards the general good – or this, at least, is what is professed.
- The preferred channels of communication with the Bundesbank are direct in nature, with the Advisory Boards and economists' roundtable as the formal and semi-formal forums. Communication via the media is an important tool, but it is used with care in order to avoid the public perception that business associations are interfering with the policies and independence of the monetary authorities.

III.3 Interest-group activity after entry into EMU

Since 1999 monetary policy in Germany – as in all other countries participating in EMU – has been determined by the ECB. The Bundesbank is a member of the ESCB and participates in formulating and implementing the ECB's policies, but a monetary policy for Germany alone no longer exists. From the perspective of national interest groups, participation in EMU therefore marks a fundamental change in their monetary policy-related task environment. It also implies that the overall policy context has changed. As a result, the question arises whether and to what extent this change affects interest groups' perceptions and activities with respect to monetary policy.

To obtain a comprehensive view of monetary policy-related interest group activity throughout the European monetary area, basically this question needs to be asked for each member state individually, as the policy contexts within which interest groups used to deal with monetary policy differed in many respects prior to monetary unification. Such differences include variations in the institutional and decision-making structures in the member states, especially with respect to their central banks, insofar as these existed at all[636]. Similarly, monetary developments and the performance of the monetary systems in the individual member states vary considerably on a historical review. Further, industrial and financial structures in the member states exhibit substantial differences, suggesting varying degrees of exposure to monetary developments for enterprises. Finally, structures, resources and activities by the national interest association infrastructures through which domestic enterprises' interests are channelled and articulated vis-à-vis policy makers differ. Given these national distinctions, a complete picture of monetary policy-related activities by interest groups in trade and industry in the euro area requires an analysis of all twelve national policy contexts.

More importantly, monetary policy – by establishing a single currency area and a single monetary policy – has, in the first place, become an EU-level policy issue. A full understanding of interest groups' activities on monetary policy in the euro area therefore also necessitates an examination of the institutional, issue and group contexts at EU level. To be sure, a final evaluation of the new environment will need to wait for a while, given that the caesura from EMU lies only a few years back. Nevertheless, initial evidence from the qualitative interviews conducted in the course of the present study yields a number of indicative preliminary results pointing towards where the future equilibrium of communication between Eurosystem central banks and the

---

[636] Luxembourg did not establish a fully-fledged central bank as a separate institution until 1998. Prior to that the circulation of money and certain other operational monetary functions were overseen by the Institut Monétaire Luxembourgeois, founded in 1983. Due to the limitations of its operational functions, the latter was not considered a central bank proper (Palmer (2001), pp. 26-27).

private sector may be located. As the following sections suggest, the problems confronting interest groups differ considerably, depending on whether they operate at national or at EU level.

The following sections take an initial step in these two directions. First, with respect to changes in the communication of interests at national level we present reactions by representatives of interest groups in Germany to the changes in the policy environment resulting from the transition to monetary union. Second, we analyse the basic parameters of interest groups' work at EU level on the single monetary policy. The most important result of this analysis, as argued below, is that at both national and EU level communication between interest groups on the one hand and monetary policy makers in their new positions and roles on the other is still evolving, suggesting that a long-run equilibrium – like the one identified in the case study on Germany – has not yet been reached in the EMU context. The observations made below therefore necessarily reflect preliminary trends in the evolution of perceptions and channels of communication.

The evidence presented below[637] is derived from two sources. First, most of the respondents from the sample of interviewees at German interest groups and at the Bundesbank referred to EMU and other major EU policy developments in their responses. The following section presents a summary of the factors related to EU economic and monetary affairs based on these statements. Subsequently, evidence from experts at EU level will be discussed with the aim of gaining a preliminary picture of the long-term consequences for interest group behaviour of shifting monetary and exchange rate policy authority to the EU level.

III.3.1 Impact on national level: evidence from Germany

In the course of the interviews conducted in the context of this study, several respondents from the sample of interest group representatives in Germany also commented on the impact of the new institutional, issue, and group environment on their monetary policy activities after accession to EMU. The respondents' reactions flag three developments in response to the caesura of the single currency. First, although generally stable over time, some perceptions of monetary affairs as a policy issue have changed. Second, patterns and channels of communication with the central bank have started to adjust to the new institutional environment. Finally, the process of adjustment has not yet been completed, so that patterns of communication have remained in a state of flux.

---

[637] Both the reactions by German and EU-level respondents are presented in qualitative terms, as the impact of EMU as such was not part of the quantitative analysis.

According to the respondents at business associations in Germany, perceptions of monetary affairs as a policy issue have generally been very stable over time. Thus, the assessment of the institutional arrangements under which monetary decisions were taken until 1998, including the backing of central bank autonomy, the perceptions of the accessibility of the Bundesbank and its independence from external political or expertise-related support enjoyed considerable continuity over the past decades. Following introduction of the single currency a number of important perceptions identified above have remained unchanged. Most importantly, according to the respondents central bank independence and the objective of maintaining a stable monetary environment continue to be trade and industry representatives' basic priorities with regard to monetary policy in general. In fact, most representatives characterised their own associations, and the German business community in general, as highly committed protagonists of a monetary order similar to that of the Bundesbank, both in the years preceding entry into the third stage of EMU and thereafter. Similarly, the assessment of the potential contributions interest associations can make to the policy process, especially in the form of political support, information, and expertise, has largely remained unchanged since 1999.

At the same time, most respondents confirmed that the new policy framework affected their perceptions of the institutional, issue, and group environments. In terms of the general assessment of interest group activities in the field of monetary policy, the majority of respondents commenting on the impact of EMU observed that the net benefits from communicating interests with respect to monetary policy had declined compared to pre-1999. As to the reasons for this view, respondents referred to both lower expected benefits and higher expected costs.

The institutional context was judged the most important factor in deterioration of the cost-benefit ratio. Respondents pointed to the modest voting power of individual national central banks, including the Bundesbank, in monetary decision making within the Eurosystem. That national central banks were not supposed to vote as representatives of their national economies was identified as another hurdle for the potential assertion of specific interests. Business representatives on the Bundesbank's regional Advisory Boards in particular considered the increased remoteness of monetary decision making from their own position as an obstacle to effective interest group work. Some respondents clearly stated that after the 2002 Bundesbank reform monetary policy was no longer a relevant issue for discussion at that level, even if a member of the bank's Executive Board participated in the meetings. Accordingly, discussions on monetary policy were considered useful only if the Bundesbank president, as the sole policy maker actually involved in monetary decisions, participated in the Board meetings.

At the same time, most respondents noted that the ECB had been provided with an extraordinary degree of independence from the political arena, an achievement they expressly welcomed. Some respondents nevertheless voiced concerns that the responsiveness of national central bankers from member states with a less pronounced "stability culture" might be higher than in Germany. A potential politicisation of monetary policy was regarded by these respondents as a serious, albeit rather unlikely, threat to euro area economic stability.

With respect to the issue context, consensus existed that formulation of the ESCB's primary objective of maintaining price stability was necessary and appropriate. Similarly, none of the respondents reported systematic deviation in their assessment of the ECB's conduct of monetary policy in its first years vis-à-vis the Bundesbank's performance. Many business representatives, however, expressed their concerns over the difficulties involved in formulating an optimal monetary policy for the entire euro area, given the structural and cyclical differences of the member economies. Noting that no serious tensions within the euro area had occurred since the introduction of the single currency, a number of respondents pointed out that internal economic imbalances could not be ruled out, and that the ECB had not yet been tested with respect to extreme economic conditions. It was mentioned that in principle an optimal euro area policy was not necessarily ideal for all member states. Given Germany's structurally low rates of growth and inflation compared to those in many other member states, respondents stressed the risk of euro-area monetary policies being tighter on average than a stance optimised for Germany alone. In so far, many respondents reserved their judgement on the performance of the single monetary policy, while stating that in principle the potential for policy conflicts was higher than before the entry into EMU as far as interest groups were concerned.

By analogy with this concern, a number of respondents perceived the group context as having changed as well, referring to the high number of stakeholders watching the ECB in its decision making across the euro area and the greater heterogeneity of interests when compared to the constituent economies. As a result of the greater pool of interests and stakeholders striving for influence on the single monetary policy in the euro area, some respondents expected the benefits from political action to be even lower than with domestic monetary policy prior to 1999.

Especially in response to the changes in the institutional and group contexts, an adjustment of patterns of communication between interest groups and the monetary authorities was considered useful in principle, especially by representatives at the federal level. Provided that the articulation of interests was sought in the first place, the respondents commenting on the patterns of communication said EU peak associations now represented important interlocutors for contacts with the ECB.

Interest aggregation at the EU level was therefore singled out by some federal-level respondents as a vital instrument for effective representation of interests vis-à-vis the ECB. At the same time, maintaining contacts with the Bundesbank, as one of the participants in monetary decision making at ECB level, was considered an equally important objective.

With regard to the latter point, it was emphasised that direct contacts with the ECB by national-level interest associations were considered difficult to establish. The ECB was said to be understood to have a particular preference for contacts with EU peak associations, so as to obtain as aggregated a picture of the state of the economy as possible. In addition, experts at the ECB pointed out that it was interested in obtaining a balanced view. Particular national perspectives were not considered relevant for the formulation of a euro area-wide monetary policy. As a result, contacts between national associations and the ECB have so far been restricted to selective individual meetings at the request of single associations. These meetings are understood to have been concerned with matters not related to monetary policy in the narrow sense.

Business representatives at the Bundesbank's Advisory Councils, in contrast, took a more passive view, recognising the diminished role of this specific channel of communication and pointing to the fact that there were no alternative channels with realistic potential for input into the policymaking process at the regional level. Some respondents at Advisory Board level remarked that given the trans-national dimension of a single European monetary policy, regional input may, in fact, no longer be useful for policy makers or meaningful for interest groups.

Finally, the responses suggest that the process of adjusting communication to the new framework conditions is not yet complete. Especially among members of the regional Advisory Boards, uncertainty was reported as to their future role. Although the new legal basis was recognised as depriving the Boards of their monetary policy mandate and limiting discussion to the remit of the Regional Offices, the Bundesbank's decision to have a member of the bank's Advisory Board participate in each Board meeting has raised hopes that the scope of discussions may nevertheless remain broad and relevant to monetary issues. At the federal level, in contrast, change has focused on whether and how the ECB can be addressed directly, and how interests in monetary policy and their articulation should be balanced between the existing channels at the federal level and via the relevant EU peak associations.

III.3.2 Perceptions and activities by EU business associations

The work of EU-level business associations on monetary issues has become an important element in the overall activity of interest groups from trade and industry in this policy field, as both the logic of the new decision making framework under EMU as such and national business associations' assessments suggest. This raises two questions. First, what perception do the relevant peak EU associations have of the institutional, issue, and group contexts? In other words, we need to analyse whether and to what extent EU associations approach monetary policy in different ways from their national counterparts, i.e. German business associations in the current context. Second, we must clarify how EU associations cope with the new issue and new institutional environment, and how they aggregate and communicate potential monetary policy-related interests to the relevant decision makers.

To answer these questions, decision makers and experts at major EU business associations were asked about their perceptions of monetary affairs in the euro area and their activities in this field of policymaking. Following the same selection criteria as in the above case of Germany, the EU-level sample of stakeholders was composed of representatives from

- the peak EU business associations in trade and industry, including industry[638], chambers of commerce[639], the retail, wholesale, and foreign trade[640], and skilled crafts[641], and
- interest associations from those sectors in the EU economy identified above as being particularly exposed to interest and exchange rate developments, including the export[642], construction[643], automotive[644], chemical[645], mechanical engineering and electronics[646] sectors.

The number of decision makers and experts at EU business associations interviewed between June 2003 and January 2004 totalled nine. Two experts at the ECB were also addressed. The composition of the sub-sample is shown in table 12[647].

Like their counterparts in Germany, EU interest-group representatives were first asked for their perception of monetary policy as an issue within their sphere of activities. As the following section shows, some indicative differences in the assessments of the two

---

638 Union of Industrial and Employers' Confederations of Europe, UNICE.

639 The Association of European Chambers of Commerce and Industry, Eurochambres.

640 EuroCommerce.

641 European Association of Craft, Small and Medium-Sized Enterprises, UEAPME.

642 The Foreign Trade Association, FTA.

643 European Construction Industry Federation, FIEC.

644 European Automobile Manufacturers Association, ACEA.

645 European Chemical Industry Council, CEFIC.

646 Liaison Group of the European Mechanical, Electrical, Electronic and Metalworking Industries, Orgalime.

647 See p. 236. In addition, one high-ranking official at the EU Commission close to the Macroeconomic Dialogue was consulted.

samples were observed, suggesting that in practice significant differences in the preferences of EU interest associations from those of their member associations in the EMU states cannot be ruled out. Second, the respondents were asked about their activities on monetary matters in practice. The results, as presented in the following, show that direct communication – the primary channel used by German interest groups with respect to the Bundesbank – is comparatively limited at Community level, with non-action or indirect interest representation occupying a stronger position. In contrast to the analysis of the evidence gained on Germany, EU-level evidence is primarily analysed in qualitative terms only, as the small size of the sub-sample renders a detailed quantitative examination inappropriate.

III.3.2.1 EU-level perceptions of monetary policy as a policy issue

With the single European monetary policy defined by the ECB, interest groups have a substantial incentive to represent their views directly to the ECB at the Community level. Peak business associations at EU level play a particularly important role in this regard, as they offer the opportunity of representing joint, EU-wide positions on policies of interest common to their members and affiliates. As a result, European business associations potentially play an influential role when it comes to aggregating and articulating monetary policy interests for enterprises in trade and industry. The question necessarily arises as to how monetary policy is approached by EU business associations in the new operational setting of EMU, and whether this approach differs from that observed at the national level, i.e. from the behaviour of German business associations in the case in point.

Evidence from the responses by the nine EU interest group representatives indicates that, while important common tendencies exist, certain differences in assessment can be identified compared to their German counterparts. Table 15 lists the numerical equivalents of the responses from EU business associations in direct comparison to those at the German counterparts discussed above[648].

As to the general assessment of interest group activity on monetary policy, the proposition that interests were not communicated very intensively was strongly confirmed by the respondents. While cross-sector peak associations reported some, albeit mostly very moderate, activity, representatives of sector-specific groups stated that they took practically no interest in monetary affairs and did not undertake any significant activity in this area. Compared with other policy fields, monetary affairs-

---

[648] Given the comparatively low number of respondents – nine in total, with some questions not answered by every respondent – the numerical values are presented here as rough indicators for the overall mapping of views, but do not lend themselves to further statistical analysis. Table 15 presents average values only, for illustrative reasons.

related activity was consequently rated by all respondents as less or much less intensive. The potential net benefits associated with such activity were – without exception – considered either low or very low.

EU and German interest group responses on central propositions

Table 15

Context	Proposition	Germany Total	Germany Federal	Germany Regional	EU Total
General	Intensity of communication of interests	4.21	4.42	4.00	4.56
General	Intensity of communication, compared with other policy fields	4.71	4.83	4.58	4.67
General	Benefits of communicating interests with respect to monetary policy	3.00	3.25	2.75	2.89
Institutional	Accessibility of central banks	2.77	2.60	2.92	3.00
Institutional	Political independence as an obstacle to communication of interests	2.63	2.50	2.75	2.75
Institutional	Central bank dependence on external political support	3.55	3.60	3.50	3.67
Institutional	Central bank dependence on external expertise and information	3.58	3.67	3.50	3.57
Institutional	Interest of central bank policy makers in interest group views	2.82	3.00	2.67	3.25
Issue	Interest group agreement with objectives of monetary policy	1.33	1.33	1.33	2.00
Issue	Interest group agreement with conduct of monetary policy	4.13	3.92	4.33	3.71
Issue	Economic effects of monetary policy	3.08	3.08	3.08	3.57
Issue	Determination of size of economic impact of monetay policy	3.96	3.92	4.00	4.29
Issue	Formation of strong preferences with respect to monetary policy	3.63	3.83	3.42	4.25
Issue	Monetary policy no priority issue on economic policy agenda	3.42	3.58	3.25	4.00
Group	Interest group resources, economic or political pressure	3.91	4.00	3.82	4.00
Group	Interest group resources, information and expertise	3.35	3.42	3.27	3.89

In their general assessment, respondents specifically referred to the extremely low impact of monetary policy on enterprises in general and on their respective members in particular, especially considering the large number of more pressing issues that associations are expected to tackle. As a result, the gross benefits of seeking to influence monetary developments were regarded by all respondents as minute. Responses also focused on the institutional hurdles to effectively influencing monetary policy, with central bank independence discouraging interest group activity. Respondents emphasised that in the case of the ECB a particularly strong form of institutional autonomy had been put in place, going even beyond the levels of independence previously practised in the member states. At the same time, a majority of respondents pointed out that their assessment hinged on experience with ECB monetary policy conducted in the opening years of the single currency. The conclusions from this experience were stressed as being preliminary, considering the ECB's relatively short period of operation and the fact that its policies had not yet been subjected to serious economic and monetary tensions. Consequently, respondents did not rule out the possibility of their organisations becoming more active in this field of policymaking if and when it assumed greater urgency in future.

In comparison to their counterparts at German interest associations, EU-level group representatives therefore arrive at a very similar general assessment, strongly confirming the propositions that communication of monetary policy-related interests is low, especially compared to activities in other policy fields. However, they do take a slightly more optimistic view of the potential overall benefits of interest group work in this area.

Asked for their specific assessment of the institutional context, EU interest group representatives judged the ECB as on the whole rather inaccessible, citing its political independence as the most important reason for this. The latter was viewed by most respondents as an obstacle to effective interest mediation, even though most of them stressed that in principle independence was not perceived as constraining the articulation of preferences as such. Like many of their German counterparts, interest groups were considered free to express their views, and it was up to monetary policy makers to decide whether and to what extent these views shape their judgment. At the same time, there was broad agreement that the ECB was not dependent on external political support, expertise, or information in the pursuit of its activities. In conformity with this judgement, ECB policy makers were, on average, considered only slightly interested in the private sector's views on their policies.

A direct comparison with the results obtained for federal-level interest group representatives in Germany with respect to the Bundesbank suggests that on average the ECB is viewed as slightly more inaccessible than the Bundesbank, even though the numerical value for the typical response is identical in both cases. At the same time, the replies on the proposition that political independence works as an obstacle to effective interest representation show that at EU level interest groups feel slightly less affected by this institutional feature than their colleagues in Germany, even though the degree of independence the ECB enjoys is generally considered greater than in the case of the Bundesbank. Analysis of the detailed responses hints at a more pragmatic approach by EU-level representatives as the most likely explanation of this difference. While many respondents in Germany pointed out that central bank independence necessitated a certain auto-limitation on the part of interest groups insofar as criticism of Bundesbank policies, especially in public, could be interpreted as an attempt to infringe the bank's independence, EU lobbyists did not consider this effect very important in their assessment. This interpretation is supported by the finding that EU interest representatives had less of a problem communicating their views on monetary policies through the media than their colleagues in Germany. Most of the EU-level respondents insisted that any activity on their part would impair the bank's political autonomy neither theoretically nor practically. In the assessment of the significance of central bank dependence in terms of external political support, expertise or information, no major differences can be identified between German and EU-level respondents. However, the interest that ECB policy makers take in interest group views on monetary and exchange rate policy was clearly judged more critically by EU respondents than by their counterparts in Germany, suggesting that the ECB's lack of accessibility is seen as being influenced by behavioural rather than institutional factors.

With respect to the issue context, overall agreement with the ECB's policy objectives and conduct was confirmed as an important reason for low interest group activity on monetary policy in general. EU business representatives reported broad agreement with the overall objectives of monetary policy as defined for the ESCB. The formulation of the bank's primary objective of maintaining price stability is generally welcomed and regarded as appropriate. At the same time, it is worth noting that agreement with monetary objectives was slightly lower than in Germany, signalling possibly higher potential for conflict with the central bank. Some respondents, however, expressed concerns that policy makers paid too little attention both legally and in practice to the secondary objectives of monetary policy, i.e. those pertaining to support for the general economic policies in the Community. More precisely, the view was expressed that monetary policy should also be designed to be conducive to growth and stimulate economic activity, especially at times of economic downturns. Individual respondents characterised this as a real problem reflected in the bank's performance record, while others considered it at least a potential challenge.

In terms of agreement with the ECB's day-to-day policy measures, all respondents said differences were rare. The majority, however, pointed out that this overall assessment for the euro area as a whole was not shared completely by all of their member associations in the member states. Thus, some respondents referred to repeated discussions with their member associations on assessment of the ECB's policies, from which marked differences in the evaluation of these policies across member states emerged, reflecting the fundamental difficulties in formulating a single euro-area monetary policy in the face of considerable structural and cyclical differences in the constituent economies.

In addition to this overall agreement with the priorities and course of policymaking, the lack of salience and urgency of monetary affairs as a policy issue was endorsed by all respondents as a second issue-related reason for low interest group activity. In general, monetary developments were regarded by business representatives as having a very weak or even negligible impact on their member or affiliated enterprises' business performance, even though precise determination of the magnitude of this impact – especially aggregated across the euro area – was considered very difficult. Interest group representatives reported clear feed-back from their member organisations – even if only by default – that monetary policy was generally considered a non-issue because of its minimal direct impact on enterprises. As in the case of respondents in Germany, however, it became evident that specification of the policy impact was considered too resource-consuming, underlining that interest representatives and their constituents do not actually know the precise magnitude of the impact. In conformity with this, preferences with respect to day-to-day monetary decisions were regarded by all respondents as either weak or very weak. As already pointed out, a majority of respondents emphasised that this assessment was regarded as preliminary, considering the ECB's relatively short track record and the fact that its policies had not yet been subjected to serious economic and monetary tensions. As a result, respondents did not rule out that monetary conditions could develop in the future in such a way as to make EU-level interest associations consider them increasingly pressing. Such a scenario was, however, generally deemed rather unlikely.

Finally, EU interest group representatives took a strong view on the relevance of monetary policy compared with other policy issues. All respondents judged monetary policy a highly irrelevant policy issue with an extremely low position on their list of policy priorities. In this context, respondents emphasised that the Community institutions were highly active legislators and regulators, especially with respect to the EU internal market, consumer protection and environmental issues. This was said to result in very tight political agendas containing numerous issues with immediate and substantial effects on enterprises in the member states. Given the low and diffuse impact of monetary and exchange rate policies, as well as the fact that no major policy controversies had reached the public agenda in general so far, monetary issues had received very little attention among stakeholders in trade and industry.

Comparing these reactions on the issue context with the responses from German interest representatives reveals a number of significant differences in assessment. Most importantly, EU-level interest representatives agree – with the average numerical equivalent of responses at 2.00 – significantly less with the overall objectives of monetary policy than their counterparts in Germany, where the numerical value is 1.33. This is corroborated by comparing typical answers, for which the median value at EU-level was 2.00 against 1.00 in Germany. This illustrates that on average European experts and decision makers were more critical of the negligible importance allocated by the Treaty and by monetary policy makers to supporting general economic policies in practice. While agreeing that maintaining price stability should be the priority objective, some respondents considered existing provisions and practices too narrowly focused on this, referring to the United States and the policies of the Federal Reserve Board as an example of a more pragmatic approach, aimed at both monetary stability as well as a policy environment conducive to economic growth. Second, the salience of monetary policy was considered much lower by EU respondents than by experts in Germany, with numerical values for the responses on the proposition that monetary policy was not perceived to have a significant impact on the corporate sector at 3.57 in the former and 3.08 in the latter case. This suggests that the gross benefits expected to accrue from political action on monetary issues is rated markedly lower at EU level than in Germany, so that incentives for EU business associations to become active in this policy area must be regarded as comparatively low. In the same vein, EU business representatives rate the strength of group preferences and the importance of monetary policy on the political agenda much lower than their colleagues in Germany. This means there are two discernible trends working in opposite directions. While there is evidence of greater potential for disagreement with the ECB's monetary policy, the overall importance of the bank's activities, and hence the potential for disagreement as such, is considered appreciably lower. So far, the former trend has not yet been so strong as to outweigh the latter.

As to the group context, EU respondents confirmed the proposition that interest groups possess the relevant information or expertise to contribute to the discourse with the central bank, or the means of exerting political pressure of any kind on monetary policy makers. It is noteworthy that EU-level business representatives were significantly more sceptical of their ability to feed expertise or information into the policy process than their German counterparts. Although emphasising their routine in terms of EU-wide data collection and analysis, most group representatives pointed out that relevant statistical information, such as surveys on business expectations, investment behaviour and planning, or views on monetary or exchange rate conditions had not been systematically collected until the late 1990s. A substantial lead on the ECB in this regard did not therefore exist in practice.

To summarise, top EU business associations approach monetary policy in a very similar way to associations in Germany: Interest group activity on monetary issues is very low owing to the insignificance of monetary developments for their constituents, the institutional difficulties in effectively representing interests vis-à-vis policy makers, and the limitations on the groups' resources of relevance to this policy area. Overall, EU groups are even more sceptical than their German counterparts about the expected net benefits of becoming active in the policy area, the relevance of monetary conditions for their members, and their own ability to make a meaningful contribution to policy discussions.

III.3.2.2 Communication of interests in practice

This sceptical assessment of the benefits and costs of interest intermediation on monetary and exchange rate issues by EU interest group representatives – very much as in Germany – does not mean that monetary policy-related interests, insofar as they exist, are not communicated to the relevant decision makers. Interest group activity with regard to monetary policy is comparatively low, but the issue is being tackled in practice, characterised by three major trends. First, some associations, especially peak cross-sectoral groups, are in the process of building up systematic coverage of monetary issues. Second, many associations, especially those representing specific sectoral interests, have remained inactive in this policy field and have no plans to the contrary. Third, communication with the monetary authorities at Community level is largely limited to the Macroeconomic Dialogue, with other channels playing a clearly minor role.

As to the coverage of monetary policy-related issues, responses from experts at EU business associations show that systematic patterns of communication with ECB policy makers are still in the process of establishment. Although most associations devoted significant resources in the 1990s to analysis and promotion of the single currency, this work was primarily focused on the period prior to the third stage of EMU, and to questions pertaining to the fundamental set-up of the single monetary policy and related policy processes such as the coordination of fiscal policies in the member states via the Stability and Growth Pact. In addition, member associations and affiliated enterprises were kept informed on the legislative and other preparatory work towards the establishment of monetary union.

In contrast, evaluating monetary conditions in the euro area, aggregating and communicating the views of the business associations and their members entered EU interest groups' political agendas only once the single monetary framework had become operational in early 1999. As a result, monetary policy represents a comparatively new issue on EU business associations' political agendas. Not all associations, however, have responded to the emergence of the new policy issue by ensuring systematic coverage of monetary issues. Based on the assessments of monetary affairs as a policy issue presented above, many business associations have decided not to get involved in monetary affairs in the first place. This is particularly true of sector-specific associations, whose representatives pointed to the generally low perceived impact of monetary policy on their member enterprises, as well as to the fact that monetary decision makers were, by definition, not concerned with particular interests within the euro area.

One important factor supporting the decision not to become active on monetary issues was said by three large industry organisations to be the reluctance of member associations at the national level to appropriate the necessary resources. The respondents stated that the question of whether to pursue systematic work on monetary questions was indeed raised within the associations in the context of discussion on EMU. In practice, national member associations often proved unwilling to contribute the necessary resources, given that many of them had never been involved in monetary questions at member-state level when national central banks were still in charge of domestic monetary policy. This logic was reported not only from sector-specific associations. One large cross-sectoral association was reportedly denied the additional resources necessary to cover monetary issues systematically, with the result that this association does not deal with that policy field at all. All the same, all respondents underlined that they would not rule out stepping up activities on monetary affairs on a case-by-case basis if monetary or exchange rates developed in such a way as to make them a matter of urgency to their constituencies.

Other large cross-sectoral business associations have become active on monetary policy, although respondents emphasised that work was still in a formative stage in a number of respects. Most importantly, some associations have reacted to the new policy issue by granting new mandates and additional resources to the internal units concerned with beefing up the relevant economic and monetary expertise and the necessary databases. In addition, coordination with member associations has been launched with a view to aggregating preferences with respect to monetary affairs across the member states. Reaching joint positions on ECB policies with member associations at national level was described by representatives from two major cross-sectoral associations as a considerable problem because of strongly diverging assessments on monetary and exchange rate conditions.

As to the means of communicating interests to monetary policy makers, EU business representatives' responses exhibit two important parallels to reactions by their counterparts at business associations in Germany. First, almost all respondents suggested that political work with regard to monetary policy and the ECB did not constitute lobbying in the narrow sense of the term, i.e. was not aimed at promoting interest group clienteles' limited, particularised interests. Rather, there was a consensus that the single monetary policy should be dedicated exclusively to the euro area as a whole, and that policy makers were neither willing to consider nor dependent upon region- or sector-specific assessments of economic and monetary conditions. As a result, communication with monetary policy makers was generally characterised as an informed exchange of information and views on overall economic and monetary conditions which, so the respondents said, differed from conventional lobbying activities in other policy areas inasmuch as it was not driven by narrow group interests. Conversely, respondents at the ECB described communication with business associations as factual and informed, and devoid of demands or pressure.

Second, a majority of respondents expressed a strict preference for direct contacts with monetary policy makers. Unlike Germany, however, this preference appears to rest more strongly on general, efficiency-related considerations. Concerns that publicly expressing policy positions on monetary policy or voicing criticism of the ECB could undermine the bank's institutional independence were not expressed as decidedly by business representatives at EU level as by their German counterparts. In contrast, at EU level the view prevails that interest groups are, in principle, free to express their preferences, and that it is up to monetary policy makers to ensure that their decisions are taken autonomously. In so far, public articulation of interests was regarded as neither violating the principle of central bank independence nor as damaging the groups' own credibility in endorsing that independence. In as far as this view applies, a certain auto-limitation on the part of interest groups with respect to communicating policy preferences to the central bank, as observed in the case of Germany, cannot be identified at EU level, or is of negligible relevance. Communication with monetary decision makers at Community level is largely limited to contacts between the major EU business associations and the ECB in the context of the EU's Macroeconomic Dialogue. As the only formalised communication forum in which both the ECB and representatives of the private sector participate, the Dialogue, in principle and abstracting from the limiting factors observed earlier, represents an important opportunity for interest groups to engage in a direct exchange of views with the ECB.

In practice, the private sector's participation in the Macroeconomic Dialogue is limited to those interest associations officially recognised by the Commission as social partners. In the case of associations representing private-sector employers, these are UNICE and UEAPME[649]. Direct formal access to communication with the ECB is consequently highly restricted, considering the large number of business associations there are at EU level. This underscores that the Dialogue was not designed as an advisory body with general private-sector involvement. Instead, its focus is determined by statute as the coordination of economic policies between the Council, the member states, the Commission and the ECB, in the context of which the social partners

[649] Besides UNICE and UEAPME, the social partners invited to participate in the Dialogue are CEEP and the European Trade Union Confederation, ETUC. CEEP, the European Centre of Enterprises with Public Participation and of Enterprises with General Economic Interest, represents public-sector employers in the EU, and was, as such, not included in the present analysis.

participate by virtue of their involvement in wage, labour market and employment policies in the member states[650].

In conformity with these framework conditions, the Macroeconomic Dialogue has been characterised by interest group representatives as an important forum for increasing the transparency of policy positions among the participants on the major topics covered in the course of discussions. With fiscal and labour market policies taking precedence, however, monetary policy was confirmed as playing no significant role in the discussions, and was reported not to have been raised actively by business representatives as an issue of concern so far. Reflecting the relatively slight perceived impact of monetary developments and overall agreement with the objectives and course of monetary policy, other issues covered in the meetings were deemed more important for the Dialogue's aims than monetary policy developments.

Nonetheless, the extended discussions were said to be appreciated for their confidential and informal character. The Macroeconomic Dialogue was perceived as offering ample opportunity to communicate interest group views on a broad range of policy issues, with the distinction between technical and political-level meetings offering contacts at both levels. As such, it was judged an important channel for representing positions on monetary issues should this become necessary. Conversely, reactions from the ECB suggest that monetary policy makers appreciate the Dialogue as increasing the transparency of policy coordination in the Community, especially since the single policy represents a relatively novel process and a regular exchange of views with the social partners was therefore seen as particularly conducive to assessing economic developments in the euro area. Finally, participants in the Dialogue emphasised that given the limited number of meetings held so far, it was too early to reach a final judgement on its operation or effectiveness as a channel for communicating policy views.

Apart from the Macroeconomic Dialogue, business representatives said they did not use any other formal or semi-formal channels of communication with the ECB or the national central banks. This also extended to the Monetary Dialogue between the ECB and the European Parliament, which was considered inadequate for the mediation of specific concerns, given that monetary policy makers were considered largely insulated from pressure from other political bodies. Instead, some respondents reported that their associations took direct recourse to informal contacts with experts or decision makers at the ECB, even though such contexts were generally characterised

---

[650] This view, based on the provisions of the Dialogue's mandate, has been confirmed in practice, as observed by Heise (2002), pp. 9-11, who reports initial evidence from the discussions in the Dialogue showing it to be centred on member-state governments' approaches to economic and employment policy.

as very rare. More commonly, a number of EU business associations forward annual reports, special reports or surveys to the ECB featuring assessments of general economic or sector-specific business conditions, information on business expectations among association members and policy recommendations of relevance to the assessment of monetary conditions by the central bank.

Finally, as with the findings on Germany, indirect channels of communication play a negligible role in the transmission of business interests to the ECB. Only one respondent reported making the occasional comment on monetary and exchange rate developments or policy decisions when approached by the media. Other respondents took no significant recourse to the media. EU interest associations do not appear to avoid public pronouncements on principle, saying instead that there was generally no reason to comment. As already pointed out, this constitutes a marked difference to the approach taken by many interest associations in Germany, where explicit public demands of the Bundesbank were treated with considerable caution.

Very much as in Germany, again, indirect political action through other political institutions and bodies such as the Council and Commission, is regarded by all respondents as ineffective, if not indeed counterproductive. This also applies to the European Parliament which – via quarterly reporting by the President of the ECB to the Economic and Monetary Affairs Committee – also enjoys direct formal access to ECB decision makers. In theory, this can be regarded as a potential indirect interest communication channel. In practice, however, indirect communication via other political institutions is recognised by business associations as highly problematic insofar as the ECB is explicitly independent of these bodies, so that potential attempts on their part to influence central bank polices are regarded as at least futile, if not illegitimate. All respondents fear attempts to use such indirect channels have considerable potential to damage private interest groups' reputations – both among ECB policy makers and the wider public. None of the business respondents therefore reported lobbying activities vis-à-vis members of the European Parliament aimed at influencing monetary or exchange rate policy so far. Instead, business representatives were said to be more interested in other macroeconomic framework conditions, such as member states' ability to fulfil their obligations under the Stability and Growth Pact or make progress on the Lisbon agenda commitments towards greater economic competitiveness, i.e. in policy developments critically and negatively influencing economic framework conditions for trade and industry.

III.3.3 Interim conclusions

The launch of the single currency has been a unique project in the economic and political development of the EU, based on the establishment of an entirely new institutional and procedural framework for monetary decision making in the

Community. Naturally, this caesura has changed the way in which private-sector interests with respect to monetary policy are aggregated and communicated to the relevant decision makers, as the results of the survey among twelve experts on monetary and exchange rate affairs from EU business associations, the ECB and the European Commission suggest.

- Most importantly, monetary policy has become a European policy issue falling within the remit of EU-level business associations. The major cross-sectoral interest associations have responded to this new issue by stepping up their work on broad macroeconomic developments and policies, and by devoting additional resources to generating monetary expertise and information. The evidence suggests, however, that this process of adjustment is not particularly forceful, with the insignificance of the policy issue and the overall agreement with monetary policy as the most important arguments put forward by EU-level representatives themselves and their member associations at national level for not devoting greater energy to monetary affairs.
- At the same time, the chances of influencing monetary decision making by the ECB, were such influence actually sought, are extremely limited – even more so than with the Bundesbank. The ECB enjoys an unparalleled degree of political autonomy, and has recourse to substantial resources within its own institution as well as the national central banks in the Eurosystem. The probability of the private sector's being able to make original contributions to the policy debate is consequently very slight. In addition, formal access to the ECB at Community level is limited to the Macroeconomic Dialogue – a policy process open to only two major associations, and not primarily conceived as a forum for exchanging views on monetary and exchange rate affairs.
- Patterns of communication are, however, still evolving. The evidence suggests that EU business associations have not yet reached a final solution on how to deal with monetary issues and the ECB. In parallel, national associations' communication with central banks at national level continues, even though the individual marginal impact on monetary decisions has fallen substantially following the shift in decision making power to the EU level. In the case of the Bundesbank, this development has been enhanced by the removal of monetary affairs from the regional Advisory Boards' agendas, cutting them off without formal replacement as a channel for discussing monetary policy with representatives of the private sector.
- Even though a new communication equilibrium has not yet been found by the stakeholders involved, the final outcome of the adjustment process is in many respects predetermined by the overall assessment of monetary policy as a policy

issue – which at EU level is very similar to that obtained from respondents in Germany. Given the broad consensus on monetary policy objectives, and provided ECB policy makers do not alter their strategy, business associations and their members regard the need for activity in this policy field as minute compared to other areas of policymaking. Disagreement with monetary policy decisions is preferably communicated in a direct, un-political, factual, and non-prescriptive manner, best characterised as an informed, expertise-oriented dialogue geared towards the general good – at least at a declaratory level.

- However, EU business associations' perceptions vary from respondents in Germany in a number of important respects, indicating that the style of communication of monetary policy-related interests at EU level differs perceptibly from that vis-à-vis the Bundesbank. Monetary policy is approached with considerable caution and sensitivity by German interest groups, reflecting their specific historical experience with the damaging impact of monetary instability as well as their appreciation of the Bundesbank's post-war achievements. Although aware of the sensitivities associated with establishing a credible monetary policy, EU interest group representatives deal with this issue in a more pragmatic manner, stressing that monetary policy does not differ essentially from other fields of policymaking. As a result, monetary policy is likely to be commented on by EU business representatives in a more critical manner – if differences in assessment arise – than in Germany, not least including open criticism in the wider public.

Concluding remarks

Summary

The preceding analysis investigated private interest groups' behaviour towards monetary policy makers and central banks, exploring the extent to which they seek to influence monetary policy and their motivations for doing so or not. Where evidence of interest group activity with respect to monetary decisions was found, the study identified the ways in which groups communicate with policy makers.

Considering the importance of monetary policies for an economy as a whole and individual firms and households in particular, the low level of interest group activity observed in practice appears puzzling at first sight. However, the theoretical analysis above suggests that there may, in fact, be good reasons for interest group activity to keep a low profile with regard to monetary policymaking.

In order to explain the conundrum, a micro-behavioural approach has been suggested with the aim of investigating the basic incentives for individuals and interest groups in the private sector to take political action on monetary questions or to refrain from doing so. The decision whether to take political action or not has been presented as a cost-benefit analysis, weighing the expected benefits of identifying, aggregating and mediating individual and group interests against the potential costs. The determinants of costs and benefits have been analysed with respect to the issue, institutional, and group contexts from which they originate.

The major theoretical findings with respect to monetary policy as a policy issue can be summarised in the form of the following core propositions:

General context

- In general, interests with respect to monetary policy are not communicated very intensively.
- In general, communication of interests with respect to monetary policy is significantly lower than in other policy fields.
- Mediating interests with respect to monetary policy does not yield sufficient benefits relative to the associated costs.

Institutional context

- Central banks are perceived as comparatively inaccessible to interests from the private sector.
- Political independence is an obstacle for the mediation of private-sector interests to the central bank.

- Given their institutional, material and expertise-based resources, central banks are not dependent on external political support in order to carry out their monetary policy assignment.
- Given their focus on aggregated economic indicators and their access to the relevant statistical resources, central banks are not dependent on external information on monetary conditions and monetary policy in order to carry out their monetary policy assignment.
- Given central banks' independence in terms of political material, and expertise-related resources and their focus on aggregated economic indicators, central bank policy makers are not interested in private-sector interest groups' views on monetary policy.

Issue context

- Individual firms or interest associations agree with the objectives and overall conduct of monetary policy.
- Interest groups may not always agree with the central bank's monetary policy decisions.
- Monetary policy is not perceived to have a significant effect on individual firms or interest associations.
- The magnitude of the impact of monetary policy on individual firms or interest associations is difficult to determine.
- Owing to the comparatively low and differential impact of monetary policy on individual enterprises, interest associations find it difficult to form strong preferences with respect to the day-to-day conduct of monetary policy.
- Given the low perceived impact of monetary developments and the importance of other policy fields, interest groups do not perceive monetary policy as a priority issue on the economic policy agenda.
- Heterogeneity of interests relating to monetary affairs within existing interest groups weakens the formation of strong policy positions in the business sector.

Interest group context

- Interest associations and their members do not have at their disposal the means of exerting economic or political pressure on the central bank.
- Individual firms or interest associations do not have at their disposal exclusive information that they can contribute to the discourse with the central bank.

To investigate the validity of these propositions, a case study has been presented on the relations between interest groups and the Bundesbank in Germany as well as on the potential impact of introduction of the single European currency and establishment of the ECB, applying these propositions as the central criteria for analysis. The case study encompasses a detailed literature-based analysis of the institutional, issue and group contexts in Germany and at EU level, complemented by qualitative interviews with a total of 58 decision makers and experts at peak, sectoral, and regional interest groups, as well as at the Bundesbank and the ECB, in the course of which the core propositions of this study were discussed.

The analysis of the institutional, issue and group contexts of business interest group activity on monetary policy in Germany and at EU level demonstrates that the task environment within which business associations and their members formulate and express their preferences with respect to monetary and exchange rate policy differs considerably from that observed in many other policy areas.

With respect to the institutional context, it was observed that the conduct of monetary policy in Germany was embedded in a well-defined institutional and procedural framework. Communication of interests was found to be facilitated in principle by the fact that monetary decisions are isolated from other policy areas and delegated to one single expert institution, the central bank. This also applies to exchange rate policies as long as no exchange rate agreements are concluded at an intergovernmental level.

At the same time, communication of interests is hampered by the special status of the Bundesbank as an institution independent of political influence, a principle safeguarded in institutional and personnel respects. This independence largely obstructs indirect influence via the surrounding political framework, especially via the government or parliament, and also reflects on potential direct relations with the Bundesbank. In addition, the Bundesbank was found to be largely self-sufficient in terms of resources, also with respect to material, informational and personnel resources. As a result of the high level of experience and expertise, in essence the bank does not rely on external input in the form of policy advice and information.

Due to its federal structure, the Bundesbank itself pre-1999 and thereafter the Bundesbank as part of the ESCB theoretically offers a multitude of institutional points of access for interest groups. Formal and semi-formal access, however, is limited in scope and restricted to an advisory role relatively far detached from the nucleus of decision making. The remoteness of these potential avenues has increased with the 2002 Bundesbank reform.

The insulating properties of the institutional framework also reflect on the behavioural patterns of Bundesbank decision makers, who regard their political independence as an essential condition for the proper pursuit of their primary objective. This is the dominating motivation behind their decisions, strengthened by strict, although not absolute, self-imposed policy rules.

Overall, this institutional framework may have discouraging effects on interest groups trying to communicate their monetary policy interests.

The issue context, in turn, is dominated by historically rooted anti-inflationary sentiment among the German population at large and in the business sector in particular. This coincides with the Bundesbank's objectives. As to the primary purpose of monetary policy, therefore, there is strong agreement between monetary policy makers and the business sector.

With respect to this primary purpose, the Bundesbank – and since 1999 the ECB – have delivered a remarkably positive performance, keeping inflation low by historical and international standards and effectively countering surges in wages and prices.

The transmission of monetary decisions into the economy has been accompanied by significant changes in the interest rate environment for businesses over the past decades. However, the impact of these changes has been small on average. This is due first to the low share of interest expenditure in German enterprises' total costs and income, and second to the low level and the stability of real interest rates.

A similar picture emerges with the impact of exchange rate developments, where the distorting effects have been weakened by the historical stabilisation and – eventually – elimination of exchange rates with the other EMU member states, Germany's most important trading partners. Stabilisation, although far less pronounced, has also been achieved with respect to the major non-EMU exchange rates.

Despite these general trends and structures weakening the involvement of business interests with monetary and exchange rate affairs, there are sectors particularly exposed to interest and exchange rate developments. These include the transport, construction, and retail sectors, where corporate financing and demand from end-customers are particularly sensitive to interest rates. Similarly, the automotive, mechanical engineering, chemical and electronics sectors are particularly involved in foreign trade. In addition, small and medium-sized enterprises are likely to be more exposed to changes in interest rates and can less easily access derivatives markets to hedge against interest and exchange rate risks.

Issue involvement is additionally weakened by the fact that monetary and exchange rate-related policy issues have, in the past years, been dominated by a whole range of other economic policy issues on the political agenda. Only in periods of strong international and domestic monetary and exchange rate pressures – and increasingly less so since the 1980s – has monetary policy assumed a significant position on the economic policy agenda.

As to the interest-group context, the aggregation and expression of interests in monetary and exchange rate issues is achieved through the existing infrastructure of business associations and their peak associations. Given its insignificance in terms of impact and urgency, monetary policy has not aroused sufficient attention to provoke the formation of dedicated cause groups. Germany's peak business associations are characterised by a wide and heterogeneous membership in terms of the size of the enterprises represented and their sectoral affiliation. This heterogeneity hampers the efficient aggregation of interests with regard to monetary and exchange rate policy. Downstream interest associations – especially the sector-specific organisations – are likely to find it easier to formulate common positions. Their importance, however, may be severely limited by the Bundesbank's strong economy-wide outlook, in which partial interests are relevant only inasmuch as they are conducive to reaching conclusions on monetary conditions in the economy as a whole. Given the Bundesbank's strong institutional status and the logic of monetary policy, the scope for exerting political or economic pressure on monetary policy makers is negligible. Nevertheless, German business associations possess substantial resources in terms of both financial and human capital and generate abundant original information of use in discourse with policy makers.

In the light of these findings, the perception of the institutional, issue, and interest group contexts was discussed with 46 decision makers and experts on monetary and exchange rate affairs from German business associations and the Bundesbank. The empirical evidence thus obtained does in fact confirm the core propositions of this study.

Interest group activity on monetary and exchange rate affairs is low, especially when compared with other policy areas, because the anticipated benefits do not justify the costs associated with more intensive activity.

Institutional accessibility is one of two major explanatory variables for low interest group activity. Political independence and ample endowment with material resources and expertise in its field of policymaking contribute greatly to the fact that the Bundesbank does not need to rely on political support or information from the private sector, and effectively insulate the bank from external influence. This is recognised by interest group representatives and enters their cost-benefit analysis on political action in this policy area.

The second major explanatory variable is the coincidence of major policy objectives between the private sector on the one hand and the Bundesbank and ECB on the other, coupled with a high measure of agreement with the monetary authorities' policies in general. Most of the time monetary policy thus becomes a non-issue as far as trade and industry associations are concerned.

Even if monetary and exchange rate developments become more urgent across economic cycles, their direct and indirect impact – where identifiable at all – is considered very low compared with that of other economic policies. As a consequence, preferences with respect to monetary and exchange rate policies are comparatively low in intensity. Despite the considerable impact of monetary policy on the economy as a whole, it is not a priority issue on business associations' political agenda.

It became apparent that the heterogeneity of interests does not play as great a role in inhibiting interest group activity on monetary affairs as suggested in theory. Preferences are perceived in a general manner and in most cases not necessarily considered contradictory.

Finally, the responses by decision makers and experts in Germany suggest that interest groups do not lobby monetary policy makers in the same way they approach decision makers in other conventional policy areas. The style of communication is rather un-political, factual, and non-prescriptive, taking the form of an informed, expertise-oriented dialogue geared towards the general good – at least at a declaratory level. The preferred channels of communication with the Bundesbank are direct in nature, with the Advisory Boards and the economists' roundtable as the formal and semi-formal forums respectively. Communication via the media is an important tool, but one used prudently in order to avoid the public perception that business associations interfere with the monetary authorities' policymaking and independence.

As from 1999, monetary policy sovereignty was transferred to the Community level by the EU member states participating in the third stage of EMU, with monetary decisions taken by the ECB. For the communication of interests, introduction of the single European currency marks an important caesura, changing the way in which private-sector interests in monetary policy are aggregated and communicated to the relevant decision makers, as the results of the survey among twelve experts on monetary and exchange rate affairs from EU business associations, the ECB and the European Commission suggest.

Most importantly, monetary policy has become a European policy issue falling within the remit of EU-level business associations. The major cross-sectoral interest associations have responded to this new issue by stepping up their work on broad macroeconomic developments and policies and devoting additional resources to generating monetary expertise and information. The evidence suggests, however, that this process of adjustment is not particularly forceful, with the insignificance of the policy issue and the overall agreement with monetary policy as the most important arguments put forward by EU-level representatives themselves, as well as by their member associations at national level, for not devoting greater energy to monetary affairs.

At the same time, the chances of influencing monetary decision making by the ECB, were such influence actually sought, are limited in the extreme – even more so than in the case of the Bundesbank pre-1999. The ECB enjoys an unparalleled degree of political autonomy and has recourse to substantial resources within its own institution as well as the national central banks in the Eurosystem. The probability of the private sector's being able to make original contributions to the policy debate is consequently very low. In addition, formal access to the ECB at Community level is limited to the Macroeconomic Dialogue – a policy process open only to two major associations, and not primarily conceived as a forum for exchanging views on monetary and exchange rate affairs.

Patterns of communication are still evolving, however. The evidence suggests that EU business associations have not yet reached a final solution on how to deal with monetary issues and the ECB. In parallel, national associations' communication with central banks at national level continues, even though the individual marginal impact on monetary decisions has fallen dramatically with the ECB's assumption of responsibility. In the case of the Bundesbank, this has been enhanced by the removal of monetary affairs from the regional Advisory Boards' agendas, cutting them off without formal replacement as a channel for discussing monetary policy with representatives of the private sector.

Even though a new communication equilibrium has not yet been found by the stakeholders involved, the final outcome of the adjustment process is in many respects predetermined by the overall assessment of monetary policy as a policy issue – which at EU level is very similar to that obtained from respondents in Germany. Given the broad consensus on monetary policy objectives, and provided ECB policy makers do not alter their strategy, business associations and their members regard the need for activity in this policy field as minute compared to other areas of policymaking. Disagreement with monetary policy decisions is preferably communicated in a direct, un-political, factual, and non-prescriptive manner, best characterised as an informed, expertise-oriented dialogue geared towards the general good – at least at a declaratory level.

However, EU business associations' perceptions vary from respondents in Germany in a number of important respects, indicating that the style of communication of monetary policy-related interests at EU level differs perceptibly from that vis-à-vis the Bundesbank. Monetary policy is approached with considerable caution and sensitivity by German interest groups, reflecting their specific historical experience with the damaging impact of monetary instability as well as their appreciation of the Bundesbank's post-war achievements. Although aware of the sensitivities associated with establishing a credible monetary policy, EU interest-group representatives deal with this issue in a more pragmatic manner, stressing that monetary policy does not differ essentially from other fields of policymaking. As a result, monetary policy is likely to be commented on by EU business representatives in a more critical manner – if differences in assessment arise – than in Germany, not least including open criticism in the wider public.

Conclusions

Motivated by the puzzle that interest groups take little interest in monetary and exchange rate issues even though their overall economic impact on enterprises is macro-economically comparable to that of other policy areas, the findings in this study suggest that the reason for this superficial discrepancy is rational rather than inconsistent behaviour on the part of interest groups. Monetary policy is an area of economic policymaking in which business associations take a very low profile, and they are perceived as having good reasons to do so.

Is monetary policy consequently a specific policy issue for interest groups? Certainly, interest groups are not dealing with a policy issue *sui generis*. The framework conditions for interest group activity are not specific in a qualitative respect. Thus, the political independence of institutions and decision makers is a mechanism implemented in one or the other form and intensity in an increasing number of policy fields – such as competition policy or financial market regulation and supervision. Even in its very pronounced form as observed in the cases of the Bundesbank and ECB, it merely serves to limit policy makers' responsiveness and accessibility to outside stimuli or even pressure. Even so, it cannot eradicate the major actors' interdependence, let alone the communication between them, given that the complete political insulation of such authorities is impossible to realise, whether in theory or in practice.

Equally, the low immediate impact of monetary developments and policy measures as subjectively perceived by the interest groups addressed here is far from an unusual phenomenon. Nevertheless, enterprises and their interest representatives have a remarkably low perception of the impact of monetary stimuli, given the potential aggregate economic impact as calculated by monetary economists, and considering that the monetary stimuli applied in these studies are regularly observed in monetary practice. The diffuseness of the transmission of monetary stimuli obviously constitutes an important explanatory variable in this context. More importantly, however, in line with the argumentation by central banks a vast majority of interest representatives hold that monetary and exchange rate policy cannot and should not be designed on the basis of the atomistic or myopic interests of partial groups in society, but rather with a view to the long-term benefits for the economy and society as a whole. In this interpretation, interest group intervention to promote partial interests is viewed by a majority of trade and industry representatives as at best illegitimate, and at worst counterproductive. In addition, business representatives seem to find solace in the logic of monetary cycles, discounting the fact that high interest rates will sooner or later turn into low rates, and that losses in competitiveness from a strong external value of the currency may before long turn into a boost for competitiveness once the currency has weakened again. In the monetary realm, policy measures with a negative impact on enterprises are likely to be followed with some certainty by more positive decisions. This contrasts quite markedly with other fields of policymaking, as accentuated by one respondent, who emphasised that unlike interest rates, he had rarely seen tax rates go down.

Similarly, monetary policy may not be the only area in which interest associations do not feel in a strong position to contribute original information or policy positions adding value for policy makers. Whenever policy makers place particular emphasis on the significance of a given decision for the general welfare, arguments motivated by partial interests are likely to fade into the background.

Nevertheless, there can be no doubt that monetary policy represents an extraordinary policy issue for interest groups, even if in a quantitative sense only, combining a number of institutional, issue, and group related specificities. Most importantly, the central banks investigated here enjoy an extraordinary degree of political autonomy, largely unequalled by other bodies within the respective polities or by other central banks in an international comparison. More generally, independent central banks do assume extraordinary institutional positions within their respective political systems. As such, they almost necessarily pose a special challenge for interest groups trying to approach monetary policy makers.

Second, it is quite unusual for business associations to agree as strongly with the overall objectives and policy measures implemented as they do with monetary affairs in Germany, and also at EU level. In the first place, this consensus results from good policymaking, in the opinion of the interest groups addressed, both with respect to the structure of the monetary systems and the way in which monetary policy makers run them. Second, it reflects the strong congruence in objectives associated with monetary policy by interest groups and those set for monetary decision makers. Finally, the strong agreement observed here bears witness to an extraordinary confidence on the part of private-sector participants in the capability of the monetary authorities and their decision makers. Based on good historical experience and at times on metaphysics, central banks enjoy an outstandingly positive reputation among private-sector commentators.

Finally, and closely connected with the previous point, central banks are the centre of competence for monetary affairs in their respective economies, and are recognised as such by business. Central bank decision making power, especially with the Bundesbank and ECB, is combined with considerable competence in their sphere of policymaking. Given far-reaching political neutrality, a high level of expertise and the extensive sources of data and statistics needed for the assessment of monetary conditions and the definition of suitable policy measures, representatives from trade and industry generally accept central bank decisions, even if the measures may not always be entirely consistent with their own preferences. From the perspective of political science, this partly reflects a substantial asymmetry between the relevant expertise in this field of policymaking commanded by the central banks, as opposed to that commanded by interest groups, with the latter at a clear disadvantage to the former. This is unusual compared with many other areas of economic policymaking, where business and business associations claim superior competence vis-à-vis policy makers, as in instances of market regulation or labour market policy.

In the light of these specificities, the question arises as to the extent to which interest groups' and monetary policy makers' perceptions and behaviour and the structures of communication between the two sides are subject to change. Based on the evidence presented above, two major sources of change are conceivable. Most importantly, the constantly low level of interest group activity on monetary affairs stems largely from the minute impact of monetary developments and policy measures as perceived by enterprises and their interest representatives. Logic dictates that interest group activity might be much brisker if this impact ever happened to be substantially greater, especially in a negative sense. And indeed, very few of the respondents addressed in the course of this study left any doubt on this point. The stability of the equilibrium in communication between interest groups and the two central banks investigated here therefore critically depends on the occurrence of policy shocks, especially external in nature, and monetary policy makers' ability to meet these challenges successfully, i.e. in a way consistent with their primary objective of maintaining price stability.

Second, stability in relations between business associations and central banks hinges on the institutional framework in which monetary policymaking is embedded. With the establishment of the ESCB and ECB mid-1998 and the introduction of the single European currency at the beginning of 1999, this institutional framework was altered fundamentally. Notwithstanding this fundamental caesura, the major change from the perspective of interest groups in Germany occurred with the shift in decision making to the Community level. The modalities of the new monetary system, however, were quite familiar to German spectators in as far as major elements, such as the independence of the ECB, its objectives, or its instruments and their formulation in the legal basis of the ESCB, were very much comparable to those of the Bundesbank.

That said, the new institutional structure does call for a new, Community-level approach to monetary issues and adjustment to the relevant communication structures. With institutional work at Community level completed before 1999, and a substantial amount of expertise, routine and reputation gained during the first years of operation of the Eurosystem, the interplay of the ECB and national central banks on the one hand and private-sector interest groups on the other has not yet found a new equilibrium, as the preceding analysis suggests. In many respects, interest group communication with policy makers in the field is still adjusting to the new institutional framework, new policy processes and the role played by the ECB and national central banks. Moreover, the approaches to monetary and exchange rate policy have been reported as differing markedly – an insight confirmed not least by the reaction of EU-level interest group and central bank representatives in the course of this study. A truly European approach to euro area monetary policymaking has yet to emerge, with national perspectives on ECB policy prevailing for the time being. Nonetheless, the major EU-level business associations have started to become active in this area of policymaking. Such an approach would enable EU interest groups to communicate with the ECB at eye-level. On the other hand, to be effective it would necessitate a more stringent aggregation of relevant interests across member or associated groups in the member states.

At the same time, national associations remain active. In the case of Germany, this is chiefly true of federal associations, which maintain any previous contacts with the Bundesbank while participating in the process of interest aggregation and communication within their respective EU peak associations. In contrast, regional associations, or more precisely the members of the Bundesbank's regional Advisory Boards, find themselves in a more awkward situation. For more than forty years, Board members enjoyed a privileged position, namely direct access to the members of the Bundesbank's highest decision making body on a quarterly basis, with the mandate to consult on monetary affairs and other issues of common concern or interest. This privilege was a somewhat puzzling arrangement. Considering that monetary policy makers are expected to take an aggregate, economy-wide view in their policy decisions and in many cases reject particularised interests in this policy area for this very reason, it may be considered unfortunate that the Bundesbank's only advisory body was – of all the constellations theoretically conceivable – composed of regional interest group representatives. While consistent with the idea of preventing the Bundesbank from being exposed to powerful political or other influences and with the concept of a devolutionary structure of the bank, the positions of interest representatives in a regionally organised advisory structure were likely to be the farthest removed from an aggregated, economy-wide view. This structure and composition was determined in the Bundesbank Act and therefore beyond the control of the Bundesbank and its policy makers. At the same time, none of them in fact considered the structure of the Advisory Boards inappropriate.

Under their new mandate, the Advisory Boards have retained their structure and composition, but their monetary *raison d'être* has been removed. Although the Bundesbank has been busy maintaining a high-ranking status for the Boards, a substantial incentive for participating in their deliberations has disappeared. It therefore remains to be seen how far it will be possible for the Bundesbank and the members to continue with the Advisory Boards as a consultative body on monetary issues, even if only on an informal basis.

This gives rise to the question what the new equilibrium of communication between central banks and interest groups in the euro area will look like in the long run. Most importantly, it remains to be seen whether a unique EU-level discourse between European business associations and the ECB will evolve. For the time being, the Community's Macroeconomic Dialogue represents the only, extremely limited, channel of communication in this regard. As to the direction of development, two countervailing forces are at work. On the one hand, the ECB's monetary policy in many ways represents the only truly single policy process in the Community, as such strongly calling for a truly Community-level form of communication with the private sector. On the other hand, the ECB's monetary policy in many ways represents the only single policy process in the Community – the most important interrelated areas of economic policymaking, such as fiscal and labour market policy, essentially remain in the hands of the member states. In addition, the national central banks in the Eurosystem continue to play a decisive role in the ECB's decision making process and in the communication of its policy measures. As result, public discourse on monetary policy continues to be influenced by strong centrifugal tendencies. Whichever of these two tendencies eventually turns out to be the stronger, the long-term structures of communication will need to integrate both Community-level and national elements in order to correspond to the quasi-federal structure of decision making within the Eurosystem.

Implications for research

This study contributes to the existing body of economic and political research in two directions. Most importantly, it complements the literature dealing with the political pressures on central banks, especially from private-sector interest groups. Systematic research into this subject was originally launched by Havrilesky, examining the influence of interest groups in the United States on decisions by the Federal Reserve Board. Recently, his approach has been developed further and applied to interest groups in Germany. The major insight of these studies is that, overall, the quantitative influence of private-sector interests on monetary decisions is very low. Insofar as a correlation was possible to identify, it ultimately remained unclear whether this was in response to political pressure from the private sector, or simply a coincidence of assessments and policy conclusions on the two sides.

While these studies investigated the ultimate impact of interest group activity on monetary decisions, the present contribution examined the extent to which such activity unfolded in the first place, how it is pursued, and why. Combining these elements yields a consistent picture, at least for non-financial business associations in Germany: Monetary policy decisions are subject to very little influence by private-sector interests, not only because central banks do not rely on private-sector views or support, but also because interest group objectives and positions on monetary policy largely coincide with those of the central bank. Even when disagreement arises, it is unlikely to be of a fundamental nature, and articulation of the relevant interests is reserved and cautious.

Scope and limitations of the analysis

Chart 112

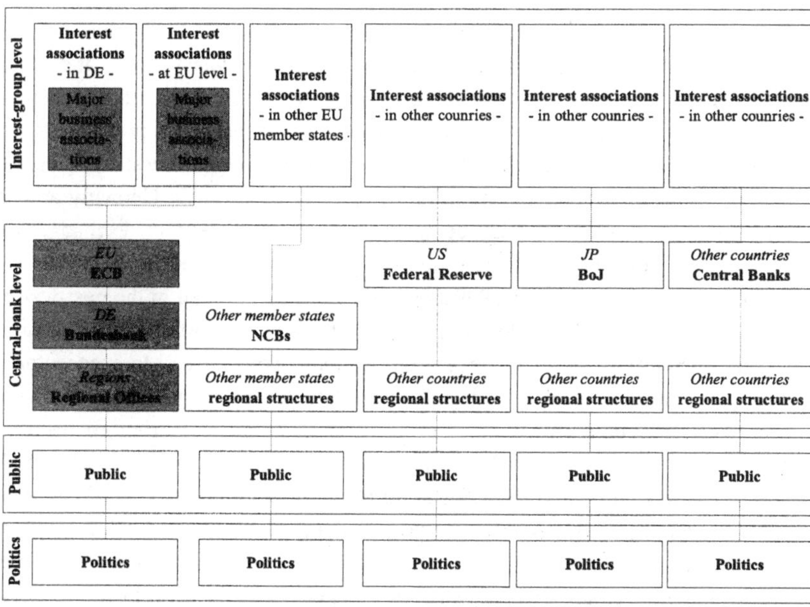

In pursuing this approach, this analysis has naturally remained limited. It has applied one method of many to investigate the political relations between interest groups and central banks. From the universe of interest groups, only those representing trade and industry have been analysed. Only Germany and the EU were investigated. Chart 112 tries to capture schematically the small area covered here – highlighted by a grey background –, and the large number of relationships omitted.

Beyond the analysis presented here, the topics could conceivably be approached from various different angles.

- The most important extension of the present study would be to investigate interest groups other than trade and industry associations, which may have preference structures and approaches towards political action other than those encountered here. This applies to trade unions in particular, which – according to many experts addressed in this study – appear to be more critical of and active on monetary policy than their industry counterparts, albeit not necessarily with greater success. Similarly, the financial sector represents a promising object of analysis, considering that it is more intricately connected to monetary and exchange rate issues and can more easily match the central bank's expertise on the related policy questions, thus overcoming one of the most important hurdles to interest communication in this policy area identified above.
- Second, it would be useful to gain a comparative perspective from other countries and historical instances in which the relations between interest groups and central banks may be different from those observed here. Given the enormous significance of the coincidence of central bank and interest group preferences with respect to monetary policy identified here, the most important question is whether the behaviour of interest groups differs from that observed in Germany and the euro area in economies with at times extreme monetary or exchange rate development. In recent history, monetary policies in the UK in the 1970s and 1980s, in Italy up to the mid-1990s, or in Greece and Portugal in the post-war era would lend themselves as interesting objects of analysis. Similarly, Japan could be an informative case with its recent deflationary experience. More accentuated examples could be found in emerging markets with recent experiences of high or even hyper-inflation, such as Argentina, Brazil, or Mexico. From an historical perspective, interest-group behaviour during the hyper-inflationary period of the late 1920s in Europe and the US should be a revealing object of analysis. Such analysis would certainly need to include Germany during that period. In as far as the institutional framework of monetary operations matters in terms of relations between interest groups and policy makers, systems with different institutional and procedural provisions are worthy of analysis. The most important example is likely to be Great Britain and the Bank of England, whose comparably brief history of political independence began in 1997, preceded by centuries of subjection to government decision making[651]. The US Federal Reserve Board represents an interesting case in point for other reasons. The Fed has had a comparatively strong tradition of seeking advice from the private sector, with the Fed's Federal Advisory Council, its Consumer Advisory Council, and its Thrift Institutions Advisory Council as the most important institutional channels.

---

[651] See Bank for International Settlements (1963), pp. 97-123.

- Third, the picture can be complemented by a more thorough analysis of the channels and means of communication available to and used by interest groups. Most importantly, this study suggests that support by the wider public has been of great concern for the Bundesbank. More detailed qualitative and quantitative research into the use and behaviour of the public with respect to monetary policy may yield additional insights into the relations between interest groups and policy makers in this policy area. Similarly, indirect communication between interest groups and central banks through the political level deserve closer inspection. As shown above, industry groups consider politicians inadequate for promoting their cause. It remains to be investigated whether this is also true of other interest groups such as trade unions, given their potentially more critical attitude towards central bank policymaking. The question also arises on the extent to which politicians cite private interests when criticising monetary policy actions – either in support of or contradiction to their own interests.
- Finally, the set of questions guiding the present study can be extended. Most importantly, research can be pursued to investigate the extent to which monetary and exchange rate policy decisions are eventually influenced by private-sector interests. This question has been faded out in the present context given the focus of the analysis on interest groups' behavioural patterns. For the study of political economics, however, the ultimate impact of such behaviour is a central concern.

Specifically with respect to the cases investigated here, what remains to be examined is whether this pattern of communication and influence taking will be carried over to the European level following introduction of the single currency. This study has presented some preliminary evidence, but a full appreciation of the effects of EMU on communication between interest groups in the euro area and the central banks of the Eurosystem in the age of Community-level monetary decision making certainly requires a longer time frame. To obtain a comprehensive picture, it will be useful to investigate the perceptions and behaviour of interest groups in this area of policymaking in the other EMU member states. Initially, we have seen that communication via the national central bank still plays a substantial role, and is set to do so for some time to come. Second, a study into the patterns of perception and communication in the member states may, in fact, yield outcomes significantly different from those obtained here, as Germany represents a unique object of analysis in important respects. German interest groups have been dealing with a central bank enjoying a comparatively great degree of political independence for a relatively long period of time. In addition, the perception of monetary developments and policy decisions in Germany is strongly influenced by historical experience with hyper-inflation and unstable monetary systems not observed on that scale in other countries.

With respect to interest group behaviour in Germany, it may furthermore be useful to subject the perceptions and activities of other samples of associations to an analysis similar to this one. Interest groups from trade and industry have been found to exhibit a strong allegiance to the Bundesbank and to agree strongly with its objectives and policy decisions. The interviews conducted in the course of this study strongly suggest that this might not be the case for other interest groups. Most importantly, trade unions have been characterised as particularly critical of the Bundesbank's position within the political system as well as of its policies. In addition, Havrilesky and Maier point out that the correlation between monetary decisions and interest-group positions is particularly significant for interest associations in the financial sector. Thus, it may be worthwhile investigating to what extent, how, and how successfully trade unions take a critical position on monetary affairs, and whether and to what extent interests in the financial markets form something comparable to a policy network or policy community with the central bank.

In addition to these implications for the study of interest groups and their behaviour in the monetary area, this study yields stimulating impulses for other fields of research. First, it underlines the importance of interest groups' perceptions of their policy environment and the policy fields they are concerned with. This becomes evident when comparing the above assessments by interest group and central bank respondents. Despite the great degree of congruence, wide differences in assessment can be observed around the mean, e.g. with respect to institutional accessibility and interest groups' ability to contribute expertise and information to the policy process. One explanation for these systematic differences may be that either side understates or overstates its views, for example with the aim of portraying greater interest in private-sector views than is actually the case. A second explanation may be seen in a potential selection bias inasmuch as the sample investigated here may exhibit a certain bias towards respondents actually interested in relations between the private sector and central banks. However, it cannot be ruled out *ex ante* that systematic differences exist in interest groups' and policy makers' perceptions, reflecting a lack of knowledge about each others' positions and views. Further investigation of this hypothesis may clarify this point and, in as far as this lack of knowledge causes inefficiencies in the interplay between interest groups and policy makers, help improve the relevant policy processes.

Second, the present findings lend strong support to the view that the institutional design of policy processes greatly influences relations between interest groups and policy makers. Most importantly, institutional independence has been found to limit interest group activity. At the same time, the precise impact of independence on interest group activity remains unclear, particularly when determining the dividing line between directly limiting effects such as legal constraints and interest groups' self restraint. Interest representatives in Germany are found to have tended to hold back with judgements on monetary affairs, due not least to the central bank's status of independence, even though this applies to the private sector in a strictly legal interpretation.

Part of this self-restraint can be traced back to the awkward position interest groups faced in argumentative terms at times when politicians criticised the Bundesbank for failing to provide monetary stimuli to economic growth. On the one hand, many entrepreneurs agree with this assessment at certain times. On the other hand, they consider such intervention by policy makers an illegitimate encroachment on the central bank's independence. As a result, business associations seem to have found themselves repeatedly in a situation in which they criticised politicians for their intervention, while tacitly agreeing with the basis of that intervention. In as far as this has been the case in the past, business associations can be regarded as strong lobbyists in the area of monetary policy, promoting the independence and objectives of the Bundesbank. Given such complex argumentative constellations in practice and the impact of institutional independence as perceived by interest groups, the precise effects of institutional provisions of this kind certainly deserve further academic attention.

Finally, interest group activity in monetary affairs seems to be a promising field of political science research on the role of information as a source of influence for interest groups. Possession of group-specific information, e.g. on the positive or adverse effects of a planned policy measure on certain segments or actors in society, has been regarded as a strong asset for interest groups in communication with policy makers. By the same token, specialised associations are often recognised not only as representatives of their members, but also as experts in a certain area of policymaking whose input or support can lend additional credibility to arguments in the political arena. This logic applies in cases when policy makers are, on average, less well informed in a certain area of policymaking than interest groups. In monetary affairs, the reverse order generally applies, giving policy makers a substantial expertise and information lead over their counterparts in the private sector. The distribution, or more precisely the demand and supply of information and expertise between policy makers and interest groups therefore has a potentially significant impact on the way in which the two sides interact. Deeper scientific insights into this part of the relationship would certainly contribute to a better understanding of policy processes, especially those concerned with intricate policy issues.

Policy implications

Given the low level of interest-group activity in monetary and exchange rate policymaking detected and explained here, we can ask whether and to what extent interest groups should do more in this respect. Assuming utilitarian decision making on the part of interest groups, all else being equal the answer to this question clearly has to be no. If – ideally – interest groups become active when, and only when, their constituents face an identifiable problem and only when the expected benefits of taking political action exceed the expected costs of doing so, then it is only rational for interest groups to leave monetary and exchange rate policy low on their political agendas in the circumstances observed here and on the assumption of limited resources. Save for isolated instances over the past three decades, monetary and exchange rate policies have had a miniscule direct, identifiable impact on enterprises in trade and industry, especially when compared to that of other public policy measures. Even if and when monetary developments were perceived to be of concern, interest groups typically found that short-term intervention could have substantial negative repercussions in the long run, and that the potential costs of influencing independent monetary policy makers could be significant – if, indeed, they stood a realistic chance of doing so at all. In so far, low interest group activity on monetary and exchange rate issues is logical and rational.

Remarkably, many interest representatives consulted here seem to have overcome the time-consistency problem underlying attempts at politically isolating monetary decision making – at least at a declaratory level: The short-term benefits of more lenient monetary conditions were regarded by the vast majority of respondents as far outweighed by their long-term costs, encouraging them to defend and support hawkish central bank policies against their critics. If such far-sighted behaviour motivates interest group activity in this policy area, then the discrepancy between immediate policy effects, medium-term economic repercussions and long-term macroeconomic equilibrium is necessarily dissipated, and myopic rent-seeking is abandoned in favour of broad agreement with the policy objectives of the central banks analysed here. How stable this consensus necessarily is, must be left unanswered at this point.

The above negative answer to the question whether interest groups should become more active on monetary matters, can be put into perspective in two respects. First, the assumptions made with regard to group behaviour can be relaxed. If agency problems exist in the principal-agent relationship between enterprises and business associations, it may, under certain circumstances, be rational for interest groups to address monetary issues even though there is no point in such action in their members' view. Second, the policy-related objectives or interest group or central bank behaviour may change. If the consensus identified here with respect to the objectives and targets of monetary and exchange rate policy were to alter on either of the two sides, it may become rational for interest groups to intensify their activities in this policy area.

Beyond these fundamental considerations, the findings of the present study carry policy implications for policy makers at the European and the national levels as well as for general issues of interest group politics. In the euro area, relations between interest groups and central banks are undergoing a process of change, as already observed. Especially at Community level, stakeholders will need to work out how close a discourse between central bankers and interest groups is desired and deemed conducive on both sides. For one thing, the ECB will need to decide whether it wishes to continue relying, on a formal and semi-formal level, on the input gained through the Macroeconomic Dialogue – involving only two private-sector business associations – and through the national central banks, or whether it wishes to work towards strengthening the discourse at Community level, for example by establishing a semi-formal roundtable as the Bundesbank did. In the latter case, the concept of monetary policy as a truly European policy process could be strengthened, both within the Eurosystem and among the wider public, and a broad and aggregated view could be obtained from peak EU interest groups. Assuming that the contemporary wisdom of depoliticising monetary policy by handing it over to independent central banks is an appropriate answer to the problems inherent in that policy process, this would, however, come at the expense of potentially politicising the debate on monetary policy, as many interest associations, a large number of which are potentially influential and might take the discussion into the wider public, would actually be prompted to formulate – potentially challenging – monetary policy positions.

In Germany, too, communication between interest groups and the central bank is undergoing a process of change, especially with respect to the future role of the regional Advisory Boards. On the one hand, the Boards' monetary policy mandate has been substantially narrowed. On the other, the Bundesbank has sought to preserve their status as far as possible by informal means. Their future role, however, remains unclear, particularly since monetary policy decisions taken at the Community level mean that regional perspectives have lost much of their relevance for the assessment and formulation of monetary policy. This argument casts doubt on the very *raison d'être* of these regional consultative bodies. In as far as this logic is deemed relevant, a more effective solution may lie in strengthening communication with the federal peak associations at national level, for instance by increasing the frequency of meetings by the roundtable of economists. Closely linked to this structural issue, there seems to be some uncertainty concerning the appropriate amount of communication. As already observed, no substantial evidence was found that either interest representatives or Bundesbank staff considered communication to be deficient. However, a significant gap in the assessment of whether the Bundesbank is interested in private sector views and in how far it appreciates external information and expertise between the two sides emerged in the course of the research. In as much as this gap does not reflect either overstatement on the part of the respondents or a selection bias, Bundesbank policy makers and interest group representatives may find it useful to consider ways of optimising communication between the two sides.

From a broader political perspective, the findings of this study suggest that establishing politically independent institutions is a viable means of keeping the relevant policy issues outside the arena of political debate. The findings also show, however, that this alone does not suffice in the long run. The example of monetary policy suggests that the Bundesbank's success as a widely recognised institution whose policy decisions meet with broad acceptance by the public at large critically rests on three additional factors. First, the objectives set for such an independent body at political level must be well defined and generally accepted. Second, policy makers in that body must pursue these objectives consistently and successfully. Third, the authority of that body can be strengthened if policy makers succeed in establishing far-reaching expertise and competence in their field of policymaking within that body. Otherwise, a great number of respondents on both sides point out that an institution as independent as the Bundesbank would not be tenable in the long run within a democratic set-up.

Select bibliography

Ainsworth, S. H., *Analysing interest groups: Group influence on people and politics*, W. W. Norton & Company, New York, 2002

Alesina, A., Summers, L. H., *Central Bank Independence and Macroeconomic Performance: Some Comparative Evidence*, Journal of Money, Credit, and Banking, Vol. 25, No. 2, 1993, pp. 151-162

Althaus, M., Meier, D. (Eds.), *Politikberatung: Praxis und Grenzen*, Lit Verlag, Münster, 2004

Amato, J. D., Morris, S., Shin, H. S., *Communication and monetary policy*, BIS Working Papers, No. 123, January 2003, Bank for International Settlements, Monetary and Economic Department, Basle, 2003

Andrés, J., Hernando, I., *Does Inflation Harm Economic Growth? Evidence from the OECD*, in: Feldstein M. (Ed.), The Costs and Benefits of Price Stability, University of Chicago Press, Chicago, 1999, pp. 315-346

Angeloni, I., Ehrmann, M., *Monetary policy transmission in the euro area: any changes after EMU?*, ECB Working Paper Series, Working Paper No. 240, European Central Bank, Frankfurt am Main, July 2003

Angeloni, I., Kashyap, A., Mojon, B., Terlizzese, D., *Monetary Transmission in the euro area: where do we stand?*, European Central Bank, Working Paper No. 114, January 2002

Austen-Smith, D., *Interest Groups, Campaign Contributions, and Probabilistic Voting*, Public Choice, Vol. 54, 1987, pp. 123-139

Austen-Smith, D., *Voluntary Pressure Groups*, Econometrica, Vol. 48, 1981, pp. 143-153

Austen-Smith, D., Wright, J., *Competitive Lobbying for Legislators' Votes*, Mimeograph, Department of Political Science, University of Rocheser, 1990

Bagehot, W., *Lombard Street: A description of the money market*, Wiley Investment Classics, Wiley & Sons, Inc., New York, 1999

Ball, L., Croushore, D., *Expectations and the Effects of Monetary Policy*, National Bureau of Economic Research, Working Paper 5344, Cambridge, November 1995

Ball, R., *Interest Groups, Influence, and Welfare*, Economics and Politics, Vol. 7, No. 2, July 1995, pp. 119-146

Baltensperger, E., *Geldpolitik bei wachsender Integration (1979-1996)*, in: Deutsche Bundesbank (Ed.), Fünfzig Jahre Deutsche Mark – Notenbank und Währung in Deutschland seit 1948, Beck, Munich, 1998, pp. 475-560

Bank for International Settlements, *Eight European Central Banks, Organization and Activities of Banque Nationale de Belgique, Deutsche Bundesbank, Bank of England, Banque de France, Banca d'Italia, De Nederlandsche Bank, Schweizerische Nationalbank, Sveriges Riksbank*, George Allen & Unwin, 1963

Bank for International Settlements, *Financial Structure and the Monetary Policy Transmission Mechanism*, Bank for International Settlements, C.B. 394, Basle, March 1995

Bank for International Settlements, *Triennial Central Bank Survey – Foreign Exchange and Derivatives Market Activities in 2001*, Bank for International Settlements, Basel, March 2002

Bank of England, *The transmission mechanism of monetary policy*, Bank of England, Monetary Policy Committee, Special Report, 2000

Bannock, G., Baxter, R. E., Davis, E., *Dictionary of Economics*, Fifth Edition, Pengiun Books, 1992

Barran, F., Coudert, V., Mojon, B., *La transmission des politiques monetaire dans les pays europeens*, Revue Francaise d'Economie, Vol. 12, No. 2, pp. 133-176, 1997

Barran, F., Coudert, V., Mojon, B., *The Transmission of Monetary Policy in the European Countries*, CEPII Working Paper, No. 96-03, February 1996

Barro, R. J., *Inflationary Finance and the Welfare Cost of Inflation*, Journal of Political Economy, No. 5, 1972, pp. 978-1001

Barro, R. J., *Recent developments in the theory of rules versus discretion*, Economic Journal, 96 (Supplement), 1986, pp. 23-37

Barro, R. J., Gordon, D. B., *Rules, discretion and reputation in a model of monetary policy*, Journal of Monetary Economics, 12 (1), 1983, pp. 101-121

Barth, M. J., Ramey, V. A., *The Cost Channel of Monetary Transmission*, National Bureau of Economic Research, NBER Working Paper 7675, Cambridge, April 2000

Bartlett, R., *Economic Foundations of Political Power*, The Free Press, New York, 1973

Bean, C., Jenkinson, N., *The formulation of monetary policy*, Bank of England, Quarterly Bulletin, Winter 2001, pp. 434-441

Beck, N., *Political monetary cycles*, in: Mayer, T., The Political Economy of American Monetary Politics, Cambridge University Press, 1990

Becker, G. S., *A Theory of Competition among Pressure Groups for Political Influence*, Quarterly Journal of Economics, No. XCVIII, No. 3, August 1983, pp. 371-399

Becker, G. S., *Public Policies, Pressure Groups, and Dead Weight Costs*, Journal of Public Economics, Vol. 28 (1985), No. 3, pp. 329-347

Becker, G. S., *Special Interests and Public Policies*, The Frank E. Seidman Distinguished Award in Political Economy, Acceptance Paper, Rhodes College, Memphis, P. K. Seidman Foundation

Becker, G. S., *The Economic Approach to Human Behaviour*, University of Chicago Press, Chicago, 1978

Beetham, D., *Bureaucracy*, Open University Press, Buckingham, 1996, 2nd Ed.

Bentley, A. F., *The Process of Government*, in: Richardson, J. J. (Ed.), Pressure Groups, Oxford Readings in Politics and Government, Oxford University Press, 1993, pp. 19-22

Berger, H., de Haan, J., *A state within the state? An event study on the Bundesbank (1948-1973)*, Scottish Journal of Political Economy, No. 1, Vol. 46, February 1999, pp. 17-39

Berger, H., de Haan, J., Eijffinger, S. C. W., *Central bank independence: an up-date of theory and evidence*, Centre for Economic Policy Research, Discussion paper No. 2353, International Macroeconomics, Centre for Economic Policy Research, London, January 2000

Berger, H., Woitek, U., *Economics or Politics: What Drives the Bundesbank?*, Münchner Wirtschaftswissenschaftliche Beiträge, No. 7, June 1997

Berger, S. D. (Ed.), *Organizing Interests in Western Europe: Pluralism, Corporatism, and the Transformation of Politics*, Cambridge University Press, Cambridge, 1981

Berk, J. M., *Monetary transmission: what do we know and how can we use it?*, De Nederlandsche Bank Staff Report, No. 15, Amsterdam, 1997

Bernanke, B., Gertler, M., *Inside the black box: the credit channel of monetary policy transmission*, National Bureau of Economic Research, Working Paper 5146, Cambridge, June 1995

Bernholz, P., *Die Bundesbank und die Währungsintegration in Europa*, in: Deutsche Bundesbank (Ed.), Fünfzig Jahre Deutsche Mark – Notenbank und Währung in Deutschland seit 1948, Beck, Munich, 1998, pp. 773-835

Beyme, K. v., *Interessengruppen in der Demokratie*, Piper, Munich, 1974

Bickerich, W., *Die D-Mark*, Rowohlt, Berlin, 1998

Bodnar, G. M., Gebhardt, G., *Derivatives usage in risk management by US and German non-financial firms: a comparative survey*, National Bureau of Economic Research, Working Paper 6705, Cambridge, August 1998

Bofinger, P., *Consequences of the modification of the Governing Council rules*, Briefing paper for the Committee for Monetary and Economic Affairs (ECON) of the European Parliament, February 7, 2003

Bofinger, P., *The Monetary Policy of the ECB under Treaty Article 105*, European Parliament, Directorate-General for Research, Working Paper, Economic Affairs Series, ECON 112 EN 04-1999, 1999

Bofinger, P. Reischle, J., Schächter, A., *Geldpolitik: Ziele, Institutionen, Strategien und Instrumente*, Verlag Franz Vahlen, Munich, 1996

Börzel, T. A., *Policy networks – a new paradigm for European governance*, EUI Working Papers, Robert Schuman Centre, EUI WP RSC No. 97/19

Börzel, T. A., *What's So Special About Policy Networks? – An Exploration of the Concept and the Usefulness in Studying European Governance*, European Integration online Papers (EIoP), Vol. 1 (1997), No. 016

Breuer, R.-E., *The role of the media: Fast and correct information as a tool for the financial markets*, Statement, European Summit of Financial Journalists, Frankfurt, 30. October, 2000

Briault, C., Haldane, A., King, M., *Central bank independence and accountability: theory and evidence*, Bank of England Quarterly Bulletin, Vol. 36, No. 1, February 1996, pp. 63-68

Britton, E., Whitley, J., *Comparing the monetary transmission mechansim in France, Germany and the United Kingdom: some issues and results*, Bank of England Quarterly Bulletin, Vol. 37, No. 2, May 1997, pp. 152-162

Brosius-Gersdorf, F., *Deutsche Bundesbank und Demokratieprinzip – Eine verfassungsrechtliche Studie zur Bundesbankautonomie vor und nach der dritten Stufe der Europäischen Währungsunion*, Schriften zum öffentlichen Recht Band 736, Duncker & Humblot, Berlin, 1997

Brown, W. M., *Keeping the Central Bank Central – U.S. Monetary Policy and the Banking System*, Westview Special Studies, Boulder, Westview Press, 1987

Browne, W. P., *Issue Niches and the Limits of Interest Group Influence*, in: Cigler, A. J., Loomis, B. A. (Eds.), Interest Group Politics, C. Q. Press, Washington, 1995, Third Edition

Brunner, K., Meltzer, A. H., *Money, Monetary Policy, and Financial Institutions*, in: Brunner, K., Meltzer, A. H. (Eds.), Money, Monetary Policy, and Financial Institutions, Carnegie-Rochester Conference Series on Public Policy, Vol. 18, North Holland, Amsterdam, 1983, pp. 1-8

Brunner, K., Meltzer, A. H., *Strategies and Tactics for Monetary Control*, in: Brunner, K., Meltzer, A. H. (Eds.), Money, Monetary Policy, and Financial Institutions, Carnegie-Rochester Conference Series on Public Policy, Vol. 18, North Holland, Amsterdam, 1983, pp. 59-104

Brunner, K., Meltzer, A. H., *The Costs and Consequences of Inflation*, Carnegie-Rochester Conference Series on Public Policy, a bi-annual conference proceedings, Vol. 15, Autumn 1981, North-Holland Publishing Company, Amsterdam, 1981, pp. 1-52

Brunner, K., Meltzer, A. H. (Eds.), *Money and credit in the monetary transmission process*, American Economic Review, 78 (2), 1988, pp. 446-451

Bryman, A., *Research methods and organisation studies*, Contemporary Social Research Series, Vol. 20, Unwin Hyman, London, 1989

Buchanan, J. M., Tullock, G., *The Calculus of Consent: Logical Foundations of Constitutional Democracy*, Liberty Fund, Indianapolis, 1999

Buchheim, C., *Die Errichtung der Bank deutscher Länder und die Währungsreform in Westdeutschland*, in: Deutsche Bundesbank (Ed.), Fünfzig Jahre Deutsche Mark – Notenbank und Währung in Deutschland seit 1948, Beck, Munich, 1998, pp. 91-138

Buholzer, R., *Legislatives Lobbying in der Europäischen Union: ein Konzept für Interessengruppen*, Universität St. Galen, Hochschule für Wirtschafts-, Rechts- und Sozialwissenschaften (HSG), Dissertation Nr. 2153, Verlag Paul Haupt, Bern, 1998

Bundesministerium der Finanzen, *Entwurf eines Siebenten Gesetzes zur Änderung des Gesetzes über die Deutsche Bundesbank*, Bundesministerium der Finanzen, May 21, 2001

Bundesverband der Deutschen Industrie, *BDI – A Good Connection*, Bundesverband der Deutschen Industrie, Berlin, 2003

Burda, M., Wyplosz, C., *Macroeconomics*, Oxford University Press, Oxford, 1993

Büschgen, H. E., *Bank-Lexikon*, Zweite aktualisierte Auflage, Verlagsgruppe Handelsblatt, Verlag Wirtschaft und Finanzen, Düsseldorf, 1997

Büsching, T., *Unabhängigkeit und Zinspolitik der Deutschen Bundesbank im Prozeß der deutschen Vereinigung (1989-1992)*, Europäische Hochschulschriften, Reihe V, Volks- und Betriebswirtschaftslehre, Band 2023, Frankfurt am Main, Peter Lang, 1997

Caesar, R., *Die Unabhängigkeit der Notenbank im demokratischen Staat; Argumente und Gegenargumente*, Zeitschrift für Politik, Jg. 27, H. 4, 1980, pp. 347-377

Caldeira, G. A., Wright, J. R., *Lobbying for Justice: Organized Interests, Supreme Court Nominations, and the United States Senate*, American Journal of Political Science, Vol. 42, No. 2, April 1998, pp. 499-523

Calvo, G. A., *On the time inconsistency of optimal monetary policy in a monetary economy*, Econometrica, Vol. 46, No. 6 (November, 1978), pp. 1411-1428

Cargill, T. F., *Central Bank Independence and Regulatory Responsibilities: The Bank of Japan and the Federal Reserve*, Salomon Brothers Center for the Study of Financial Institutions, Monograph Series in Finance and Economics, Monograph 1989-2, Leonard N. Stern School of Business, New York University, New York, 1989, pp. 1-78

Casper, J. D., *Public Opinion and the Supreme Court: Introductory Remarks*, Northwestern University Law Review, Vol. 84, Nos. 3-4, 1990, pp. 983-984

Cecchetti, S. G., *Legal structure, financial structure, and the monetary policy transmission mechanism*, National Bureau of Economic Research, NBER Working Paper 7151, Cambridge, June 1999

Chatelain, J. B., Generale, A., Hernando, I., von Kalckreuth, U., Vermeulen, P., *Firm investment and monetary policy transmission in the euro area*, Deutsche Bundesbank, Economic Research Centre, Discussion Paper 20/01, December 2001

Chouraqui, J.-C., Driscoll, M., Strauss-Kahn, M.-O., *The effects of monetary policy on the real sector: an overview of empirical evidence for selected OECD economies*, OECD, Department of Economics and Statistics, Working Papers, No. 51, April 1988

Chubb, J. E., *Interest Groups and the Bureaucracy – The Politics of Energy*, Stanford University Press, Stanford, 1983

Cigler, A. J., *Interest Groups: A Subfield in Search of an Identity*, Paper presented at the annual meeting of the Midwesterm Political Science Association, Chicago, 1989

Cigler, A. J., Loomis, B. A., *Introduction: the Changing Nature of Interest Group Politics*, in: Cigler, A. J., Loomis, B. A. (Eds.), Interest Group Politics, C. Q. Press, Washington, 1995, Third Edition

Cigler, A. J., Loomis, B. A., *Organized Interests and the Search for Certainty*, in: Cigler, A. J., Loomis, B. A. (Eds.), Interest Group Politics, C. Q. Press, Washington, 1995, Third Edition

Cigler, A. J., Loomis, B. A. (Eds.), *Interest Group Politics*, C. Q. Press, Washington, 1995, Third Edition

Clamen, M., *Le Lobbying et ses secrets: guide des techniques d'influence*, Dunod, Paris, 1995

Clarida, R., Gali, J., Gertler, M., *The science of monetary policy: a new Keynesian perspective*, NBER Working Paper No. 7147, National Bureau of Economic Research, Cambridge, 1999

Clausen, V., *Asymmetric Monetary Transmission in Europe*, Springer-Verlag, Berlin, 2001

Clements, B., Kontolemis, Z. G., Levy, J., *Monetary Policy under EMU: Differences in the Transmission Mechanism?*, IMF Working Paper, WP/01/102, August 2001

Collignon, S., Schwarzer, D., *Private Sector Involvement in the Euro – The power of ideas*, Routledge Advances in European Politics, Routledge, London, 2003

Congleton, R. D., *Information, special interests, and single-issue voting*, Public Choice, 1991, Vol. 69, No. 1, pp. 39-49

Conradt, D. P., *The Germany Polity*, Fourth Edition, Longaman, New York, 1989

Coughlin, P., Murrell, P, Mueller, D. C., *Electoral Politics, Interest Groups, and the Size of Government*, Economic Inquiry, 28 (1990), 4, pp. 682-705; Reprinted in: The Public Choice Approach to Politics, Edward Elgar, Aldershot, 1983, pp. 320-343

Council of the European Union, *Broad economic policy guidelines for the period 2003 – 2005*, Council of the European Union, Brussels, June 2003

Coutinho, L., *Monetary policy rules and the international monetary transmission*, CEPS Working Document No.191, The Centre for European Policy Studies, Brussels, October 2002

Cukierman, A., *Central Bank Strategy, Credibility, and Independence: Theory and Evidence*, The MIT Press, Cambridge, Massachussetts, 1994

Cukierman, A., Webb, S. B., Neyapti, B., *Measuring the Independence of Central Banks and Its Effects on Policy Outcomes*, The World Bank Economic Review, Vol. 6, No. 3, 1992, pp. 353-398

Cukierman, A., Meltzer A. H., *A theory of ambiguity, credibility, and inflation under discretion and asymmetric information*, Econometrica, Vol. 54, No. 5, September 1986, pp. 1099-1128

Czada, R. M., Windhoff-Héritier, A. (Eds.), *Political Choice: Institutions, Rules, and the Limits of Rationality*, Campus Verlag, Frankfurt am Main, Westview Press, Boulder, Colorado, 1991

Dagger, S., Greiner, C., Leinert, K., Meliß, N., Menzel, A. (Eds.), *Politikberatung in Deutschland – Praxis und Perspektiven*, VS Verlag, Wiesbaden, 2004

Daumann, F., *Interessenverbände im politischen Prozess – Eine Analyse auf Grundlage der Neuen Politischen Ökonomie*, Walter Eucken Institut, Untersuchungen zur Ordnungstheorie und Ordnungspolitik, No. 38, Mohr Siebeck, Tübingen, 1999

Dawson, G., *Inflation and Unemployment: Causes, Consequences and Cures*, Edward Elgar Publishing Limited, Aldershot, 1992, pp. 89-133

Daxhammer, R., *Special Interest Groups and Economic Policy in Democratic Societies: Theoretical Foundations and Empirical Evidence*, Peter Lang, European University Studies, Series V, Economics and Management, Vol. 1677, Frankfurt am Main, 1993

De Bondt, G. J., *Credit and asymmetric effects of monetary policy in six EU countries: an overview*, De Nederlandsche Bank Staff Report, No. 23, Amsterdam, 1998

De Bondt, G. J., *Credit Channels and Consumption in Europe: Empirical Evidence*, BIS Working Papers, No. 69, June 1999, Bank for International Settlements, Monetary and Economic Department, Basle, 1999; also: DNB Staff Reports 1999, No. 39, De Nederlandsche Bank, 1999

De Bondt, G. J., *Credit channels and consumption: European evidence*, DNB Staff Reports 1999, No. 39, De Nederlandsche Bank, 1999; also: BIS Working Papers, No. 69, June 1999, Bank for International Settlements, Monetary and Economic Department, Basle, 1999 de Grauwe, P., *The Design of the European Central Bank*, Kredit und Kapital, Sonderheft, pp. 295-315

De Grauwe, P., *The Economics of Monetary Integration*, Second Revised Edition, Oxford University Press, Oxford, 1994

de Haan, J. (Ed.), *The History of the Bundesbank: Lessons for the European Central Bank*, Routledge International Studies in Money and Banking, No. 9

De Nederlandsche Bank, *The importance of financial structure for monetary transmission in Europe*, De Nederlandsche bank, Quarterly Bulletin March 2000, pp. 33-40

Dedola, L., Lippi, F., *The monetary transmission mechanism: Evidence from the industries of five OECD countries*, Centre for Economic Policy Research, CEPR, Discussion Paper, International Macroeconomics, No. 2508, July 2000

Deutsche Bundesbank, *Bankbilanzen, Bankenwettbewerb und geldpolitische Transmission*, Deutsche Bundesbank, Monatsbericht September 2001, pp. 51-70

Deutsche Bundesbank, *Bankbilanzen, Bankenwettbewerb und geldpolitische Transmission*, Deutsche Bundesbank, Monatsbericht September 2001, pp. 51-70

Deutsche Bundesbank, *Bundesbank Act and Statute of the European System of Central Banks and of the European Central Bank*, Banking Regulations 1, Deutsche Bundesbank, Frankfurt am Main, June 1998a

Deutsche Bundesbank, *Die Tätigkeit der Deutschen Bundesbank: Strukturreform*, Deutsche Bundesbank, Geschäftsbericht 2002, Frankfurt am Main, März 2003a

Deutsche Bundesbank, *Ergebnisse der gesamtwirtschaftlichen Finanzierungsrechnung für Deutschland 1991 bis 2000*, Deutsche Bundesbank, Statistische Sonderveröffentlichungen 4, September 2001

Deutsche Bundesbank, *Europäische Organisationen und Gremien im Bereich von Währung und Wirtschaft*, Deutsche Bundesbank, Frankfurt am Main, Mai 1997

Deutsche Bundesbank, *Monetary strategies in the countries of the European Union*, Deutsche Bundesbank, Monthly Report, January 1998, pp. 33-48

Deutsche Bundesbank, *Real interest rates: movements and determinants*, Deutsche Bundebsank, Monthly Report, July 2001, pp. 31-47

Deutsche Bundesbank, *Realzinsen: Entwicklung und Determinanten*, Deutsche Bundesbank, Monatsbericht Juli 2001, pp. 33-50, 2001b

Deutsche Bundesbank, *Seventh Act amending the Bundesbank Act*, Deutsche Bundesbank, Monthly Report, May 2002, pp. 5-18, 2002a

Deutsche Bundesbank, *The monetary policy of the Bundesbank*, Deutsche Bundesbank, special publication, October 1995

Deutsche Bundesbank, *Überlegungen und Vorschläge zur künftigen Organisationsstruktur der Deutschen Bundesbank*, Deutsche Bundesbank, Monatsbericht, Juli 1999, pp. 5-16, 1999a

Deutsche Bundesbank (Ed.), *Fünfzig Jahre Deutsche Mark – Notenbank und Währung in Deutschland seit 1948*, Beck, Munich, 1998

Dieckmann, A., *Empirische Sozialforschung: Grundlagen, Methoden, Anwendungen*, Rowohlt, Reinbek, 1997

Dunleavy, P., *Democracy, Bureaucracy, and Public Choice*, Harvester Wheatsheaf, Hemel Hempstead, 1991

Edinger, L. J., *Pressure Groups Politics in West Germany*, in: Richardson, J. J. (Ed.), Pressure Groups, Oxford Readings in Politics and Government, Oxford University Press, 1993, pp. 175-190

Eggert, R., *Bundesbank zwischen europäischer Geldpolitik und regionaler Verantwortung*, HWWA Wirtschaftsdienst, Hamburg, November 2001, reprinted in: Deutsche Bundesbank, Auszüge aus Presseartikeln, Nr. 52 vom 28. November 2001, pp. 10-13

Ehrmann, M., *Firm size and monetary policy transmission: evidence from German survey data*, ECB Working Paper No. 21, European Central Bank, May 2000

Ehrmann, M., Gambacorta, L., Martínez-Pagés, J., Sevestre, P., Worms, A., *Financial systems and the role of banks in monetary policy transmission in the euro area*, Deutsche Bundesbank, Economic Research Centre, Discussion Paper 19/01, December 2001b

Ehrmann, M., Worms, A., *Interbank lending and monetary policy transmission: evidence for Germany*, Deutsche Bundesbank, Economic Research Centre, Discussion Paper 11/01, July 2001a

Eichener, V., Voelzkow, H. (Eds.), *Europäische Integration und verbändliche Interessenvermittlung*, Metropolis-Verlag, Marburg, 1994

Eijffinger, S. C. W., *Independent central banks and economic performance*, Edward Elgar, Cheltenham, 1997

Eijffinger, S. C. W., *The new political economy of central banking*, Paper presented at the conference "Monetary Theory as a Basis for Monetary Policy", International Economic Association, Trento, Italy, September 4 to 7, 1997

Eijffinger, S. C. W., Hoeberichts, M. M., *Central Bank Accountability and Transparency: Theory and Some Evidence*, Deutsche Bundesbank, Discussion Paper 06/00, Economic Research Centre of the Deutsche Bundesbank, Frankfurt, November 2000

Eijffinger, S. C. W., Onno de Beaufort Wijnholds, O., Hoogduim, L. H. (Eds.), *A Framework for Monetary Stability: Papers and proceedings of an international conference, Amsterdam, October 1993*, Kluver Academic Publishers, Dordrecht, Financial and Monetary Policy Studies, Vol. 27, 1994

Eijffinger, S. C. W., Schaling, E., *Central bank independence in twelve industrial countries*, Banca Nationale del Lavoro Quarterly Review, Nr. 184, March 1993, pp. 49-89

Eijffinger, S. C. W., van Keulen, M., *Central bank independence in another eleven industrial countries*, Banca Nationale del Lavorno Quarterly Review, Nr. 192, March 1995, pp. 39-83

Eijffinger, S., Schaling, E., Hoeberichts, M., *Central bank independence: A sensitivity analysis*, European Journal of Political Economy, Vol. 14, 1998, No. 1, pp. 73-88

Elgie, R., Thompson, H., *The Politics of Central Banks*, Routledge Advances in International Relations and Politics, Routledge, London, 1998

Englert, M., *Der Handlungsspielraum der amerikanischen Bundesbank im Regierungssystem der Vereinigten Staaten*, Schäuble Verlag, Rheinfelden, Historische Forschungen 23, 1988

Eun, Soong-Pyo, *Die rechtliche Stellung der Deutschen Bundesbank und Währungsstabilität – eine rechtstheoretische Untersuchung*, Köhler-Druck, Tübingen, 1994, pp. 1-275

European Central Bank, *Characteristics of corporate finance in the euro area*, European Central Bank, Monthly Bulletin, February 2001, pp. 37-50

European Central Bank, *Developments in the debt financing of the euro area private sector*, European Central Bank, Monthly Bulletin, November 2003, pp. 47-57

European Central Bank, *Economic fundamentals and the exchange rate of the euro*, European Central Bank, Monthly Bulletin, January 2002, pp. 41-54

European Central Bank, *Financing and financial investment of the non-financial sector in the euro area*, European Central Bank, Monthly Bulletin, May 2001, pp. 75-82

European Central Bank, *Issues related to monetary policy rules*, European Central Bank, Monthly Bulletin, October 2001, pp. 37-50

European Central Bank, *Monetary policy transmission in the euro area*, European Central Bank, Monthly Bulletin, July 2000, pp. 43-58, 2000a

European Central Bank, *Recent findings on monetary policy transmission in the euro area*, European Central Bank, Monthly Bulletin, October 2002, pp. 43-54

European Central Bank, *Report on Financial Structures*, European Central Bank, Frankfurt, 2002

European Central Bank, *The accountability of the ECB*, European Central Bank, Monthly Bulletin, November 2002, pp. 45-57

European Central Bank, *The ECB's relations with institutions and bodies of the European Communities*, European Central Bank, Monthly Bulletin, October 2000, pp. 49-64, 2000d

European Central Bank, *The ECB's relations with institutions and bodies of the European Community*, ECB Monthly Bulletin, October 2000, European Central Bank, Frankfurt, 2000b

European Central Bank, *The ECB's relations with institutions and bodies of the European Community*, European Central Bank, ECB Monthly Bulletin, October 2000, pp. 49-64

European Central Bank, *The ECB's relations with international organisations and fora*, European Central Bank, Monthly Bulletin, January 2001, pp. 57-76

European Central Bank, *The economic policy framework in EMU*, European Central Bank, ECB Monthly Bulletin, November 2001, pp. 51-65

European Central Bank, *The European Constitution and the ECB*, European Central Bank, Monthly Bulletin, Frankfurt am Main, August 2004, pp. 51-64, 2004

European Central Bank, *The external communication of the European Central Bank*, European Central Bank, Monthly Bulletin, February 2001, pp. 59-66

European Central Bank, *The information content of interest rates and their derivatives for monetary policy*, European Central Bank, Monthly Bulletin, May 2000, pp. 37-56, 2000c

European Central Bank, *The institutional framework of the European System of Central Banks*, ECB Monthly Bulletin, July 1999, European Central Bank, Frankfurt, 1999

European Central Bank, *The Monetary Policy of the ECB*, European Central Bank, Frankfurt, 2004

European Central Bank, *The Monetary Policy of the ECB*, European Central Bank, Frankfurt, 2001a

European Central Bank, *The outcome of the ECB's evaluation of its monetary policy strategy*, European Central Bank, Monthly Bulletin, Frankfurt am Main, June 2003, pp. 79-92, 2003a

European Central Bank, *The stability-oriented monetary policy strategy of the Eurosystem*, European Central Bank, Monthly Bulletin, January 1999, pp. 39-50

European Central Bank, *The stock market and monetary policy*, European Central Bank, Monthly Bulletin, February 2002, pp. 39-52

European Central Bank, *Transparency in the monetary policy of the ECB*, European Central Bank, Monthly Bulletin, November 2002, pp. 59-66

European Commission, *Co-ordination of economic policies in the EU: a presentation of key features of the main procedures*, European Commission, Directorate-General for Economic and Financial Affairs, Euro Papers, Number 45, July 2002

Faith, R., *Lobbying and the measurement of conventional welfare cost*, Public Choice, 1991, Vol. 72, No. 1, pp. 23-36

Falkner, G., *Interest Groups in a Multi-level Polity: The Impact of European Integration on National Systems*, EUI Working Paper, RSC No. 99-34, 1999

Favero, C. A., Giavazzi, F., *Monetary Policy Transmission in the Euro Area*, European Parliament, Directorate-General for Research, Working Paper, Economic Affairs Series, 1999a

Favero, C. A., Giavazzi, F., Flabbi, L., *The Transmission Mechanism of Monetary Policy in Europe: Evidence from Banks' Balance Sheets*, NBER Working Paper No. 7231, National Bureau of Economic Research, Cambridge, 1999b

Feldstein, M. (Ed.), *The Costs and Benefits of Price Stability*, University of Chicago Press, Chicago, 1999

Felgenhauer, M., Grüner, H. P., *Committees and Special Interests*, European Central Bank Working Paper Series, Working Paper No. 293, November 2003

Fisch, S., Rudloff, W. (Eds.), *Experten und Politik: Wissenschaftliche Politikberatung in geschichtlicher Perspetive*, Schriftenreihe der Hochschule Speyer, Band 168, Duncker & Humblot, Berlin, 2004

Fischer, K. H., *Lobbying und Kommunikation in der Europäischen Union*, Berlin-Verlag A. Spitz, Berlin, 1997

Flick, U., *Design und Prozess qualitativer Forschung*, in: Flick, U., Kardorff, E. v., Steinke, I. (Eds.), Qualitative Forschung, Rowohlt, Reinbek, 2000, pp. 252-264

Flick, U., Kardorff, E. v., Steinke, I. (Eds.), *Qualitative Forschung*, Rowohlt, Reinbek, 2000

Forder, J., *The case for an independent European central bank: A reassessment of evidence and sources*, European Journal of Political Economy, Vol. 14, 1998, No. 1, pp. 53-71

Franke, G., *Notenbank und Finanzmärkte*, in: Deutsche Bundesbank (Ed.), Fünfzig Jahre Deutsche Mark – Notenbank und Währung in Deutschland seit 1948, Beck, Munich, 1998, pp. 257-306

Franke, J., Dobson, L. D., *Interest groups: the problem of representation*, Western Political Quarterly, 38 (1985), 2, pp. 224-237

Franke, S. F., *Politik und Wirtschaft: Eine notwendige, aber reformbedürftige Verbindung*, in: Lobbyismus und Politik, HWWA Wirtschaftsdienst 2000/III, pp. 149-152

Fratianni, M. U., Spinelli, F., *A monetary history of Italy*, Cambridge University Press, Cambridge, 1997

Fratianni, M. U., von Hagen, J., Waller, C. J., *Central banking as a political principal-agent problem*, Economic Inquiry, Vol. 35, No. 2, 1997, pp. 378-393

Friedman, M., Schwartz, A. J., *A Monetary History of the United States 1867-1960*, Princeton University Press, Princeton, 1963

Frowen, S. F., Pringle, J. R., *Inside the Bundesbank*, Macmillan, Basingstoke, 1998

Galati, G., Melick, W., *Central bank intervention and market expectations*, Bank for International Settlements, Monetary and Economic Department, BIS Papers, No. 10, April 2002

Ganley, J., Salmon, C., *The industrial impact of monetary policy*, Bank of England Quarterly Bulletin, Vol. 36, No. 3, August 1996, pp. 288-298

Gardner, J. N., *Effective Lobbying in the European Community*, Deventer, Kluwer Law and Taxation Publishers, 1991

Gleske, L., *Organisation, Status und Aufgaben der zweistufigen Zentralbanksysteme in den Vereinigten Staaten von Amerika, in der Bundesrepublik Deutschland, in der künftigen Europäischen Währungsunion*, Weber, A. (Ed.), Währung und Wirtschaft – Das Geld im Recht: Festschrift für Prof. Dr. Hugo Joseph Hahn zum 70. Geburtstag, Nomos, Baden-Baden, 1997, pp. 123-140

Goodhart, C., *Central banking*, in: Newman, P., Milgate, M., Eatwell, J. (Eds.), The New Palgrave Dictionary of Money and Finance, St. Martin's Press, New York, 1992, pp. 321-325

Goodhart, C. A. E., *Money, Information and Uncertainty*, Second Edition, Macmillan, Basingstoke, 1989

Goodhart, C. A. E., *The Central Bank and the Financial System*, Macmillan, Basingstoke, 1995

Goodhart, C. A. E., *The Evolution of Central Banks*, MIT Press, Cambridge, Massachussetts, 1988

Goodhart, C. A. E., *Whither Central Banking?*, Mimeo, Financial Markets Group, London School of Economics, 2001

Goodhart, C. A. E., Hoffmann, B., *Asset Prices, Financial Conditions, and the Transmission of Monetary Policy*, Paper presented at the Stanford Institute for Economic Policy Research and the Federal Reserve Bank of San Francisco Conference, "Asset Prices, Exchange Rates, and Monetary Policy", Stanford University, March 2-3, 2001

Gordon, R. J., *The Demand for and Supply of Inflation*, Journal of Law and Economics, Vol. 18, 1975, pp. 807-836

Görgens, E., Ruckriegel, K., Seitz, F., *Europäische Geldpolitik: Theorie, Empirie, Praxis*, 2. Auflage, Werner Verlag, Düsseldorf, 2001

Gramlich, L., *Bundesbankgesetz, Währungsgesetz, Münzgesetz: Kommentar*, Carl Heymanns, Berlin, 1988

Gray, V., Lowery, D., *To Lobby Alone or in a Flock: Foraging Behavior Among Organized Interests*, American Politics Quarterly, Vol. 26, No. 1, January 1998, pp. 5-34

Greenwood, J., *Representing interests in the European Union*, MacMillan, Basingstoke, St. Martin's Press, New York, 1997, The European Union Series

Greenwood, J. R., *Interest Groups in the European Polity*, Current Politics and Economics of Europe, 2 (1992), 3, pp. 149-170, 2

Greenwood, J., Grote, J. R., Ronit, K. (Eds.), *Organized Interests and the European Community*, SAGE Publications, London, 1992

Gündisch, J., *Rechtsetzung und Interessenvertretung in der Europäischen Union*, Boorberg, Stuttgart, 1999

Haiss, P. R., *Lobbying für Universalbanken: Chancen und Risiken vernetzter Unternehmensstrukturen*, in: Lobby Management, Scheff (Ed.), Vienna, Linde, 1998

Hall, S., *Credit channel effects in the monetary transmission mechanism*, Bank of England, Quarterly Bulletin, Winter 2001, pp. 442-448

Harding, R., Jaks, J., van Paridon, K., Szomburg, J., *Wo versteckt sich der ostdeutsche Tiger? Über die Wirtschaftsperspektiven der neuen Bundesländer*, Gutachten, Hamburg, 2002

Härtel, H.H., *Makroökonomische Politik in der Europäischen Währungsunion*, Institut für Weltwirtschaftsforschung Hamburg, HWWA, Wirtschaftsdienst Nr. 2, 1999

Havrilesky, T., *Central bank autonomy, central bank accountability and inflation performance*, Mimeo, Duke University, February 1995

Havrilesky, T., *Monetary policy signalling from the administration to the Federal Reserve*, Journal of Money, Credit, and Banking, Vol. 20, No. 1, 1988, pp. 83-101

Havrilesky, T., *The influence of the Federal Advisory Council on Monetary Policy*, Journal of Money, Credit, and Banking, Vol. 22, No. 1, 1990, pp. 37-50

Havrilesky, T., *The political economy of monetary policy*, European Journal of Political Economy, Vol. 10, 1994, pp. 111-134

Havrilesky, T., *Tracking the influences of politicians on monetary policy*, American Banker, 1992

Havrilesky, T. M., *A Partisanship Theory of Fiscal and Monetary Regimes*, Journal of Money, Credit, and Banking, Vol. 19, No. 3, August 1987, pp. 308-325

Havrilesky, T. M., *The Pressures on American Monetary Policy*, Kluwer Academic Publishers, Financial and Monetary Policy Studies 13, Dordrecht, 1993

Hayo, B., *Inflation culture, central bank independence and price stability*, European Journal of Political Economy, Vol. 14, 1998, No. 1, pp. 241-263

Heclo, H., *Issue Networks and the Executive Establishment*, King, A., The New American Political System, pp. 87-124, MacMillan, Washington, 1978

Hefeker, C., *Federal Monetary Policy*, CESifo Working Paper No. 422, February 2001

Hefeker, C., *Interest Groups and Monetary Integration: The Political Economy of Exchange Rate Choice*, Westview Press, Boulder, 1997, pp. 1-161

Hefeker, C., *Interest Groups, Coalitions and Monetary Intergration in the XIXth Century*, The Journal of European Economic History, Vol. 24 (1995/1996), No. 3, pp. 489-536

Heipertz, M. K. G., *How strong was the Bundesbank? A case study in the policy-making of German and European Monetary Union*, Centre for European Policy Studies, Working Document No. 172, September 2001

Heise, A., *The Cologne Process: a neglected aspect of European employment policy*, Friedrich Ebert Stiftung, International Politics and Society, No. 2, 2002

Henry, N., *Public Administration and Public Affairs*, Prentice Hall, Englewood Cliffs, Sixth Edition, 1995

Hentschel, V., *Die Entstehung des Bundesbankgesetzes 1949-1957. Politische Kontroversen und Konflikte (Teil I)*, Bankhistorisches Archiv, Zeitschrift für Bankengeschichte, 14. Jg., H. 1, June 1988, pp. 3-31

Hentschel, V., *Die Entstehung des Bundesbankgesetzes 1949-1957. Politische Kontroversen und Konflikte (Teil II)*, Bankhistorisches Archiv, Zeitschrift für Bankengeschichte, 14. Jg., H. 2, December 1988, pp. 79-115

Hermanns, H., *Interviewen als Tätigkeit*, in: Flick, U., Kardorff, E. v., Steinke, I. (Eds.), Qualitative Forschung, Rowohlt, Reinbek, 2000, pp. 360-368

Herrnson, P. S., Shaiko, R. G., Wilcox, C. (Eds.), *The Interest Group Connection: Electioneering, Lobbying, and Policymaking in Washington*, Chatham House Publishers, Chatham, 1998

Hirschman, A. O., *Exit, Voice and Loyalty*, Discussion Paper, Harvard University, Harvard Institute of Economic Research, Harvard University, Cambridge, Massachussetts, 1973, No. 281

Hoffmeyer, E., *Decisionmaking for Economic and Monetary Union*, Group of Thirty, Occasional Papers No. 62, 2000

Holtfrerich, C.-L., *Geldpolitik bei festen Wechselkursen (1948-1970)*, in: Deutsche Bundesbank (Ed.), Fünfzig Jahre Deutsche Mark – Notenbank und Währung in Deutschland seit 1948, Beck, Munich, 1998, pp. 347-438

Holtham, G. H., Kato, H., *Wealth and Inflation Effects in the Aggregate Consumption Function*, OECD, Department of Economics and Statistics, Working Papers, No. 35, OECD, Paris, 1986

Hopf, C., *Qualitative Interviews – ein Überblick*, in: Flick, U., Kardorff, E. v., Steinke, I. (Eds.), Qualitative Forschung, Rowohlt, Reinbek, 2000, pp. 349-359

Hoppenstedt, *Adreßbuch Wirtschaft 1999*, Heyner Verlag, Munich, 1998

Houben, A. C. F. J, *The Evolution of Monetary Policy Strategies in Europe*, Dissertation, Rijksuniversiteit Groningen, 1999

Hubbard, R. G., *Is There a 'Credit Channel' for Monetary Policy?*, National Bureau of Economic Research, Working Paper 4977, Cambridge, December 1994

Issing, O., *Einführung in die Geldpolitik*, Fünfte Auflage, Vahlen, Munich, 1993b

Issing, O., *Einführung in die Geldtheorie*, Neunte Auflage, Vahlen, Munich, 1993a

Issing, O., *The European Central Bank as a new institution and the problem of accountability*, in: de Haan, J. (Ed.), The History of the Bundesbank: Lessons for the European Central Bank, Routledge International Studies in Money and Banking, No. 10, 2000, pp. 143-156

James. H., *Die Reichsbank 1876 bis 1945*, in: Deutsche Bundesbank (Ed.), Fünfzig Jahre Deutsche Mark – Notenbank und Währung in Deutschland seit 1948, Beck, Munich, 1998, pp. 29-90

Jarchow, H.-J., *Theorie und Politik des Geldes – Geldtheorie*, Achte überarbeitete und ergänzte Ausgabe, Vandenhoek und Ruprecht, Göttingen, 1990

Jordan, G., *The Pluralism of Pluralism: An Anti-theory?*, in: Richardson, J. J. (Ed.), Pressure Groups, Oxford Readings in Politics and Government, Oxford University Press, 1993, pp. 38-70

Junius, K., Kater, U., Meier, C.-P., Müller, H., *Handbuch Europäische Zentralbank: Beobachtung, Analyse, Prognose*, Uhlenbruch, Bad Soden, 2002

Kalckreuth, U., *Monetary transmission in Germany: new perspectives on financial constraints and investment spending*, Deutsche Bundesbank, Economic Research Centre, Discussion Paper 19/01, December 2001

Kaltenthaler, K., *German Interests in European Monetary Integration*, Journal of Common Market Studies, Vol. 40, No. 1, 2002, pp. 69-87

Kaltenthaler, K., *Germany and the Politics of Europe's Money*, Duke University Press, Durham, London, 1998

Kaltenthaler, K., *Institutional Sources of German Moentary Policy Dynamics*, Journal of Public Policies, No. 3, 1997, pp. 269-297

Kaltenthaler, K., *The Sources of Policy Dynamics: Variations in German and French Policy Towards European Monetary Co-operation*, West European Politics, Vol. 20, No. 3 (July 1997), pp. 91-110

Kane, E. J., *External Pressure and the Operations of the Fed*, in: Lombra, R. E., Witte, W. E. (Eds.), Political Economy of International and Domestic Monetary Relations, Ames, Iowa State University Press, 1982

Kashyap, A. K., Stein, J. C., *The Impact of Monetary Policy on Bank Balance Sheets*, National Bureau of Economic Research, NBER Working Paper 4821, Cambridge, August 1994

Kashyap, A. K., Stein, J. C., *The role of banks in monetary policy: A survey with implications for the European monetary union*, Economic Perspectives, Federal Reserve Bank of Chicago, Chicago, 1997, pp. 2-18

Kashyap, A. K., Stein, J. C., *What do a million banks have to say about the transmission of monetary policy?*, National Bureau of Economic Research, Working Paper Series, No. 6056, Cambridge, Massachussets, 1997, also: The American Economic Review, Vol. 90, No. 3, June 2000, pp. 407-428

Keefer, P., Stasavage, D., *Bureaucratic Delegation and Political Institutions: When are Independent Central Banks Irrelevant?*, The World Bank, World Bank Policy Research Working Paper No. 2356, February 2001

Kelle, U., Erzberger, C., *Qualitative und quantitative Methoden: kein Gegensatz*, in: Flick, U., Kardorff, E. v., Steinke, I. (Eds.), Qualitative Forschung, Rowohlt, Reinbek, 2000, pp. 299-308

Kettl, D. F., *Leadership at the Fed*, New Haven, Yale University Press, 1986

Keynes, J. M., *The general theory of employment, interest and money*, MacMillan, London, 1936

Kieler, M., Saarenheimo, T., *Differences in Monetary Policy Transmission? A Case not Closed*, European Commission, Economic Papers, No. 132, Commission of the European Communities, Brussels, November 1998

Kimber, R., *Interest Groups and the Fallacy of the Liberal Fallacy*, in: Richardson, J. J. (Ed.), Pressure Groups, Oxford Readings in Politics and Government, Oxford University Press, 1993, pp. 38-48

Kindleberger, C. P., *A Financial History of Western Europe*, Oxford University Press, New York, Second Edition, 1993

Köhler, C., *Transmissionskanäle der Geld- und Kreditpolitik*, Vortrag von Prof. Dr. Dr. h.c. Claus Köhler, Mitglied des Direktoriums der Deutschen Bundesbank i. R., im Willy-Brandt-Haus, Berlin, am 27. Oktober 2001, reprinted in: Deutsche Bundesbank, Auszüge aus Presserartikeln, Nr. 49 vom 7. November 2001, pp. 16-2

Köhler, H., Kees, A., *Die Verhandlungen zur Europäischen Wirtschafts- und Währungsunion*, in: Waigel, T. (Ed.), Unsere Zukunft heißt Europa – Der Weg zu Wirtschafts- und Währungsunion, Econ, Düsseldorf, 1997, pp. 145-174

Kohler-Koch, B., *Interessen und Integration. Die Rolle organisierter Interessen im westeuropäischen Integrationsprozeß*, Kreile, M. (Ed.), Die Integration Europas, Politische Vierteljahresschrift, Sonderheft, (PVS-Sonderheft), No. 23, pp. 81-119

Kohler-Koch, B., *Organized Interest in the EC and the European Parliament*, European Integration online Papers (EIoP), Vol. 1 (1997), No. 009

Kollman, K., *Outside lobbying: Public opinion and interest group strategies*, Princeton University Press, Princeton, 1998

Kopper, H., *Von der D-Mark zur gemeinsamen europäischen Währung*, in: Waigel, T. (Ed.), Unsere Zukunft heißt Europa – Der Weg zu Wirtschafts- und Währungsunion, Econ, Düsseldorf, 1997, pp. 175-192

Köppl, P., *Public Affairs Management: Strategien und Taktiken erfolgreicher Unternehmenskommunikation*, Linde, Vienna, 2000

Kowal, S., O'Connell, *Zur Transkription von Gesprächen*, in: Flick, U., Kardorff, E. v., Steinke, I. (Eds.), Qualitative Forschung, Rowohlt, Reinbek, 2000, pp. 437-446

Kreile, M., Münkler, H., Schmidt, M. G., Streeck, W. (Eds.), *Staat und Verbände*, Politische Vierteljahresschrift (PVS), Sonderheft Nr. 25, 35. Jahrgang, Westdeutscher Verlag, Wiesbaden, 1994

Krottenmüller, G., *Die Österreichische Nationalbank – Ihre organisatorische und funktionale Stellung in der Wirtschaftsverwaltung*, Institut für Angewandte Sozial- und Wirtschaftsforschung, Jupiter-Verlag, 1971, pp. 1-175

Küppers, M., *Banken in der geldpolitischen Transmission – Eine Untersuchung der Kreditvergabe deutscher Geschäftsbanken*, Schriften zur angewandten Wirtschaftsforschung, Mohr Siebeck, Tübingen, 2000

Kydland, F. E., Prescott, E. C., *Rules Rather than Discretion: The Inconsistency of Optimal Plans*, Journal of Political Economy, 1977, Vol. 85, No. 3, pp. 473-491

Lagerlöf, J., *Lobbying, information, and private and social welfare*, European Journal of Political Economy, No. 13, 1997, pp. 617-637

Landeszentralbank in Hessen, *The Role of the Land Central Banks within the European System of Central Banks*, Frankfurter Finanzmarkt-Bericht, November 1998, No. 32, pp. 1-9

Lee, D. R., *Marginal lobbying cost and the optimal amount of rent seeking*, Public Choice, 1985, Vol. 45, No. 2, pp. 207-213

Leech, B. L., Baumgartner, F. R., *Basic Interests*, Princeton University Press, 1998

Lepsius, M. R., *Interessen, Ideen und Institutionen*, Westdeutscher Verlag, Opladen, 1996

Levačić, R., Rebmann, A., *Macroeconomics – An Introduction to Keynesian-Neoclassical Controversies*, Second Edition, Macmillan, Basingstoke, 1991

Liebl, F., *Strategische Frühaufklärung: Trends, Issues, Stakeholders*, R. Oldenbourg Verlag, Munich, Vienna, 1996

Lindley, J. T., *An Analysis of the Federal Advisory Council of the Federal Reserve System, 1914-1938*, Garland Publishing, New York, 1985

Lindsey, D. E., Wallich, H. C., *Monetary policy*, in: Newman, P., Milgate, M., Eatwell, J. (Eds.), The New Palgrave Dictionary of Money and Finance, St. Martin's Press, New York, 1992, pp. 741-748

Lippi, F., *Central bank independence and credibility: Essays on delegation arrangements for monetary policy*, Erasmus Universiteit Rotterdam, Dissertation, Rotterdam, 1997

Lippi, F., *On the Costs of Central Bank Independence*, Tinbergen Institute TI 1-95-227, 1995

Lohmann, S., *Federalism and Central Bank Independence – The Politics of German Monetary Policy, 1957-92*, World Politics, No. 50 (April 1998), pp. 401-446

Lück, M., *Zentralbankpolitik in Italien*, Peter Lang, Reihe V, Volks- und Betriebswirtschaft, Vol. 2246, Frankfurt am Main, 1997

Mack, C. S., *Business, Politics, and the Practice of Government Relations*, Quorum Books, Westport, 1997

Maier, P., *Political Pressure, Rhetoric and Monetary Policy – Lessons for the European Central Bank*, Edward Elgar, Cheltenham, 2002

Maier, P., *Pressure on the Bundesbank*, Kredit und Kapital, Heft 4/2000, pp. 468-497

Maier, P., de Haan, J., *How independent is the Bundesbank really? A survey*, in: de Haan, J. (Ed.), The History of the Bundesbank: Lessons for the European Central Bank, Routledge International Studies in Money and Banking, No. 10, pp. 7-42

Maier, P., Sturm, J.-E., de Haan, J., *Political Pressure on the Bundesbank: An Empirical Investigation Using the Havrilesky Approach*, Working Paper, SSRN, November 2000

Marsh, D., *Die Bundesbank – Geschäfte mit der Macht*, Zweite Auflage, Bertelsmann, Munich, 1992

Marshall, M., *The Bank – The Birth of Europe's Central Bank and the Rebirth of Europe's Power*, Random House, London, 1999

Märtz, T., *Interessengruppen und Gruppeninteressen in der Demokratie: Zur Theorie des Rent-Seeking*, Lang, Frankfurt am Main, 1990

Masciandaro, D., Spinelli, F., *Central banks' independence: institutional determinants, rankings, and central bankers' views*, Scottish Journal of Political Economy, Vol. 41, No. 4, November 1994, pp. 434-443

Mayer, M., *The Fed*, The Free Press, New York, 2001

Mayer, T., *The Political Economy of American Monetary Politics*, Cambridge University Press, 1990

Mazey, S. P., Richardson, J. J., *Interest Groups in the European Community*, in: Richardson, J. J. (Ed.), Pressure Groups, Oxford Readings in Politics and Government, Oxford University Press, 1993, pp. 191-213

Mazey, S., Richardson, J. (Eds.), *Lobbying in the European Community*, Oxford University Press, Oxford, 1993

McAdam, P., Morgan, J., *The monetary transmission mechanism at the euro-area level: issues and results using structural macroeconomic models*, European Central Bank, Working Paper No. 93, December 2001

McCallum, B. T., *Crucial issues concerning central bank independence*, NBER Working Paper No. 5597, National Bureau of Economic Research, Cambridge, 1996

Mehnert-Meland, R., *Central Bank to the European Union: European Monetary Institute, European System of Central Banks, European Central Bank – Structures, Tasks and Functions*, Kluwer Law, London, 1995

Meltzer, A., *The Transmission Process*, Paper presented at the conference The Monetary Transmission Process: Recent Developments and Lessons for Europe, hosted by Deutsche Bundesbank, Frankfurt, March 26 and 27, 1999

Mény, Y., *Government and Politics in Western Europe*, Second Edition, Oxford University Press, 1993

Middlemas, K., *Orchestrating Europe: The Informal Politics of European Union 1973-1995*, Fontana Press, London, 1995

Miller, G. P., *An Interest-Group Theory of Central Bank Independence*, The Journal of Legal Studies, Vol. XXVII (June 1998), pp. 433-453

Milner, C. R., *Interest Groups and Policy Formulation*, Greenway, D., Bleaney, M., Stewart, I., (Ed.), Companion to contemporary economic thought, London, Routledge, 1991, pp. 697-712

Minkkinen, P., Patomaki, H., *The Politics of Economic and Monetary Union*, in: Minkkinen, P., Patomaki, H. (Eds.), The Politics of Economic and Monetary Union, The Finnish Institute of International Affairs, Kluwer Academic Press, Dordrecht, 1997, pp. 7-18

Miron, J. A., Romer, C. D., Weil, D. N., *Historical Perspectives on the Monetary Transmission Mechanism*, National Bureau of Economic Research, Working Paper 4326, Cambridge, April 1993

Mishkin, F. S., *The Channels of Monetary Transmission: Lessons for Monetary Policy*, National Bureau of Economic Research, Working Paper 5464, Cambridge, February 1996

Mitchell, W. C., Munger, M. C., *Economic Models of Interest Groups: An Introductory Survey*, American Journal of Political Science, Vol. 35, No. 2, May 1991, pp. 512-546

Mitchell, W. C., Simmons, R. T., *Beyond politics: markets, welfare, and the failure of bureaucracy*, Westview Press, Boulder, 1994, Independent studies in political economy

Moe, T. M., *Towards a Broader View of Interest Groups*, Journal of Politics, Vol. 43, 1981, pp. 531-543

Mohtadi, H., Roe, T. L., *Growth, lobbying and public goods*, European Journal of Political Economy, Vol. 14, 1998, No. 3, pp. 453-473

Mojon, B., *Financial Structure and the interest rate channel of ECB monetary policy*, European Central Bank, Working Paper No. 40, November 2000

Mojon, B., Peersman, G., *A VAR description of the effects of monetary policy in individual countries of the euro area*, European Central Bank, Working Paper No. 93, December 2001

Mucciaroni, G., *Reversals of Fortune: Public Policy and Private Interests*, The Brookings Institution, Washington, 1995

Mueller, D. C., *Perspectives on Public Choice*, Cambridge University Press, 1997

Mueller, D. C., *Public Choice*, Cambridge University Press, New York, 1979

Mueller, D. C., *Public Choice: A Survey*, Journal of Economic Literature, No. 14, June 1976, pp. 395-433, Reprinted in: Mueller, D. C., The Public Choice Approach to Politics, Edward Elgar, Aldershot, 1983, pp. 447-488

Mueller, D. C., *The Public Choice Approach to Politics*, Edward Elgar, Aldershot,

Mueller, D. C., Murrell, P., *Interest groups and the size of government*, (1) Public Choice, Vol. 48, (1986), No. 2, pp. 125-145; (2) Reprinted in: The Public Choice Approach to Politics, Edward Elgar, Aldershot, 1983, pp. 344-364

Munger, M. C., Roberts, B. C., *The Federal Reserve and its institutional environment: a review*, in: Mayer, T., The Political Economy of American Monetary Politics, Cambridge University Press, 1990

Neumann, M. J. M., *Geldwertstabilität: Bedrohung und Bewährung*, in: Deutsche Bundesbank (Ed.), Fünfzig Jahre Deutsche Mark – Notenbank und Währung in Deutschland seit 1948, Beck, Munich, 1998, pp. 309-346

Ng, Y.-K., *Welfare Economics*, Revised Edition, Macmillan, Basingstoke, 1992

Niskanen, W. A, *Bureaucrats and Politicians*, Journal of Law and Economics, Vol. 18, (1975), pp. 617-643

Niskanen, W. A., *Bureaucracy and public economics*, Edward Elgar, Aldershot, 1994

Niskanen, W. A., *Bureaucracy and Representative Government*, Aldine Atherton, Chicago, 1971

Nölling, W., *Unser Geld – Der Kampf um die Stabilität der Währung in Europa*, Ullstein, Frankfurt am Main, 1993

OECD, *Monetary Policy in a Changing Financial Environment*, OECD Economic Outlook, No. 67, OECD, Paris, 2000, pp. 225-239

Olson, M., *The Logic of Collective Action*, in: Richardson, J. J. (Ed.), Pressure Groups, Oxford Readings in Politics and Government, Oxford University Press, 1993, pp. 23-37

Olson, M., *The Logic of Collective Action: Public Goods and the Theory of Groups*, Harvard University Press, Cambridge, Massachussetts, 1965

Olson, M., *The Rise and Decline of Nations*,

Olson, M., Zeckhauser, R., *An Economic Theory of Alliances*, Review of Economics and Statistics, Vol. 48, pp. 266-279, 1966

Opper, S., *Der Stand der Neuen Institutionenökonomik*, Hamburgisches Welt-Wirtschafts-Archiv, Wirtschaftsdienst 2001/X, 81. Jahrgang, Oktober 2001, pp. 601-608

Palmer, M., *The Banque Centrale du Luxembourg in the European System of Central Banks*, Banque Centrale du Luxembourg, May 2001

Pedler, R., *The Management of Public Affairs*, ECPA Occasional Papers, No. 2, January 1995

Peele, W. E., Southern, D., *Governing Germany*, Blackwell, Oxford, 1991

Peersman, G., Smets, F., *The industry effects of monetary policy in the euro area*, European Central Bank Working Paper Series, Working Paper No. 165, August 2002

Peersman, G., Smets, F., *The monetary transmission mechanism in the euro area: more evidence from VAR analysis*, European Central Bank, Working Paper No. 91, December 2001

Peters, B. G., *The politics of bureaucracy*, Longman, London, 4th Ed., 1995

Petracca, M. P., *The Politics of Interests: Interest Groups Transformed*, Westview Press, Boulder, 1992

Petracca, M. P., *Federal Advisory Committees, Interest Groups and the Administrative State*, Congress and the Presidency: A Journal of Capital Studies, 1986 Vol. 13, No. 1 (Spring), pp. 83-114

Pijnenburg, B., *EU lobbying by ad hoc coalitions: an explanatory case study*, Journal of European Public Policy, 5 (1998), 2, pp. 303-321

Pöhl, K. O., *Der Delors-Bericht und das Statut einer Europäischen Zentralbank*, in: Waigel, T. (Ed.), Unsere Zukunft heißt Europa – Der Weg zu Wirtschafts- und Währungsunion, Econ, Düsseldorf, 1997, pp. 193-209

Pohl, M., Freitag, S. (Eds.), *Handbook on the history of European banks*, Aldershot, 1994

Pollard, P. S., *A look inside two central banks: The European Central Bank and the Federal Reserve*, The Federal Reserve Bank of St. Louis Review, January/February 2003, pp. 11-30

Posen, A. S., *Is Fighting Inflation a Just War?*, Conference paper, prepared for the International Finance/IMF/World Bank conference "The Future of Monetary Policy", July 11, 2000, Washington, D.C., Institute for International Economics, Washington, 2000

Potters J., Sloof, R., *Interest Groups – A Survey of Empirical Models that try to assess their influence*, Tinbergen Institute TI 95-85

Potters, J., *Lobbying and pressure: theory and experiments*, Amsterdam Thesis Publishers, Tinbergen Institute Research Series No. 36, Subseries A, General Economics, University of Amsterdam, Dissertation, 1992

Potters, J., van Winden, F., *Lobbying and asymmetric information*, Public Choice, 1992, Vol. 74, No. 3, pp. 269-292

Potters, J., van Winden, F., *Modelling Political Pressure as Transmission of Information*, European Journal of Political Economy, Vol. 6, 1990, pp. 61-88

Potters, J., von Winden, F., *Models of interest groups: four different approaches*, Amsterdam, Tinbergen Institute, Discussion Ppaer No. 93/204, Tinbergen Institute

Quintyn, M., Taylor, M. W., *Regulatory and Supervisory Independence and Stability*, International Monetary Fund, IMF Working Paper, WP/02/46, March 2002

Ramey, V. A., *How Important is the Credit Channel in the Transmission of Monetary Policy?*, National Bureau of Economic Research, Working Paper 4285, Cambridge, March 1993

Remsperger, H., *Geldpolitik – was wird von ihr erwartet, was kann sie leisten?*, Speech by Prof. Dr. Hermann Remsperger, reprinted in: Deutsche Bundesbank, Auszüge aus Presseartikeln, Nr. 26, Frankfurt am Main, June 10, 2003, pp. 5-9

Rheinisch-Westfälisches Institut für Wirtschaftsforschung, *Mehrwertsteuererhöhung und Senkung der Sozialabgaben: Beschäftigungs- und Verteilungseffekte*, RWI-Konjunkturbrief, Nr. 3, November 1997, Rheinisch-Westfälisches Institut für Wirtschaftsforschung, Essen

Richardson, J. J. (Ed.), *Pressure Groups*, Oxford Readings in Politics and Government, Oxford University Press, 1993

Richardson, J. J., Jordan, A. G., *Governing under Pressure: The Policy Process in a Post-Parliamentary Democracy*, Government and Administration Series, Martin Robertson, Oxford, 1979

Roberts, R., Kynaston, D. (Eds.), *The Bank of England: money, power, and influence 1694-1994*, Oxford University Press, Oxford, 1995

Romer, C. D., Romer, D. H., *Institutions for Monetary Policy*, NBER Working Paper No. 5557, National Bureau of Economic Research, Cambridge MA, 1996

Romer, C. D., Romer, D. H., *New Evidence on the Monetary Transmission Mechanism*, Brookings Papers on Economic Activity, No. 1, 1990, pp. 149-213

Rowley, C., Tollison, R., Tullock, G., *The political economy of rent-seeking*, Kluwer Academic Publishers, Boston, 1988

Rüdiger, R., *Die Unabhängigkeit der Bundesbank: Analyse und Materialien*, Athenäum Verlag, Kronberg, 1978

Salisbury, R., *Interest Groups*, in: Greenstein, F. I., Polsby, N. W. (Eds.), Handbook of Political Science, Volume 4, Nongovernmental Politics, Vol. 4, Addison-Wesley, Reading Masachussetts, 1975

Salisbury, R. H., *Putting Interests Back into Interest Groups*, in: Cigler, A. J., Loomis, B. A. (Eds.), Interest Group Politics, C. Q. Press, Washington, 1995, Third Edition

Salisbury, R. H., Heinz, J. P., Laumann, E. O., Nelson, R. L., *Who works with whom? Interest group alliances and opposition*, American Political Science Review, Vol. 81, No. 4, December 1987, pp. 1217-1234

Salmon, P., *The logic of pressure groups and the structure of the public sector*, European Journal of Political Economy, 3 (1987), 1/2, pp. 55-86, 7

Samm, C.-T., *Die Stellung der Deutschen Bundesbank im Verfassungsgefüge*, Schriften zum Öffentlichen Recht, Band 63, Duncker & Humblot, Berlin, 1967

Schell, R., Hill, P. B., Esser, E., *Methoden der empirischen Sozialforschung*, Sechste Auflage, R. Oldenbourg Verlag, 2000

Scheuch, E. K., *Lobbyismus und Verbandswesen in unserem politischen System*, in: Lobbyismus und Politik, HWWA Wirtschaftsdienst 2000/III, pp. 145-149

Schmidt, C., *Analyse von Leitfadeninterviews*, in: Flick, U., Kardorff, E. v., Steinke, I. (Eds.), Qualitative Forschung, Rowohlt, Reinbek, 2000, pp. 447-455

Schnell, R., Hill, P. B., Esser, E., *Methoden der empirischen Sozialforschung*, R. Oldenbourg Verlag

Schubert, K., *Politikfeldanalyse: Eine Einführung*, Leske und Budrich, Opladen, 1991

Schütt-Wetschky, E., *Interessenverbände und Staat*, Darmstadt, Primus Verlag, 1997

Sekkat, T., *Exchange rate variability and EU trade*, Final Report to the Commission of the EU, DG II, November 1997

Sgherri, S., *Monetary Transmission Channels, Monetary Regimes and Consumption Behaviour*, De Nederlandsche Bank Staff Report, No. 53, Amsterdam, 2000

Shapiro, B. P., *An Introduction to Cases*, Harvard Business School, Review No. 10, 1988, Harvard

Shapiro, M., *Interest Groups and Supreme Court Appointments*, Northwestern University Law Review, Vol. 84, Nos. 3-4, 1990, pp. 935-975

Shughart, W. F., Tollison, R. D., *Preliminary evidence on the use of inputs by the Federal Reserve System*, American Economic Review, Vol. 73, 1983, pp. 291-304

Simmert, D. B., Welteke, E. (Eds.), *Die Europäische Zentralbank – Europäische Geldpolitik im Spannungsfeld zwischen Wirtschaft und Politik*, Deutscher Sparkassenverlag, Stuttgart, 1997

Sloof, R., *Game-theoretic Models of the Political Influence of Interest Groups*, Thesis Publishers Amsterdam, Tinbergen Institute Research Series No. 143, Amsterdam, 1997

Sloof, R., *Lobbying when the Decision-maker can acquire Independent Information: A Comment*, Tinbergen Institute TI1-95-233, 1995

Smets, F., *Central bank macroeconometric models and the monetary policy transmission mechanism*, in: Bank for International Settlements (Ed.), Financial Structure and the Monetary Policy Transmission Mechanism, Bank for International Settlements, Monetary and Economic Department, C.B. 394, Basle, March 1995, pp. 225-258

Smets, F., Wouters, R., *The exchange rate and the monetary transmission mechanism in Germany*, De Nederlandsche Bank Staff Report, No. 35, Amsterdam, 1999

Smith, B. C., *Bureaucracy and Political Power*, Wheatsheaf Books, Brighton, 1988

Smith, E. O., *The German Economy*, Routledge, London, 1994

Smith, V. C., *The Rationale of Central Banking*, Liberty Fund, Indianapolis, 1990

Smits, R., *The European Central Bank: Institutional Aspects*, Series: International Banking and Finance Law Series, Vol. 5, Kluwer Law International, 1997

Stark, J., *Reflections on the Maastricht process from one of the architects*, Speech by Dr. Jürgen Stark, reprinted in: Deutsche Bundesbank, Auszüge aus Presseartikeln, Nr. 26, Frankfurt am Main, June 10, 2003, pp. 3-5

Stern, K., *Die Notenbank im Staatsgefüge*, in: Deutsche Bundesbank (Ed.), Fünfzig Jahre Deutsche Mark – Notenbank und Währung in Deutschland seit 1948, Beck, Munich, 1998, pp. 141-198

Streeck, W., *Interest Heterogeneity and Organizing Capacity: Two Logics of Collective Action?*, Czada, R. M., Windhoff-Héritier, A. (Eds.), Political Choice: Institutions, Rules, and the Limits of Rationality, Campus Verlag, Frankfurt am Main, Westview Press, Boulder, Colorado, 1991, pp. 161-198

Streit, M. E., *Die deutsche Währungsunion*, in: Deutsche Bundesbank (Ed.), Fünfzig Jahre Deutsche Mark – Notenbank und Währung in Deutschland seit 1948, Beck, Munich, 1998, pp. 675-720

Swank, O. H., Dur, R. A. J., *Producing and Manipulating Information*, Tinbergen Institute Discussion Paper, TI 2001-052/1, January 2001

Swank, O. H., Dur, R. A. J., *Why Do Policy Makers Give (Permanent) Power to Policy Advisors?*, Economics and Politics, 13(1), 2001, pp. 73-95

Swank, O. H., Suurmond, G., Visser, B., *Vanity in Politics*, Tinbergen Institute Discussion Paper, TI 2002-123/1, March 2003

Swank, O. H., Visser, B., *On Committees of Experts*, Tinbergen Institute Discussion Paper, TI 2005-028/1, March 2005

Swank, O. H., Visser, B., *The Consequences of Endogenising Information for Herd Behaviour*, Tinbergen Institute Discussion Paper, TI 2003-021/1, March 2003

Swank, O. H., Wrasai, P., *Deliberation, Information Aggregation and Collective Decision Making*, Tinbergen Institute Discussion Paper, TI 2002-006/1, December 2003

Swank, O. H., Wrasai, P., *Policy Makers, Advisors, and Reputation*, Tinbergen Institute Discussion Paper, TI 2004-037/1, November 2004

Szász, A., *50 years of the Bundesbank – Lessons for the ECB*, in: de Haan, J. (Ed.), The History of the Bundesbank: Lessons for the European Central Bank, Routledge International Studies in Money and Banking, No. 10, 2000, pp. 1-5

Szász, A., *Die Währungspolitik in der EG – aus Sicht der Niederländischen Zentralbank*, Deutsche Bundesbank: Auszüge aus Presseartikeln, Nr. 45, June 1989, pp. 5-8

Szász, A., *The Road to European Monetary Union*, Macmillan, London, 1999

Teivainen, T., *The Independence of the European Central Bank: Implications for Democratic Governance*, in: Minkkinen, P., Patomaki, H. (Eds.), The Politics of Economic and Monetary Union, The Finnish Institute of International Affairs, Kluwer Academic Press, Dordrecht, 1997, pp. 55-75

Terkildsen, N., Schnell, F., Ling, C., *Interest Groups, the Media, and Policy Debate Formation: An Analysis of Message Structure, Rhetoric and Source Cues*, Political Communication, 1998, Vol. 15, No. 1, 45

Thurber, J. A., *Dynamics of Policy Subsystems in American Politics*, in: Cigler, A. J., Loomis, B. A. (Eds.), Interest Group Politics, C. Q. Press, Washington, 1995, Third Edition

Tollison, R. D., *Rent Seeking: A Survey*, Knopf, New York

Tollison, R. D., McCormick, R. E., *Politicians, Legislation, and the Economy*, Martinus Nijhoff, Boston, 1981

Toma, E. F., Toma, M., *Central bankers, bureaucratic incentives and monetary policy*, Kluwer Academic Pub., Financial and Monetary Policy Studies 13, 1986

Toma, E. F., Toma, M. (Eds.), *Central Bankers, Bureaucratic Incentives, and Monetary Policy*, Financial and Monetary Policy Studies, Vol. 13, Kluwer Academic Publishers, Dordrecht, 1986

Toniolo, G. (Ed.), *Central Banks' Independence in Historical Perspective*, Walter de Gruyter, New York, 1988

Toolsema, L. A., Sturm, J.-E., de Haan, J., *Convergence of Monetary Transmission in EMU: New Evidence*, CESifo Working Paper No. 465, April 2001

Triesch, G., Ockenfels, W., *Interessenverbände in Deutschland*, Olzog, Munich, 1995

Truman, D. B., *The governmental process: political interests and public opinion*, Borzoi Books, Knopf Publishers, New York, 1971, 2nd. Ed., 1993

Tullock, G., *The politics of bureaucracy*, Public Affairs Press, Washington, 1965

Uhlenbruck, D., *Die verfassungsmäßige Unabhängigkeit der Deutschen Bundesbank und ihre Grenzen*, Bankrechtliche Schriften des Instituts für Bankwirtschaft und Bankrecht an der Universität zu Köln, Band 4, C. H Beck, Munich, 1968

van den Bempt, P., *The Political Aspects of Economic and Monetary Union: A View from Brussels*, in: Minkkinen, P., Patomaki, H. (Eds.), The Politics of Economic and Monetary Union, The Finnish Institute of International Affairs, Kluwer Academic Press, Dordrecht, 1997, pp. 19-54

van Paridon, C. W. A. M., *Auf dem richtigen Kurs? Betrachtungen zur Standortdiskussion Deutschlands*, Nomos Verlag, Baden-Baden, 1996

van Schendelen, M. P. C. M., *EU Committees as Influential Policy Makers*, Ashgate, Aldershot, 1998

van Schendelen, M. P. C. M., *EU Committees as Influential Policymakers: 12 Case Studies*, Ashgate Publishing, Aldershot, 1998

van Schendelen, M. P. C. M., *Learning from Recent Interviewing of Dutch MPs*, European Journal of Political Research, No. 11, 1983, pp. 413-426

van Schendelen, M. P. C. M., *Machiavelli in Brussels – The Art of Lobbying the EU*, Amsterdam University Press, 2002

van Schendelen, M. P. C. M. (Ed.), *National Public and Private Lobbying*, European Centre for Public Affairs, Aldershot, Dartmouth

van Sinderen, J., Roeland, T. J. A., *Policy Implications of Endogenous Growth Models*, in: Brakman, S., van Ees, H., Kuipers, S. K. (Eds.), Market Behaviour and Macroeconomic Modelling, Macmillan Press, New York, 1998, pp. 341-358

van Sinderen, J., van Bergeijk, P. A. G., Vollaard, B.A., *Structural Reform: The Issues*, in: P.A.G. van Bergeijk, et al., Structural Reform in Open Economies: A Road to Success?, Edward Elgar, Cheltenham, 1999, pp. 1-14 van Waarden, F., *Dimensions and Types of Policy Networks*, European Journal of Political Research, No. 21, 1992, pp. 29-52

van Winden, F., *On the economic Theory of Interest Groups: Towards a Group Frame of Reference in Political Economics*, Tinbergen Institute TI 1-97-117/1, 1997

Vaubel, R., *The bureaucratic and partisan behavior of independent central banks: German and international evidence*, European Journal of Political Economy, No. 13, 1997, pp. 201-224

Verband Deutscher Maschinen- und Anlagenbau, *VDMA – 100 Jahre im Dienste des Anlagenbaus*, Maschinenbau Verlag, Frankfurt am Main, 1992

von Alemann, U., *Organisierte Interessen in der Bundesrepublik*, Opladen, 1987

von Arnim, H. H., *Staat und Verbände*, in: Lobbyismus und Politik, HWWA Wirtschaftsdienst 2000/III, pp. 139-142

von Bonin, K., *Zentralbanken zwischen funktioneller Unabhängigkeit und politischer Autonomie, dargestellt an der Bank von England, der Bank von Frankreich und der Deutschen Bundesbank*, Studien zum Bank- und Börsenrecht, Band 4, Nomos Verlagsgesellschaft, Baden Baden, 1979

von Delhaes-Guenther, D., Hartwig, K.-H., Vollmer, U., *Monetäre Institutionenökonomik*, Schriften zu Ordnungsfragen der Wirtschaft, Band 67, Lucius, Stuttgart, 2001

von Hagen, J., *Geldpolitik auf neuen Wegen (1971-1978)*, in: Deutsche Bundesbank (Ed.), Fünfzig Jahre Deutsche Mark – Notenbank und Währung in Deutschland seit 1948, Beck, Munich, 1998, pp. 439-474

von Hagen, J., Hayo, B., Fender, I., *Geldtheorie, Geldpolitik, Finanzmärkte*, in: Zimmermann, F. (Ed.), Neue Entwicklungen in der Wirtschaftswissenschaft, Physica-Verlag, Heidelberg, 2002, pp. 1-42

von Hagen, J., Süppel, R., *Central bank constitutions for federal monetary unions*, European Economic Review, Vol. 38, 1994, pp. 774-782; CEPR Discussion Paper, London, 1994

von Hagen, J., Waller, C. J., *Regional Aspects of Monetary Policy in Europe*, Kluwer, Boston, 1998

von Kardoff, E., *Qualitative Evaluationsforschung*, in: Flick, U., Kardorff, E. v., Steinke, I. (Eds.), Qualitative Forschung, Rowohlt, Reinbek, 2000, pp. 238-251

von Schmädel, D., *Führung im Interessenverband: Probleme der innerverbandlichen Willensbildung*, Untersuchungen über Gruppen und Verbände, Band 7, Duncker und Humblot, Berlin, 1968

Waechter, K., *Geminderte demokratische Legitimation staatlicher Institutionen im parlamentarischen Regierungssystem – Zur Wirkung von Verfassungsprinzipien und Grundrechten auf institutionelle und kompetenzielle Ausgestaltungen*, Schriften zum öffentlichen Recht Band 667, Duncker & Humblot, Berlin, pp. 183-217

Walsh, J. I., *European Monetary Integration and Domestic Politics: Britain, France, and Italy*, Lynne Rienner Publishers, Boulder, London, 2000

Walter, C., *Das Federal Reserve System, die Deutsche Bundesbank und das Europäische System der Zentralbanken/die Europäische Zentralbank im Vergleich*, R. S. Schulz, Starnberg, 1994, pp. 1-285

Weimer, W., *Deutsche Wirtschaftsgeschichte*, Hoffmann und Campe, 1998

Weintraub, R. E., *Congressional Supervision of Monetary Policy*, Journal of Monetary Economics, No. 4 (1978), pp. 341-362

Welteke, E., *Politische Unabhängigkeit der Notenbanken als Voraussetzung für stabiles Geld*, in: Theilacker, B., Banken und Politik – Innovative Allianz für die Zukunft, Frankfurter Allgemeine Buch, Frankfurt, 2000, pp. 23-47

Welteke, E., Stark, J., *Stellungnahme zum Entwurf eines Siebenten Gesetzes zur Änderung des Gesetzes über die Deutsche Bundesbank (7. BBankGÄndG), zur Vorbereitung auf die Anhörung im Finanzausschuss des Deutschen Bundestages, in Berlin, am 26. November*

2001, Deutsche Bundesbank, Auszüge aus Presseartikeln, Nr. 52 vom 28. November 2001, pp. 7-10

Wheelen, T. L., Hunger, J. D., *Strategic Management and Business Policy – Entering the 21st Century Global Society*, Sixth Edition, World Student Series, Addison-Wesley, Reading, 1998

White, L. H., *The Theory of Monetary Institutions*, Blackwell, Oxford, 1999

Willett, T. D., Keen, E., *Studying the Fed: toward a broader public-choice perspective*, in: Mayer, T., The Political Economy of American Monetary Politics, Cambridge University Press, 1990

Wilson, G. K., *American Interest Groups*, in: Richardson, J. J. (Ed.), Pressure Groups, Oxford Readings in Politics and Government, Oxford University Press, 1993, pp. 131-144

Wilson, G. K., *Business and Politics: A Comparative Introduction*, Chatham House Publishers, 1990

Wilson, G. K., *Interest Groups*, Comparative Politics, Oxford, Blackwell, 1990

Wilson, J. Q., *Bureaucracy: what government agencies do and why they do it*, BasicBooks, New York, 1989

Wonnacott, T. H., Wonnacott, R. J., *Introductory statistics for business and economics*, Fourth Edition, John Wiley, New York, 1990

Woolley, J. T., *Monetary Politics – the Federal Reserve and the Politics of Monetary Policy*, Cambridge University Press, 1986

Yoho, J., *The evolution of a better definition of 'Interest Group' and its synonyms*, Social Science Journal, 1998, Vol. 35, No. 2, pp. 231-255

Studien zu Internationalen Wirtschaftsbeziehungen

Herausgegeben von Prof. Dr. Michael Frenkel

Band 1 Christiane Nickel: Insider und Outsider bei der Osterweiterung der Europäischen Währungsunion. 2002.

Band 2 Georg Stadtmann: Noise-Trader auf Devisenmärkten. Viel Lärm um Nichts? 2002.

Band 3 Wolf-Heimo Grieben: Trade and Technology as Competing Explanations for Rising Inequality. An Endogenous Growth Perspective. 2003.

Band 4 Alexander Mende: Order Flow Analyses and Foreign Exchange Dealing. 2005.

Band 5 Torsten Wezel: Determinants of Foreign Direct Investment in Emerging Markets. An Empirical Study of FDI Flows from Germany and its Banking Sector. 2005.

Band 6 Steffen Kern: The Behaviour of Interest Groups in Trade and Industry Towards Monetary Policy and Central Banks. Theory and Evidence on Germany and the Euro Area. 2006.

www.peterlang.de

Torsten Wezel

Determinants of Foreign Direct Investment in Emerging Markets

An Empirical Study of FDI Flows from Germany and its Banking Sector

Frankfurt am Main, Berlin, Bern, Bruxelles, New York, Oxford, Wien, 2005.
XII, 189 pp., num. fig. and tab.
Studien zu internationalen Wirtschaftsbeziehungen.
Edited by Michael Frenkel. Vol. 5
ISBN 3-631-53343-8 / US-ISBN 0-8204-7658-7 · pb. € 39.–*

Emerging markets frequently feature strong economic growth but also unique risks – political instability, legal uncertainty and corruption – which constitute barriers to foreign direct investment (FDI). This study analyzes empirically whether superior investment profiles of recipient countries matter for German FDI in addition to typical determinants such as labor costs, level of income and market openness. The specifics of banking FDI are also examined, notably the impact of incipient banking crises abroad and the risk-mitigating property of multilateral development banks acting as stakeholders in individual FDI projects. The concluding part highlights recent initiatives of international organizations to lower investment barriers, fight corruption and strengthen financial system stability.

Contents: Determinants of German Foreign Direct Investment in Latin America and Asia · Foreign Bank Entry into Emerging Economies: Determinants and Risks · Does Co-Financing by Multilateral Development Banks Increase "Risky" FDI?

FSC
www.fsc.org
MIX
Papier | Fördert
gute Waldnutzung
FSC® C083411

Zeitfracht Medien GmbH
Ferdinand-Jühlke-Straße 7
99095 Erfurt, Deutschland
produktsicherheit@kolibri360.de

Druck:
CPI Druckdienstleistungen GmbH
im Auftrag der
Zeitfracht Medien GmbH
Ein Unternehmen der Zeitfracht - Gruppe
Ferdinand-Jühlke-Str. 7
99095 Erfurt